Peer-to-Peer: Building Secure, Scalable, and Manageable Networks

D1568140

ABOUT THE AUTHORS

Dana Moore is currently a senior Scientist at BBN Technologies with over 25 years of research and development experience. He was previously the Chief Scientist for Roku Technologies, a P2P software startup. He is a popular conference speaker and university lecturer, and an expert on software agent systems and P2P collaboration. Dana has authored articles for numerous publications.

John Hebeler has over 20 years of distributed computing experience. He is currently investigating streaming multimedia for Arbitron. Previously, he was Vice President of Engineering for Roku Technologies, a P2P software startup. He is a popular speaker on advanced technologies, and is also an adjunct professor at Loyola College, where he teaches advanced technology courses for the MBA curriculum.

ABOUT THE TECHNICAL REVIEWER

Mark Newcomb is currently a consulting engineer at Aurora ConsultingGroup in Spokane, Washington. He has four years experience working withnetwork security issues and a total of more than 20 years experiencein the networking industry. Mark is a frequent contributor andreviewer for books by Cisco Press, New Riders, Macmillan Technical Publishing, McGraw-Hill, and Coriolis.

Peer-to-Peer: Building Secure, Scalable, and Manageable Networks

DANA **MOORE** AND JOHN **HEBELER**

McGraw-Hill/Osborne

New York Chicago San Francisco
Lisbon London Madrid Mexico City
Milan New Delhi San Juan
Seoul Singapore Sydney Toronto

McGraw-Hill/Osborne
2600 Tenth Street
Berkeley, California 94710
U.S.A.

To arrange bulk purchase discounts for sales promotions, premiums, or fund-raisers, please contact McGraw-Hill/Osborne at the above address. For information on translations or book distributors outside the U.S.A., please see the International Contact Information page immediately following the index of this book.

Peer-to-Peer: Building Secure, Scalable, and Manageable Networks

1234567890 CUS CUS 01987654321

ISBN 0-07-219284-4

Publisher
  Brandon A. Nordin
Vice President and Associate Publisher
  Scott Rogers
Acquisitions Editor
  Franny J. Kelly
Project Editor
  Elizabeth Seymour
Acquisitions Coordinator
  Alexander Corona
Technical Editor
  Mark Newcomb
Copy Editor
  Andrew Saff

Proofreader
  Marian Selig
Indexer
  Irv Hershman
Computer Designers
  George Toma Charbak,
  Lauren McCarthy
Illustrators
  Lyssa Wald, Michael Mueller
Cover Design
  Greg Scott
Series Design
  Kelly Hume

This book was composed with Corel VENTURA™ Publisher.

For Jane: You are the love for a lifetime, my True North.
And for Caitlin of the windy yellow hair: Lithesome child, all my hope
and love for you, my Caitlin of the windy yellow hair.
—Dana Moore

To my wife, partner, and friend: Christi,
whose boundless patience with my efforts in writing this
book is exceeded only by her love for our children
Emily, Sean, and James,
and for myself.

—John Hebeler

AT A GLANCE

CONTENTS

ACKNOWLEDGMENTS

The authors gratefully acknowledge the intellectual leadership of Dr. Clay Shirkey, considered by some to be Peer-to-Peer's most eloquent spokesperson, and a lucid writer. Dr. Shirkey, in provocative essays and the occasional conversation, has helped the authors gain greater insights into the critical issues that are helping to shape and define peer-t- peer computing and collaboration. His essays on the "Dark Matter of the Internet" and "The Great Re-wiring" stand out as especially thought-provoking treatises on the changing face of the Internet.

We especially appreciate the contributions of colleagues and friends who wrote insightful and knowledgeable sidebars to the book:

John Flynn, who wrote "Peer-to-Peer Computing and Agent Technology" in Chapter 9, is a Business Development Director at BBN Technologies in Arlington, VA. He also serves as the Program Manager for the DARPA Agent Markup Language (DAML) integration project. John is a graduate of the U.S. Naval Academy and has a master's degree in computer science from the Naval Postgraduate School. While at the Naval Postgraduate School, he developed the first high-level block-structured language and compiler (Algol-M) to execute on a microcomputer. Mr. Flynn retired from the Navy with the rank of Captain.

Richard Kilmer, who penned "Creating a Personal Web Services Engine" in Chapter 9, is CEO of InfoEther, and former CTO of Roku Technologies. His contributions to Peer-to-Peer computing include co-founding Roku and conceiving of the idea of a "context engine" as a design center for Peer-to-Peer collaboration.

Prasad Kunchakarra and Tushar Hazra , senior consultants, provided insightful research, ideas, and commentary.

Tom Dietz, Vice President at Arbitron, believed and supported our project in many ways, helping to make it possible.

Ed Greengrass, a senior Computer Scientist with the Department of Defense section, wrote two , "The Content Addressable Web for P2P" in Chapter 4, and "P2P as an Information Utility" in Chapter 9. His research interests include data bases, information retrieval, agent technology, and data mining. He has been active in the computing field in industry and government for 40 years.

The authors acknowledge the influential writings of pioneers in documenting or defining the evolution and advance of Cyberspace, especially Sherry Turkle for her thoughtful book, *Life on the Screen: Identity in the Age of the Internet* (Touchstone Books, 1997). And thanks to Steven Johnson, whose *Interface Culture: How New Technology Transforms the Way We Create and Communicate* (Basic Books, 1999), challenged our world view about the way our relationships with computing and technology change and redefine us.

We also thank various musical artists for providing the sound track that accompanied our many late nights of writing. Without the Indigo Girls, Nanci Griffith, Strawbs, Renaissance, R.E.M., and Bruce Springsteen, our long nights would have been far longer.

Finally, we gratefully acknowledge the infinite patience of our spouses and children for putting up with the long hours of research, experimentation, and writing that went into this book.

INTRODUCTION

Peer-to-Peer (P2P) is yet another technical buzzword—a buzzword for a technology so important that this book is devoted to it. Do you need to stretch your vocabulary to include yet another acronym? Will we take you on a tour of absurd facts and little-known applications? In short: No. We will explain to you, using straightforward examples, how you can leverage the ultimate power of being connected to peers. We will provide you with the tools and skills with which to master an exciting new exchange medium—a medium that dwarfs the current Web by order of magnitude.

The P2P medium provides an unprecedented number of ways to obtain information, acquire useful services, and vastly improve collaboration. To establish these exchanges, you must address a multitude of business and technical issues. Our objective is to provide you with the information and the confidence to take advantage of a powerful new way to use the Internet. Our step-by-step approach clearly illustrates the "what, why, and how" of this new Internet paradigm. Rather than dwelling on the buzz associated with P2P, we focus on the tremendous usability of the P2P world. Popularity comes and goes. Solving real problems is our focus.

WHAT MAKES P2P IMPORTANT?

What is it about P2P that has everyone buzzing? Why is it important to study, understand, and implement? Why is it a model that will be the basis for many applications in the near future?

Napster and Gnutella are dissimilar P2P applications, yet they each reveal much that is common to all P2P applications. Both Napster and Gnutella are being called fundamentally new network models. Let's take a quick look at each to gain some insights into the entire class of P2P applications.

Gnutella

Gnutella is a P2P file-sharing system distributed across each of the peers in the Gnutella community. It enables you to search and download the files of other community members. All the personal computers within the Gnutella community know very little about each other. Although the community can span the world, each personal computer within the community knows only about the other personal computers to which it's directly connected. Discovery of each participant is possible, but the makeup of the community is largely invisible to any user. There is no real hierarchy, in that the community empowers each of its personal computers equally. Your personal computer is not known to anyone not directly connected unless you offer a file that interests another person.

Searches into the community propagate "virally"—a personal computer sends the query to all the connected computers, each forwards the message to all the computers to which it is connected, and so on. Although P2P does not guarantee the anonymity of a given personal computer, each computer tends to be "hidden in the numbers." No central repository lists all the files in the community of connected users. When a user request for a file gets a positive response from a computer somewhere in the community, the two nodes connect directly and transfer the file. This meandering parade through the peers can be quite time-consuming.

Napster

Napster is also a distributed P2P file-sharing system. However, Napster specializes in music files, specifically MP3 files. Napster allows a user to search and download any MP3 file stored on another Napster user's personal computer. Any personal computer connected to Napster connects to a centralized server that interrogates the machine for the MP3 files that the machine's owner is willing to share.

Each computer in the Napster community knows about the Napster server to which it's directly connected. Napster users are largely visible and easily located by interrogation of the servers in the system. Although there is some level of hierarchy in the sense that a Napster server facilitates music searching, Napster still equally empowers each computer in the community. Your computer is unknown to anyone not directly connected to you unless you offer to share a file.

Queries into the community terminate at a Napster server that returns a list of the computers holding the music files of interest to the requester. Anonymity of a given member of the community is generally a moot point until a file is requested for download, at which time the computer is easily discovered, as the identity of the file's owner is usually attached to a file. Users in the system can bookmark a site that they find especially interesting and members can chat with one another.

The Napster servers act as central repository that lists all the files in the Napster community of every user machine. When a user request for a file gets a positive response from a node somewhere in the community, the two nodes connect directly and transfer the file. Interestingly, the actual music files move only from one peer to another. The centralized Napster server only holds information about the music files or metadata.

What These P2P Applications Have in Common

From these descriptions, Gnutella and Napster might seem quite different, but the characteristics that they share demonstrate the P2P model. We could describe any number of different P2P applications, not just these two distributed file-sharing applications, and most of the same conclusions would still apply.

First, Gnutella and Napster both put the power of information sharing back into the hands of ordinary users. Even though it is contrary to the intent of the original designers and implementers of the Internet and the Web, Internet service providers (ISPs) such as America Online (AOL) have tended to take control over the flow of information and the availability of content, using it as leverage. P2P applications such as Gnutella and Napster return some measure of control to the user.

Second, both Napster and Gnutella treat every computer in the community as both client and server. Whether or not some level of server assistance is involved, as in Napster, the personal computer takes on new responsibility, doing the "heavy lifting" of the application and the responsibility for controlling the uploading and downloading of data.

Both applications use a variant of the open instant messaging protocol (Internet Relay Chat, or IRC) as the transportation protocol. Open system instant messaging platforms enable anyone who can understand the programming interface to create whatever application software they wish. Software developers are not locked out of creating better versions of the client software or new applications because a corporation controls the transportation system. This approach to standards enables rapid innovation.

Both systems create a search engine that searches a small fraction of the total Internet (although it searches the part that means the most to you). They also create a file-serving system. The combination of a search engine and a file-serving system makes all participants clients *and* servers of the files. This combination illustrates the principle of creating loose communities in which the interested parties play a large part in the overall success of the system. The products of the system (searching and file management) use the available cycles of client machines rather than burdening huge server farms in the network. It doesn't really matter that Napster's search capability is a central service whereas Gnutella's is more distributed; both rely on user input and computer capability at the edge of the Internet.

To make the service work reliably all the time, both applications rely on the redundancy of many similar systems rather than expensive robust servers closer to the center of the network. Even though variable connections (computers may go online and offline unpredictably) are the rule, the system maintains its overall integrity and robustness because many computers hold the same content. Thus, variability and unpredictability are expected and compensated for by the sheer scale of the distributed system. Previously, the personal computer was considered the center of the computing universe, but in the P2P model, the network is front and center. As long as users are willing to dedicate some portion of their computing and bandwidth resources to network or community use, the system works.

Both applications treat user machines as servers without any required setup by networking gurus or information technology (IT) specialists. Each computer simply provides its piece of the overall functionality, and lets the other personal computers in the community do theirs.

What Do These P2P Applications Teach Us?

P2P applications teach a number of lessons about the next stages in the maturing of the Internet. In hindsight, technologists and users got hung up on the browser model. They tried to stretch the client/server model so far that it began to break down. They tended to forget that the Internet and the Web were meant to facilitate something more like a conversation and less like a television network (several television networks already present passive entertainment; we don't need to turn the Internet into another source of it). P2P redresses some of this imbalance between user and provider and makes us all more participants than spectators. P2P brings the Internet (which was originally created to be a groupware enabler) closer to its roots.

Additionally, P2P gives Internet users much more of a voice because no central enforcing authority controls the system. P2P addresses many of the difficulties of having centralized servers in the mix. The major downside of single centralized services is that they create significant hardware and bandwidth costs.

Further, they tend to attract parasitic regulation and litigation. The irony of Napster is that, even though the end user's behavior may be in violation of intellectual property laws, only Napster's aggregation of metadata (data about the data on the computers within the user community) has become a legal point of attack. It seems unfortunate to hold Napster accountable for creating an online catalog that simply points to files residing at an otherwise unknown location.

Similarly, European courts may order Yahoo to prevent surfers from browsing certain types of listings, but they cannot stop P2P communications from taking place without bringing down the entire Internet.

So, while central services may be attractive in extracting profits, they also eventually attract regulation and taxation that ultimately interfere with the services' operation. Consider that the real value of eBay, the Internet auction site, for the Internet user. eBay's value to the user may lie less in the online auctions than in the side conversations initiated because your presence as a bidder becomes known to someone who wants to offer you a deal privately. The side conversations are pure P2P.

As you learn more about P2P, it begins to look more like infinitely scalable distributed computing. Even staid Microsoft, by suggesting in its .Net initiative that P2P resources are available in the Internet for you to use, may finally be getting the idea. In the words of their business rival, Sun Microsystems: "The network is the computer."

What Does This All Mean for You?

P2P allows you to reach into and interact with a boundless source of information that exists at the Internet edge—the personal computer. This source provides a multitude of new information *and* services. The information taps directly into the source of most information today—again, the personal computer. The services enable you and your fellow personal computer users to collaborate. This collaboration could be between close, well-known associates working on an important project or an unknown person sharing a common interest or activity.

OUR APPROACH TO P2P

Hopefully, you are excited about P2P and how you can take advantage of it. This book will help you do just that.

The book is divided into four parts:

▼ **What is P2P and why is it valuable to you?**   Part 1 gets you excited about the potential of P2P. It defines P2P and its associated opportunities. It also raises awareness of both the benefits and the risks of entering into a new way of exchanging information and services.

■ **What are the fundamentals of P2P?**   Part 2 establishes the value and technical foundations for P2P. These include making the business (and personal) case and exploring the key technology enablers.

■ **How do you build solutions that incorporate a P2P approach?**   In Part 3, you begin building practical P2P solutions step by step. This part begins with designing the overall P2P architecture and its many dimensions. You will explore a combination of readily available applications and simple steps that you can take to address your specific goals. Part 3 details several specific solutions that you can implement today.

▲ **How can you best take advantage of what is coming next for P2P?**   Part 4 addresses future direction and issues with P2P. It establishes the new ground of P2P as it evolves into the mobile world and beyond.

The four parts build on each other, with each giving you the information and skills needed to move onto the next. They include code and configuration examples that you can customize to your particular needs.

Let's get started!

CHAPTER 1

P2P Defined

Definitions are important. Technical jargon is too often rich with deception and distorted by marketing whims. These distortions trivialize the hard work required to gain the full benefits of the technology. The excitement generated by illusive language and marketing techniques encourages only surface evaluation and quickly leads to disappointment and disillusionment when the new technology doesn't solve all the world's problems. We need to scrape away misconceptions and plain untruths if we are to enable you to maximize the benefits of P2P. This starts with defining the technology.

DIRECT EXCHANGES BETWEEN PEERS

Currently, most people transact these exchanges on the Web, going to one location that aggregates information from other sources. You then conduct a transaction with the web site, which coordinates the transactions among multiple clients. The process is technically complex and often failure prone—Gartner Group estimates have concluded that about 75% of all online "shopping carts" are abandoned during the process, possibly owing to the complexity of working through the complexities of the exchange process.

In contrast, P2P implies direct exchanges. If you have something I want, I go directly to you and obtain it. Likewise, I may have something you want, in which case the process reverses. In many cases, the exchange is mutual—*quid pro quo*. The "something" could be a file that contains a picture or a sound or real-time information like your son's soccer scores. It could be a service such as a storage capability or file conversion. The beauty of conducting exchanges amongst peers is that the participants view each other as equals, and roles can shift as the need requires. There is no permanent dividing line between "client" and "server," between producer and consumer. Unlike using the Web, P2P makes it as easy for you to publish as to consume, to create as well as enjoy. Today you may be an information consumer, tomorrow and information or service provider. P2P based applications don't force you to make or to understand arbitrary distinctions.

People instinctively seem to understand peer networks, frequently resort to peer exchanges to get things done, and systems operating outside the formal organizational structures are the rule rather than the exception. Acquiring an understanding of peer networks seems to be a part of the human maturation process.

Before P2P existed, the authors were novice engineers developing an advanced real-time messaging system that required a new technical approach. As employees of Bell Laboratories, we had at our fingertips extensive technologies—if we could find them! We had two choices for acquiring the technology we needed. To put it in the vernacular, we could go peer-to-peer by bouncing requests off friends and associates, or go server-based by finding our way through the vast centralized bureaucracy. The former solution sounded inefficient at best; the latter sounded plain intimidating.

There were two additional constraints: We needed the technology quickly (with support to boot), and we had no funds. In our conformist approach, we first attempted to go through the daunting management chain of command. After dealing with politics and egos, we finally received our response. It had a repetitive ring: *nyet, nyet, nyet, nyet*. In the industrial age, where change was suspect and often expensive, working through the chain of command was a viable approach. Today, such an approach just doesn't work.

So after wasting time with the management parade, we had to think creatively. We decided to contact the developers of the technology directly. Through a diverse network of friends and intermediaries, we found the lead developers. The phone call was memorable. We asked one of the developers sheepishly, "Could you send us the executable code, source code, and documentation?"

"No problem," the developer responded. "By the way, who are you?"

We then asked, "Could we work with you to refine the technology?"

Since then, we have loved peer-to-peer; although the catch phrase did not yet exist. As we grew wiser with the passing years, we did everything through an informal network of peers. This approach got the job done, simply and directly.

Our early P2P network accomplished our development goals. We received critical technology rapidly, with the necessary support. Since it was from the original producers, it was up to date. The suppliers then worked with us to advance their product successfully. We established a P2P partnership that exchanged value in ways other than monetary. Since this path lacked the expensive markups and delays of a management chain, marginal exchange rates were very low; the benefit-to-cost ratio was acceptably high. Thus, new releases, features, and documentation kept coming our way. Our relationship, along with the technology, flourished. The technology was called the Tuxedo transaction processing system. Today, such efforts can be amplified because of the universal connectivity brought by the Internet combined with P2P applications.

The pre-P2P anecdote aptly illustrates P2P. P2P represents the movement of information and services from one individual or peer *directly* to another individual or peer. Over time, such a relationship forms a bidirectional flow— *quid pro quo*. Our example focused on a network of friends and associates along with basic human protocols. P2P migrates this dynamic to the computer world. The intermediaries, although essential, do little more than carve out a path between peers. The peers represent the real exchange end points between the producer and the consumer. The intermediaries in the Internet translate to network services such as the Domain Name Service (DNS). They are essential for coordinating and finding peers, but the real action is with the peers.

Another example of P2P is Napster's centralized metadata service. Metadata is information about information. In Napster's case, the metadata is the filename, file size, and recording qualities. A later chapter will cover metadata in depth. Metadata is a key ingredient in successful information and service management.

P2P AND THE INTERNET

The Internet is the ultimate peer-to-peer mechanism. The user can easily reach and interact with virtually any computer. Why does this concept seem so new? Actually, the Internet started out as P2P. (Never confuse the Internet with the World Wide Web.) A small group of researchers wanting to share information agreed on protocol standards, and linked via a network. The researchers were roughly equivalent in technical know-how and maintained a balance between consumption (reading stuff) and production (writing stuff). Within today's definition, this network was almost pure P2P. The ultimate potential of the early Internet went unheralded due to the small number of participants as well as the technical jargon that obfuscated the network's communication value.

Then a new Internet age came along, featuring web browsers and Hypertext Markup Language (HTML). This technology enabled an unsophisticated client to obtain information. All the user had to do to access the information was simply point and click. The browsers hid complex addresses and network peculiarities from the user's view. Although the Web, as it became known, enabled simple client access, it did not enable simple publishing. Whereas a consumer need only master a mouse, a publisher had to master HTML, DNS registration, web servers, Common Gateway Interface (CGI), and a litany of other acronyms and buzzwords. This shifted the original P2P balance between consumers and producers: Big organizations had the time and skills to master the production complexity, while individual users became pure consumers. The Internet became a TV set with a shopping cart (no jiggly wheel, though).

Almost unnoticed, the Internet continued to evolve. Although people loved the browser, and were often dazzled by the graphic glitz of HTML pages, the Internet capability they depended on most was e-mail, which many cite as the seminal P2P application. E-mail as simple text exchange became the Internet's killer application. The P2P nature of e-mail is largely a technical debate. E-mail achieves P2P goals with some limitations, by delivering information from one person to another. It perfectly balances easy production and easy consumption. As studies show, e-mail is the one Internet function that would be difficult for users to give up.

A CONCISE P2P DEFINITION

Can we state with conviction an unambiguous definition of P2P? Are we getting closer to defining P2P? Like many technologies, from "push," to XML, P2P has quickly acquired quite a buzz, and buzzwords come and go. Our goal is to remove the fuzziness and buzziness of the word and give you the power to use P2P to accomplish your communication and information goals. Therefore, let's declare a basic, concise definition:

Peer-to-Peer (P2P): The action of mutually exchanging information and services directly between the producer and the consumer to achieve purposeful results

Let's examine each one of the words to explore the definition fully.

▼ **Action** The P2P process is not static. P2P dynamically exchanges real-time information and capabilities. It does not behave like a fixed web site offering the same static information. Many web sites arguably have dynamic features, but for the most part, the dynamic information originates elsewhere.

■ **Mutual exchange** P2P is not a one-way street. The value of P2P is exchange. Traditional web sites offer only one type of exchange: dollars for product or service. P2P offers much more interesting exchanges: a song for disk space; a picture for a video; and so on. You may get value by just participating in a P2P network. The exchange can be between parties that vary from anonymous to highly trusted, depending on the sensitivities and applications involved.

■ **Information**   Most valuable information, such as programs, music, documents, and presentations, is created on a peer personal computer system. The peer represents the ultimate destination and repository of information. P2P enables users to get to the most timely and valuable information available. The very notion of "publishing" reveals the flaw of the Web. The term *publishing* infers that the information already exists somewhere and that the act of publishing just makes it available. Publishing information to a web site is fraught with delays and difficulties, and anything that delays information availability erodes its value. Information and services must also reside somewhere. Like a turtle, P2P travels with its own resources. There is no need to allocate space on a server. P2P offers instant information scalability.

■ **Services**   Peer systems are treasure troves of services, especially with today's server-class personal computers. Peer systems offer raw computing resources, such as file storage, network bandwidth, and processing cycles. The average utilization of these resources is quite low. What is your personal computer with a 1MHz processor, 60GB hard drive, and broadband-connected computer doing right now? As I write this chapter, my computer is managing the daunting task of recognizing which key I am pressing. A typical user's personal computer is more involved with screensavers than anything else. In contrast, a typical Yahoo web site server is very busy. Also, peer systems are loaded with advanced software applications—applications that can create music, videos, presentations, and more.

■ **Directly**   Peer systems exchange information and services directly. The P2P participants do not have to endure a hierarchy of locations and format translations. In P2P, there is no middleman, so users benefit from the speed and efficiency of dealing directly with the desired participant.

■ **Producer and consumer**   Producers create and allow access to information and services, which consumers then use. In P2P, each personal computer or peer is *both* a consumer and a producer. Any peer may offer services and information, and any peer can consume them.

▲ **Results**   P2P is about results. It is not about the network. P2P delivers you the information or services you need. Without real results, P2P is an *interesting* technology. This book focuses on results of P2P, not its philosophy.

Where does P2P "live" (if any technology can be said to "live")? That is, where is the architectural and computing center of P2P? Who are the producers and consumers? They are you and I. Where do you do your computing? For most users, the answer is a personal computer. Most of those personal computers run Microsoft Windows, although a few run Macintosh. P2P does not require these specific platforms. P2P could just as easily exist on Linux or UNIX or even the monolithic IBM mainframe. Although P2P exchanges are platform-independent, the vast majority of P2P exchanges take place between two personal computers, for several simple reasons. First, most of the information and services exist on personal computers. If you want to share and interact with others instantly, the exchange is likely to go more smoothly if you are using a personal computer.

Therefore the architectural and computing center of P2P is determined by the location of useful information and services—more often than not, the most useful things are found on your personal computer. Second, many P2P applications require software on both sides of the exchange. Software developers write for the most popular platforms first, and here the personal computer easily wins.

Your personal computer can be thought of as a device residing on the "edge" of the Internet, unlike the big web servers that offer HTML pages or act as a front end to e-commerce services which are considered to exist in the "center" of the net. Like the universe, the edge has been expanding rapidly. Further, the PC is not the only edge device participating in the P2P revolution. The edge also encompasses the plethora of mobile devices that are also "Internet-enabled." Mobile edge devices can be first rate participitants in P2P applications, as you will see.

To summarize our definition of P2P, let's compare a P2P information exchange to a web site information exchange (see Figure 1-1). In P2P, a peer makes a request directly to another peer precisely where the source information exists. A web site creates a two-step

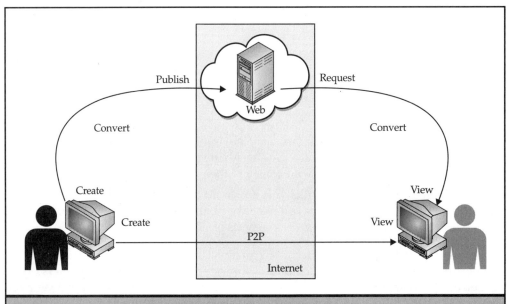

Figure 1-1. Contrasting a Web Site Exchange with a P2P Transfer

process. First, a site with appropriate resources must be constructed. Then the information is created elsewhere (most likely on a personal computer) and "published" to the site. The information waits at the site for a request. After receiving a request, the site transfers the information to the requester.

Table 1-1 outlines the differences between P2P transfers and web sites. The table summarizes topics that subsequent chapters explain in detail. Note the significant differences and their impact. P2P offers a more scalable, robust approach than traditional web servers while enabling direct access to any information or service. P2P also offers a higher degree of privacy and control, as the information or service never really leaves your personal computer. This is not to imply that P2P is perfect for everything. Web sites can provide the same information and service to everyone quite efficiently, and will continue to play a valuable role in electronic commerce. P2P just opens up a new direct channel between individual users for exchanging their information and services.

Factor	P2P	Web Site
Exchanges between consumer and producer	Symmetric	Asymmetric
Availability of content and services	Commonplace	Complex
Number of users making content and services available	Many	Few
Requestors of content and services	Many	Many
Ability to scale quickly and efficiently	Unlimited	Limited
Privacy	Maintained	Vulnerable
Formality and control	Low	High
Focus	Lots of different, dynamic requests	Lots of similar requests
Architecture	Fully distributed	Client/server
Format	Any	HTTP and HTML
Availability	Distributed	Concentrated
Machine type	Any	Large server

Table 1-1.   Contrasting Factors Between P2P and Web Sites

WHY IS P2P IMPORTANT, AND HOW IS IT IMPLEMENTED?

Let's examine two aspects of P2P in greater detail: the value and the technical aspects of P2P. Value aspects explain the excitement individuals and organizations feel for P2P.

Essentially, the value aspects define *why* P2P is important. P2P solves real business and personal problems while offering new opportunities for both individual productivity and entertainment applications and enterprise level business applications. The technical aspects cover the implementation of P2P—the *how*. Recent technical advances created powerful P2P foundation technologies, and developers have built simple-to-use P2P applications upon this foundation.

The Value of P2P

P2P's potential to meet many business and personal needs are generating interest in the technology. When you examine P2P from a business perspective, you realize that the same issues impact your personal life. How has your life and business changed in the last decade? People are more time-constrained, more event-driven, and much more mobile. They are also still human and thus strive to remain connected to each other despite these improvements. The Internet offers both increases in productivity for individuals and businesses as well as new ways to communicate. Hyperbole is rampant regarding the Internet—but just a few years ago, how could anyone have imagined an inexpensive, instantaneous connection to virtually everyone? The Internet is filled with information and information processing tools. That is where the fun begins.

P2P Offers the Information and Services That Are Most Important to You

Information is a generic word that covers many items in the digital world—pictures, music, video, and presentations, to name just a few. It also represents communication via a birthday card to your sister, a schedule change for the baseball game, and a notification of stock price. Processing information represented by services includes displaying a picture, playing a song, and sending an e-mail.

Information represents more than business data. It entertains, informs, and drives our decisions. More and more digital information is replacing more traditional media such as paper. The vast majority of digital information does not reside on big corporate servers. Most of the people who want to communicate do not sit behind big corporate servers either. The preponderance of information and communication exists on personal computers—the Internet peers. The goal of P2P is to get you to the information and people you care about the most. This goal defines the huge potential of P2P.

P2P Incurs Minimum Cost

Another key determinant of value is cost. How much does it cost to get information or communicate with one another? Cost has many dimensions beyond just dollars and cents. It encompasses time, required skills, standards, and accessibility.

Let us start this exploration with the traditional cost—dollars. The computing platform of the personal computer consists largely of a sunk cost. The raw material for P2P—the processing power, memory, and disk storage—are already purchased. Thus, P2P can ride on tracks already paid for, and the net cost is zero. But the cost does not stop there. The next step is information and communication tools. Again, these tools already exist on most computers or are available for nominal cost, often with a simple download. Hence, the raw materials for producing useful information, services, and communication are also essentially paid for.

The network, however, does have a recurring cost. For most network users, the cost of network access is offered at a flat monthly rate. Therefore, the marginal cost of sending information or services is essentially zero, as are the direct dollar costs for P2P. If you look only at direct cost, any marginal value gained from P2P would be worthwhile. Unfortunately, you cannot look just at cost, although it is a good place to start and explains some of the enthusiasm for P2P.

Let's contrast P2P costs with a traditional web site's costs. Web site costs include connectivity costs, programming costs, operating system maintenance, and the hosting hardware. A traditional web site is an entire new resource—a resource that must be paid for. The web site cost could be direct through billing, packaged as part of a service, or deferred through forced advertising. All three are used extensively. The web site also requires the movement of the information and re-creation of the services on another platform. These tasks are time-consuming and complex. Sites that offer the creation of services rather than just static information can be very costly indeed. Sites that come packaged as part of an Internet service, such as the sites included with America Online and Erols, do not allow any user-installed services and offer very limited information storage.

P2P Saves Time

Cost has many other factors, such as time. The time it takes to process, move, or use information determines much of its value. Yesterday's news is yesterday's news. Any delay in moving or processing information incurs an additional cost. As the time sensitivity rises, as is the trend today, the costs go up. P2P enables you to connect directly to the information you need, eliminating any delays. This direct connection ensures that you receive the information from the definitive source and thus decreases the chance of obtaining a questionable copy.

Another time factor is how long it takes the user to acquire the knowledge and skill required to access and use the information or service. Almost any ancillary information detracts from the value. The average user does not want to have to learn how to use techniques and tools to acquire the information he or she needs; he or she simply wants to know how to access that information as quickly as possible.

In the past, mostly engineers invested in these electronic information tools. Engineers actually find it fun to wind their way through the complex electronic maze to uncover a rather bland e-mail message at the end. This complexity is a major hurdle to users who have larger concerns, such as raising a family or making payroll. They have no time or patience for such nonsense. And since they are really running things and doing things, such users control the most interesting information and communications.

This is where the story of the Web has a happy ending. Whereas web sites succeed because they make viewing simple, P2P will succeed because it makes publishing information, services, and communication easy. P2P is still rather complex, but it is rapidly becoming simpler. As it becomes less complex, the rest of the world (the owners of the interesting information) will jump in. In deciding to invest in this book, you have distinguished yourself as one of the first to test the emerging P2P waters. The purpose of this book is to make P2P simple for your needs.

P2P Gives You Control

Control over your valuable information is also an important factor. You need to be able to control who can use your information and services and when they can use it. You also need to be able to update and change your offerings easily, and know instantly that the updated version is available. The less control a technology offers, the lower its value and price.

P2P provides publishers with total control. The information resides on your personal computer, giving you far greater control than if you were to move your trusted information to a web site server. Once you move your information to a server, it is under someone else's control. The web site can make promises and establish "privacy policies," but the fact remains that someone else now controls your information as well as all the data collected about that information, such as who accessed it and when. Privacy policies are only as good as the company enforcing the policies. Besides, have you ever read the legalese of a web site's policy statements?

History has demonstrated that the tempting assortment of information is hard to resist and that web site policies are not to be fully trusted. eToys, the once-promising toy site, eventually put all of its "protected" information up for sale. Ultimately, this loss of control will limit the availability of information. If you were developing a patent, would you trust it to a large web site? Would you trust the site with pictures of your two-year-old?

P2P Offers the Full Richness of the Internet

Variety is also a key value issue. In the P2P world, you can make available *any* information or service. Web sites are very limiting unless you get into the inner workings of a web server. The web site domain often limits the information format to HTML and disallows service offerings completely.

When setting up an advanced technology class for a graduate education program, Dana gave his requests to the Information Technology staff one by one. Each request was happily approved until the last one. The last request was to enable a student to build a service, not just create a static information resource. The normally accommodating staff put their answer quite simply: no. They stated that a poorly written service could crash the entire site, affecting thousands of users. No student would ever be allowed to create such a crisis.

This inherent vulnerability limits service offerings of web sites. Hundred of sites will accommodate HTML files, but few allow service offerings. This vulnerability also explains the level of approval and skills required to offer active web services. These restrictions lead directly to less innovation and experimentation.

P2P Offers Virtually Universal Accessibility

Accessibility is also key value dimension. If the tools and technologies are not readily available, as was the case early in the history of the Internet, success is limited. The Internet and its associated technologies become more and more accessible each day. The network itself is reasonably priced and comes delivered via a multitude of agents that range from satellites to simple phone modems. Often, having multiple access points is crucial to keeping yourself connected, in case one or more of these access points is not working. This also is a problem with P2P: Technical problems can prevent the user from accessing the service or information. This book features a large section with suggestions on fully addressing this apparent Achilles' heel of P2P. P2P offers a wealth of readily available tools to fix such problems.

When value exceeds costs, it is a good deal. More and more peers or personal computers hold valuable information and services. P2P builds an inexpensive, simple path to this treasure trove. In establishing this path, P2P opens rich communication paths between peers. The combination of easy-to-use, accessible technology with interesting information and services adds up to tremendous value for P2P.

The Technical Value of P2P

Now let's explore the technical side. This all starts with the foundation of the Internet—its network. You need not explore all the technical peculiarities, but some are essential in understanding where P2P fits in and where it can go.

P2P Leverages Internet Openness

At its core, the Internet is a network—but not just any network. Most networks of the past, such as the phone system, were highly sensitive to what traveled across them. The phone system was designed for human voice conversations that had statistically average connection times and frequency ranges. Stuffing data across this phone system design was awkward—hence the eerie squeaks and clicks when a digital modem connects over a phone line. A phone modem must translate the computer world of bits and bytes to human frequencies. The phone system network also has another problem: It is connection-oriented. This means that when you make a phone call, first the system establishes the connection path. Your conversation travels down this fixed path. Individual pieces of the conversation depend on this path. If, due to the dynamics of phone calls, another path would prove better, an existing conversation cannot take advantage of it.

The Internet is not like that at all. First, it is completely indifferent as to "what" travels, "where" it is going and coming from, and "how" it is getting there. This apparently simple aspect of the Internet offers tremendous power to P2P. The Internet provides an inexpensive communication path to the world *and* does not care about the content that flows through the path. Any type of information can flow over Internet pathways. Second, since they are not fixed, the communication paths are highly available. If multiple points suddenly fail, the information smoothly adjusts around the nonoperational points. The Internet, at its core, is simply a delivery system that works. It delivers whatever you want and quickly adjusts to any problems.

Since the Internet doesn't care about what is sent, you are free to send anything at all. Only the sender and receiver participants care about the specific format. This freedom leads to a challenge: The sender and receiver must agree on the information's format. Just like the human world, the computer world depends on protocols and formats. Humans typically use simple informal protocols, like greeting someone with "Hello" before trying to sell that person something. Of course, the format used for such communication is the local language and vernacular. The Internet differs only in formalities. Anyone who struggles with the letter *l* or the number one (*1*) in an e-mail address understands the rigidity of digital world's rules.

The Internet also has specific protocols and formats to achieve communication. To initiate successful communication, users must agree on the protocols and formats. Internet web sites agreed on the protocol of HyperText Transmission Protocol (HTTP) and the format of HyperText Markup Language (HTML). These standards led directly to widespread adoption. Standards also drive the two ends of the communication: Both the sender and receiver must understand the same protocol and format. Again, the Internet itself doesn't care about protocols and formats. You are free to change and update them *as long as* both the sender and receiver stay in step. Both HTML and HTTP have gone through many arguable improvements, which is one of the major reasons that you must regularly update your browser. If you failed to upgrade, only the older features of HTML and HTTP would operate, and thus you would be unable to interact with the new functionality at a given web site.

This freedom presents both opportunities and challenges for P2P. P2P is free to deploy any type of interaction formats and protocols. This freedom can quickly produce waves of innovation. As you explore the existing P2P landscape, you will quickly see the power of unleashing creativity. However, there is a challenge: Unlike in *Star Trek*, there is no universal translator. If you devise an effective new communication protocol, you must convince your P2P associates to download and install a program that understands this protocol. If you control your associates—for example, if they work for you— this task is relatively easy: You simply order them to install the program. (Coercion is always effective!) If your communication opportunity demands a larger P2P audience, the Internet can be either very generous or cruel—the best programs win, the bad ones sink into oblivion.

Good examples of P2P's widespread adoption include all the forms of instant messaging. Instant messaging contains a specific protocol; there is one for each well-known brand such as America Online (AOL), Microsoft Service Network (MSN), and so on. These

Internet service companies demand that each user download and install their version of an instant messaging program. The millions of adopted users prove that adoption can happen quickly. Many good applications go begging for an audience simply because they never achieve the critical mass needed to demonstrate real value.

The first technical point is that you can deploy any type of communication on the Internet. The catch is that you must convince each user to handle your communication's protocol and format.

P2P Leverages Technology Standards

The second technical area is standards. They offer a solution to the openness of Internet networking. Standards free P2P from forcing users to adopt "your" protocols and formats. If users all agree to certain technical standards, they need not struggle with unique applications that understand and translate protocols and formats.

The development of standards has progressed rapidly and is becoming a great enabler of P2P. Many working groups are rapidly solving the few remaining problems. Standards in protocols and formats allow P2P participants to operate above the nuts-and-bolts level to achieve their information and service goals directly. In addition, the protocols and formats continue to grow, offering new advantages in performance and features.

Not everyone is interested in standards. A nonstandard but highly adopted approach such as AOL instant messaging brings a captive audience to the holder of the proprietary standard. Such an approach is not evil, but a light caution is in order. Subsequent sections will fully explore the various standards and their use in P2P. For now, know that standards are a good thing that makes your communication burden much lighter.

Standards exist on several levels. Formal standards published by a standards body are on solid ground. Another standards type is *de facto*. De facto standards are not as rigorous and thorough as formal standards, but they get the job done. They come into existence due to their inherent merit and/or strong support from a vendor.

P2P Leverages Personal Computer Hardware

The third technical point is the personal computer itself. Following Moore's law,[1] the personal computer has grown from an engineer's toy to a business class machine capable of performing efficient multitasking, storing staggering amounts of data, and handling high-speed network communications. Capabilities once reserved for carefully guarded corporate rooms, serviced by men in white coats, now sit demurely next to your desk.

As explored in later chapters, your personal computer can form a highly available, robust computing platform that can outperform many corporate setups. The amount of raw resources available is huge. All the corporate servers in the world cannot even touch the combined capabilities of the Internet edge of personal computers. Not surprisingly, the

---

1   Moore's law is not really a law but more an observation that has held true for decades. Moore's
       law promises a doubling of computer processor speed every eighteen months for the same or
       lower cost.

Level	Type	Value
1	Raw computing resources	Disk space, processing, network bandwidth
2	Information	Files and databases
3	Services	Applications

Table 1-2.   P2P Resource Levels

resources contained in the personal computer have grown to be the major producer and analyzer of critical information—information on which you depend. P2P simply frees these resources to others.

Your P2P resources can be unleashed on three major levels. You could choose to offer raw resources by allowing simple resource services such as file storage or number crunching. You could also choose to unleash your information in the form of databases or files. You could even go as far as providing application services that run on your system. Table 1-2 above summarizes the various levels of resources. P2P applications and exchanges can cross all three levels, depending on your needs and offerings.

The technology supporting each of these levels is advancing rapidly. Moore's law drives the creation of additional processor resources and thus drives level one. The sheer usability of personal applications drives levels two and three. Thus a P2P application constructs a firm bridge between peers that offers peer resources in one or all of the three levels. Napster, for example, shares the first two levels. At level one, you store files for others as well as yourself. At level two, you offer musical resources as information.

P2P Leverages Personal Computer Information and Application Services

The fourth technical area is the ability to create useful information or powerful services. This ability lies in your software applications. Personal computer applications have grown in power, usability, and cost-effectiveness. Many are even free. These applications leverage the largely untapped personal computer hardware capabilities.

Production capabilities have moved from the hands of the bourgeoisie to the proletariat: you and me. Decades ago, the powerful applications existed only on the "powerful" server machines. Who would have thought a decade ago that an individual user could become a distributor and producer of high-quality CDs or photos? Formerly, only big businesses, with expensive factories, could make such a claim. In fact, many modern large businesses have failed to take notice of this powerful personal computer ability.

Today, tools and applications exist all over the personal computer landscape. These tools, with their fantastic creation facilities, have a very limited voice on the Web. They have been forced to find other outlets and have produced limited success stories such as Napster. Tools and applications have grown to harness the raw hardware power available. Users can create high-quality music and photos—even art—and then burn and distribute the content on a digital CD. You can even duplicate professional packaging through CD labels and insert printing. These capabilities are so good that second-hand swap shops must insist that a CD is an original—whatever that means.

Metcalfe's law,[2] which speaks of the value of networking, drives personal computer applications further. The large number of P2P participants create high value for current and potential software applications. The breadth of the participant community offers a promising future for P2P.

P2P Offers a Fully Distributed Symmetric Architecture

Computer architectures abstract overall services and reliability. This abstraction allows designers to focus on key issues such as reliability and integrity. Later chapters will fully explore the many dimensions of architecture. For now, simply note that P2P is very different from a web site architecture. A web site runs a client/server architecture. The web site is the obedient server; your browser is the demanding client. Many simultaneous requests bombard a popular web site. A single web site failure produces many disappointed clients. Since a web site client can only make requests and not service them, a web site failure causes exchanges to fail completely.

A web site administrator can take steps to improve the site's reliability. Such steps include the use of redundant CPUs or disk drives. These steps are very costly and produce only marginal improvements. P2P, by nature, is completely different. Each peer is simultaneously a client and a server. Thus if one server is down, a multitude of peers can fill the void. Whereas a web site may have two or three backup systems, P2P may have thousands. A popular P2P application can be as reliable as an elaborate web fail-over mechanism. This points to an interesting irony: Although each individual peer is most likely less reliable than a web site server, the combination of thousands of peers creates reliability that may exceed that of a web site. There is strength in numbers.

The technical aspects of P2P are all harbingers of its success. The foundation begins with the basic operation of an indifferent, ubiquitous communication medium—the Internet. This medium combines with powerful personal computers and tools. Standards then knit the medium, hardware, and software together without messy and complex communication arrangements.

THE P2P VALUE PROPOSITION

Clearly, P2P offers value in many areas for both individuals and businesses. This section examines some P2P value models to explore this further.

---

2   The value of a network increases exponentially as the number of nodes on the
     network increases.

To examine the value proposition, we categorize P2P into three value concepts: one to one, one to many, and many to many.

One-to-One P2P Value

One-to-one P2P applications enable you to access your peers. That is, you can remotely obtain your information and services. Thus P2P publishes services and information for you to access from remote or mobile devices (other peers). After all, the information and services are yours, and hence the most valuable to you. Many remote access applications allow you to obtain portions of your peers' information and capabilities. An anonymous peer, such as a conference hall computer, can thus obtain your important information and services.

In our mobile, hectic world, the value of one-to-one P2P is clear. Although you could always publish your important information to a web site server, today's frenzied world is hardly so orderly that you could ever anticipate which information or service will be in demand at any instant. You could also use a synchronization application to publish the information or service automatically. Both of these approaches are fraught with difficulties and hidden complexities. Neither allows the publication of services or huge amounts of information. Have you ever tried to synchronize your entire collection of MP3s or all your family photos? Would you ever want to?

One-to-Many P2P Value

One-to-many P2P applications enable the controlled sharing of your information and services with "trusted peers." Many groups collaborate together, and that collaboration results in schedules, contact information, documents, presentations, and the like. Examples of small trusted groups range from corporate project teams to soccer teams.

These types of applications enable the dynamic creation of a collaboration space—a space that is up to date, easily accessible, and protected from any centralized oversight. Today, most small, ad hoc groups depend on traditional means for collaboration—paper. The dynamics of modern technology, and the fact that web site collaboration is needlessly complex, make it necessary for users to make countless phone calls, generate new hard copy, and so on."

Many-to-Many P2P Value

Many-to-many P2P applications enable the anonymous publishing and sharing of information. The user can then tap directly into the richest vein of information anywhere. Web search engines search only web sites, which constitute only the tip of the Internet iceberg. Many-to-many P2P applications enable the harvesting of the Internet edge—your personal computer. Anyone familiar with searching for a song on the Internet recognizes the value of the Napster P2P application. Search attempts often produce thousands of peers that have that desired song. The many-to-many P2P value is the most discussed simply because such applications offer common information that reflects most users' interests. Many-to-many P2P represents the mass market and taps into the hordes of files, information, and services scattered throughout the network edge.

P2P Context Value

Context value forms an interesting corollary to the three value concepts. Context represents information associated with the direct information or resource. A simple example is this P2P book. Context surrounding it would include the book's price, the authors, and so on. Depending on your perspective, the contextual information can be very valuable. Again, here the peer offers some hidden value.

For example, suppose that you are interested in a new musical group—the Peers. Context can help you decide whether you want to listen to and own the group's recording. You might be influenced by technical context issues such as the quality of the recording. Your choice could also be affected by associative information such as the fact that your friend Joe has the Peers' CD and your musical taste is usually similar to Joe's. Context enriches the direct information and can offer powerful indicators to help you decide what action to take.

Every celebrity understands how information can be taken out of context. Web searches often find information that is devoid of context. Rich context—the inherent interrelationship between documents (e-mails, word processing documents, html pages)—exists on the peer. The peer is electronic ground zero, where you do all your transactions, exchanges, and creations. P2P applications can tap into this rich context to make your services and information even more powerful. This is especially true when examined across the three P2P application concept areas. The closer the relationship between peers, the more value context holds. Figure 1-2 illustrates the relationship.

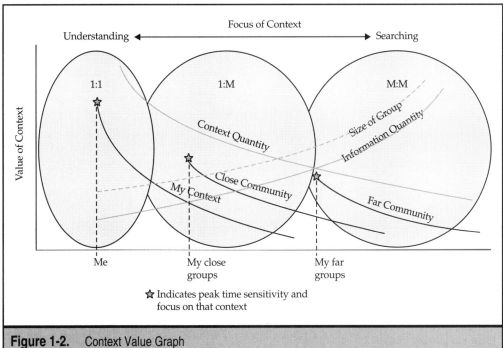

Figure 1-2. Context Value Graph

Although P2P applications don't yet harvest the rich context of the peer, they will soon. Web sites cannot harvest the peer's information, but must constantly ask you questions and make guesses. Each independent site bombards you with text boxes demanding answers. Aren't you tired of that? Also, do you trust sites that demand such information? Finally, how long does your context information stored on a web site remain accurate?

REAL-WORLD EXAMPLES

To build a working, understandable definition further, this section briefly examines a few real-world examples beyond those with which you are likely to be most familiar, music sharing applications like Napster or Morpheus. For a variety of reasons, Napster and P2P are often considered to be synonymous terms. Napster captured considerable mindshare, and in a world of hard-to-learn, hard-to-use applications, the site seemed almost miraculously easy to use. Napster's model is an inspiration to software designers and developers, but Napster is only one type of application in a broad range of unique and interesting P2P applications. This section discusses a small sampling of interesting P2P applications.

SFLAN

On January 3, 2001, Microsoft and Starbucks announced a joint venture that seemed beyond the scope of their core businesses. The duo announced that henceforth the corporations would join forces to offer wireless Internet access in most Starbucks coffee bars. Patrons could sip latte and surf the Web using a technology unglamorously called 802.11b. Starbucks is trying to capitalize on this technology for commercial reasons. In San Francisco, however, an organization called SFLAN is using 802.11 for a much more ambitious strategy: to knit together communities. As SFLAN explains in its "manifesto" (http://www.sflan.com):

> *Imagine a citywide wireless LAN that grows from anarchistic cooperation. From a laptop in any park, from a PC in any house, from any handheld assistant on the street, you can get at the Internet at blazing speed. From there, imagine a phone that uses your base station when you are in your house, but uses the net when you are out of range.*

The basic idea behind SFLAN is that, as the use of broadband connections grows, people will create LANs in their houses using small, inexpensive hubs into which they can plug in their computers. They will also be able to plug in a tiny radio beacon (a *wireless access point*, or *WAP*) so that anyone within range—roughly a couple blocks' radius—can piggyback on their broadband Internet connection. Eventually, this "anarchistic cooperation" creates a citywide equivalent of a multimegabit-per-second LAN for the benefit of all, at a very small cost for each user.

SFLAN is an example of using P2P as a shared resource provider. It demonstrates that people might be willing to dedicate some portion of their resources (in this case, their bandwidth) to community use, if others are willing to do the same thing for the common good.

Roku

Roku is a P2P platform that operates with traditional desktop tools to give you access to your information. The platform helps you achieve goals with the tools even if you are working remotely from the desktop on which the tools (and Roku) are installed.

When you first install Roku, it gathers information from address books (such as those in Microsoft's Outlook or the Palm desktop), e-mails, documents, and calendars, and then uses a "context engine" to figure out how the information is related. The context engine creates links between the information so that, for example, if you were on the road with nothing but a mobile phone or PDA, and you wanted to look up a phone number for a friend, you could contact your Roku and search for the number.

Roku is an example of *person-to-system* P2P, where one on the members of the conversation is a person (you) and the other is a software agent. With Roku, a resource that is not available when you are away from it (such as your PC at home or work) can work for you no matter where you are and no matter what access method (remote web browser, wireless PDA, cell phone, or pager) is handy.

Groove

Groove is the 800-pound gorilla of corporate P2P computing. It is a platform that software developers can use to build cooperative collaboration environments.

Groove exemplifies a P2P *collaboration space*. When you and your team members install Groove on your PCs, your team creates a "virtual space." In this virtual space, you can interact with members of your group and collaborate on projects in real time. Although Groove is a software development platform, it includes several capabilities and tools that all users can benefit from right off the shelf. These capabilities include the following:

▼ Communications features such as live voice over the Internet, instant messaging, text-based chat, and threaded discussion (such as you might find in a news server or discussion server)

■ Tools for sharing documents, pictures, contacts, and activities (for example, a shared white board that a number of people can doodle on at the same time)

▲ A shared text pad that you can use to brainstorm

In addition to this basic platform, Groove provides a specification to add new tools and manage the group (inviting people to join the group, for example, or changing their permissions).

SETI@home

Applications such as Roku and Groove enable you to collaborate either with your computer(s) and/or with other people, making use of your computing resources and networks to create an environment where you use your computer to achieve personal goals. In the case of Roku, you use your own network and PC as a personal server when you are physically remote. With Groove, you use your own PC and the PCs of others in your circle to create a private network to do personal and group work. The Search for Extraterrestrial Intelligence (SETI) at Home (SETI@home) project borrows your computer when you are not using it to achieve larger, nonpersonal scientific goals.

The basic premise of SETI@home is that most home computers sit around doing little more than consume electricity, when they could be doing something useful for all humankind—analyzing the mountains of data from astronomers as they search the heavens for life in the universe. University of California, Berkeley researchers working on this project faced the problem of analyzing all the data continuously collected from the large radio telescopes at Arecibo and other places in the world. They realized that it would take a complex of supercomputers cranking away day and night to keep pace. They also knew that SETI programs could never afford to build, buy, or access that kind of computing horsepower.

Instead, the researchers arrived at one of those ideas that occur once in a lifetime. Rather than installing a few huge computers to do the job, they break apart the problem and use many smaller computers like yours to work on each part. They parcel out computations (which they call "work units") from the Seti@home server over the Internet to people around the world to analyze. When your home PC finishes working on its bit, it ships the results back to the SETI server and picks up the next work unit. Through this P2P application, SETI has built a massively parallel computer (using the collective intelligence of your computer, and mine, and eventually millions of others) to work on a large problem, and in return we might be instrumental in solving one of humankind's greatest questions: "Is there life out there?"

SETI@home is an example of *infrastructural* or *architectural* P2P, where members of the P2P community are not even necessarily aware that someone other than themselves is using their resources, and where a self-organizing network is created from the voluntary participation of people and machines all over the regular Internet.

Jabber

Jabber is a next-generation instant messaging (IM) platform. Instant messaging platforms (such as AOL Instant Messenger or Yahoo! Messenger) have been around for a while, but Jabber is unique in that it is also a platform for building other kinds of applications. All IM platforms are P2P in that they operate in a private space that springs up among the peers talking to one another. Jabber, however, allows a software developer to create applications for that private space that might have nothing to do with textual chatting with another person. For example, an online shopping application might use your Jabber information to complete an online form with shipping information. Another application might examine your presence information (whether you are online or offline) to decide whether it should send you an instant message or call to inform you that your spouse's flight will be delayed.

Jabber is an example of P2P *messaging as a platform* upon which many kinds of applications can be built, including those where people communicate with people or with applications, or where an application communicates with applications.

SOCIAL IMPACTS OF P2P

In addition to creating new technical and business opportunities, P2P computing also has the potential to effect social change. Some of these impacts are already changing the way people think, and some of the impacts are not yet in full flower. As this section explains, they are powerful and have enormous potential for changing the way people live, play, work, interact, communicate, and use information.

A Part of the Woodwork

P2P applications such as instant messaging work their magic in subtle ways so that you are not even aware of them and their effect. They demonstrate an interesting social aspect of P2P, about which little has been written. That is, P2P tends to become a common part of your daily life, often disappearing into the structure of your day so that you hardly notice that it's there. This is true of e-mail, the most basic P2P application. You take for granted the existence of your e-mail connection, as though it was something akin to water or electricity—seemingly free and ubiquitous. Napster, for example, makes publishing and subscribing obtainable by a novice within minutes of installing the application (many users remain unaware that they are actually publishing their own music to other Napster users).

The following sections continue to examine the social impact of P2P. They also suggest ways in which the Internet needs to be more like P2P.

Modes of Interaction

The first time you send or receive an instant message with one of the popular P2P IM applications, you perceive the power of P2P. Traditional telephony, or a face-to-face meeting, forces structure to the interaction. There are setup considerations (dialing or setting up a physical place and time); there is a protocol ("What do I want to talk about?" "What tone is appropriate—business or social?" "How do I start the conversation?" "How do I handle pauses?" "What does that raised eyebrow mean?"); and, of course, there is the discipline of paying or feigning attention.

With IM, communication moves to a whole new mode of interaction. The talk is more casual, for one thing. The rhythm of the conversation changes as well; gaps (possibly long) are tolerated and even expected. Conversations are more staccato and less structured; ideas and emotion are blurted out, perhaps not even in full sentences, perhaps not even in words. Acronyms such as "LOL" (laughing out loud) or the ubiquitous smiley-face family of emotions serve as a new language for P2P.

Conversations are more open-ended, possibly continuing for hours. Indeed, on college campuses, IM connections tend to stay up all day long, and conversations potentially never end. Dorm-mates can be seen sitting back to back, ignoring one another while holding half-dozen simultaneous conversations with friends who are only "virtually" there. Whether this kind of communication is a *good* thing or a *bad* thing is beyond the scope of this discussion and this book. What we suggest is that it is a *different* thing, very much a *P2P* thing, and very much a driving force behind P2P. Clearly, P2P creates a social shift, and that the shift, at its heart, involves people interacting with one another over a distance.

Further, the shift represents a new level of immediacy, intimacy, utility, and control in dealing with people and systems, while at the same time weaving new and dynamic capabilities into the fabric of our lives.

Immediacy

In the short history of the computer, significant changes have occurred in the role of the computer and our relationship with the computer. Up until the mid-1980s, computers were used in very data-centric ways. Phalanxes of data-entry clerks and highly skilled computing professionals fed and tended to mainframes. Results were seldom interactive or communication-centered, because of the structure of computing, networking, and the types of problems being handled by computers. The relationship between humans and computers was human-to-database.

1980s: The Document Is King

In the 1980s, the Macintosh and Windows ushered in an era in which the document became paramount. With the advent of more sophisticated networking and the desktop graphical user interface (GUI) metaphor, the relationship between humans and computers became human-to-document. During this era, which is only now coming to an end, the personal computer was dominant due to its ability to present simple graphical interfaces for creating, manipulating, printing, and circulating documents.

The Next Generation: Events Are King

Today, suddenly, the computer is being thrust into a novel and unfamiliar role—that of communications server. The relationship between humans and computers is becoming human-to-agent, where the computer acts as an agent capable of notifying people of important events, new information arrivals, and the virtual presence of friends or contacts.

Data and documents remain important in supporting real-time interactivity and collaboration between people, but personal computers have gained a new role as communication devices for an increasingly mobile and event-driven life style in the developed world. The ability to act immediately upon goals and targets of opportunity has higher status in our collective consciousness than the orderly management of data or document production.

Thus, computing has evolved socially from a place where data entry was important, to a document-centric model of computing, to one in which handling events and communicating and collaborating with team members are perceived to be the most important functions of computing.

The P2P client computer is beginning to replace or at least supplement traditional server functionality. Servers at the core of the Internet cannot, by themselves, scale up to provide the level of responsiveness necessary to support the immediate alerting that users require for a seamless experience in which immediacy is the prize.

Intimacy

Intimacy might sound like a strange attribute to ascribe to the P2P phenomenon. But companies and researchers are beginning to recognize the value of the intimacy that P2P provides with other people (whether known beforehand or discovered in a community of interest) and with your own information.

If the traditional Web and application servers at the core of the Internet are inadequate to provide sufficient immediacy, they are also inadequate to provide a personalized information experience.

You've probably had the experience of surfing to a portal site and reading through the news articles there. You can leave that page and return to it as many times as you like, but you will always return as somewhat of a stranger. Cookies and history features help, but the recognition level falls short of our expectations. The site just doesn't know you. Its perspective is limited to the relatively small number of interactions that you have with the specific site. Your countless hours surfing elsewhere on the Internet are lost to the site's view. Even powerful Amazon.com doesn't really know you; otherwise, the site wouldn't consistently push books and music that you don't want.

The Internet of today tends to be less than useful as a personal outpost in cyberspace. Sites can't be bothered with learning much about you and your interests, unless there's a clear economic motivation. All the economic incentives for the Web lead sites to treat you as a viewer in a largely non-interactive experience. Toward the end of the last century, the business forces behind the Web wanted to shift the purpose of the Web to re-create television and serve up largely one-way interactions. Further, they wanted to create a specific kind of television—the equivalent of television's home shopping network, wherein you were allowed interactivity only to the extent that you could type in a delivery address, a quantity, and credit card information.

The Internet as experienced via the Web is not a very inviting place to put your intimate data, such as your e-mails and your contact information. Unless you are the "deer in the headlights" of a web e-commerce provider who drops an occasional web cookie onto your hard disk, the Internet tends to treat you as a faceless, nameless nonentity. The Internet doesn't have to be this way. Both the research and commercial sectors are working to improve the level of intimacy. Later chapters will cover these efforts.

Intimacy and Knowledge Spaces—I Need My Data

Knowledge spaces are your collection of personal information. A knowledge space may reside anywhere. For example, a personal computer indiscriminately harbors your knowledge space through its assortment of applications such as e-mail, scheduling, and even tax software. Web sites and Internet service providers (ISPs) also may contain pieces of your knowledge space through your various trips through their resources. An ISP or web site could potentially retain this knowledge space.

But even if an ISP had a strong motivation (whether commercial or, less likely, altruistic), it could never conveniently hold enough of your important information to allow you on-demand access to your intimate information to make that a viable option. First of all, you now have too much "stuff" on your personal computer—the pictures you create with your digital camera, your MP3 collection, your contact lists, your calendar, your collected documents. What motivation would your ISP or a web site have to provide you a data haven for free or for the purpose of getting you to look at web banner advertising?

Second, loading or synchronizing all that "stuff" to an ISP requires an act of will. You would have to plan, set aside time, and execute an upload. You have to make decisions about what to synchronize and what to leave out. That decision is almost always based on a mental snapshot of what you *might* need at some time in the future when you are away from your PC. In contrast, your personal, broadband-connected PC is an always-available data haven, and the right server software can provide you with real-time access independent of whatever device you happen to hold in your hand. Later chapters will discuss the architectures and applications that allow this level of intimacy with your knowledge stores.

Intimacy and Virtual Presence

As we suggested previously, instant messaging fosters a casual and immediate style of interaction with others, and at the same time it allows a higher level of communication between users who may be thousands of miles apart. A single glance at an IM "buddy list" reveals which of your associates are "present" (online rather than offline), and a sweep of the eye across their status messages can reveal which of them are "available" (willing to talk rather than busy). A simple "U there?" message to a friend present and online can be the gateway to a useful exchange. Messages can create instant communities of interest. The technology cannot ensure any user's actual identity. Thus, the user must authenticate the identity through various indirect means.

Recently, in a company strategy meeting, we were surprised to see an instant message pop up on our wireless iPaq PocketPCs. One of the other executives in the meeting sent us a message to the effect that the speaker was "talking nonsense." How refreshing to see the time-honored primary school experience of intimate note passing reborn in the adult world and the Internet age. We agreed with the executive and formulated a strategy to neutralize the speaker's silly babbling. Although we didn't realize it at the time, we had been parties to a time-of-event formation of a community of interest.

Intimacy, People, and Communities

Clay Shirky, noted P2P pundit, remarks that Napster "showed us the shape of the next generation Internet." Whether Napster survives its legal challenges or not (the outcome was very much in doubt in mid-2001, as this book was being written) is not relevant in the larger scheme of things. But we believe that Shirky's comment is right on target on a number of grounds. In particular, the next generation Internet will be a far more intimate place where the focus will be on people communicating and interacting with each other. This focus is in contrast to that of the previous generation Internet, which was gluing visitors' eyeballs to the advertising banners on a web site, and tracking visitors like a deer in season.

Every time a Napster user performs a song search and discovers that several other people downloaded the same song, the site creates a relationship. A friend recently discovered that someone was downloading some arcane song from their PC over Napster. Our friend had been in the act of disconnecting from Napster for the night, but delayed doing so until the downloader was finished, on the grounds that the other person (presumably a complete stranger) had to be a "cool person" because he or she shared our friend's eclectic taste in '80s pop. Voilá! Instant formation of a community of interest and mutual respect.

Utility

As we further discuss the technology reach of P2P, it will become clear that the traditional edge device of the client/server network, the personal computer, no longer limits our ability to interact with other people or with systems across the Internet. For over a century, people have enjoyed tethered (wired) person-to-person voice communication, and more recently, this has extended to wireless, on-the-go communication. With the emergence of P2P, meaningful person-to-system communication is possible as well.

In the earlier incarnation of mobile data access, the effort centered upon moving the mass media communications model of the web experience onto mobile handsets. This effort failed for the obvious reasons—shrinking the web experience, with all of its attempted TV glitz and glamour, onto a four-line display at the end of a slow data connection is simply a silly idea. Apparently, this was not quite as obvious to many Internet and telephony executives, who should have known better, but spent millions of dollars fielding these generally useless systems. Instead of forcing users to navigate the Web with an all but useless nine or ten button keypad, these executives should have concentrated on transporting alerts, notifications, and critical e-mail from our work and home personal computers, and from our peers, onto our mobile handset.

Users have moved from interacting with cyberspace at a tethered PC to interacting while on the move and responding to real-time events, alerts, and notifications ("events are king"). Rather than navigate the Web on a tiny handset to find a summary of the latest professional soccer scores, users would much rather know whether someone is ringing their front doorbell at home and be able to interact with that person (if it's the washer repair person, open the door; if it's the neighborhood burglar, call the police). Several P2P projects are under way to do precisely these kinds of things, and upcoming chapters will cover these efforts.

The ability to receive alerts, messages, and notifications independent of device and location is something that simply was not readily available even a few years ago. P2P access, sharing your knowledge space with yourself and achieving actionable goals, redefines the role of computer and networking technology; it also changes your ability to be productive any time and anywhere, something that the next section and later chapters will discuss.

Control

P2P technology also returns to the individual some measure of personal control over the myriad digital scraps of information we are forced to remember in the modern login and password era. In the era before society went online, you could hold all the numbers and contact information you needed in a little paper address book, or on assorted scraps of paper. The required set of information seems to have multiplied significantly.

Now we have telephone numbers for our spouses at work, and for their mobile devices; mobile and pager numbers and e-mail addresses for our kids; at least a couple e-mail addresses; and multiple login and passwords, for work and e-commerce sites. A friend of ours keeps all her logins and passwords stowed on her Palm V (surely an act of misguided faith); whenever she needs to log in from any machine, she pulls out the list and enters the information. The size of the information space relevant to our lives has grown to such an extent that the PC acting as a personal information server, available to you wherever you happen to find yourself, becomes a realistic need.

Digital Butterflies

Additionally, we create information wherever we happen to be at the moment. Perched at our work computer, we create reports, draft analyses, write business e-mail, generate meeting requests, record sales contacts, and produce myriad other kinds of business documents. On the go, we record into our nifty PCS phone a telephone number for later retrieval. We flit to our home machines and record interesting web sites into our bookmarks, write e-mails to relatives, and build our MP3 collections. On holiday, we create digital photos or short films and later upload them to our multimedia Macintoshes to edit and share with the grandparents. Like cyber-butterflies, we flutter from one information context and information manipulation tool to another, and never consider how trapped we are by the very tools that create and maintain our digital experience.

Trapped by Tools

Your tools don't talk to one another, and they don't talk to you, except under very special circumstances—you have to be using a certain hardware platform and/or be in a specific place. You have to learn all about their limitations and quirks, and they respect none of yours. You have to remember exactly where you created the information—on what machine, in what folder, in what format. Getting to your own data often becomes a formidable obstacle in achieving what should be a simple goal. P2P has some prescriptive remedies for the control problem of having too many identities and tools. This book will explore these remedies.

In summary, P2P has the potential to create positive social change, foster a new era in productive use of the Internet, and give back some measure of control of your information.

THE DARK SIDE OF P2P

P2P is not a panacea. Although we are enthusiastic about P2P's potential, several trouble-some areas exist. The chapters ahead explore some solutions that can mitigate some of these problems. Others are not as easily dismissed. These problem areas include:

▼ **Unpredictability**   Most P2P applications lack any centralization. This makes it very difficult to predict anything about a P2P application. How much bandwidth will it take up and when? What will be the overall performance? These and many other questions make predictability a real concern.

■ **Integrity**   Some P2P applications depend on essentially anonymous peers. The content they share or services they offer are not subject to any level of validation or certification. A song entitled "GreatSong.mp3" may not be such a great song; it may not be a song at all. The magical P2P proliferation of content can make removing poor information extremely difficult. In a short period, "GreatSong.mp3" could be resident on thousands of peers.

■ **Availability**   P2P services and applications depend on a peer, not a web server. Peers come and go. The peer that had valuable information yesterday may crash today. Critical services may not be available when you need them.

■ **Peer control**   Many P2P applications exert little control over the peers. A P2P application may exercise a little central authority or none at all. Lack of control creates fears of anarchy. This lack of control can make enemies out of traditional IT groups. A P2P application may inadvertently tie up valuable IT resources such as bandwidth, or force IT to make additional firewall compromises.

▲ **Security**   Many P2P applications offer direct access to your information and services. Most peers are personal computers owned and controlled by other users like you and me. We are not full-time security specialists. The P2P application could have security holes, or improper administration could create one. In either case, this serious vulnerability deserves your attention. Subsequent sections in this book describe and demonstrate effective security measures.

P2P raises serious concerns, but no activity or technology is 100 percent safe. This book's goal is to make you aware of these concerns and forge solutions or workarounds to ensure your success with P2P. Some risks can never be completely eliminated. Your awareness enables you to best evaluate the risks and benefits. You are often protected just by the sheer magnitude of participants. Why would someone target you? To crackers, you are much less valuable than the jewels contained in a web site, such as thousands of credit card numbers.

Concerns such as these bring to mind a story about two lawyers and a bear. Two lawyers[3] are hiking through the woods. Off in the distance, they see a bear charging at them. One lawyer quickly begins changing his hiking boots into his running shoes. "You can't outrun a bear!" the other lawyer injects. The first lawyer replies, "I don't have to. I only have to outrun you!" To be safe, you need not build a virtual Fort Knox, you just need to show a little more concern than all the others do. This book's solutions will make sure that you do.

WHAT MAKES P2P IMPORTANT TO *YOU*

P2P is interesting technically and has many exciting applications. Many new businesses and intriguing personal uses are being planned that take advantage in one way or another of P2P computing. But why is P2P so important?

An earlier section discussed some of P2P's social impacts. P2P allows people greater immediacy, intimacy with the information they create and the devices they use, greater utility from their tools, and control over how accessible their identity is in cyberspace. All of these impacts add up to one thing: Returning to people the power that they lost to the complexity of using computers and computerlike tools. Regaining power becomes especially important in an age where automobiles are half machine and half computer, where mobile phones are tiny computers that must be programmed to deliver the functionality that makes them useful at all, and where home alarm systems require programming that only a Ph.D. or a six-year-old could master.

One thing that people in the developed world now particularly lack is *time*—time for their families, time for each other, time for themselves. If P2P has half the impact that we anticipate, people will gain both power and win back time for themselves.

A friend's school-age daughter wanted to try out for a role in the musical play *Godspell,* but she had never heard any of the musical selections from it. Her father really wanted to help her to gain knowledge of the music, but as he only learned of it after the dinner hour, he was in a quandary as to what to do. He couldn't go to the local CD store; they would be closed, and in any event might not have the CD or tape, since it wasn't a current "top 40" selection. Brick-and-mortar businesses have to carry actual inventory, and are loath to carry a selection for very long. He couldn't purchase it from an online store either; delivery would take at least a couple days.

In desperation, he turned to the most well-known P2P application, Napster. Within an hour, he had downloaded the significant songs from the musical and burned a CD for his daughter. Whether this was theft of intellectual property was not the big issue for him—he would more than likely have been overjoyed to use a "legal" site (controlled by the recording industry) had there been one. What was important for him was that he gained *power* over the situation, and was able to gain mastery over time. He got back a piece of his life.

---

3   Actually this joke works with almost any profession so substitute one of your choice.

In the months to come, you will hear more about new and possibly arcane concepts, such as P2P online-shopping experiences (SmartPeer), P2P context engines, P2P currencies (MojoNation), P2P software agents (Consilient), P2P collaboration (Groove Networks, Ikimbo), P2P file sharing (Freenet), and many others. However, everything that qualifies as P2P conforms in some way to the spirit of giving the user back some power over his or her own life and enabling the user to share that power with others.

SUMMARY

P2P builds a direct bridge between users. This bridge links their work and play efforts into direct collaboration. It also links their information and services to form a new, rich Internet resource—a resource containing up-to-date, useful, and pertinent information and services. Previously, the rules of web servers constrained Internet collaboration and information sharing. P2P breaks free of these constraints and opens up an entirely new Internet dimension. It is also a dimension that the user can control. There is no need for privacy policies from a third-party web site. P2P is not without its faults and risks, but with careful guidance, you can avoid or mitigate many of them.

This chapter has outlined the basics of P2P. The next chapter continues your P2P journey by taking a strategic tour of the current landscape.

CHAPTER 2

The P2P City Tour: Existing Solutions Ready Now

This chapter and the next take you on a tour of P2P solutions and possibilities. This exploration is by no means comprehensive, but rather a representative sampling of the major types of P2P solutions that exist today. Your tour consists of two parts: a city tour and a rough jungle safari. The first tour surveys the P2P civilized territories. These consist of P2P solutions that you can buy or obtain "out of the box"—ready-made solutions, services, and products that allow you to use P2P approaches. Such solutions enable you to participate in the P2P revolution without hacking through a raw landscape. The second tour delves deep into the jungle of P2P possibilities, offering an overview of the raw materials of the P2P revolution. This tour consists of the building blocks and frameworks that enable you to begin constructing the next new revolutionary P2P city stop.

THE P2P CITY TOUR: EXISTING SOLUTIONS READY NOW

The first tour has all the comforts of a frontier city—some nice spots, but many unpaved and unproven roadways and destinations. The tour divides the P2P city into two neighborhoods. Our first neighborhood examines P2P resource sharing products and services. You'll make several stops to explore file sharing. File sharing applications were the first set of tools that established P2P as a real alternative. The rest of the initial neighborhood includes sharing other computing resources such as distributed computation and distributed searching solutions.

The second neighborhood tour examines P2P collaboration product and services. You will see the sights of basic collaboration products, gaming, and instant messaging tools. Surprisingly, the huge success of instant messaging is rarely attributed to its P2P roots. Finally, you begin to understand the city's customs by evaluating the common business and technical themes along with important pitfalls surrounding today's P2P out-of-the-box solutions. On the city tour, you will see what is possible now. The city's successes, failures, and challenges open up the path to new possibilities.

THE P2P SAFARI: POSSIBILITIES AND PROMISES

The second tour is not for the timid P2P explorer. Simply exploring the P2P city, with all its creature comforts, makes for a fascinating trip. However, P2P is going much further, and you'll want to explore this frontier. This tour starts with the raw materials in the P2P jungle. The discoveries include the players who offer the building blocks and frameworks to build advanced custom P2P solutions. The tour also offers a view into upcoming P2P products and services.

Your safari stops will take you to several challenging and dark areas. The first area is P2P infrastructure. Successful P2P solutions depend on a multitude of services such as security and communication. Incorporating these raw but powerful infrastructure services into your solution rapidly improves its overall functionality and performance. The next area is P2P distributed objects. The capability to execute remote functionality greatly enhances a P2P solution. Distributed objects enable you to get at the lowest level of functionality in the P2P solution. The toughest terrain that you will traverse leads you to P2P development frameworks. This area integrates the best from distributed objects and infrastructure services to offer a comprehensive P2P construction environment.

The last stop on the safari takes you to the strange, paradoxical area of in-the-net P2P services. This topsy-turvy area incorporates servers to strengthen overall P2P solutions. Servers offer the proverbial "street corner" that enables efficient and timely peer communication and collaboration. The street corner acts as an efficient means of exchanging information amongst peers. Street corners may be a little premature while we still traverse the P2P jungle but vendors are hoping to get an early start. The safari ends with a jungle campfire story that outlines the common pitfalls and challenges in this jungle terrain—lessons that summarize today's P2P enablers and the challenges that they hold for your solutions.

What You'll Learn Along the Way

Your tour through these landscapes has two purposes: It illustrates what you can do now with P2P and also begins to reveal a framework to establish your own P2P solutions. The landscape is quite varied and dynamic. Surely much will have changed between our writing this book and your reading it. The dynamics of P2P will undoubtedly change specific implementations in the form of product and service offerings. However, the basic information and collaboration needs addressed by P2P will evolve more slowly and naturally. Your expeditions balance both points—specific implementation issues and the core, strategic benefits. These two major tours begin to build your P2P tool chest and outline your possibilities in applying P2P to address your needs.

The first of our two tours—the civilized one—uncovers both the implementation and value of the P2P products. Each tour reveals the ways in which companies have turned current technology into something immediately useful. You could decide to use these products directly or, by taking the second expedition, delve deeper into the foundation technologies to build your own P2P solution. The safari expedition in the next chapter will assist you in deeper explorations of fundamental P2P technologies.

Regardless of which tour you choose to take, keep one basic observation in mind: P2P offerings will succeed or fail based on the value that they provide to the consumer. The bursting of the Internet investment bubble in 2000 was a clear signal that the number of users doesn't count, the number of dollars taken in profit does. To make a profit, P2P products and services must prove to be of value to the consumer. Many of these offerings have yet to show a profit and hence may not survive, but as they struggle to provide value to consumers, you should take advantage of the opportunity to explore the products. Each product or service we examine offers insights into today's implementations and points the way towards Tomorrow's P2P solutions—Tomorrow's value equation.

You do not want to meander aimlessly across this P2P landscape. Explorations of these types often leave you confused with a long litany of disorganized sites, products, and services. This flawed approach leaves the reader grappling to make sense of the complexity. It is like visiting a city by quickly jumping from place to place. Each jump appears to have no connection to the previous place. The tourist is left with a lot of pictures, often blurred, but no feel for the place. In order to avoid placing such on burden on you, our journey starts with a map that contains a two-level hierarchy tied to the P2P definition from Chapter 1. The map tells you where you are and where you came from. It provides context that allows comparisons and eases the understanding of the various P2P players and their roles.

As a savvy tourist, you will make judicious stops along the way. You explore each P2P locale, as your guides highlight the key issues and distinctions between the various P2P offerings. We standardized each tour to provide consistency between stops. Each tour stop first presents an overview of the P2P product or service, then details the specific benefits to you, the supporting technologies and their corresponding architecture, any interesting issues, and conclusions.

Finally, your guides summarize the landscape for each tour. The summary identifies the commonalities and key differences between the examined sample of P2P products and services. We also note the common themes that spell success or failure. This summary sets the stage for the next section, which builds a comprehensive view of P2P. The comprehensive view details all the requirements and features needed for successful P2P computing for your personal or business adventures. This view will help you establish full P2P functionality for advanced, comprehensive solutions customized to your individual or business needs.

So let's get started on your P2P tour. As with any tour, some places (or products) are more interesting than others, so certain stops will be quick and to the point. But you will linger longer at the more interesting spots to appreciate the possibilities.

THE CURRENT LANDSCAPE MAP FOR P2P

Let's begin the landscape P2P tour by outlining the map. Your map builds on the *P2P def-inition* from Chapter 1:

> *Peer-to-Peer Computing (P2P): The action of mutually exchanging information and services directly between the producer and the consumer.*

Your map consists of a two-level hierarchy of categories. The first level illustrates the three major threads that define P2P: resources, collaboration, and P2P enablers. Resources are what you want. Collaboration establishes methods to work and play together. Finally, P2P enablers provide the superstructure to build engaging, powerful P2P applications quickly. P2P enablers represent the raw materials of P2P, and you explore them in your second tour, the safari, in Chapter 3. Figure 2-1 illustrates the high-level categories.

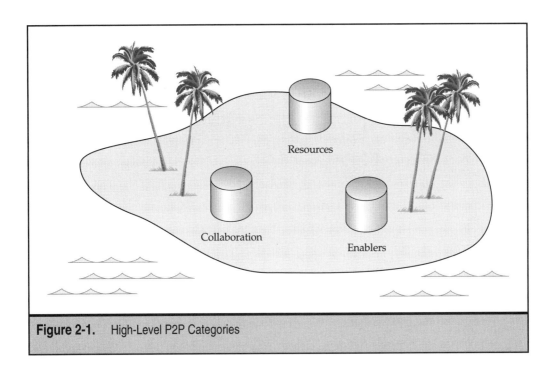

Figure 2-1.   High-Level P2P Categories

The following are the high-level categories:

▼   **P2P Resource Products and Services**   This category represents the interesting "stuff" that each peer owns and controls. Products in this category make the stuff available to you remotely, to your close associates, or to the world. The stuff could include raw computing resources, formatted or unformatted information, or capabilities of your applications. Table 1-2 briefly covers resources, and our P2P definition refers to them as *information and services*.

▲   **P2P Collaboration Products and Services**   A major P2P goal is to communicate with your fellow peers so that you can work (and play) together. These products and services help you accomplish your business or personal goals, and vice versa. Again we are reminded of the P2P mantra: quid pro quo. Many products and services tie groups of peers together to exchanges ideas, work on projects, and the like. Our P2P definition referred to this as *mutually exchanging*.

The specific P2P products and services on this tour all fall into one of these two categories. Figure 2-2 illustrates this area of the tour.

Figure 2-2.   P2P Products and Services

Let's begin your first tour. It introduces each area and its subcategories. Then each tour stop illustrates one of the areas.

P2P RESOURCE PRODUCT AND SERVICES

▼ **File Sharing**   This category forms the first noted P2P success. It allows you to access information in the form of raw files that resides on someone else's computer. This simple capability of grabbing someone's files lit the P2P fire. It instantly demonstrated the powerful information reach discussed in Chapter 1. The P2P tour includes the file-sharing product Freenet.

■ **Distributed Computation**   This category taps into the rich P2P vein of underutilized raw computing resources. Distributed computation products knit together the diverse P2P hardware platforms to create a virtual supercomputer at a bargain basement price. Chapter 1 discussed a major distributed computation initiative, SETI@home. This tour makes a stop to explore United Technologies.

▲ **Distributed Search** This category harvests the rich resources of P2P. Effective searching mines the sheer vastness of P2P for you to find the proverbial needle in a haystack. Ultimately, these product offerings could prove the most valuable category of all. The vastness of P2P clearly offers loads of valuable information and capabilities, but you need to be able to find them among the millions of peers. These tools unlock P2P's richness. Your P2P tour stops to visit the distributed search tool OpenCola.

File Sharing

File sharing taps the vastness of P2P file resources. As you explore these solutions, several issues come up quickly. Most files are not indexed or categorized in any way. Microsoft Word allows you to add a category or keywords. Frankly, though, few users know how to use this capability to search the information. A file can contain any type of information, such as a school history report, a business case, or a travel journal. Files may also contain multiple formats; for example, a text document might include embedded graphics. Aside from opening the file, you have only limited means to discover what a file might contain. Even opening the file presents challenges; users depend on the file extension to indicate which application can decode the file's contents.

Users try to maintain some indexing and categorization by using creative filenames along with organizing the files intelligently in file folders. However, these persnickety details slip from the mind. We often have trouble finding our own files despite our best attempts to create meaningful names and directories. P2P file sharing opens up all these unique ad-hoc indexing systems to the world.

These limitations strangely enough allow great freedom in moving files from peer to peer but create quite a challenge in finding and interpreting a desired file. Since users need not categorize files or adhere to any naming convention of the files, they produce a lot of files without creating an easy path to find them. Files offer content clues only with their filenames, extensions, and content types. These clues guarantee little and often send users on a wild goose chase, much like results found from a web search engine. Future solutions may demand some additional descriptive structure for files. For now, let's make a tour stop at Freenet—quite an interesting P2P neighborhood.

Freenet

Although you can think of the Internet as an enormous shared content repository, the role of most users of this information is that of a content consumer. In contrast, Freenet enables users to act as a publisher as well as a consumer by using the combined computational and storage capabilities of peer computers to create the world's largest information store. Freenet allows anyone to publish or consume information, unfettered by a central authority such as an ISP, multinational corporation, or government. That's a tall order, but when Ian Clarke and a contingent of brilliant collaborators proposed Freenet in a paper in mid-2000, many regarded the proposal an eminently sensible and desirable way for the Internet to operate. The collaborators' paper described Freenet as:

> ...*an adaptive peer-to-peer network application that permits the publication, replication, and retrieval of data while protecting the anonymity of both authors and readers. Freenet operates as a network of identical nodes that collectively pool their storage space to store data files and cooperate to route requests to the most likely physical location of data. No broadcast search or centralized location index is employed. Files are referred to in a location-independent manner, and are dynamically replicated in locations near requestors and deleted from locations where there is no interest. It is infeasible to discover the true origin or destination of a file passing through the network, and difficult for a node operator to determine or be held responsible for the actual physical contents of her own node.*

A moment's reflection over the collaborators' goal reveals a very radical change from the way things operate currently. For one thing, Freenet would provide users total anonymity. While this might mean on the one hand that pornography would flow through Freenet without embarrassment to its purveyors, it also means that political dissent can flow just as unencumbered without penalty or prosecution. It also means that (because no central servers are involved) plausible deniability exists for anyone who happens to store information temporarily on his or her machine as a result of being a node in the path of information creators or consumers.

Further, a denial-of-service attack is a lot less possible in an architecture like the Freenet network because it lacks central server as an attractive target. As Chapter 1 pointed out, the Napster system became vulnerable to legal challenge from the record industry because it centrally stored information about the information often referred to as metadata being held by its users. They did not store the files themselves but all the necessary information to find and download them. Napster could then be accused of aiding and abetting the commission of a crime. By decentralizing the functions of the system, Freenet could be far more resistant to all kinds of attack, much like the overall structure of the Internet itself.

Benefits   Freenet's creators are concerned with the potential erosion of the ability to disseminate information freely, even within a democratic society. In every era in which media conglomeration occurs, whether it's the Hearst era in newspaper publishing or AOL's acquisition of Time-Warner, it is important to have a counterbalancing force. If everything the public sees or hears is filtered through the spinners and opinion shapers, then democracy is potentially under assault. Freenet's philosophy is ostensibly to act as a counterweight to media control and aggregation, to allow two or more people who want to share information (whether it's music, pictures, or social opinion) to do so.

These are the philosophical benefits, but there are practical benefits as well. Freenet creates what is essentially a virtual public publishing network with very little setup of the kind that one would have to do to publish on the traditional Web. Your information is *free* immediately. There is no need for special conversions or esoteric linking.

Technology   The Freenet protocol is one of the more fascinating parts of the Freenet story. It's a simple message passing protocol in which "neighboring nodes" pass messages to one another. Any neighbor can pass a message requesting a file, or transferring a file, or simply telling its neighbor, "Here I am." The network built upon this basis is very adaptive, with nodes possibly coming and going dynamically. Significant redundancy exists among the many nodes that store a given file, so losing a single node in the system is inconsequential.

Nodes in the system talk only to neighboring nodes, but the term "neighbor" does not necessarily connote geographic closeness. Neighborhoods form spontaneously based on a built-in discovery system that freely associates cooperating computers into small groupings or neighborhoods. Computers, within a given neighborhood, work together on many activities such as sharing popular files. This often eliminates the need to seek out the global set of Freenet users and makes many activities fast and efficient.

The Freenet system does not contain clients or servers. Neighbors simply pass messages to one another. Nodes have no idea whether the node to which they just passed a message is the ultimate destination for a file, or simply another connecting node in the system. Thus a given node cannot "profile" another node in terms of the files it publishes or consumes.

The architectural imperative of Freenet is straightforward: to store documents and allow others to retrieve them. Serving this imperative, each node maintains files accessed by a Freenet generate key. The key is just a numerical representation of the file enabling easier indexing and searching. What a given node stores is initially random, but over time similar files tend to accumulate at the same node. Several of these similar nodes tend to form in the network, and in this way the system achieves redundancy and reliability. The system clusters nodes based on how the octets in a file resolve into a key via a hashing algorithm. There is no notion of closeness in meaning, thus two photographs of the same public monument, although representing the same object, would not necessarily be stored at the same node. Thus popular material doesn't always wind up at the same PC, and bottlenecks or hot spots are unlikely.

Issues   Any communication strategy without some assistance from servers in the network can result in very uneven performance. Napster offers a much more predictable performance than Gnutella for this very reason. Gnutella and Freenet can appear slow; in systems without a hierarchy, the overhead for locating a piece of information can be quite high. Less popular information is less replicated and thus can take a lot longer to find and deliver.

A nontechnical issue is that of acceptance—critical mass. Without a high level of popular support, a Freenet network offers rather sparse content. Without a larger number of nodes and a large amount of content, Freenet would be destined to be a curiosity only. Each Freenet participant adds value; each defector takes value away. Freenet is merely a framework to allow contributions, and your contributions give it its value. If users find it cumbersome and difficult, Freenet will fail and another *better* approach will take its place.

Conclusion   Freenet has the potential to create a new geography for the Internet, one based on cooperating peers rather than on large media conglomerates. In an Internet where content publishers use tricks as devious as single-pixel cookies to profile users, the implications of Freenet for anonymity, privacy, and free expression are too important to ignore. However, the anonymity of peers offers little branding or context to enable you to trust the information.

We have downloaded many files that were not what we thought they were. These have included music files that were flawed and papers that did not cover the desired topic. Corporations spend plenty to establish their brand, as an established brand indeed has real value in establishing the consumer's trust. P2P must find its own branding methods if it is to build and establish trust. Do not fall into the trap of believing that big business is always bad and that peers are always good. This prejudicial view is flawed in many ways. For now, remain cautious but still very curious.

Distributed Computation

The next tour stop gets at the raw computing resources of your computer—the disk space, processing power, memory, and bandwidth. You could think of this stop as a subway tour below the busy streets above.

Unlike busy corporate servers, most peers have an easy life. A peer, for most of its life, acts much like someone with a big inheritance lying around drawing screensavers and every now and then checking e-mail—oh, the tough life of a peer. Distributed computing taps into this largely idle resource. Clearly, allowing someone to access your raw resources is threatening at best. It also must overcome tough technical challenges to integrate diverse, unrelated hardware successfully to cooperate for some higher goal. Turning our personal computers into the largest, most robust supercomputer is somewhat fantastic and yet quite achievable. In Chapter 1, you actually visited one tour stop in this category, SETI@home. For another example, let's visit a United Technologies approach.

United Technologies

United Technologies is setting up over 100,000 personal computers with P2P software to work on complex scientific calculations and modeling problems. The software runs during off hours, when typically the personal computers are getting their beauty sleep. Current exercises include design simulations for aircraft parts. This approach could halve the time and money required to develop turbine engines by eliminating costly prototypes.

Benefits   United Technologies taps into the many computing cycles left idle after the employee heads for home. This instantly creates value out of a wasted resource.

Technology   The United Technologies' P2P software solution has a major advantage over most P2P solutions. United Technologies determined a standard configuration for each P2P contributor. This eliminated the many possible combinations typically found in a distributed P2P solution, which must accommodate a wide range of operating systems and hardware configurations. If a computer did meet the standard, it could not participate. This simplified the P2P solution but also constrained the number of P2P participants.

United Technologies developed its own middleware to pass messages directly between each peer. It does not require a centralized server. The United Technologies developers are currently debating the use of a standardized messaging protocol.

Issues   United Technologies undertook such a venture due to the maturing of the personal computer. The PC's computing power is now huge, having advanced from handling a few million instructions per second to billions. This computational power allows computers to work on several tasks simultaneously. United Technologies also noted the PC's ability to remain up and available. The personal computer has finally arrived as a powerful and dependable ally.

United Technologies quickly discovered a P2P challenge related to such a solution: How do you debug it? Unless the problem is correctly decomposed, errors are extremely difficult to locate. United Technologies' tools may enable multiple computers to work together, but unless a problem is well understood and assigned, the result may be chaos.

Conclusions   United Technologies' software enables users who were using less than 5 percent of their potential computing power to increase that utilization to more than 85 percent. United Technologies' solution raises significant challenges. It requires that a personal computer conform to United Technologies' standards to simplify development and deployment, and the company constructed a proprietary middleware for P2P message passing. The solution also demands creative problem decomposition. The hurdles were tough, but all those free computing cycles compose quite a prize.

Distributed Search

Now that you have all these tools to access your files and raw resources, a basic problem exists: How do you *find* the files and computing resources you want? Searching across the vast and dynamic P2P landscape can be quite daunting. Where do you start?

The first generation of P2P search products is somewhat simplistic but still quite powerful. These products are burdened with searching through unstructured references to the files and resources typical of a peer environment discussed earlier. There are no standards to refer to a particular file or resource. A user is free to make a file reference or commonly referred to as a file name anything they want. This is compounded by the addition of file directories, which also maintain no standards. There is simply no Dewey decimal system for P2P files and resources. Some naming conventions do emerge but they guarantee little.

Unstructured file names existing on peers is a two-edged sword. By its nature, the lack of structure enables quite a bit of freedom. This means that users can easily create new files and directories. In addition, many files are composites. Almost any content—such as graphics, texts, and even video—can be inserted into a document, presentation, or spreadsheet. Devoid of structure and rules, users easily create files. And there are a lot of them. However since they maintain no filing structure, once created they can be very difficult to find.

In their mad rush to produce a report, people neglect its structure in the name of speed. But inefficiencies have a strange way of biting users later. ("Hey, where did I put that file?" "Which file was it that had that great line graph?") P2P has the same problem, but on a much bigger scale. These initial P2P searching products make bold attempts to rein in and organize the P2P frontier. Let's get on with the tour of OpenCola.

OpenCola

The traditional way that you find something relevant on the Web is to use a search engine. You type in a couple of words, then the search engine uses your phrase as a lookup index to its collection of indexed pages. This type of search strategy is often called *content-based filtering*, because it uses features of the pages it has visited and indexed to resolve your query and to estimate how close a given page is to being what you really want to see.

Another type of searching and filtering, *collaborative filtering*, is possible, and P2P is the key to making it possible. Suppose that you could create a folder on your PC's desktop and drop in some sample web documents that exemplified the types of things that you are interested in seeing. Then, without doing anything else, you note the next time you look in the folder that it holds, as if by magic, more documents that are topically relevant. Such an experience would be unusual for most users, who are used to searching, navigating, and analyzing the content of the Web pretty much on their own. This is the experience that OpenCola attempts to create for you.

If that experience seems like something from a science fiction novel, perhaps it's appropriate that the chief evangelist and spokesmodel for OpenCola is celebrated science fiction writer Cory Doctorow. However, OpenCola is much more science (or more appropriately, technology) than fiction, and it's based on a simple premise: People who are alike enjoy similar things. People who are alike also tend to find and read similar things on the Web.

For example, while working together, the coauthors of this book discovered that we both like a brand of pudding called Kozy Shack. We ended up getting into a far-too-long discussion about its creamy texture, sweet taste, and other fine virtues. In short, we formed a community of sorts based on something that we both liked and could authoritatively discuss. Suppose that a third party wanted to know more about this delicious treat. That user could search the Web with a multi-engine searcher such as Copernic, but other than the official www.kozyshack.com site, the user would get few other useful hits. On the other hand, if we could advertise our enthusiasm in some way—perhaps by writing a little paean about Kozy Shack, or typing out our favorite recipes using the product—and then drop these little advertisements into a folder that others in cyberspace could see, then the third party would be able to take advantage of our deep pudding knowledge.

Benefits   OpenCola doesn't *quite* work like the pudding example, but the story does exemplify many of the ideas behind its technology strategy. OpenCola's new world order for information would be based on the contributions of "super-recommenders," people with the time, passion, or expertise to gather great collections of information on a particular topic. Such people might gather esoteric collections of information ostensibly for personal use, but might have no intent to publish (either because the difficulty of publishing is too high, or because the information collector feels that the potential interest is too low).

Nonetheless, these private collections of information have a higher potential for "goodness" than a random selection of sites returned from a search engine, exactly because someone has already gone through the exercise of finding the most relevant material. Moreover, the fact that someone actually went to the trouble of saving it (or a link to it) almost assures that the material is "good." In our professional research and preparation for this book, we have collected literally hundreds of reference URLs and downloaded a large number of articles from them on the topic of P2P, web services, and software agents. If there were no cost involved with publishing that information, we could produce a far more relevant collection than any search engine would be likely to return. The collection would have no direct benefit to the publisher (just as making a song collection available on Napster has no benefit for the individual), but either act would have relatively little cost. Cost-free altruism is a model that actually works

Technology   OpenCola takes advantage of an idea called COLA (collaborative object lookup architecture), which uses a strategy to view the Web as a set of object-oriented XML documents. The "Open" part of the name refers to the idea that the company uses the open source model as a way of attracting outside contributors to its effort. Thus, the base architecture might allow a developer to write an agent that interlopes in Internet Relay Chat (IRC) rooms, to monitor chat histories and alert you when your name is mentioned or find discussion groups that you would be most interested in joining. Thus, the architecture encourages the development and inclusion or other nontextual relevance engines, so that an interested developer might contribute an algorithm that lets you drop in an MP3 file as a seed, and find other similar songs by the same or other artists, not by title, but by style of music.

A significant feature of OpenCola's Folders implementation is that it uses autonomous, distributed search agents to do its heavy lifting. In addition, OpenCola offers an interface to train a search robot. A user can "program" a personal agent without having to be a programmer. Thus, a user can modify a query and the content changes according to the reinforcement of the trained search robot.

A user could start off with a document about Captain Cook, and the search agent, not really understanding language, might bring back 500 documents, some of them involving Mt. Cook National Park, some Cook County Illinois, some Peter Cook and Dudley Moore. Some might even have the precise combination of words, but actually be far off-topic. Ordinarily, you can't correct the bad guesses of search engines. With a strategy such as OpenCola, you can then tell an agent, "I really want documents like *this*, not like *that*." The agent would then act to correct its understanding of what you really want.

As mentioned previously, the OpenCola architecture is based on *autonomous agents.* The agents in the system are called Folders. Agents are bits of software that can run for relatively long periods of time unattended and remember their working history. Because the agents can work unattended, the software doesn't require constant supervision to do its work, and it can cooperate with other Folders to find better answers. Because the agents can remember their history, you can train a Folder to bring back better documents (based on your subjective evaluation).

Folders use distributed storage strategies, recognizing that some documents need to be stored locally on your hard disk to be useful (MP3 files, for example). Others can be left where they are and are small enough to be fetched as needed (for example, you might choose to store a site's URL, but not the content of the site).

Figure 2-3 depicts the architecture of Folders. The *Scheduler* is the primary controller for the system, telling the system when to perform a task. It receives messages from any node (a remote Folder, for example) and can fire up an activity on behalf of the message's sender. The *Link Ripper* controls the local *Fetcher*, requesting it to fetch files from the network, then passes any files gathered to the *Relevance Engine*. The Relevance Engine determines each file's content type (common types are text, mp3, xml, html, and mov), then passes the document to a plug-in module that can analyze the document. The engine can evaluate some material based on its metadata (data describing the content of the file) even before passing the material on to a plug-in.

Plug-ins are built specifically for the type of data that they analyze. For example, since MP3 files have a tag that identifies the artist, the title, and sometimes the lyrics, the song document can be scored for relevance based on the training you give the system. By dragging a sample document (or several of them) into a Folder, you create the relevance criteria; the plug-ins use the same techniques to understand the sample data as they do to understand the fetched documents. Because OpenCola uses an open source approach, plug-ins can be developed for almost any analytical purpose. Suppose that a system needs a translator module to analyze a document written in German. A developer could

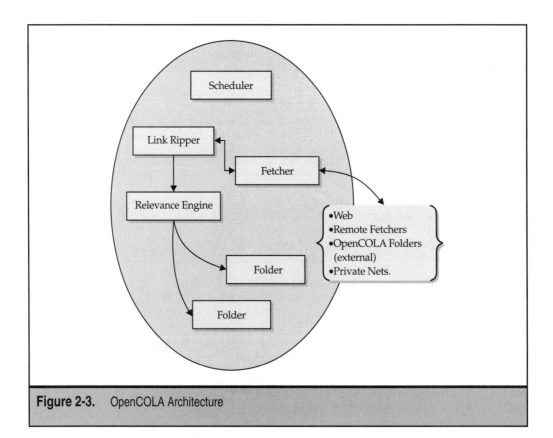

Figure 2-3.   OpenCOLA Architecture

write just that piece, which would then be available for everyone to use; suddenly the system has new overall capabilities.

Issues   The Xerox PARC Internet Ecologies Area (http://www.parc.xerox.com/istl/groups/iea/) published an analysis entitled "Free Riding on Gnutella," in which the authors established that among Gnutella users, most (70 percent) didn't share files, and even more (90 percent) didn't cooperate in answering queries. They also found that people who were willing to share files were not necessarily the ones with the most desirable files. This apparent stinginess exists despite the fact that the price of sharing is negligible. The reasons for this stinginess appear to be social rather than technical, but if these findings are legitimate, they tend to threaten significantly the notion of cooperative sharing.

These findings also seriously threaten the idea that if enough people share, no one person can become the target of legal action, because the size of the community allows each user to hide his or her identity in the numbers. If only a few people are willing to be the nexus for an unpopular political view, then they are in effect the "server" for the entire body of people subscribing to that view, and can be singled out for harassment or prosecution. No one wants to be a "poster child" for prosecution.

The study points out that a major weakness in systems that use cooperative sharing is that a "tragedy of the commons" will develop over time, with information seekers constantly hitting a set of fewer and fewer contributors. A system such as OpenCola, however, hosts such a sufficient diversity and level of participation that the number of contributors is more than sufficient. There are ways to automatically gain participation. Napster, for example, recognizes all files in a folder with a well-known name (by default). Thus when a user downloads a file, it is automatically shared, with no intervention or active steps required on the individual's part. Another potential way to induce users to participate is to offer economic incentives, which is how the P2P resource sharing system MojoNation operates.

Conclusion   OpenCola combines P2P networking and collaborative expertise. It allows you to build any number of single-purpose streaming search engines built on a single-purpose network of cooperating searchers that can aggregate their results for you. In all, OpenCola is a pretty neat package.

P2P COLLABORATION PRODUCT AND SERVICES

Now the tour moves to the wilder, fun side of the P2P city. You move on to the interactive stuff—P2P collaboration product and services. The wilder side consists of three subcategories:

▼   **Basic Collaboration Products and Services**   This category offers the services to coordinate a workspace. Working together electronically has many challenges. Have you ever wiped out a document by overwriting the new version with the old? Do you have a file that requires sharing among your project team or family? These tools enable seamless flow of information and communication among a group. They create a P2P information space that is up-to-date and synchronized with each group member's contributions. Your P2P tour stop here is the large and ever-friendly Groove.

- ■ **Gaming**   Whereas basic collaboration focuses on a goal, gaming focuses on just fun and entertainment. Interestingly enough, gaming has many of same challenges as basic collaboration, just with better graphics. This is an explosive area of P2P, since playing a Web server is not nearly as exciting as playing a peer. Gaming offers direct interaction with peers (people) of various skill levels and interests. The P2P technical advantages assist fast and fun gaming. Your P2P tour stops include two products: Net-Z and the game Star Craft Multiplayer by Blizzard.

- ▲ **Instant Messaging**   At its core, P2P is all about communication. Communication in the form of instant messaging established the second major success of P2P. Instant messaging may eclipse e-mail as the killer application of the Internet. It enables you to access your friends and associates instantly without being rude. It is the ultimate electronic tap on the shoulder. Instant messaging has grown from a small, interesting base to something fought over in the largest software companies. The fight is over the ability to establish the new instant messaging standard and its associated advertising possibilities. The upcoming safari explores the fundamentals of instant messaging. For now, the tour explores Ikimbo's instant messaging tool, Omniprise.

Basic Collaboration Product and Services

The tools in this category tap into users' desire to work together from a distance. But since you are *there* and I am *here,* we run into many communication and collaborative challenges. Most electrical solutions just seem to muddy the works. In my electronic collaboration attempts, I seem to spend more time sifting through network settings and menu items than actually communicating with my associates. In an unfortunate sense, I collaborate with the tool rather than the person.

Despite cool interfaces and graphics, electrical solutions to long-distance collaboration usually pale to their human equivalents, lacking such communicative cues as vocal inflections, facial expressions, and gestures. However, electronic exchanges often beat a five-hour plane ride or a 90-minute commute. These tools will never replace human interactions but they can wonderfully augment them. Your tour of these tools begins with a big boy: Groove.

Groove

In the fall of 2000, with a great deal of flourish, Groove Networks announced the results of three years of research and development. In the kingdom of collaborative tools, Groove was poised to become the newly crowned king. Ray Ozzie, whose previous triumph, Lotus Notes, had changed how people look at corporate workflow forever, explained to the press and analysts that Groove would do all that Notes had done and more.

Although Notes worked beautifully with highly structured information, users turned to other strategies to handle most real-world problems such as unstructured data and event-driven collaborations. For these, users usually employed a much different set of tools (such as e-mail, phone, or fax). Thus, while part of a given solution might rely on Notes, much of the interaction between the human participants was not being served at all by Notes, or any other tools.

While pondering this fact, Ozzie noticed one of his kids playing an online game with some friends. He found it remarkable that the game (*Quake*) was being played in just the kind of interactive space he was beginning to envision. Moreover, the kids had reworked the game space to create a new game—one that hadn't been a part of the original version of *Quake*.

This experience demonstrated the qualities that would be desirable in a next-generation collaborative space:

▼   A group could be self-forming and self-managing.

■   It would be easy to attack problems that the software didn't anticipate.

▲   It would be possible and even easy to add tools and reconfigure the space to do things that the software designer had not originally imagined.

Groove's forte is that it offers a group of people a private space in which they can interact. Groove allows an individual to create a P2P space and invite others to participate in the space. The space's creator can outfit the space with appropriate "out-of-the-box" tools (for example, a shared white board in the discussion area).

Groove starts with a pure P2P model. When one person does something on one computer, it happens transparently and simultaneously on all computers. Thus, Groove creates a shared context that transcends the usual muddle of mounting network drives on a local area network (LAN) or the loose confederation of working collaboratively by e-mail.

Groove can integrate legacy tools (at least Microsoft COM-compliant tools) and provides an application programming interface (API) that enables a developer to add new tools as well.

Benefits   The fundamental capability offered by Groove is that it connects you with the peers that you most interact with. Thus, Groove connects you with the information and services that are most important to you.

Chapter 1 declared that P2P will succeed because it makes publishing information, services, and communication easy. Groove exemplifies this in many aspects, whether in its enterprise version (which is loaded with additional administrative tools) or in its free personal edition. The idea may seem a little foreign at first, but once you've used a personal space to collaborate, the idea will seem intuitively obvious, just as instant messaging did. We, in fact, used Groove's collaborative spaces to coauthor this book.

Groove's tools let you create secure shared spaces where you make instant and direct online connections with others to share information and collaborate. Early enterprise adopters are using the platform to implement customer relationship management (CRM), distributed marketing efforts, and supply chain management. Families are experimenting with Groove as a way of closing the distance between far-flung family members.

Communications capabilities include live voice over the Internet (using a "push-to-talk" strategy), traditional instant messaging and text-based chat, threaded discussions, tools for sharing (files, pictures, music), and simple activities (drawing, Web browsing, using a rich-text notepad). Groove has other interesting capabilities that make it extremely attractive for use:

▼ **Personas**   A persona represents a theme in someone's life. It organizes all the information or state and capabilities along lines that make life a bit easier for the chosen theme. Groove allows you to maintain multiple personas, nicely isolated from one another. The advantages may not be obvious at first, until you realize that you actually do have many distinct personae or roles in your life, and that you spend a lot of time servicing each of them. You might be a soccer parent, business professional, and university lecturer, for example, all rolled into one. In each of these roles, you create content and interact with distinct and different networks of associates, coworkers, or students. In one persona, you might host a shared space in which the invitees are family members contributing photos to the shared scrapbook or genealogy project; in another, you might collaborate on the monthly sales forecast. Thus, keeping the different roles separated from one another for manageability (or just for sanity sake) is often important, and Groove enables you to do so.

■ **Extensibility**   Groove includes a number of tools that you can choose to add to the space to reconfigure its capabilities. Groove's intention is to build a deep treasury of applications that conform to its framework.

■ **Autosynchronization**   If a space member is disconnected from the space, a fellow Groove participant acts as a proxy for the missing person, keeping them in sync with all the other members of the shared space. Further, if someone makes changes to his or her space while disconnected, the content and changes are saved on the member's PC. When the member reconnects, all changes and additions are sent to all other members. Additionally, all changes that other members have made in the meantime are immediately sent to the reconnected member's space as well. In this way, Groove does not require or penalize variable connectivity. Existing on more than one computer is not a problem either, because autosynchronization comes to the rescue here as well. Most users don't stop working at the traditional "five o'clock whistle" and find that their work and home lives often blend together and spread over many computers—desktops at work, laptops on the go, home systems. You can share a space over many computers in sync. Further, the loss of a single computer is no longer a catastrophe, because you can fully restore its replacement from existing spaces.

▲ **Persistence**   Since the possibility exists that one or more parties in a space might suddenly go offline, Groove doesn't have anything like a save command. This omission might seem unusual to PC users, who quickly learn to "save early and save often." Every action by any user is immediately saved in a platform-neutral XML storage system on all systems connected to the space. Thus, if necessary, the other members could restore a user. We can see echoes of the Napster ideal of reliability and high availability through redundancy and sheer numbers of the participants within each Groove space.

Technology   Groove is inherently P2P. This means that the machines included in a Groove space do the heavy lifting of maintaining the seamless connection between invited members of the space. Every participant must have the Groove client application consisting of a transceiver, a tool framework, and instant messaging tools.

The Groove architecture, depicted in Figure 2-4, is a modified model-view-controller (MVC) architecture. In simple terms, MVC divides a computer application into its information model (the information *model*), a user experience piece (one or more graphical *views* of the information), and the piece that enables the user to manipulate the application's configuration and data (the *controller*).

Groove sits in the middle of this MVC model and makes certain that local changes to the model are propagated to everyone else sharing the space, and are "persisted" or made permanent in both the application's storage area and, when necessary, in Groove's own

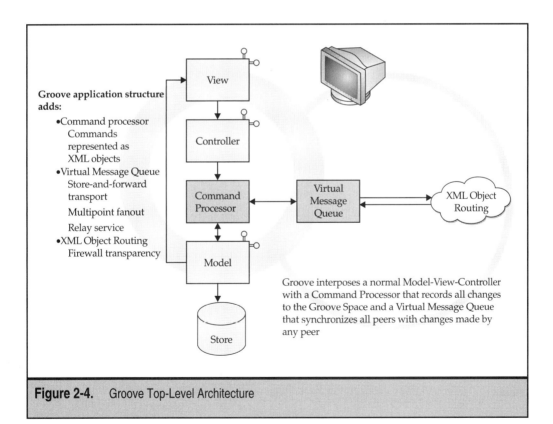

Figure 2-4.   Groove Top-Level Architecture

XML-based storage area. This double-persistence is especially critical for assuring that everyone sharing the space, even when he or she is offline, gets all changes to the space, and that each user's changes are propagated to everyone else too. Groove must therefore mimic what the actual underlying tool does to control its and possibly the user's view of the data, interposing all control changes to the actual tool mimic. The additional architecture components of Groove represent P2P concepts that you'll see repeatedly, and you'll learn about these components shortly.

Groove uses an encrypted Extensible Markup Language (XML) format to pass data between engines. An XML format is a standard, formal data format often used for exchanging information. Every change, large and small, that must be communicated has a cargo of XML data. Whenever possible, Groove uses a proprietary direct (instant) messaging protocol to communicate, but converts the data to HTTP to attempt to traverse firewalls. Groove uses the same communication protocol to converse with resources in the local instance of Groove as it does distant instances.

The component architecture of Groove spans a number of functions common to many P2P engines:

▼ **LifeCycle Services**   These are the basic services provided by any framework. The services include startup and tool loading and initialization, as well as management of all the tool components.

■ **Dynamics Services**   This is the formal name applied to the idea of "sitting in the middle" of everything going on in the space, as explained previously in the description of the overall architecture. As Groove's architecture document explains the concept:

Dynamics services maintains a deterministic, distributed consistency model for all tool components. It provides delta management for all endpoints (combination of member and device) in a shared space. It also handles processing, dissemination, receipt, and recovery of all shared space data. It coordinates and orders execution of changes to each tool's data model via the tool's engine component.

■ **Security Services**   Groove's security services are transparent, which means that you don't have to do anything to use them. They include authentication (determining whether members are actually who they say they are) and on-the-wire encryption.

■ **Member Services**   This component tells a local Groove space (that is, the one running on the local computer) who the members of the shared space are, and what their contact information says about them. The component also propagates to everyone in the space any changes that a member makes to his or her contact information.

■ **Access Control Services**   You use this component to administer a space to decide who gets to see what.

▲ **Component Services**   This component automatically updates Groove itself and any included software components. It makes certain that versions are up-to-date and that they are updated from a valid source.

Figure 2-5 illustrates the P2P sharing using a Groove space.

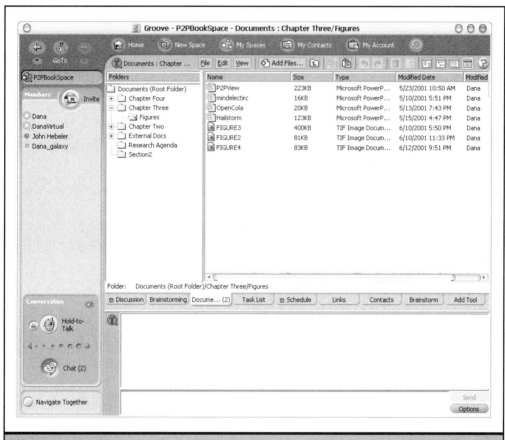

Figure 2-5.   P2P Sharing with a Groove Space

Issues You should be aware that Groove is a work in progress and has missing functionality. That doesn't mean Groove is not worth using as is, or that basing your next killer application on it is a bad idea; it simply means that you should be aware that the applications are early "alpha" quality, but will certainly become better over time. Groove and the scores of developers committed to making this idea work will make sure that new and exciting tools emerge for this platform. The developer documentation is uniformly of high quality and will allow developers to start their efforts efficiently.

Even though the tools are immature, there's already a lot to like. For example, the instant messaging capability allows you to record, send, and receive voice messages, send URLs, send files, and address one or more recipients. This slick capability alone would seem to justify installing and using Groove. As Steve Gillmor, editor–in–chief of *XML*, says in the editor's notes of the April/May *XMLOnline* magazine (www.xmlmag.com):

> *To my eye, it's peer-to-peer e-mail. When our corporate mail server goes down because of the latest Outlook virus attack, I switch to Groove mail. There's no spam, because only people I invite have my address. It's a private IT-free communications network built on top of encrypted XML—extensible and viral in the best sense. And free is very hard to top.*

Conclusion The Groove story is so sophisticated that some people may not fully understand it immediately; that's one of the challenges that any sophisticated new infrastructure platform has to face. Once people start to use Groove, they quickly harness the power of the functionality built on top of the Groove foundation. They need not necessarily understand the inner workings. Few Instant messaging users understand or even care about its inner workings. As drivers of increasingly sophisticated and complex automobiles, all we really need to understand is how to use the steering wheel, throttle, and brake pedal. The goal is to make using software just that easy.

Gaming

This tour stop taps into people's desire to play together. Humans, for the most part, have always outdistanced a computer-playing partner. P2P has many technical strengths that lend themselves to outstanding gaming. Each peer can store and load the large graphics required for a modern game, and local processing power easily tackles the tough three-dimensional (3-D) drawing. The communication between gaming peers can be minimal. For example, just a few hundred bytes might send in a large troop movement. This size would hardly tax even an outdated phone modem. Gaming satisfies our longings for escape and fun—this is a category to watch. Your tour stop in this category is Net-Z and the game Star Craft Multiplayer by Blizzard.

Net-Z

Net-Z offers a rich collaborative environment focused directly on Internet P2P gaming. Its extensive gaming platform enables the full creation of games. The gaming environment offers a high level of services that allow fault tolerance, load balancing, monitoring, and platform independence.

Technology   Net-Z adds its own gaming twist at organizing gaming collaboration and setting up the corresponding communication paths. It defines high-level objects that form gaming abstracts such as monsters and weapons. The object's descriptions are captured in the Net-Z Data Description Language. The language describes at a high level how objects get published and re-created across the network. It automatically marshals[1] and unmarshals objects as they move across your screen to fellow players.

   Net-Z offers extensive performance monitoring and load balancing routines to ensure that your army doesn't stutter across the screen. The load can be shifted to other players automatically to keep everything running smoothly. Gaming depends on performance consistency to enhance realism.

   Net-Z also offers an intuitive bandwidth adjuster to allow play on many speeds and line qualities. The bandwidth adjuster allows you to simulate games at different speeds to identify possible bottlenecks or sub-optimal playing conditions.

Issues   The underlying technology is proprietary to Proksim Software. This gives the developers, not you, complete control over the technology's future. You may benefit from the services that a gaming foundation provides, or you could get trapped in a foundation that burdens you with unwanted directions. We visit this dilemma in upcoming explorations. A foundation is truly a double-edged sword. The foundation offers extensive functionality to solutions built on top of it but the solutions are forever trapped into evolving with the foundation.

Conclusion   Gaming is a unique form of collaboration. It differs from working on documents and such in many ways. Gaming provides a critical edge to P2P services. Gaming must be fast and efficient. Whereas a user may easily put up with a delay in sending a message, delays take all the fun out gaming—and fun is what gaming is all about. A platform to launch games holds a lot of promise, but only if it fulfills the basic promise of smooth, efficient performance across the participating peers.

Star Craft Multiplayer by Blizzard

Star Craft is a very popular game that has built-in P2P features. It is a war and strategy game that emphasizes the latter. Three species fight for survival at the edge of the universe. Aside from providing sheer fun, Star Craft offers a combination of features to allow players to meet, exchange ideas, and play.

Technology   Star Craft offers four methods to enable the user to play with users on other computers: a local area network using the IPX protocol, phone modems, a direct null-modem cable, and coordination via a web server, battle.net. The battle.net web site interfaces with a web browser built directly into the game, so the user need not ever leave the game interface. Once the player arrives at the web site, the game enables the player to select several possible games under way and indicates the available network bandwidth for

---

1   Marshalling is the ability to extract the key data elements needed to re-create an object.
      Un-marshalling re-creates the object given the extracted data elements.

each game. Players may also use a built-in chat feature before and during a game. They can choose their games to be public or even to be private by requiring a password.

The rich graphics, so key to successful games, reside locally for all players. Therefore, there is no need to send large graphics files across the network. The game exchanges only small amounts of information and therefore works even across poor, slow networks and connections.

Issues   Advanced games such as Star Craft create their own P2P world with players and communication methods. This game is an example of a P2P island with its own set of logins, protocols, and interfaces. The local storage of graphics and local processing of rendering logic make Star Craft an excellent example of P2P distribution.

Although the games allow players to participate over slow lines, a player's line speed has an impact. Many gamers ban slow-line participants altogether. Such bans are an early sign of the emergence of two classes of gamers: the slow dial-ups and the high-speed broadbands.

Conclusion   Gaming is a natural match with P2P—gaming is where the players are. Each player can arrive ready to go with local graphics and processing power. Players can also take advantage of the other communication channels to set up and monitor games. As with so many other P2P applications, games are evolving into independent islands that require participants to create a new identity and use with a new application protocol. A more uniform or standardized solution would enable rapid game participation and thus more fun.

Instant Messaging

You could never complete your tour without first visiting the common, yet powerful, P2P tool of instant messaging. Whereas file sharing is the obvious P2P success story, instant messaging is much less recognized for its P2P characteristics. Instant messaging arrived prior to P2P, and clearly the development of network services has greatly assisted the development of instant messaging. Therefore, many users don't think of P2P in the same breath with instant messaging. However, instant messaging couldn't be more closely associated with P2P. Instant messaging enables users to locate their peers, provides a direct P2P communication path, and even offers an informal status of a peer's availability.

This simple tool now commands quite a bit of respect. Major software vendors are fighting mightily to forge their software's identify through the software's form of instant messaging. These vendors' struggle to establish their own unique IM identities is causing some problems. Each commercial instant messaging solution has its own unique protocol. This creates communities but each is trapped within its chosen instant messaging domain. The different formats can be frustrating to master. Some of your friends may be on AOL instant messaging, some on Yahoo instant messenger, and other rebels may insist on Jabber. Each requires a different download and a desktop application (even with its own advertisements). Jabber has a different twist, which Chapter 3 explores.

Even with its faults, instant messaging is here to stay. You need only achieve a small critical mass among your friends and associates to see its value.

For now, let's make a tour stop not as familiar as the instant messaging services previously discussed: Ikimbo.

Ikimbo's Omniprise

If Groove is the Cadillac of collaboration technologies, then surely Ikimbo's flagship product, Omniprise, is the Volkswagen Beetle. For just as Groove is large and complex, Omniprise seeks to be lean and mean. Whereas Groove's developers seek to create a platform that encourages writing of new tools that can effectively capture value by using the underlying platform capabilities, Omniprise's developers tend to believe that the essence of good collaboration is a little simpler. They reckon that instant messaging (which can reveal both presence and possible availability) and cross-device file sharing are really more important. Where Groove's developers seek to create the next generation of Microsoft NetMeeting, Omniprise's developers have the more modest ambition of extending simple instant messaging beyond the desktop and into the wireless world. They understand that the explosion of wireless is a force to be reckoned with—one that has not yet begun to serve business well beyond the voice communications capability.

Omniprise is a little like other instant messaging programs in that it shows presence information for members of a given collaboration group. Ikimbo understood that the grass-roots adoption of instant messaging would represent a challenge for corporate information groups (attempting to provide a highly reliable, secure, high-grade service environment) and for users (selecting a standard platform and determining what capabilities to provide to a user).

Omniprise reveals which of your contacts are online, and also indicates whether each contact is connected to a personal computer, a personal digital assistant such as a palm pilot, or web-enabled phone. Users on the wireless devices can compose short responses to messages; users on a portable device can see only the descriptive data about files attached to e-mail. Attachments are saved at a central server until you can connect via a PC client, an arrangement that is both sensible and useful. You can exchange a file simply by dragging and dropping the file on a name in the contact list. If you want to initiate a group chat, simply drag multiple contact names to a chat window. Some of these capabilities exist in certain forms in many popular IM programs, but Omniprise also handles the big problems that IT and organizations are beginning to be much more concerned about: the security and legal issues.

Because instant messaging (AIM, Yahoo Messenger, MSN) has entered the corporation through individual adoption, without the blessing or support of corporate information services groups, it has become a wild card. Instant messaging is a blessing because it lowers the barrier to communication and collaboration, by reducing communication time and costs (infrastructure costs and more importantly social costs) to near zero. On the debit side of the ledger, corporate information technology managers are becoming increasingly concerned that instant messaging serves as an ungoverned, unauthorized exit point for corporate information.

The instant messaging experience is like a casual and seemingly innocent conversation. Individuals inside a corporation can unthinkingly transmit files, make legally attributable statements, or unwittingly reveal sensitive corporate data. On the receiving end of the conversation, there is no real and authoritative guarantee that you are talking to the person whom you believe is at the other end of the line. Likewise, you have no way of knowing who might be overseeing the conversation.

The case against software giant Microsoft at the end of the last decade rested largely on the evidence gathered from its e-mail communications. If instant messaging is the e-mail of the new century, then certainly its users will be held equally accountable legally. Further, the trend toward increased substitution of instant messaging for e-mail or other "official" communications will certainly grow without bounds.[2] The use of instant messaging as a corporation-to-external (supply chain, partners, customers, and so on) collaboration tool is expected to top 181 million users by 2004.[3]

Benefits   Omniprise's primary benefit is that the user interface organizes the user experience extremely well. The product goes beyond simple instant messaging to provide a more collaborative environment to exchange ideas and thoughts.

Among Omniprise's other features and benefits are that it's a unified application, offering instant messaging, file sharing (either server-based or peer-based), and e-mail management in a very easy to use and administer interface. Ikimbo also realized that privacy and authentication are important to users as well, so Omniprise offers end-to-end encryption and digital signing as well.

Technology   Ikimbo uses a combination of server-based information management with a client tailored to deliver the user experience. The presence of a server does not make an application "less P2P." Servers in the flow of data can significantly enhance the throughput of the P2P experience and can act as proxies for group members not available at a given moment. For example, you can choose to keep your portion of project files on a trusted server rather than your own desktop, which makes them available to other group members, even when your machine is not online. You can permit a trusted server to hold your data or e-mail so that should you need wireless access, your PCs need not be online.

Issues   Issues with Omniprise are business-related rather than technical, but they do highlight something you should be aware of when deciding on any technology. Whenever a technology offering attempts to compete against the large players (such as Microsoft and AOL) on the one hand, and free software (such as Jabber) on the other, the variety of competitors can easily challenge the long-term value of the technology. As of mid-2001, Omniprise seems to be vulnerable to attack from both fronts.

---

2   According to Esther Dyson's reckoning, AOL reported a total population of 61 million AIM users in mid 2000, of whom 20 million were active at any given moment. ICQ had roughly 70 million with roughly the same number active. Yahoo Messenger and MSN had both topped 10 million users by July 2000.

3   This figure is according to an August 2000 report by IDC.

Conclusion   Ikimbo's Omniprise offers an example of a P2P collaboration that is neither as simple as vanilla instant messaging nor as complex as Groove. Like Groove, Omniprise can be tied into back-end systems via an API. Another significant feature is that Omniprise is easy to deploy remotely without firewall changes, which complies with many corporations' strict security policies. Like Groove, Omniprise has an e-mail-based invitation mechanism. When you download the installer, it updates your group membership settings and contact lists for the group.

CITY TOUR SUMMARY

Your civilized city tour now comes to an end. Figure 2-6 summarizes the landscape, noting the highlights.

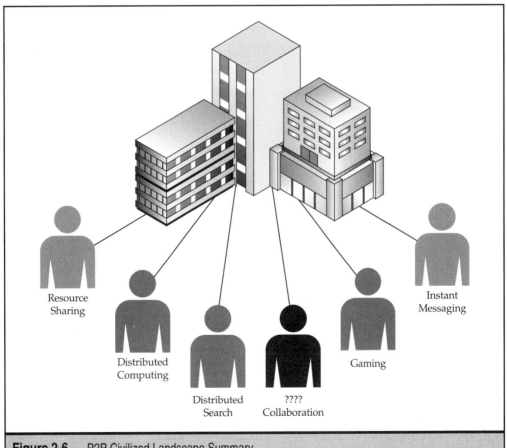

Figure 2-6.   P2P Civilized Landscape Summary

Your tour consisted of a range of stops at technologies that are ready today. They quickly reveal the power of P2P. You started by visiting the beachhead of P2P—sharing files. You moved on to sharing raw computing resources, and then to large-scale distributed searching. These three technologies combine to find and share the vast resources of P2P. Next you moved on to collaboration. You started with basic collaboration and then moved on to the intense collaboration found in gaming. Your last stop is always a P2P favorite: instant messaging. This city section expanded the power of P2P beyond resources to meaningful exchanges among users—the true peer endpoint.

Before moving on to the next tour, let's make some observations about the cityscape:

▼ **P2P Power** P2P offers unprecedented ways to find, publish, and exchange information with the new locus of the Internet: the peer. You can easily tap into a growing body of resources and communication paths. You can also quickly and easily offer all of your resources to your friends, associates, or the world. P2P is here.

■ **Independent P2P High Rises** Most of that P2P power is stand-alone. The products are built from the ground up with their own protocols, environments, and security. This is to be expected from the early players. Their goal was to get to the market, not to form standards committees. Selfishly, all hope to establish de facto standards just by the sheer critical mass of their product's popularity. This early and independent launch forces you to familiarize yourself with the alien interfaces and multiple logins that each product contains. Early adopters are willing to struggle with these differences, but real success will ultimately require a little more cooperation.

■ **Immaturity** Many of the tour stops are still in their early stages. The technology is not yet robust, nor is the market direction clear. In your investigations, make sure to kick the tires and test the technology on real problems. In most cases, you can easily do so with a simple download. Often the products will pleasantly surprise you.

■ **User Friendliness** Many products have not addressed the complexity, usability, and privacy concerns of the nontechnical P2P user. The vast majority of peers are nontechnical users. If the market continues to offer solutions that confuse and scare them, P2P will never reach its full potential.

■ **Expanding Diversity** P2P products and services continue to grow and diversify. This brief tour visited only the highlights. Much more is out there and a lot more is to come. Keep an eye on new offerings. They could quickly solve that tough problem you are facing.

▲ **The Big Time** The P2P marketplace has clearly raised the interest of the big players in computing. Microsoft, Sun, and IBM, just to name a few, are all valiantly pursuing advances.

Say goodbye to genteel city life. Now the tour turns to the wild country: the P2P jungle, teeming with customized solutions and the foundation for P2P's offerings.

CHAPTER 3

A Safari into the Software Developer's World

Y our tour continues with a safari expedition into the P2P frameworks and tools that make up the raw materials of P2P solutions. Many of the safari stops are in truly wild and untamed terrain and by no means represent finished products ready for the marketplace. They do offer some tantalizing P2P possibilities for both today and tomorrow.

Since this is only a tour, your stops may not fully satisfy your needs. Don't worry: Future chapters cover the necessary technologies in depth. In a few instances, the raw materials have found early favor with developers and have already produced an abundance of derivative products. Thus they can easily be confused with end products. The reverse can also be true.For example, Chapter 2 covered Groove as a collaboration tool product, but it's *also* an enabler with an extensive programming interface for building customized tools. Like most everything in the Internet space, things morph with great speed and regularity from tool to product to service and back again. With this caveat in mind, let's begin your safari.

P2P ENABLERS

The P2P jungle is home to many enablers of potential P2P applications and frameworks. Enablers form the foundation for the resource-sharing, messaging, and collaboration products discussed in the civilized tour.

Many of P2P products visited in the city tour require services such as security and communication. P2P enablers bundle these services into foundation products that form the raw material of P2P. You or a P2P product vendor can effectively build upon these enablers, allowing you to deliver customized solutions faster than you could by building from scratch. In addition, enablers evolve and advance independent of your efforts. Thus you can offer enhanced capabilities without writing much (or any) new code. For example, the underlying framework may offer a new version with enhanced printing capabilities. By linking your value-added pieces with the newer version of the framework, you suddenly offer your product users better print capabilities without having to do anything in particular in your code.

Unfortunately, enablers do have a downside. They can trap your solutions into the constraints and choices of the enabler. The enabler may support only certain languages, platforms, or protocols. Also, their bugs become *your* bugs. Their release schedule becomes the gating factor for *your* release schedule. The shortcut that enablers present through the P2P jungle may be strewn with quicksand pits. As your tour guides, we will make sure to point out these risks.

Essentially, P2P enablers provide a computing environment that can help you develop P2P solutions rapidly. As we suggested earlier, enablers are never an end in themselves. You should judge them by the wonderful applications developed upon them. Effective enablers offer a diverse toolkit of useful capabilities and thus free software developers to focus on creating unique products rather than assembling the underlying nuts and bolts.

The enabler jungle consists of five areas:

▼ **Infrastructure**   These are the basic building-block components of P2P. Components consist of discrete services that address a basic P2P requirement such as communication or security. By leveraging P2P infrastructure, you quickly solve many basic P2P challenges and are then free to develop and deliver advanced, higher-level solutions. Infrastructure components evolve independently and often rapidly. Thus, they continue to enrich the products that incorporate the infrastructure component. The only danger is the constraints that the infrastructure might place on the products that use it. Your P2P safari stops at the infrastructure product Microsoft Hailstorm.

■ **Distributed Objects**   Distributed objects enable a P2P solution to decompose application services resident on the personal computer, such as all or part of your application logic, into discrete computing resources. You can then offer these resources as P2P services available to you or your friends remotely. This is a step beyond information sharing into the realm of *capability* sharing. Your P2P safari stops include Sun's JXTA (also known as *Juxtapose*) and Microsoft's .NET.

■ **Development Frameworks**   Development frameworks construct an overall P2P environment that potentially includes infrastructure and distributed objects. P2P solutions reside within the framework. A framework integrates necessary P2P capabilities (for example, life cycle management, persistence, access controls, authorization, information structuring) via an API (application programming interface). An effective framework enables users to develop fully functional P2P applications quickly. These applications remain bound (some would say trapped) to the framework. A framework can be a prison or a powerful ally. It all depends on the goals of your P2P application and the goals of the framework. Your P2P safari stop here is the Mind Electric.

■ **Messaging Frameworks**   Instant messaging, discussed in the city tour, is only the beginning of the communication possibilities of P2P. Messaging frameworks rapidly construct new communication paths between peers. They facilitate everything from simple chat to large formal communication exchanges from peer machine to peer machine. Messaging frameworks can loosely connect peer frameworks, distributed objects, and infrastructure through trusted communications. Messaging frameworks offer two interesting safari stops: Jabber Instant Messaging and BXXP protocol.

▲ **In-the-Net Services**   In-the-net services exist outside of a particular client machine and provide services to a community of users. This may seem slightly heretical, since in the doctrine of "pure" P2P, "all participants are equal." However, while it may be true that all participants are equal in terms of their right to publish, access their private communities, and be first-class participants in the community's activities, it is also true that not all devices are equal in terms of bandwidth and compute capacity. Thus, it is often architecturally practical to have server-based computers in the net or in the flow that do some of the "heavy lifting," to offer assured service availability, and to offer common services. Address lookup and translation service are typical of these kinds of services. Therefore, in-the-net services tend not to be destinations but rather act as catalysts to bring together peers. In-the-net services act as assistants to make P2P more efficient. Your P2P tour stops include the Dynamic Domain Name Service (DDNS) offered by DtDNS, and a streaming multimedia technology, Chaincast.

Infrastructure

P2P infrastructure covers a lot of jungle territory. Rich, effective P2P applications require a treasure trove of underlying services or infrastructure. This section does not allow a full exploration, only a quick visit. Watch the weather and button up: Your next stop is Microsoft's Hailstorm.

Microsoft Hailstorm

Although Microsoft's announcement in March 2001 of its Internet personalization initiative, called Hailstorm, was more vapor than substance, many P2P innovators held their breath to see what substance was behind the announcement. At the core, Microsoft seemed to be saying that the technology behind Hailstorm would make online privacy a non-issue. During the announcement, Microsoft proclaimed, "[Hailstorm] starts with the fundamental assumption that users own and control their personal information so only the users decide with whom they share their information and under what terms."

Hailstorm creates a user-centric architecture that combines with a set of XML services. It attempts to integrate the islands of information and capability in a typical personal computer. Microsoft based Hailstorm on an authentication system, which they call "Passport." Passport's goals are to allow single sign-on for web services and to provide and authentication system that permits application and services to act in concert.

Benefits   The goal of Hailstorm is to turn personal computer applications such as Microsoft Outlook into Internet services available remotely. This remote availability includes access via mobile phones and wireless Internet appliances. Microsoft promises that users will need no special proprietary software to interact with Hailstorm and that it will be platform-independent. These promises certainly seem to signal a new openness from a company that has not traditionally been an enthusiastic proponent of the open source model. Hailstorm works via SOAP (Simple Object Access Protocol). SOAP uses XML (eXtensible Markup Language) to create remote procedure calls in such a way that any Internet-connected application, device, or service can take advantage of the platform's personalization capabilities. Some of the early proponents of Hailstorm envisioned it as being able to increase the usability of web services:

▼   American Express stated that Hailstorm would enhance its customer relation management (CRM) capability by allowing the credit card giant to create a better personal experience for members.

■   Click Commerce, a company involved in supply chain management, stated that using Hailstorm will enable companies to collaborate more seamlessly with their distribution partners by "providing real-time information any time, any place and on any device."

▲   eBay, the famous auction site, said that it intends to use Hailstorm as an additional API (application programming interface) to give developers additional ways to embed eBay into applications.

Hailstorm, which doesn't exist in any tangible form as this book is being written, seems to be almost a universal panacea for protecting privacy, offering a unified persona in cyberspace, context sharing, and a remote-access user experience.

Technology   Hailstorm is based on a larger set of technologies that Microsoft has dubbed .NET (discussed shortly). The .NET architecture is very similar to Mind Electric's GLUE (also described later in this chapter), except that GLUE is more Java-centric, whereas .NET is intended to be more language-neutral. At the heart of Hailstorm is a permission-based system called Passport, which holds the details of peoples' identities (for example, names, addresses, credit card numbers, logon names and passwords). These details, in effect map your real-world identity into the digital world.

Working with Hailstorm, Passport knits the disparate architectures of legacy applications together under a single controlling entity, so that you can access them from a single machine, which may be a desktop browser or a mobile device. A big bonus of the single digital identity technology is that manual synchronization of information between devices like PocketPCs and PCs, and manual data entry, the bane of many users, become nonissues. Thus when you change your contact coordinates (or when one of your contacts does), you don't have to update your identity in myriad places, as you currently do. A travel scenario using this set of services would work like this:

1.   You give consent for the service to access pieces of your digital profile (but only those pieces). The service then accesses your booking preferences and your credit card information.

2.   The identity you give could be one of many digital personae that exist for you. For example, your corporate identity might use a different credit card, and might have additional constraints based not on your own preferences, but on the requirements of the identity profile of the group to which you belong. Because you explicitly create a link between yourself and your company, you exist partially as an individual identity and partly as a member of a group. The profile combining personal facts added from your corporate data would be exposed to the travel provider. Thus you would be able to pick from fares and airlines that meet your personal preferences, and still be limited by the tighter constraints imposed by the corporate travel office.

3. The service would also be able to access your .NET/Hailstorm-compliant calendaring program to examine it for conflicts, or to put the itinerary on your schedule.

4. Finally, through wireless gateway services, you would be able to access your calendar (which Hailstorm has turned into a Web service) from a device, receiving live updates on delays or cancellations.

Hailstorm is analogous to the graphical user interface (GUI) services that Microsoft provides in its operating systems. Prior to Windows, developers would have to write specific nonstandard interfaces for their applications. With the advent of the Microsoft Windows Foundation Classes, developers could use a common and well-supported set of visual fixtures for their applications without much effort, and concentrate instead on implementing the business rules. In much the same way, Hailstorm handles many of the details of working with the basic elements of a user's digital experience, such as calendars, location, preferences, and profile information. Disparate entities are consolidated via SOAP for remote object access, via XML for message passing and data representation, and via the .NET architecture layers for transport and security.

Figure 3-1 shows the Hailstorm services planned to ride atop the .NET service layer. The components form a complete digital portrait of a user. A clear concern is what technical mechanisms are in place to ensure that this information's availability is limited to people of the user's choosing (for example, the friendly travel agent in the preceding scenario). Currently details are sketchy, but Microsoft says that "legal and technical" protections will be in place, and that information will have limited scope, availability, and life span.

Issues   While the protection of personal information seems to be an overriding concern, Hailstorm poses the larger issue of whether a corporation can or should be entrusted with the keys to our personal kingdoms. Some people might feel better if Hailstorm were an open source project supported with a standards body. Microsoft is proposing Hailstorm as an "open access" model—developers can access it freely, but not alter it freely. Microsoft (and possibly an inner circle of developers who have a financial stake in Hailstorm) must approve all alterations to Hailstorm's core.

The vision for Hailstorm is extremely ambitious. Microsoft hopes that the Hailstorm infrastructure will give the corporation unprecedented control over the individual's web experience. Hailstorm is likely to remain in the "vaporware" category for some time, however, especially since Sun Microsystems has formed a competing effort with several partners to provide an open source model of Passport style services.

Microsoft will host Hailstorm services, which raises concerns among rival vendors, who maintain that the company is trying to establish a dominant market position in the Internet in the same way that it has long dominated PC operating systems. Microsoft's applications and software development tools have long been intimately tied to Microsoft's operating systems in a way that disadvantages potential rivals. If the corporation repeats the same model for new operating systems such as Microsoft XP, then software vendors and ordinary users may have reason to fear Hailstorm.

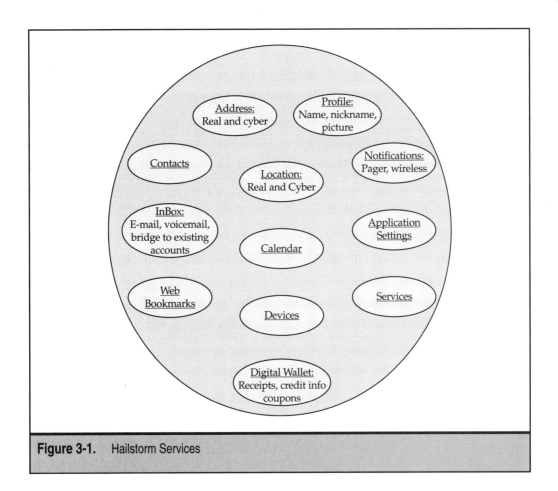

Figure 3-1. Hailstorm Services

Microsoft has announced that one objective of Hailstorm is to generate revenue, possibly via a subscription model. For users who consider the Internet a free information superhighway, the potential of a single company turning the net into a toll road is discomforting. Thus, Hailstorm seems to face problems with acceptance right from the start.

Hailstorm also poses some interesting technology issues. Many professionals involved in distributed computing feel that Hailstorm will have difficulties in scaling up to serve up millions of digital passports securely and with acceptable performance. Scaling performance beyond the ability of the centralized networks of server class machines or "server farms" is one of the reasons that designers and forward thinkers are turning away from highly centralized models.

Conclusion   Microsoft's idea of using Hailstorm to host the identity of everyone using the Web, and acting as a go-between for every electronic transaction in the e-commerce marketplace, seems overambitious. However, even if only a piece of Hailstorm succeeds, it may well represent a new era of Web service in which usability for the individual is paramount.

Distributed Objects

Distributed objects are a certain type of P2P infrastructure. The technology enables users to execute a program or parts of a program remotely. In the modern programming model, the *object*, a construct meaning data and program methods collected together into an abstraction, can represent any kind of real world article or idea. It is appropriate to think of an object as an *executing unit*. For example, an object may convert U.S. dollars to English pounds. An executing unit maintains some information or state about the action that it performs. In the example of converting dollars to pounds, the object state would contain a method for doing currency conversion, and the currency conversion factors.

The object model is often trapped in its hosting application. Thus, for example, an ActiveX object may only be accessed via a remote program that interoperates with a Microsoft operating system. Java objects generally have to use Java's RMI (remote method invocation) interface. Restrictions such as these, locking you into specific computing choices such as the operating system or programming language that you use, have a large impact on your selection of a distributed object mechanism. But if you use distributed objects correctly, you could enable a P2P application to tap directly into the capabilities of the applications already resident on another machine. Distributed object technologies can make existing personal computer applications available to peers as resources.

Developers can sometimes delude themselves regarding tools that enable distributed objects. Use of a particular tool to address real-world problems often reveals the inflexibilities or deficiencies that make using the distributed mechanism difficult or even impossible. Be aware of this possibility before you invest serious effort. Distributed objects magnify your skills; they don't *provide* the skills. They provide a strong foundation upon which you can build. As in any foundation, if the distributed objects change, you must also. Basements don't usually move (at least on the East Coast), but distributed object mechanisms will. Your first safari stop for distributed objects is Sun's JXTA.

Sun Microsystems' JXTA

Sun Microsystems loves the Java programming language (as do most software developers, according to many surveys). The company also loves alliteration and tends to start all Java-associated technologies with a J. The name JXTA derives from the word *juxtapose*, meaning to place side by side—a P2P-compatible concept. JXTA is a set of protocols—rules of communication that enable interoperability among distributed clients.

Chapter 1 emphasized the importance of Internet standards to tame some of the net's chaos. Without standards, each participant is forced to load a unique application feature just to understand each unique protocol. As previously stated, this problem currently exists among the various instant messaging protocols such as AOL, MSN, and ICQ. Standard protocols such as JXTA do not dictate implementation details such as programming language or operation system platform, although Sun will doubtlessly release an implementation in the Java programming language. Instead, such protocols offer a high-level map to guide implementations.

Benefits   The benefits that JXTA provides to the P2P world all surround the value in using well-accepted and well-supported standards to exchange information and services. An accepted standard, now sorely missing, could drive innovation and encourage developers to adopt the standardized technology, by freeing each P2P application developer from having to define the nitty-gritty details of communication and interaction. JXTA not only defines interoperability standards but also details standard services, for example discovery of resources, and federating devices and services together.

Technology   The key to JXTA is its modular, extendable architecture. Figure 3-2 illustrates the JXTA architecture, which consists of three primary layers: JXTA core, JXTA services, and JXTA applications.

The JXTA core layer consists of services for establishing and maintaining logical groupings or peer groups. The core enables policy control between groups and within groups, peer *pipes* to establish communication channels, and monitoring services to control behavior and access between members within peer groups. The JXTA core defines all the major protocols for peer interactions and exchanges including the discovery of specific peers, information about available peer resources, and membership security policies.

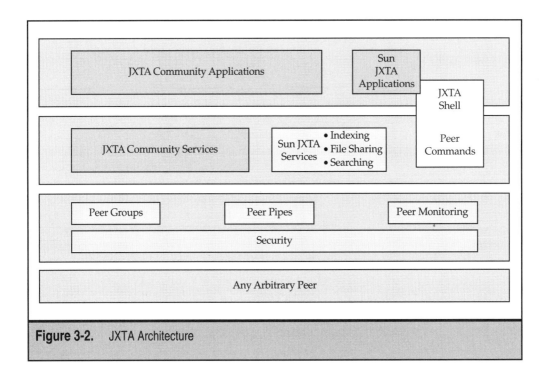

Figure 3-2.   JXTA Architecture

The JXTA services layer builds and expands on the basic services contained in the JXTA core. These higher-level services include parallel searching across multiple peers, secure messaging, and communication persistence, to name just a few. This layer establishes the higher-level services that JXTA applications can leverage. Thus the JXTA services layer forms the application programming interface to interact with P2P objects.

The JXTA application layer is where it all comes together. Specific applications are built on top of the JXTA core and JXTA services to address resource sharing and collaboration applications. This layer also contains a scripting language that enables programmers to assemble JXTA components rapidly.

The three layers form a modular environment that enables you to rapidly find remote objects or units of execution on any JXTA-supporting peer, and then to interact with them.

Issues   JXTA is in its infancy in a still young P2P world. Therefore, the direction and implementation success of JXTA is far from clear. It does offer a comprehensive view of services and products to fulfill P2P potential and does not demand any specific language or operating system platform. JXTA is a technology to watch and one that with Sun's backing will continue to evolve.

Conclusion   P2P requires extensive services to enable the rapid construction of powerful applications. JXTA offers a framework to accomplish just that. In addition, Sun has the muscle to establish the standards and build the critical mass of applications and services to make a viable, growing framework. JXTA is technically a standard that will allow implementations in many languages and platforms, including Microsoft's own proprietary "Java killer" language, C# (C-sharp).

Microsoft .NET

Your next safari stop introduces you to a cantankerous jungle neighbor of JXTA. Microsoft's .NET has many similarities to JXTA but has a distinct Microsoft emphasis (rather than a Java emphasis). The .NET framework consists of a set of software libraries that enable you to turn application features into P2P services rapidly. Since .NET builds on the extensive services offered in the Microsoft operating system platform, it doesn't need to be as comprehensive as JXTA. This architecture imposes a constraint: P2P solutions that leverage the .NET framework must reside on the Microsoft Windows platform. However, since most peers run a Microsoft Windows platform, this constraint is not as serious as it sounds. Figure 3-3 illustrates the .NET framework.

The .NET framework consists of run-time services that your P2P application calls activate. You can build your application using any language that supports the Microsoft Windows platform. Such languages include Visual Basic, Visual C#, and Visual C++, as well as other lesser Microsoft languages such as Python and Perl. All implementations, regardless of language constructs, call the same .NET services. This ensures consistency across all language implementations.

Benefits   Microsoft's .NET offers a consistent programming model across multiple languages. The simplified programming model isolates much of the operating system

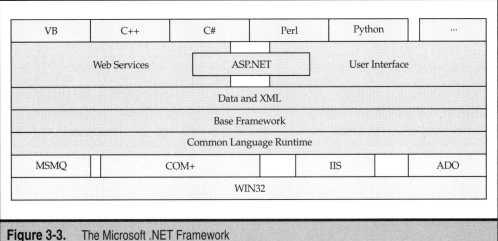

Figure 3-3.   The Microsoft .NET Framework

complexity and runs on all Microsoft platforms. .NET contains features that simplify deployment by avoiding the Windows shared libraries and their .dll (dynamic load library) approach to implementing objects.

.NET offers standard interfaces and data formats and is built on top of familiar tools to ease adoption. In addition, .NET integrates into a large set of powerful server-based (in-the-net) services to handle persistence, workflow, and transcoding to Internet appliances.

Technology   The .NET effort assembles a large number of new classes that Windows applications see as services. These classes make it faster for any Windows application to leverage the .NET services. All applications, regardless of language,[1] use the identical .NET service. This ensures a high level of consistency. The services include a security model that is based on roles, not just simple user accounts. This allows the application to accept incoming access on two levels, referred to as authentication and authorization. The former identifies each user, whereas the latter indicates what services and activities the user is allowed to perform.

The data formats are all XML-based. This allows a standardized approach that can easily integrate with other applications. The extensibility of XML encourages a smooth, graceful innovation path. .NET uses the XML-based SOAP for requesting service execution. SOAP standardizes remote execution of application objects. Applications that take advantage of SOAP can easily distribute themselves. Thus a local application can move to a remote application running on another peer and still access the now-remote services without making any significant changes.

---

1   Not quite true. Microsoft's list of supported languages conspicuously excludes Java.

Issues   The .NET initiative is still in its infancy. This exposes you to a high level of risk. A .NET application will likely stay bound to the Microsoft Windows platforms (however they evolve). .NET will arrive in Windows platforms with quite a blast. It demands quite a bit of change for Windows programmers. This demand may be met with applause or boos. If it is the latter, Microsoft may quickly change direction and threaten any .NET initiatives. Customer acceptance is not currently clear.

Conclusion   .NET, like Sun's JXTA, makes a lot of promises. It is unclear whether the initiative with deliver all of its promises or when it will deliver them. The .NET initiative promises to make network-center services essential to P2P easy to construct, deploy, and support. The Windows-only support of .NET is a moot point for most peers, and any tools that make writing services only enrich P2P offerings. If .NET meets its promise, many new P2P applications will soon arrive.

Development Frameworks

Now the safari moves on to the more formal area of development frameworks. Development frameworks live in a rarified climate apart from other software. Frameworks are software on which other software gets built. They are unique and highly valuable, but only to a very small community—that of software developers. To the rest of the world, frameworks are invisible, like the plumbing in the walls, but software developers look at a new framework with the appreciation of the craftsperson for a new tool, examining every nuance and facet. They marvel over things that would put normal folk to sleep, praising fine distinctions and lamenting missing features. Let's make a tour stop at Mind Electric's GLUE.

Mind Electric's GLUE

When software mastermind Graham Glass left behind his company ObjectSpace and his esoteric software agent product, *Voyager* to turn his attention to a P2P framework, excitement ran high. When results began trickling out of his small, focused effort (a company called the Mind Electric), developers discovered that their interest was certainly justified. What was emerging was a platform, called *GLUE*, that could take much of the pain out of building highly distributed applications and make P2P distributed applications as easy to develop as more mundane ones. Earlier, you learned that software developers can build new applications on foundational P2P products such as Groove. But there are some limitations on how far from the look and feel of Groove the developer's applications might be able to stray. If a developer is more determined to write an application with its own look and feel, GLUE fills the need.

Benefits   GLUE is a Java-based platform that allows a software developer to create web services from smaller parts. Compared to the average Microsoft application, GLUE is positively tiny. A framework such as GLUE turns a PC into a server. Web services become peer services. (Web services are actually quite complex. They demand mastery of technical "alphabet soup" that would baffle the average person—EJB, J3EE, XML, SOAP, WDSL, and UDDI are among the technologies that web services might require.)

Software frameworks (at least the ones related to communications) are often shown in a "protocol" stack, rather like a software layer cake, and GLUE is no exception. Figure 3-4 depicts the GLUE layer cake. Note that GLUE sits atop a lot of complexity and manages that complexity for you.

Technology If you decode all the acronyms and jargon, a clearer picture of what works together to create a full-featured P2P implementation emerges. Let's break apart the model and see what lurks beneath. To help make the discussion concrete, let's demonstrate translating Fahrenheit to Centigrade, which requires a trivial algorithm. The following shows the algorithm as a snippet of Java code, inside the simplified class wrapper.

```
1. public int calc( int centigrade )
2. {
3. return (((9 * centigrade)/5) + 32 );
4. }
...
5. int f = calc( 100 );
```

The first line declares that a function called calc is public (that is, another piece of code can invoke it). It consumes an integer (int centigrade) and emits an integer as a result of being called. Lines 2 and 4 define the limits of the function, and line 3 does the heavy lifting of performing the calculation, and returns the answer as well. Line 5 shows the calculation in action; after calc gets called, the integer f contains the value 212. That's pretty simple stuff. Next comes the real challenge. Suppose that calc is a part of a running program

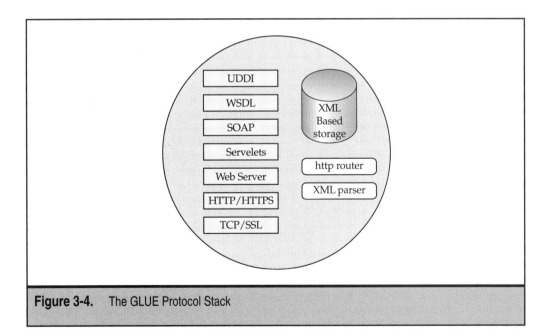

Figure 3-4.   The GLUE Protocol Stack

on another computer somewhere in the network and you want a peer to invoke it from another peer. (As was previously mentioned, P2P is all about computers talking to other computers.) How would you accomplish this?

Here is how GLUE organizes the solution. At the highest level, GLUE uses *UDDI* (Universal Description, Discovery, and Integration). UDDI is a specification that allows computer entities to find one another, possibly even adding other kinds of useful (non-address-related) information. UDDI would register the whereabouts of this little code as a resource, in such a way that other programs would be able to find it. After finding the converter, you need a way to invoke it—that is, to pass the integer to the converter so that it has a number to process.

That's where *WSDL* (Web Services Description Language) comes in. WSDL is a language used to describe a service on the network using XML messages—a key component of GLUE. The messages are meant for computer programs rather than for humans to read. The messages contain parameters that can be used as the input to procedures inside programs on a network. One language-neutral way to implement WSDL is via SOAP, the Simple Object Access Protocol. The following listing shows a SOAP message that invokes the Peer function.

```
1. <?xml version="1.0"?>
2. <SOAP:Envelope xmlns:SOAP="urn:schemas-xmlsoap-org:soap.v1>
3. <SOAP:Body>
4. <calcResponse>
5. <Value>212</Value>
6. </calcResponse >
7. </SOAP:Body>
8. </SOAP:Envelope>
```

The following listing illustrates the function's response.

```
1. <?xml version="1.0"?>
2. <SOAP:Envelope xmlns:SOAP="urn:schemas-xmlsoap-org:soap.v1>
3. <SOAP:Body>
4. <calcResponse>
5. <Value>212</Value>
6. </ calcResponse >
7. </SOAP:Body>
8. </SOAP:Envelope>
```

So far the system discovers resources using UDDI and passes the important information back and forth via SOAP. You still must address several other issues to form a complete solution. GLUE integrates additional capabilities to cover more of a solution's architecture.

SOAP stops short of defining how peers send and receive messages (that's left to the software developer). Also, the SOAP specification doesn't define how a message, once received, will create an instance of an object and execute the method. Finally, it doesn't specify transport mechanisms.

The lower layers of GLUE provide these definitions and specifications. GLUE creates Java servlets, which are responsible for decoding the XML messages and mapping them to methods (such as the temperature converter) and returning the appropriate result. GLUE also provides a built-in Web server that handles HyperText Transfer Protocol (HTTP).

Benefits   You now have a complete solution for offering your temperature converter to the world, or just to yourself remotely, or for building your next IPO-worthy P2P applications. The rub is that you will need to be a software developer to make all this work. The nifty part is that if you are a software developer, you won't need to be a genius or a networking guru to be successful. It's always an important asset for software developers to have a complete and sophisticated library in their toolkit; most developers get something up and running so that they can study how best to use and extend it. GLUE gives developers a tall platform to stand upon.

Conclusion   GLUE is significant for a variety of reasons; most of them qualify as ingenious "plumbing." GLUE is a complete library for building and invoking distributed web services. It has a tiny footprint—an embeddable collection of services that is less than 500KB. Distributed as a Java .JAR file (which is similar to a compressed .ZIP file), GLUE allows you to turn an otherwise unmodified Java object into a P2P web service instantly.

GLUE is platform-, protocol-, and transport-neutral. Thus you can implement your P2P service on Linux, Windows, or Macintosh machines without affecting the service's users. A service written to this specification leverages the features of SOAP, Microsoft's upcoming .NET framework, and IBM's evolving Web Services Toolkit (WSTK).

GLUE includes a microweb server, a Java servlet engine, SOAP processor, XML parser (Electric XML), and a dynamic WDSL generator, as well as a UDDI client and UDDI server. Also, GLUE supports mobile communication via Wireless Application Protocol (WAP). You never can tell when you're going to need to convert temperatures on the go, using your data-enabled cell phone.

GLUE uses a lightweight XML persistent storage database system. Finally, the Mind Electric gives you a way to deploy your P2P web service using a web browser, which allows you to install your application across a network dynamically. GLUE is good evidence that good things can come in small packages.

Messaging Frameworks

Your next stop takes you to the building blocks of messaging. Messaging addresses the basic need to share information with peers. Messaging frameworks tackle two distinct problems:

▼   **Communication**   The direct exchange of information.

▲   **Presence**   The ability to determine that someone is actually there to receive the communication.

The second characteristic is not a requirement. You can still send information (in most communication frameworks) without someone being present to receive it. Still, it is nice to know that the person is actually there and may be able to respond quickly to your communication. Presence ensures that all the electronic signals reach an actual human being. This feature can quickly provide the status information for all your peer associates.

Messaging frameworks leapfrog many of the limitations of e-mail. Effective communication is both synchronous (you wait for an answer, as when you ask, "Do you want to go to lunch now?") or asynchronous (you do not wait for an answer, as when you pass the declarative message, "The new version of *xx* is available"). Initially, simple exchanges formed the popular communication method known as "chat." The various forms of chat, whether IRC (Internet relay chat), or other chat applications often are referred to as *instant messaging* to distinguish them from e-mail, which is not instantaneous. But as the messaging products evolve and broadband becomes more commonplace, new types of communication will leverage the messaging framework. You can use messaging frameworks to send and share files and even make phone calls.

Messaging must solve a sticky electronic communication dilemma: how to provide a unique name and corresponding location for each communication participant. This general problem is referred to as *naming*. Each communication resource or peer must have a unique name or identifier. These names are then dynamically bound to specific locations, enabling participants to jump from machine to machine or allowing the machine itself to jump from address to address. These naming/location directories can be problematic. The Universal Resource Location (URL) addresses combined with Dynamic Naming Service (DNS) attempt to solve this situation for fixed Web sites. But this technique works poorly for P2P.

P2P computers often depend on Dynamic Host Configuration Protocol (DHCP) to assign an IP address. Thus every time you connect as a peer, you may be assigned a different IP address. For this reason, an individual PC may not be registered in the static DNS system. In short, DNS, the main Internet naming scheme, is but one method of namespace definition. Instant messaging utilizes a parallel namespace to map people and the machines they use to communicate. For this reason, P2P namespaces are sometimes referred to as the "dark matter" of the Internet. DNS is part of a paradigm that recognizes peers as only recipients of information, not publishers.

Let's get a sense of how the part of the Internet not directly plugged into traditional DNS is used to create a messaging framework by visiting our next stop on the tour, by visiting Jabber, an open source instant messaging solution.

Jabber

Jabber is an instant messaging and presence framework developed within the open source community. The framework is easily extensible to develop more powerful communication methods and integrates into complementary technologies. Jabber can directly integrate with most major proprietary instant messaging systems such as AOL, MSN, and ICQ. It can also integrate with any nontraditional messaging systems such as wireless and paging systems.

Benefits   Jabber establishes instant and buffered communication between peers. It can selectively indicate presence information on your peer friends and associates. Jabber is extensible to different types of communication beyond simple chatting. The framework is inclusive to all other messaging types including proprietary and nontraditional types. Because Jabber is open source (see the section "Open Source Software—What's It All About?" later in this chapter) and available for free, you can customize it to your specific needs. The free source characteristics also promote an environment of innovation.

Technology   Jabber technology is highly modularized and scalable. The overall architecture follows the e-mail architecture, which is fully distributed. Like e-mail, Jabber requires a Jabber server. (As mentioned previously, a server often plays a critical role in coordinating P2P activities.) You will learn more about server elements shortly. In line with P2P's objectives, the Jabber servers communicate with other servers as peers, forming higher-level P2P or server-to-server (S2S) communication.

Jabber participants connect only with their Jabber server. Their Jabber server determines whether the communication is local or must go to another Jabber server. This parallels the successful e-mail architecture. Like e-mail, Jabber is highly scalable. A small Jabber server could serve a small client base, yet still connect with all the other Jabber servers, thus offering access to a virtually unlimited number of users.

Jabber builds its communication foundation and format on XML. XML allows you to standardize and extend the communication format. This directly addresses the unformatted information problem discussed in Chapter 2, yet XML still allows extensions. These extensions allow the applications to grow into new areas without losing support for earlier communication formats. The XML extension could contain a simple chat exchange or something much more detailed. This flexibility allows Jabber to step up to much higher types of communication such as machine-to-machine requests for peer services.

Jabber also allows translations, called *transports,* between other types of communication flows. A transport is a standard way of translating between Jabber and a foreign communication method such as AOL Instant Messenger. Many transports are available, and the documentation explains how you can build additional ones.

Issues   Jabber has all the advantages and disadvantages of open source. These issues are fully discussed in the upcoming section, "Open Source Software—What's It All About"?

Jabber modularity and loose coupling of major architectural pieces afford both flexibility and extensibility. The data adapters enable integration of many sources but must be kept up to date if that source changes. Foreign sources, such as AOL, may change just to avoid Jabber integration.

Conclusion   Jabber is an excellent messaging product worth watching. It is useful merely as a universal chat client that integrates all your AOL and MSN buddies. But its capability to enable quick, complex information exchanges opens up a world of communication possibilities. You can establish your own private messaging and communication system by establishing a peer as the common Jabber server. (If that sounds confusing, don't worry; later chapters will go into full detail.) Finally, you can write your own extensions to a Jabber client or Jabber server to address your unique communication needs. In short, Jabber provides a very powerful communication framework for P2P.

Blocks Extensible Exchange Protocol (BXXP)

The next safari stop goes to a lower, more basic level of communication. BXXP (pronounced *beep*) solves many problems inherent to Internet communication. HyperText Protocol (HTTP), the protocol of Web sites, essentially facilitates one-way communication. HTTP is adequate for many Web sites, but falls short in the dynamic, bidirectional world of P2P. BXXP steps into this void to offer a new protocol that directly addresses the needs of P2P.

The three major concerns of BXXP are authentication (correctly identifying communication participants), transport security (disallowing any spying), and the actual communication.

Benefits   BXXP uses message-oriented exchange using a request and response similar to Web exchanges. However, BXXP is bidirectional, enabling either participant to make or service a request regardless of which one initiated the connection. This bidirectionality serves P2P well. In addition, BXXP enables multiple, asynchronous messaging requests. You do not have to wait for one request to complete before making a new request.

BXXP is fully extensible due to its XML foundation. BXXP extensions are formally defined in BXXP profiles. These definitions make it easy for peers to understand your particular XML formats. Currently, many profiles exist for different communication needs.

Like Jabber, BXXP is open source and available for free. Because it is open source, you can customize BXXP to your specific needs. Its open source orientation also makes BXXP an environment of innovation.

Technology   BXXP is actually a comprehensive communication framework that details all necessary basic protocol operations. These include incorporating features, such as authentication, that the actual applications usually maintain. Authentication is the feature that identifies you as you. Because each application typically performs authentication, if you use 100 applications, you probably have 100 passwords. Sometimes applications share a directory such as LDAP, but in such cases the library's reach is limited to local area network participants. BXXP fully addresses authentication as a protocol. All applications using BXXP rely on its authentication, so you need only a BXXP password. Any messaging application built on BXXP need not worry about authentication.

The ability to handle simultaneous exchanges makes useful P2P solutions possible. In addition, a peer can both initiate conversations and respond to them. Typically, web sites only respond and are not permitted to initiate a request. Web sites only serve. Thus if a web site knows something that you should know—for example, that your stock portfolio just dropped 20 percent—it must wait until you ask. BXXP allows bidirectional communications. A BXXP service on a peer can both notify and be notified, which is a clear advantage.

Issues   BXXP is a new protocol with some intriguing features. A protocol's viability and value are assured only when the protocol is in use by a critical mass of users. BXXP has not yet reached that critical level of popularity. Still, the protocol solves some problems that must be addressed, so stay tuned.

Corporate security and protocols are often at odds. It is unclear whether large corporations will allow the proliferation of such a powerful protocol.

Conclusion   Although BXXP addresses many P2P problems, offering efficient symmetrical communications between peers, it is still in infancy. Symmetrical communications, absolutely necessary for P2P applications, require a full revamp of thinking about how applications communicate. Certainly, HTTP whose model assumes a server in the flow and a thin client (whose primary responsibility is to display output from a server or to fill in forms to be transmitted to a server) is not the right design center for peer applications. To the extent that BXXP can supplant protocols such as HTTP, it will become an important part of the new P2P Internet landscape.

OPEN SOURCE SOFTWARE—WHAT'S IT ALL ABOUT?

Open source software is a new and growing category in software. It is software freely available in both executable form and in source code. Thus you can use it instantly or customize it to your particular needs. An open source development team loosely coalesces to own and advance an open source software product. Contributions to the source code, intended to advance the software, come from all over the world.

Open source software has tackled some of the toughest software problems, from operating systems with Linux, to Web servers with Apache, to many P2P solutions. The software has laid the foundation for many mission-critical business applications as well as many successful personal applications. The Apache web server, for example, runs more than 50 percent of web sites. Open source software is a large innovation catalyst to the P2P world as well as the larger computer world. Many of the examples explored in this chapter are open source and freely available.

Open source does come with some rules:

▼   **Free Redistribution**   Developers cannot sell any modification for profit and must continue to distribute modified source freely. This rule prevents a short-term gain for one group at the expense of the software's advancement.

■   **Source Code Availability**   Although you could distribute just the executable version, a user must always have a means to acquire the source code easily. In addition, you cannot purposely create confusing code meant to hinder understanding (although with some programmers, determining intentional violations of this rule can be a tough call).

■   **Derived Works**   All works deriving from the original must adhere to the same restrictions. Unofficial modifications must be clearly distinguished from the base effort.

▲   **No Discrimination**   Open source strives to be written in such a way that there is little or no dependence on proprietary underpinnings, or operating systems.

Advantages and Disadvantages of Open Source Software

Open source offers some valuable advantages, including price, control, innovation, and support.

Price

Clearly a huge advantage is the price. But always keep in mind that a price includes all the installation, support, and training to operate the software. So although the initial dollar price may be low, the other price factors can drive your overall costs much higher.

Control

Because you can download the actual source code, you can control your own destiny (if you have the necessary skills). You need not worry about whether the software supports a direction unique to your efforts. For example, you may need certain performance improvements for your particular use. A standard, commercial software application would not enable you to make such changes and you would be out of luck.

On the other hand, because control is initially in the hands of anonymous developers, software users may find it difficult to trust the basic functionality and security of the software.

Innovation

The free software community includes hundreds of programmers who contribute ideas (and code) on a very regular basis. Popular free software programs such as Linux advance very quickly. They achieve free software success by attracting a critical mass of developers to ensure rapid progress.

Support

Support comes in two distinct flavors. Free support comes from the army of developers interested in advancing the software. You will be amazed at how quickly and accurately they respond. You can also search the many newsgroups for answers to your questions. Second, you can use support services that charge a support fee. These services spring up to give higher levels of support for critical business needs.

Getting Involved

You can contribute to free software either by advancing an existing software application or starting your own. Visit one of the many free source sites or one of the collaboration sites such as collab.net. These collaboration sites manage all the logistics of developing open source software.

In-the-Net P2P Services

The last stop in the P2P jungle exists on the fringe of P2P. A discussion of in-the-net services, usually resident on large servers at well known DNS addresses appear out of place in the discussion of the P2P world. In-the-net services perform such tasks as address resolution

(Jabber,) meta-data (Napster,) or workflow coordination (SETI@home.) The coordination between P2P edge devices and traditional large Web servers can be quite beneficial to both. Whereas peers are great at creating content or communicating with users, they are not great at serving as a gigantic information switchboard.

There is often a role for centralized servers in the flow of information from peer to peer. P2P architectures can take one of two directions with respect to services that are best centralized. They can make one peer the server (sort of a super peer) or just create a real server with a known DNS address. Servers, therefore offer a universal name and location for important information. Napster discovered this role and aggregated meta-data song titles and P2P client addresses in a centralized server farm. As a result, Napster searches were very responsive, quickly providing query responses in the same manner as dedicated Web servers. Once the music was located, you could use the meta-data to select a peer to whom you could direct your download request.

In-the-net services can be essential partners to the smooth operation of many overall P2P solutions complementing and significantly advancing the goals of P2P systems. Upcoming chapters explore the many services available to launch a more powerful P2P application via in-the-net services. Let's take a quick visit with DtDNS, a dynamic domain name service, and then move on to an interesting streaming company, Chaincast.

DtDNS's Dynamic Domain Name Service

Naming is a critical component of any P2P solution. If you can't find a peer, you can't use any of the peer's services and information. Web sites have the luxury of fixed IP addresses. They register a name like www.fun.com and their IP address with a Domain Name Service (DNS). The DNS then takes requests for the web site and provides the IP address.

Registering the name and IP address costs the web site money. DNS registration and its costs are too much of a burden for a small peer system. Peers are often forced to use the Dynamic Host Configuration Protocol (DHCP) to obtain an available IP address. DHCP dynamically assigns an available IP address from a preallocated pool of addresses. The peer has no assurance that he or she will ever obtain the same address. Therefore, basing P2P addressing on a static, non-dynamic address space, such as DNS is not a viable solution.

What is needed is a dynamic system that attaches the same virtual name to a dynamic IP address. This is what DtDNS Corporation's product DtDNS (http://www.dtdns.com) offers. It provides a dynamic virtual address, not a static one. Upon receiving an IP address, the peer simply registers the address with the in-the-net service, DtDNS. The registered name then follows the peer, which thus does not need a fixed IP address. Regardless of the physical address, the peer's virtual address is always correct.

Conclusion   Dynamic DNS offers a valuable solution to the challenges in locating a moving target. This is a concern that traditional naming services such as DNS simply ignored. Currently, DtDNS virtual naming remains free and universally accessible in the net service, but, with the economic viability of all "free" services having been affected by the "Dot com" implosion beginning in 2000, this may not always be the case.

Chaincast P2P Multimedia Streaming

Chaincast is a thrilling jungle stop—it is the stuff of movies, music, and breaking-story newscasts. Streaming enables the Internet to go beyond static pages to achieve movement and sound by delivering audio and video instantly over the Internet.

Streaming had a less than auspicious start; many users remember the jerky images and rudely interrupted sounds of the early efforts. An early watershed moment was the February 3, 1999, streaming event of a Victoria's Secret fashion show. All the excitement even brought one of the author's wives, normally uninterested in the Internet, into the fray. However, after only a few seconds watching, she was puzzling whether the image was a woman, a bra, or something else. Many potential visitors didn't even get to see that much, because the services failed for many. Clearly, streaming had promise but it also had a long way to go.

Streaming is now beginning to take advantage of the advances in processing technology and improvements in bandwidth. Eventually a truly advanced, *interactive* multimedia experience should be possible between peers. Streaming still is somewhat in the jungle, but it is a fun place. The experience goes far beyond "television for the Internet." It enables a customizable, two-way multimedia adventure that TV will never achieve.

Streaming overcomes the need for the huge downloads usually associated with complex multimedia. The first digital pieces of your selected audio or video establish a local multimedia buffer. The buffer size depends on your network speed and other factors. The buffer adapts to the unpredictable instantaneous bandwidth of the Internet. When the network suddenly slows down, the multimedia player uses a larger amount of buffered data. When the network speeds up, the buffer is replenished. The filling of the buffer continues throughout your viewing or listening experience.

A flaw in this approach is that the average delivery of digital pieces or network packets must match your viewing pace. Streaming is less sensitive to instantaneous rates but *very* sensitive to overall rates. You cannot fit a video viewed at 200KB/sec into a 100KB/sec network sack. This limitation presents a significant challenge to suppliers of streaming multimedia.

The originator of the streaming event must deal with the multitude of paths to all the receivers of the event. Although many paths may be just fine, many will not be. The presence of problematic paths can result in a very unpredictable streaming event that is almost impossible to solve from a server perspective. The challenge is to move the streaming information closer to the receiver and form a content relay. Chaincast addresses this issue by enabling two peers to serve as the content rely point. Chaincast appropriately calls its technique *chaincasting*. Chaincasting makes each peer both a receiver and a transmitter. Receivers with extra bandwidth create a virtual multicasting router, sending the stream efficiently to adjacent receivers.

Benefits Chaincast ultimately improves the streaming experience and the associated costs. The product achieves these improvements by significantly reducing server network bandwidth and processing requirements. The distributed P2P network handles much of the streaming, which lowers costs and also lowers the barriers to peers who want to provide streaming. Chaincast distributes the load of offering up the stream across a P2P network rather than large, expensive server farms. This distribution leverages P2P to achieve fantastic scalability. It also makes it possible for peers to stream multimedia events that thousands of users can view.

Technology   Chaincast consists of several components that deliver a high-quality streaming experience. Chaincast consists of a network topology engine that tracks the listening experience to determine continually the best path for each participant. The servers encode streaming content to allow players to take advantage of Chaincast. Content accelerators provide a middle tier to boost the streaming process. Finally, the end point is the Chaincast player. An add-on to existing players, such as Windows Media Player, the Chaincast player receives and sends steaming information to nearby participants. A Chaincast manager component watches over the streaming and provides security.

These components combine to form the Chaincast platform, which is illustrated in Figure 3-5. The platform consists of the content creators (VRM servers), the content

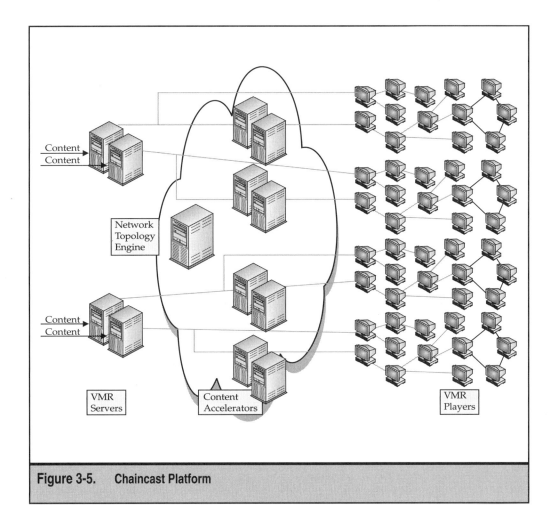

Figure 3-5.   Chaincast Platform

accelerators, and the VRM players. The VRM players communicate with other players to distribute the streaming content.

Conclusion   Streaming remains an auspicious but raw Internet technology. Many peers have the raw multimedia material through experimentation with the flood of video cameras and microphones. The content is just waiting to be set free. Streaming, however, is currently still a novelty to many. It remains complex and out of reach for most peers. Chaincast provides a promising approach to advance streaming on the backs of P2P. This approach raises several troublesome issues. Chaincast leverages P2P but really does not acknowledge P2P's leadership. Peer participants unknowingly advance someone else's goals. The technology is bent on a very non-P2P goal of extending a server view through the exploitation of P2P resources. However, technologies such as Chaincast could easily change to allow peers to leverage the technology. Let's hope so. Until then, Chaincast remains in the jungle.

JUNGLE TOUR SUMMARY

Now that you have reached the end of your jungle safari, it is time to gather around a campfire and discuss some of the common issues that you faced in your journey:

▼   **Immaturity**   If the applications discussed in Chapter 2 can be thought of as immature, then the tools being used to build them are even more so. Since, unlike more mature Web-based applications, there is no canonical definition of a P2P application, few tools and development environments have emerged. The platform that is best for you depends on your overall needs. If you're building a collaboration application using P2P, your needs will be very different from those of someone building a photo-sharing application using P2P. It's also too soon to determine whether one platform will be significantly better than others. Likewise, no one yet knows for certain whether a technology such as Groove, .NET, or GLUE will lead P2P developers to a more enabled state or into a blind alley.

■   **Riding the Tiger**   An ancient Chinese adage holds that whoever seeks to ride the back of the tiger often ends up inside. For nearly two decades, the experience of other companies riding the back of the Microsoft tiger has demonstrated the truth behind this saying. It is entirely possible that by aligning themselves with any initiative championed by Microsoft, that a whole new set of companies will discover the same thing. Although most analysts agree that the Hailstorm initiative overreaches even Microsoft's ambitions, the real questions focus on what happens to the industry and to the state of competition if the initiative *does* succeed, even partially. Will Hailstorm's success upset the balance of power such that other approaches disappear altogether? Will P2P-based applications grow to look like simple extensions of Office XP applications? Will innovation suffer? Microsoft alone may hold the answers to these questions.

- ■ **Unity or Anarchy**   Many forces are working to unite the P2P space with frameworks, distributed objects, and the like. The standards will develop, and ultimately the marketplace will prevail. But P2P tools face major hurdles. Not all frameworks and standards will win. Many will depend on reaching a critical mass of users and programmers. So place your bets carefully. The sheer demands of markets often work against the unity that can sometimes enable developers to seize opportunities or maintain a competitive advantage.

- ▲ **Standards**   Rather than using existing standards, many enablers are trying to establish their own P2P standards to take P2P to the next level. It is not clear which if any will win. They all offer interesting insights into creating a better, easier P2P world. One clear trend has emerged: XML in all its various forms will no doubt form the communication format of P2P.

TOUR CONCLUSIONS

After your whirlwind tours of the two P2P landscapes, you now return to civilization with a greater understanding of the projects currently carving out new spaces within the Internet. In some cases, innovators are trying to create new products for end users (Napster and Freenet), in some cases new tools strictly for tool makers (GLUE), and in other cases both (Jabber and Groove). Before you move on to the next level of complexity, let's make some observations about the tours.

New Paradigms Require New Thinking

In his 1997 book on human-computer interaction, *Interface Culture*, author Steven Johnson says

> *At the threshold points, near the birth of any technology, all types of distortions and misunderstandings are bound to appear—misunderstandings not only of how the machines actually work, but also of more subtle matters: what realm of experience the new technologies belong to, what values they perpetuate, where their more indirect effects will take place.*

The growth of the suburbs in the United States was a secondary effect of the program that built the system of interstate highways. No one foresaw that the suburbs would change our living, commuting, and shopping patterns; would hollow out the cities; would foster cultural homogeneity; would create insatiable demands for infrastructure and energy; and would change the face of American society like nothing that had occurred before, since the migration from the agricultural economy that created urban America in the first place.

In a similar vein, P2P is a secondary effect of the increasing ubiquity of high-speed wired and wireless networks and high-performance computing equipment at the network's edge. We think that we can see some of the secondary side effects of P2P, but can we really? What we *appear* to know already is that the "Wintel" community (consisting of

Microsoft, Intel, AMD, Compaq, Dell, Hewlett-Packard, and the like) seems pretty happy. During most of the 1990s, a new release of Microsoft's desktop operating systems and office tools required a lock-step PC upgrade. The Pentium class machine changed all that. Even with normal software bloat, machines were more than adequate to handle ordinary desktop processing. Fewer PC users had incentives to upgrade. Profits fell, and the technology sector suffered tremendous setbacks. Now, conventional wisdom suggests that P2P holds the potential to change the picture significantly.

Chip makers and PC manufacturers feel that P2P applications will create the need for newer and more powerful chipsets, feature cards, displays, and disk capacity. Many users are already addicted to e-mail, chatting, and other forms of live content (see the section "Live Content Addiction" later in this chapter), and P2P will facilitate even more interactivity. Thus, the anticipated need to support video and audio streaming will drive an increase in the level of all PCs to "server-grade" machines.

New Paradigms Require Old Thinking

When the Internet was first conceived by BBN Technologies and DARPA (the Defense Advanced Research Projects Agency,) the idea was of a network that was inherently distributed and inherently P2P. The Internet of the early 1980s could be drawn on a single piece of paper, as shown in Figure 3-6. As this figure indicates, the design implied a peer orientation for the network. The network was to have no second-class citizens; everyone was to be both a client and a server. Thus the answer to whether distributed applications and P2P are new paradigms is both yes and no.

Because distributed computing is a venerable concept, designers and developers must remind themselves of some "old thinking" about the essential characteristics of distributing applications across a network and some invalid assumptions. A feature of P2P generally taken for granted is that the network is essentially abstracted away; that is, the network between the pieces of an application is assumed to be non-existent. In a perfect world where networks would behave in a deterministic fashion, so-called network effects (like any latency or link failures) would be transparent.

Ideally, a network would work as well as the plumbing in your house, and likewise would not be something to which you would ever need to give much thought. Of course, if something were to go wrong with your house plumbing, the effect would be very noticeable, wreaking havoc on your life. Much the same can be said of the network in a networked architecture. Peter Deutsch at Sun Microsystems points out that naïve developers make eight fatal assumptions when they build distributed architectures. Working to combat them is what makes P2P and similar application frameworks "interesting" to work with:

1. The network is reliable.
2. Latency is zero.
3. Bandwidth is infinite.
4. The network is secure.
5. Topology doesn't change.

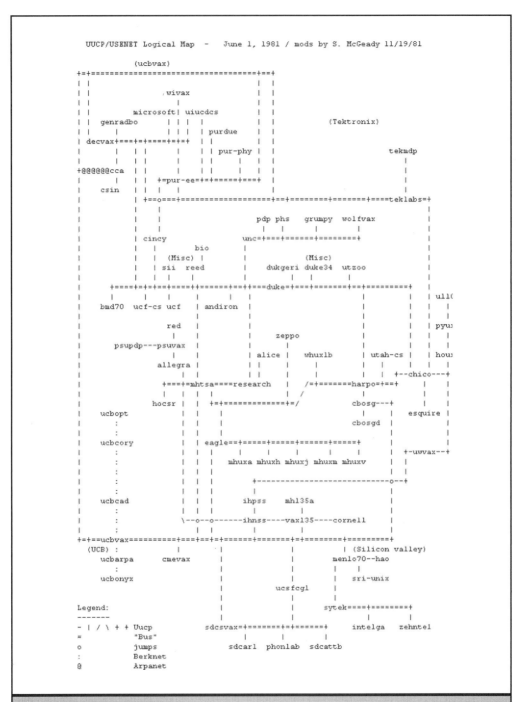

Figure 3-6. The Early "Internet"

6. There is one administrator.

7. Transport cost is zero.

8. The network is homogeneous.

As developers design new kinds of systems, they must consider an important set of design criteria—the Eight Great Standards of Good P2P design:

1. The network must be *self-defining* and *self-establishing,* capable of coming together without much in the way of network administration or intialization.

2. The network must be *self-repairing,* capable of losing losses of some number of participants without degrading anything (except perhaps for performance).

3. The network must use a *dynamic namespace,* capable of dynamically growing and changing, and be able to tolerate users who are behind firewalls, or who have DHCP addresses assigned by their organization or ISP.

4. The network tolerates *variable connectivity,* enabling users to join or quit at any time without affecting the overall quality of the P2P experience you are trying to provide to them.

5. The network doesn't have a problem with *latency.* Users can run wired or wireless, fast or slow. It shouldn't matter, and shouldn't affect the overall quality of the experience.

6. The network is *appropriately engineered.* It divides labor. There is an appropriate division of labor between servers and clients.

7. The network has *message-oriented communications,* allowing a wide variety of applications to be built.

8. The network does *"just enough."* That is, servers and routers manage their functions (such as routing, or lookup, or metadata storage), and then get out of the way of the peer devices at the network's edge.

New Paradigms Require Unconventional Wisdom

The World Wide Web was the earliest topology of cyberspace that actually worked well enough for people to begin to sit up and take notice. The Web was (and still is, to a large degree) about smart but heavily burdened servers in the flow of data, and dumb but underwhelmed PCs at the edge, showing pretty arrangements of pictures and text, or forms for end users to fill up with data. With the advent of the P2P model, the landscape has changed such that smart clients at the edge are talking to other smart clients.

In the early 1990s, Intel launched an experiment to join peers so that they could yield to medical researchers their available computing power. Few would have guessed then that during the first two months of the experiment 600,000 people would donate over a 100 million hours of processing time. Such an effort is pretty unconventional, but in truth many (perhaps most) of the new and innovative applications will initially be seen as unconventional. Who would have foreseen that textual chatting would have become (next to e-mail) the fastest growing indoor sport for most people on the net? Live content and live interaction hold a magnetic attraction for people, and P2P nurtures person-to-person interchange as significantly as the telephone did a century ago.

In a nascent marketplace, at least a few of the ideas being developed will not survive their infancy. But all of them will challenge the status quo and contest staid thinking. The genie can never be put back in the bottle, and P2P's possibilities will forever change the course of the Internet's evolution.

CHAPTER 4

Of Names and Addresses

In this chapter, you learn why finding people and things either by their names or their addresses has been a "big deal" ever since civilization got big enough to matter, and why the Internet only acted to compound the problem. This chapter explains how P2P architectures lead the way toward a different kind of Internet[1] where users can directly access people and resources by who or what they are rather than by an invented abstraction. Further, you learn about mobile devices and how P2P helps bridge the mobile world and the Internet. Finally, the chapter discusses how P2P is helping to define what Tim Berners-Lee, inventor of the World Wide Web, terms the "Semantic Web," a redefinition of cyberspace where information has higher meaning, and people and computers work in greater cooperation.

THE NAMING OF THINGS

According to the Book of Genesis, the first task the Almighty gave to Adam in the Garden of Eden was the naming of things. Fortunately for the first man, he wasn't created in the Internet era. When people talk about naming in P2P, they are really referring to addressing or at least something closely analogous to addressing. In the Internet sense, naming is a way of figuratively referring to something distant—a way of uniquely identifying something while at the same time concealing the fact that a network is between you and the object that you wish to find.

Historically, telecommunications has forced people to deal with a second level of abstraction in which they use an address of some kind (a telephone number or a URL) to represent the resource they actually want. P2P strives to deliver to the average user a world in which the user really doesn't need to be so concerned about all the cryptic numbers and addresses that represent the name of the resource that he or she wants to access, manipulate, or interact with. What Napster gives the average user, for example, is the ability to configure his or her own network. Through Napster, the user can set up a network based on accessing the actual thing that the user wants by name (a song called "Closer to Fine," or all the songs of the Indigo Girls, for example) without having to worry about all the mechanics of how to connect to the person who has a file containing the song(s).

This kind of access capability, where the user just names something and it becomes available, is called a *content-addressable Web*. It's actually the model that Berners-Lee had in mind when he conceptualized the World Wide Web.

When people talk about addressing in the modern Internet, they are actually talking about addressing either working resources or possibly other human beings. Sometimes the distinction may seem unclear or even unimportant. You may think that you are sending correspondence to a person when you type in a long e-mail addressed to Joe.Blow@AnISP.com, when in actual fact you are addressing a mailbox (a resource) at Joe's ISP. The distinction is

---

1   Although this chapter touches lightly on architectural ideas, Chapter 5 will delve deeper into
     P2P architecture concepts.

not really moot, however; you really have no idea if or when Joe will actually read your e-mail message. On the other hand, if you send Joe an instant message, you have a really clear idea about the questions of if and when.

IS THERE A DIFFERENCE BETWEEN A NAME AND AN ADDRESS?

Humans have a long history of blurring the distinction between naming and addressing as a distant communications concept. Washington D.C.'s *Newseum* includes a palm-sized clay tablet from ancient Sumeria circa 2100 B.C., bearing the message, "your loving wife has had a child" (see Figure 4-1). This communication reached its intended recipient, the message traveled from a source address (the new mother's proxy) to the intended recipient (the happy father).

You can see some parallels with modern Internet communications from this exchange. This example is perhaps the purest form of content addressing—delivering content directly from the source to the hands of the recipient.

Names inevitably become entwined with addresses because people and resources have physicality; thus naming and addressing *seem* to be very nearly the same thing. Connecting to a distant person or a needed resource requires an ability to navigate the vagaries of the wires or the ether between.

Figure 4-1.   Early Sumerian Clay Tablet

We do not know how many hands the tablet passed through, or how many weeks it took to deliver this message (or in truth whether it reached the new father at all). The message did not get broken into packets (the tablet seems intact), but it probably did experience switching, being handed off from messenger to messenger, just as messages now experience multiple hops across the net. Thus, we can't directly compare either "level of service" or "quality of service" with the modern Internet. In the time-tested model of a communications network strung together via humans acting as nodes, the message had to be hand-delivered or verbally delivered to a specific person, thus the address and the person were one and the same.

The goal of the communication is the conveyance of personally relevant information. Requests for resources may have been the subject of the communication, but they could not be addressed directly. Whether the mechanism for conveying intelligence across distance was signal fires, couriers, or carrier pigeons, not a lot happened with the concept of addressing for a very long time.

TELEGRAPHY—THE VICTORIAN INTERNET

Even in more modern models of networked communications, addressing was still pretty simple. Fast forward to the 18th century, to the earliest visual telegraphy networks in England and France (such as the one shown in Figure 4-2). Nodes in the net were place on adjacent hilltops and operators manipulated shutters or other articulated signaling devices to move the message along to the next node. When the message got sufficiently close to its physical destination, it was transcribed to paper and hand-delivered to its physical destination and recipient. This model certainly resulted in faster delivery than the Sumerian model. Still, security, reliability (especially on a foggy day), and error correction were pretty suspect, but those are issues for another chapter.

Achieving even greater speed than optical telegraphy was the Morse-style telegraph, where electricity carried the message forward. The insertion of multiple electrically connected nodes created a new kind of multi-hop network that replaced the messenger-to-messenger hand-offs of the short-lived Pony Express.

However, Morse-style telegraphs changed nothing regarding addressing. The "last-mile" portion of the communication path, in which the transcribed message was hand-carried to the named recipient, was still a feature of the naming architecture. The target address was assumed to contain (or at least be associated with) the named recipient (the receiving resource). The messenger had to resolve addresses manually, and thus had to be extremely knowledgeable about local geography. Although telegraphy implemented a simple store-and-forward architecture from network edge to network edge, the messenger might also receive a reply message for the message originator, thus creating an analog to a not-so-instant messaging system.

Telegraphy created a system in which addresses were partly pure abstraction (within the network) and partly physical. The interior of the network, in which the local telegraph offices were separate nodes, was a completely synchronous point-to-point addressed

Shutter Style Optical Telegaphs in Great Britain (above)
and Articulated Arm Style in Napoleonic France (below)

Figure 4-2.   Optical Telegraphy

topology, very closely resembling a modern instant messaging system where telegraphers sent and received messages (either personal or revenue-bearing) and received replies in real time. Nodes in the interior didn't deal with any address other than the address of the next node. Operators at the telegraph offices actually resolved the endpoint address by inspecting the message header. If the message was intended for a local recipient, the office transcribed the message and handed it to a messenger; otherwise, the operator simply passed the message to the next office along the trunk line until it reached one of several large branch offices.

The larger branch offices were aggregation and switching points where local trunks terminated. At the branch office, a large number of interconnects were available to other branches, and again the operator made a switching decision, "hooking" the message (hanging it on a hook on a conveyor belt) for transmission to a specific branch by relay telegraphers. Alternatively, he or she[2] might retransmit the message to another local trunk radiating out from the branch office.

The interior of the telegraph network somewhat presaged P2P in one sense: Each node knew only about its interconnected nodes, and had "always-available" access to its neighbors. As our discussion of the Gnutella architecture noted, this is precisely the undercarriage that Gnutella uses to link users' machines together. There was, however, no edge-to-edge communication within the system other than that among the human resolvers in the loop. The ultimate resolver was of course the faithful Western Union delivery boy, whose diligence finished the final lap of the person-to-person connection. The achievement of the era of the telegraph, the "Victorian Internet," as it is sometimes called, was to decrease the time required for long-distance personal communications. The system achieved this speed through a complex orchestration that turned names into addresses both inside and outside the network.

THE TELEPHONE AGE—REACH OUT AND ADDRESS SOMEONE

The very first telephone call demonstrates P2P in its pure form: direct person to person communications, collaboration, and resource access. When Alexander Graham Bell uttered the now famous words, "Watson, come here. I want you," he demonstrated exactly what we find so utterly appealing about the P2P paradigm:

▼ Direct access to resources

■ (User-perceived) simplicity

■ No need for either participant to record or remember a long string of characters representing the desired resource

■ No need to learn and navigate a complex protocol or complex software

▲ "Always-on, always-available" access

Unfortunately, as soon as Bell needed to speak to someone *other than* Mr. Watson, things once again became complex. With the broader adoption of Bell's marvelous invention, the need for naming conventions to allow unambiguous addressing rushed at engineers headlong. Built upon the telegraphy backbone, and then extended by copper wires into almost every inhabited place, the early telephone network was the first application that associated an abstract address (a telephone number) with a physical one. Thus a person or group of people (a family residence) was associated with a communications endpoint and represented by a number.

---

2   Because telegraphy was one of the first "information age" jobs, in which muscle power was not a differentiator, almost as many women as men were telegraphers.

Still, in the earliest days of the telephone, the local party line was relatively P2P. You listened for a distinct ring that meant the call was for you; when you wanted to call someone, you spoke to a human operator who set up the call for you. The operator connected you directly to the resource of interest, usually a neighbor or local business. The price you paid is well known to anyone who ever watched *The Andy Griffith Show*. The ever-present and ever-prying telephone operator pretty much guaranteed that you would never want for company during a conversation, and that you would never have any privacy. Even if the operator wasn't listening in on the shared party line, your closest neighbor might be. Thus, you experienced the same level of privacy as an Internet chat room would offer a half-century later. On the party line, you were known by name and your personal business belonged to everyone.

Even after the demise of the party line, when personal and private long-distance end-to-end personal communications became a possibility for the first time, the system of naming wasn't perfect. You could be assured that your device would connect with the device at a certain physical address, but you couldn't necessarily be assured that you would connect with the right person.

You might actually have to converse with an assistant, a spouse, or the person's two-year-old daughter. This was not always what you wanted, and it forced a certain etiquette extraneous to the real intent of the communication. That is, you had to wrap the information exchange in the form of a conversation. Rather than being a simple information exchange, you might have to talk in complete sentences, feign interest, create a human connection, when all you wanted to know was the answer to the question, "Did you get the Bigglesworth report done on time?" Still, the wired telephone system, built on the foundation architecture of electric telegraphy, marched us one step closer to being able to specify, unambiguously, to whom you wished to connect and with which resource.

In voice telephony, the addressing scheme for U. S. telephones (called the 3-3-4 system: three-digit area code, three-digit exchange, and four-digit extension) came about as a result of the physical architecture of something called crossbar switching, an artifact of 1940s telephone technology. When you dialed a 3, the area code was transmitted to a large crossbar switch (see Figure 4-3). Sets of bars in the switch could move left and right, up and down, backward and forward. As you continued to dial, for example, 0 and 1 to complete the prefix for the 301 area code, the other bars of the crossbar moved into place.

In this way, an area or prefix code in the range 000 to 999 (not all numbers were used) could be handled via a crossbar's "translator," which slid the crossbars into place and made the proper electrical connection to a distant switch. The far-off switch received the remainder of the numbers (for example, a prefix of 555 and an exchange address of 1212) and did a similar kind of brute force lookup to set up the call.

The method by which the physical construction of the switch implemented a lookup table to hand off long-distance calls dictated an addressing scheme called the North American Numbering Plan (NANP). People who grew up in the United States became ingrained with a mental model of a telephone model representing access to a distant resource. In the early 1980s, the Bell System (later AT&T) spent millions of dollars creating a data network (called Net1000) based on its circuit-switched technology.

Figure 4-3.   Crossbar Switch from the Telephony Museum

The way that the corporation chose to name resources should surprise no one: A resource was named and accessed via a 10-digit number called a "network standard address," which recapitulated both in function and in spirit the NANP telephone system named resources in voice telephony. Net1000 experienced an early demise at the hands of the BBN (Bolt, Baranek, and Newman, the original architects of the Internet) University of Southern California, and Stanford University engineers working on something they called an "internet," a network of networks.

FINALLY, THE INTERNET

Naming a resource on the Internet worked much as it did on the phone system. The Internet required a different numbering system,[3] but a numbering system nonetheless. The way that early users of the Internet accessed a resource was, once again, not by the resource's name, but by its number. As a convenience, users could *alias* the number to a string of letters, giving the Internet a slightly more human-friendly face. This continuing

---

3   The numbering scheme, which allocated 2^{32} in four different ways of representing subnetworks, was thought to allow more numbers than anyone could ever imagine using. By 1999, it was recognized that the system was on the verge of running out of addresses.

use of numbers should be unsurprising, as the Internet was being built upon the copper wires of the telephone backbone network.

Naming and addressing have always been a problem of numbers. Naming was certainly a good deal simpler when the world was simpler. It could not have been very difficult to find the correct recipient for that Sumerian tablet. Some biblical scholars maintain that the "throng" or "multitude" of people present at the Crucifixion amounted to five or six people. In the 1666, the year of the Great Fire, the entire population of London was 350,000 people. Today, it's over 7.2 million. That's a totally different scale. When the entire machine population of the Internet could be listed on the back of a napkin as depicted in Figure 9 in Chapter 3, the naming problem was much easier to solve. Each machine on the Internet simply maintained a file listing the name and IP address for every other machine.

The numbers game of the early Internet resembled the earliest era of telephony in yet another way: In the age of mainframes and departmental minicomputers, one physical device would have multiple users. There was really no way of directly naming and accessing a resource. Only after BBN's Ray Tomlinson invented e-mail could one user dream of communicating directly "by name" with another human (albeit indirectly and asynchronously) on the Internet. The Internet was finally beginning to achieve the goal of enabling users to refer to a resource by its name.

Even so, the sheer size of the Internet became its own worst enemy. It seems ironic that *cyber*, a part of the word *cyberspace*, comes from the Greek word meaning "to pilot"—ironic, because it's so hard to pilot your way through the tangle of dots, slashes, tildes, and often funny names in the URL/URI space. The very scale at which the WWW exploded in its first decade made naming resources even more important. Toward the end of the first generation of the Internet, in the early part of the new century, formal naming for the "official" part of the Internet, the World Wide Web, became a major issue, with names becoming increasingly weird or silly just because the namespace became so overpopulated.

ALTERNATIVE NAMESPACES

With Napster, you could finally get something you wanted without first having to understand Internet addressing, a concept difficult for most people to grasp because the address space has become so complex and unbounded.

As long as most other applications were wedded to the Domain Name System (DNS), users had to remember that (at some level) they were still tied to an indirect naming-by-addressing scheme. Prior to the advent of the P2P era, DNS had a remarkable run as the only glue that held the infinite reaches of cyberspace together. In its first 16 years, Network Solutions, the *de facto* czar of naming/addressing, registered 23 million unique domain names. Each of these domain names represented the name of a resource of potential interest to someone. Finally, Internet users were approaching the level of intimate distant access heretofore offered by long distance telephony.

The coming of P2P put the final pieces in place. P2P ushered in the era of the personal resource-by-name Internet. PCs, which had earlier been relegated to acting as browser support for the "official" Internet, were the catalyst. PCs were not considered appropriate in the role of servers, in the 1980s and early 1990s, but now the operating systems were distinctly more robust, with large amounts of data and computing capacity.

A thousand U.S. dollars bought a server class machine that far surpassed the VAX 11/780 departmental computers of the mid-1980s. PCs were suddenly recognized as "the place where the cycles lived." The aggregate compute capacity of all U.S. personal computers in 2000 was estimated to be $10*10^9$MHz per second with a storage capacity of $10*10^5$TB (terabytes) of data. PCs were now, in the words of noted P2P pundit Clay Shirkey, a part of the "dark matter of the Internet." By this he meant that the real power of the Internet was beginning to transcend the "official" limits of DNS.

By early 2000, 23 million Napster users were part of an alternative namespace that coalesced without a central registering authority in the first 16 *months* (not 16 *years* as the official Internet had). By 2000, well over 200 million people and systems were included in the non-DNS instant messaging address space. By mid-2001, the free AOL IM system alone had over 100 million users generating 500 million IMs a day.

P2P finally freed our thinking and heavily supplemented (some would argue that *supplanted* might be a better word) the model of reality, forced upon us by telecommunications, where "person" and "machine" had precisely the same meaning. Only when ICQ, the first P2P instant messaging application, first appeared on the scene did we begin to understand and accept the idea that intermittent connectivity and "movable presence" were possible and presented no real problem in human-to-human (or system-to-system) communication over the Internet.

The need to create movable presence, where users could move from one PC to another and still maintain instant messaging capability, forced the creation of the new addressing model in which machines eschewed DNS in favor of a new application-specific namespace. Today, Groove, Napster, NetMeeting, AIM, Yahoo Messenger, Jabber, and many other P2P applications all use a similar strategy to create their own namespaces. A later section will discuss how these applications create these spaces.

WHAT'S NEXT?

Although P2P is markedly improving naming in cyberspace, it has not conquered all the challenges. Some suggest that by creating an alternate namespace that is still dependent on and branched off from the "real" DNS system, that:

▼ Alternative spaces are only delaying the inevitable.

■ Users will inevitably run out of ways to name the myriad devices that they will want to address.

■ While PCs number in the hundreds of millions, embedded devices, from smart door knobs to smart light bulbs, will number in the billions.

■ Users will not want to have to name the upstairs closet light bulb.

▲ Naming schemes are notorious for not working with one another.

Each of these concerns may have some truth behind it, but certainly we are several steps further along the path of being able to directly address things than we were a mere 10 years ago. The fact that users are just beginning to understand the naming schemes many years after the invention of the Internet simply demonstrates how close to infancy the Internet still is, and how little users, even now, understand about the real nature and potential of the Internet beast. In his book *Interface Culture,* writer Stephen Johnson remarks:

> At the threshold points, near the birth of any technology, all types of distortions and misunderstandings are bound to appear—misunderstandings not only of how the machines actually work, but also of more subtle matters: what realm of experience the new technologies belong to, what values they perpetuate, where their more indirect effects will take place.

Certainly this has proven true in the last century. For example, when construction of the interstate highway system was launched in 1956, no one could have guessed that the secondary results would be a nation on wheels, the decline of the cities, and the sprawl of suburbia. Similarly, few people could have foreseen that television would become so much more than (and different from) visual radio. We must similarly wonder what is the real nature and potential of both P2P and the Internet in general.

DEALING WITH ADDRESSING

By enabling the user to address content directly by name, P2P helps to remove many of the difficulties of finding and connecting to people and resources in cyberspace. But P2P doesn't eliminate the need to operate using the Internet's addressing scheme. Instead the various in-the-flow and on-client applications that create P2P's internal plumbing handle the addressing.

The Role of Internet Protocol

Until and unless some other addressing scheme supplants IP, the Internet Protocol, system developers and architects need to understand and interoperate with IP. A replacement for IP is rather unlikely; the Internet has been up and running continuously since its inception in 1969, continuously evolving and growing. The net has evolved from connecting mainframes over an all-copper infrastructure, to connecting workstations and PCs over a largely fiber networking fabric, to connecting wireless devices over a hybrid network. It has never had to "reboot" or receive emergency medical attention, and in fact the only other things that are as robust as the Internet are biological organisms.

Neither the Internet nor the way that users address things on the Internet are likely to go away.[4] Thus, whatever new paradigm may emerge to connect people in cyberspace

---

4   The next generation of IP, the Internet Protocol called IPV6, will almost certainly change many of the dynamics of the Internet, including bandwidth reservation and possibly the way that users address machines.

will use Internet-style addressing. Even mobile devices must translate their conversational protocol into IP packets, as we will discuss shortly.

The Role of Hypertext Transfer Protocol

HTTP is also unlikely to go away. An open, well-documented protocol, HTTP has grown from an infancy, in which it was a simple scalable implementation of serving static content from remote file systems, to a mature family of technologies capable of scaling excellently and hosting enterprise applications.

HTTP allows any programming language or operating system to participate as long as it respects the on-the-wire protocol. With only three request primitives (HTTP-Get, HTTP-Post, and HTTP-Put) and a single response type (HTTP-Response), HTTP makes it easy to arrange and maintain programmatically the conversation between notional clients and servers. Throughout the book, we describe peers as simultaneously supporting the capabilities of both clients and servers (so perhaps a proper name for this model would be the *servent* model—that is, part *serv*er and part cli*ent*). Even so, in a given HTTP conversation, one party usually assumes the role of server for the conversation, and the other party the role of client.

Dynamic DNS Addressing

Because peers can converse via HTTP, they can establish a conversation even though neither may know *a priori* the other's IP address. In one popular strategy that uses HTTP, each potential participant in a conversation could register its IP address with a server in the flow. For example, let's imagine that Derrick Doorstop has a home PC running one of the popular P2P remote access applications.

If Derrick's is one of the millions of homes served by a high-speed digital subscriber loop (DSL) service, a potentially random IP address will be assigned every time the PC reconnects to the network.[5] This common practice is known as Dynamic Host Configuration Protocol (DHCP). If Derrick is unaware of the address of his home machine, how will he be able to connect with it while on the road or from his office? Derrick's desire is not to have to fiddle with things like IP addresses. Like most users, he just wants to be able to talk with his home machine's applications, access files, look at his calendar, or accomplish myriad other useful things.

A common and useful P2P strategy would work as shown in Figure 4-4.

Derrick's home machine might send a unique identity and its IP address (DerrickDoorstop.HomePC, 192.168.1.100) to a machine that we might call a *dynamic* DNS name resolver or server (DDNS). Let's imagine for a moment that the DDNS name resolver is at the URL http://PeerLocator.com/RegisterMe, where the RegisterMe part of the URL following the final slash (/) connects the machine to a Java servlet, Perl script, or other glue

---

5   If you live in the Chesapeake Bay area (or places other than Southern California) where there is "real weather," this will happen frequently in the stormy summer months.

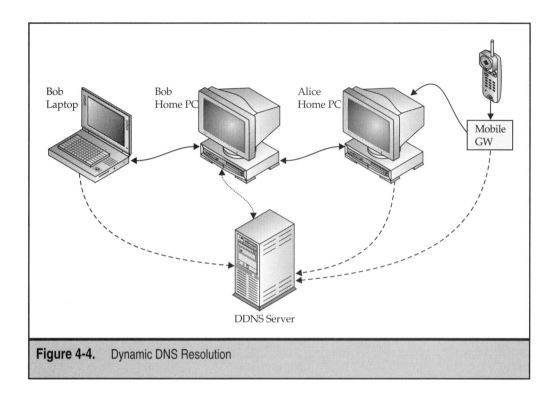

Figure 4-4. Dynamic DNS Resolution

code that connects the user to a back-end service. Derrick's machine connects his browser to the well-known URL of the dynamic DNS server, but with a little twist.

The P2P application on his machine would actually use a URL like http:// DerrickDoorstop.HomePC. 192.168.1.100. PeerLocator.com/RegisterMe, where a portion of the URL is used to embed additional information about the machine's location. The DNS system points all requests of the form *AnythingAtAll*.PeerLocator.com directly toward PeerLocator.com. The system itself doesn't know or care about the *AnythingAtAll* part of the address, assuming that PeerLocator.com will know what to make of the phrase once traffic has arrived there. In this case, the system is right. The DDNS service records the machine name and its IP address, so now Derrick knows how to browse to it.[6]

Note that registering with a dynamic DNS server like this whenever Derrick's machine connected to the net serves a dual purpose. In addition to telling the DDNS server its assigned IP address, Derrick's machine is also letting the server know that it's reconnected to the net and ready to accept incoming requests from Derrick. Even with

---

6   It isn't a very good idea to send the phrases DerrickDoorstop.HomePC and 192.168.1.100 in the clear as shown in this example. Such phrases make it too obvious and easy for a malicious hacker or automated system to decipher the meaning. The Security section talks in more detail about ways to secure many aspects of P2P.

high-speed cable modem services, where IP addresses are usually fixed, letting the server know this *presence* information is a critical part of P2P.

Meanwhile, as Derrick's PC has been holding its own conversation with the server, Derrick arrives at work and now wants to access his home PC remotely to get that presentation he forgot to copy to a writable CD and shove into his backpack. No problem. He points his browser to the well-known URL of the dynamic DNS server, but again with a little twist. This time, the address he uses embeds some additional information into the URL to indicate his eventual target.

Using the dynamic DNS server PeerLocator.com, Derrick's browser at work sends an HTTP-Get request to http://DerrickDoorstop.HomePC.PeerLocator.com/LogMeIn. The DNS system again parses the URL from right to left, ignoring everything to the right of the slash and everything to the left of PeerLocator.com. The server then redirects his request to his actual home machine (generally removing itself from the conversation altogether). Derrick's home system might then offer him a login screen so that he could continue the dialog with his resources.

Peering Through the Firewall

In the preceding example, nothing impeded Derrick's home machine from responding to his HTTP-Get request. Both parties were on the open Internet, where conversation is unrestricted. What happens when one or both parties are behind firewalls—hardware and/or software that restricts incoming communications?

P2P networks can handle this difficult situation too. When machines are behind a firewall, either party can make only an outbound HTTP request.[7] An outbound HTTP request is effectively an HTTP-Get request, and the other party must respond to it appropriately. A pair of HTTP-Get requests would collide in the network and never generate an appropriate response.

If Derrick is browsing from a work PC behind the corporate firewall, where it can make only an HTTP-Get request, there is still not a significant problem. The browser can actually reach out to an address like http://DerrickDoorstop.HomePC.PeerLocator.com/LogMeIn, and the DDNS server will simply act as a forwarding service. When both parties are behind a firewall, life gets a little more complex.

When Derrick's work PC and his home PC can both make only an outbound request, the intermediary in the net takes on the additional responsibility of turning around the respective requests. It crafts a response to each party to which its peer partner appears to have been directly addressing. This server (in addition to doing DDNS duties as described previously) would again act as a proxy for both the parties involved, injecting enough intelligence into the dialog that each party gets a correctly formatted response.

---

7   A firewalled network that blocks both inbound and outbound requests would be the functional equivalent of no network at all. Some information technology departments selectively block certain outgoing requests, too. Such blocking can be an exercise in frustration, given the expansion rate of the World Wide Web.

In P2P usage, a home or office machine might do an HTTP-Get perhaps three or four times a minute to the proxy server. When no one is interested in connecting (such as when Derrick is stuck in traffic on the way to the office), the request simply times out and Derrick's home machine goes into sleep mode for several seconds.[8] When Derrick finally drags himself to his cubicle (not even appreciating all this hard work that's been occurring on his behalf), he points his browser to http://DerrickDoorstop.HomePC.PeerLocator.com/LogMeIn, and the DDNS name resolver creates a proper HTTP-Response to both parties.

Other Protocols

All this talk of HTTP and dynamic DNS as protocol engines for P2P should not be taken as a slight to other protocols. Depending on the particular application, other protocols are certainly valid and useful. For example, Gnutella-style applications use a protocol much like Internet Relay Chat (IRC), which ferries simple text around a self-forming network. There are a number of other interesting open protocols, such as XML-RPC and IIOP, a way of handling ORBs (Object request brokers) in an Internet infrastructure.

However, you should consider the advantages of both DNS and HTTP. In the case of DNS, the protocol is extremely lightweight and is seldom blocked either as incoming or outbound traffic. In fact, experimenters have used DNS as an undercarriage for bearing other protocols, including HTTP. An advantage that HTTP has over just about any other protocol[9] is that it can express semantic meaning. Any intermediary in the net (such as the proxy server previously described) or the target at the network's edge capable of responding to an HTTP request knows how to deconstruct the message being sent and decide whether it is an appropriate target for the message. No special decoder ring is required.

Architectures for Connecting Resources

Certain fixed realities will remain a part of the Internet for the foreseeable future. Given these legacies, let's explore how addressing in this new part of the Internet is accomplished. In the P2P world, there are only a few ways of successfully conjoining resources: a fully centralized architecture (as exemplified by SETI@home), a mediated architecture (exemplified by Napster), and a full decentralized architecture (exemplified by Gnutella and its variants).

Centralized P2P Architectures

In a fully centralized architecture, all resources identify themselves to a server in the information flow, as shown in Figure 4-5.

---

8   Getting the correct polling interval, the elapsed time between successive outbound requests
      from the home system, is a bit of fine art. The P2P system doesn't want to keep someone
      waiting for a login to pop up, but on the other hand, too high a request frequency will not
      permit the system to scale beyond a small number of users.
9   A number of semantic protocol-like languages are beginning to emerge, including software
      agent languages like KQML (Knowledge Query Manipulation Language) and DAML (DARPA
      Agent Markup Language).

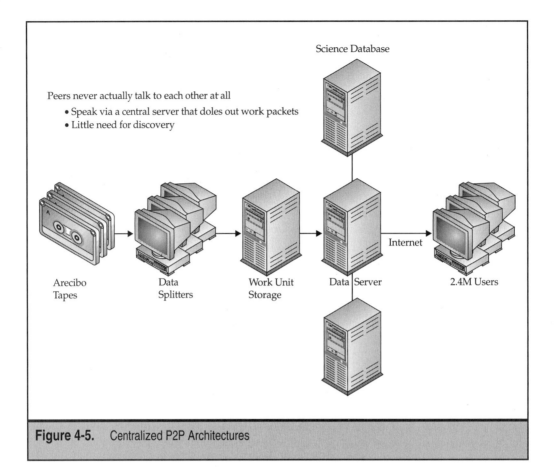

Peers never actually talk to each other at all
• Speak via a central server that doles out work packets
• Little need for discovery

Science Database

Arecibo
Tapes

Data
Splitters

Work Unit
Storage

Data Server

Internet

2.4M Users

Figure 4-5.   Centralized P2P Architectures

In SETI@home, the computers at the edge of the network do not even know of one another's existence. When they go online, the software supplied to them from SETI registers their IP address with the central SETI server complex.

Another computer at the SETI server complex receives data streams from the large radio telescopes at Arecibo, Puerto Rico, and breaks them down into work units. The system parcels out the work units to cooperating home PCs that then crunch the numbers while their owners are asleep or otherwise away from their machines. Since the work unit server knows the IP addresses of its community members, this system works quite easily.

The otherwise idle PCs have downloaded from SETI some software that understands the work unit data format and can analyze the signals that they receive from the central server. When they finish with a work unit, the PCs send the result back to the central server, which then may send them additional work units.

This sort of P2P architecture might seem peculiar to you, especially if this book has led you to believe that P2P is more about people communicating and collaborating directly with other people than about software generating with spreadsheets or performing other solitary activities. However, such a model does fit at least some of the qualifications of P2P in the sense that:

▼ Large distributed communities of sometimes connected users are formed informally, without the users having to do anything explicit.

■ Individual users are volunteering a portion of their own resources for the use of a collective community.

▲ Collaboration is occurring—even though individual PC users may not be aware of it, any more than individual cells in your fingers are aware that you are in the process of using them to achieve some higher goal such as throwing a baseball or playing Mozart.

Mediated P2P Architecture

A more common architecture is what we might call a *mediated architecture*. In such an architecture, a server in the network manages some functions on behalf of the community of peers. Typically in mediated architectures, the server performs a specific function, then gets out of the way of the peers at the edge of the network. Consider how unobtrusively Napster performs its role for millions of users.

In the architecture of the music-sharing program Napster, each new user downloads the Napster program from Napster's web site. Once the simple installation is complete, the user chooses which folders on his or her hard drive to share with other members of the network. The Napster server records the list of music titles that each user offers for sharing. On connection to one of Napster's servers, its brilliance and simplicity becomes readily apparent to the Napster user, and that brilliance is part of Napster's architectural design.

When a user searches for a music file, the central server inspects its cached playlist, and then returns the username, filename, and Internet connection type of each user who is online and has the file of interest. The user then selects the user from whom to download the file, and the server establishes a direct connection between the two users. The Napster server was not involved in the interaction between the users other than acting in an advisory and informational role. As shown in Figure 4-6, simultaneous downloads could be going on all over the network with only minimal help from the Netscape server.

The genius of the Napster design was manifold:

▼ Context and community formation was simplicity itself—song titles, artist names, and user IP addresses were all the threads needed to stitch together a worldwide community.

■ Napster is just "decentralized enough." It is cleverly split along functional lines. In acting as a virtual table of contents and matchmaker, Napster centralized only the role of maintaining a coordinated set of actions.

▲ On the other hand, Napster decentralized the aspects of the community that could a make use of the compute power in the users' devices—the actual sharing, uploading, and downloading of files.

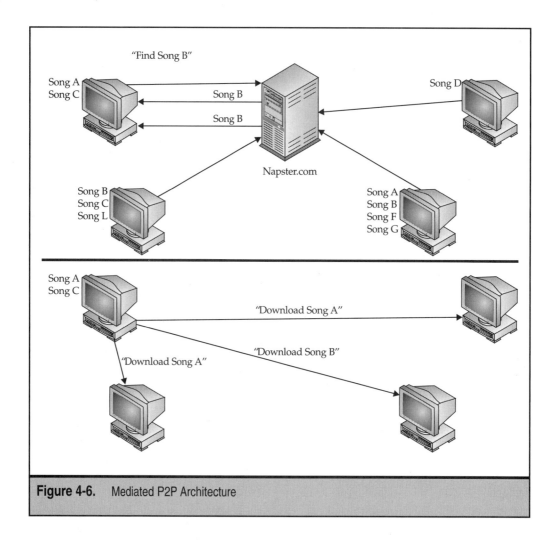

Figure 4-6. Mediated P2P Architecture

Groove, another mediated architecture, uses in-the-net servers both to locate users via dynamic DNS and to cache synchronization transactions for communities of users, whose members may come online and go offline at indeterminate times. Each Groove peer is equipped with a Virtual Message Queue Server that performs routine synchronization (for example, of an updated file that a peer is sharing). If the Virtual Message Queue Server can't synchronize with one or more peers (because they are off the network), then a relay server in the net stores updates of the file until the peer comes back online. Interestingly, the way that Groove works has parallels with the way that Napster works.

Groove also decentralizes just enough of its operations to allow the network resident portion to scale to large numbers of users, and forces the heavy lifting of keeping all users synchronized to the peers making changes.

▼ Groove matches users of a particular space (in Groove parlance, virtual communities are called *spaces*) to their current IP addresses. It informs users when other users of the same space are online or offline.

Groove, like Napster, splits functionality along operational boundaries, once again offering just enough utility as needed within the net to knit communities of users together.

Decentralized P2P Architecture

Architectures that don't rely on servers in the network at all are possibly the most faithful to the P2P vision. Typically these kinds of networks (exemplified by Gnutella-style[10] applications) don't use servers to do routing, caching, file sharing, recording of search results, or any other peer activities. Gnutella is an ongoing experiment in the most extreme style of decentralized P2P networking and as such continues to evolve architecturally (see Figure 4-7). For example, some variants of Gnutella do morph certain peers into the role of "reflectors," servants that will cache the answers to certain popular queries so that network traffic is somewhat reduced. Suppose that a user asks for the mp3 "Like a Virgin" by Madonna. Instead routing the user over a large part of the entire Gnutella community, a reflector servant will return the IP address of a machine with that song, having cached the answer previously.

Overall though, Gnutella-style networks don't use a central server to keep track of user files. To share files via the Gnutella model, a user starts with a networked computer A equipped with Gnutella servant software. Computer A connects to a neighboring Gnutella-networked computer, B. Computer A then announces that it is "alive" and available to computer B, which in turn announces to all the computers to which it is connected—C, D, and E—that A is alive.

Computers C, D, and E then announce to all computers to which they are connected that computer A is alive. Those computers continue the pattern and announce to the computers to which they are connected that computer A is alive. Although the reach of this network is *potentially* infinite or at least very large, in reality it is limited by "time-to-live" (TTL) or number-of-network-hops constraints—that is, the maximum number of forward links that the request will reach. Most Gnutella servants will reject any network messages that have TTLs that are more than seven hops away from computer A.

Once computer A has announced that it is "alive" to the various members of the peer network, it can then search the contents of the shared directories of the peer network members. This is part of the resource discovery and federation ability of a Gnutella-style network. If computer A is searching for a picture of Samuel Morse, the network sends the search request to all members of the network, starting with, B, then C, D, and E. These recipients, in turn, send the request to the computers to which they are connected, forwarding the request to the maximum number of hops allowed by the protocol.

---

10   A number of applications use this style of networking. Gnutella, a distributed search and file-sharing application, first demonstrated such a network. For convenience, we will refer to the entire class of applications—including Freenet, Gnutella, Limewire, and InfraSearch—as "Gnutella-style" applications.

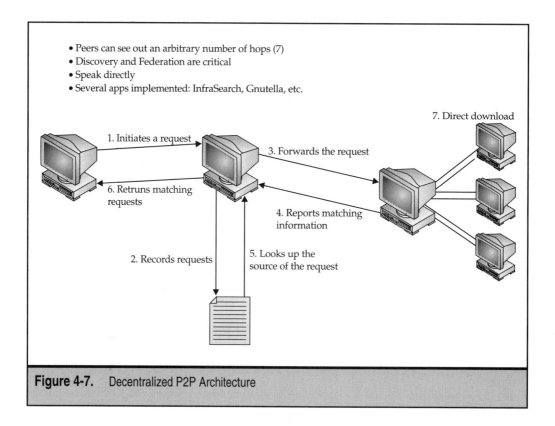

- Peers can see out an arbitrary number of hops (7)
- Discovery and Federation are critical
- Speak directly
- Several apps implemented: InfraSearch, Gnutella, etc.

1. Initiates a request

3. Forwards the request

7. Direct download

6. Retruns matching requests

4. Reports matching information

2. Records requests

5. Looks up the source of the request

Figure 4-7. Decentralized P2P Architecture

If one of the computers in the peer network, such as E, has a file that matches the request, it transmits the file information (name, size, and so on) back through all the computers in the pathway toward A. Computer A's display then shows a list of files matching the search request. Finally, computer A opens a direct connection with E and downloads Samuel Morse.jpg directly from E. Thus, a Gnutella-style application enables file sharing without using peers that do not actually directly serve content themselves.

From this review of the most popular P2P architectures, you can see that no one style fits all, and that very different models can still be accurately referred to as P2P. When mobility enters the picture, an additional layer of complexity is required to enable small wireless devices to play as equal peers.

We have thus far characterized P2P in terms of computing archetypes—network architectures, clients, servers, and so on. The following section presents a very different perspective on P2P.

The Content-Addressable Web for P2P

So far this chapter has looked at information and P2P from the traditional perspective of naming and addressing. The following essay asks what the Internet might be like if we could achieve the goal of what is called the "semantic Web." In such a conception of the

Web, its loosely organized and difficult-to-search chaos would be much different, replaced by the ability to address Internet content directly.

Content addressing

Our friend Ed Greengrass is an expert on the topic of content addressing. Here are his thoughts:

"Currently, Web-based and P2P communities can be used to create applications like searching for popular music recordings by title or by artist name. It would seem that this capability might extend to any works of art or intellect that can be identified by title, or which might have textual meta-data associated with it. The Google picture photograph search, for example, catalogs images contained in web pages by using the picture's title as the search key. This neat cataloging trick works reasonably well over a limited subset of the total content of the Internet's riches. Consider, though, that Napster can't successfully navigate the subtly varied content of the classical music world, and that Google's picture and photo navigation is completely dependent upon the web page author supplying accurate titling along with the Web art or photograph.

"Consider what happens if you don't *know* the title, or the author-supplied meta-data is non-descriptive. What if you are looking for some kind of information that doesn't *have* a title? What if the information you want is spread over (and embedded in) many documents and databases? What if the pieces you want haven't been conveniently tagged by the terms that occur to you when you initiate a search? Conversely, what if you are *offering* information to the P2P community, but it didn't occur to you which parts would interest other peers, or how they would choose to express their interest?

"If P2P is to achieve its full potential, it is necessary that peers be able to tell the P2P communiti(es) to which they belong what information, services, or other resources —in a word what 'content' —they possess and offer to the community. This means that they need a vocabulary and language for posting or broadcasting a description of this content. This same language can be used for requesting content. Therefore, we call this approach *content addressing*.

"Content addressing, as we use the term here, means that a peer registers by using terms describing its semantic content, in contrast to merely registering its logical or physical address (such as a web site's URL). Content addressing offers important advantages, but also raises additional difficulties and costs.

"Content addressing should not be confused with the services provided by web retrieval engines today. Most Web Information Retrieval (IR) engines (in particular those that provide automated indexing,) scan the Web via robot agents, and index each candidate page on the basis of terms found in the page itself, or in URLs pointing to the page. Such techniques have limitations well known in IR, limitations that result from the fact that the indexing systems do not bring human understanding to the indexing task.

"On the other hand, Web IR services like Yahoo provide human indexing. However, this brings its own set of limitations. Humans cannot keep up with the volume of data continually being added to the Web. Professional indexers are typically limited by the controlled vocabulary of terms currently in use by the given index service. Worse, even a set of professional indexers cannot hope to be domain experts in all the many complex application domains available on the Web.

"In the future, peers (not just web sites) would register their wares by content descriptors rather than URLs and IP addresses. Or what comes to the same thing, the URLs would morph into content descriptors, and relations among those descriptors—in a word, a 'language.' This language would be useful not only for peers describing the content they offer, but for peers formulating search queries, and mobile agents trying to execute those queries. Of course, as we suggested earlier, content addressing already exists to some extent; services like Napster offer content addressing in a narrow, specialized (but important!) domain such as popular music. P2P will realize its full potential only when peers can advertise and request content of many types, from many domains.

"However, the advantages of content addressing come at a price. Registering a peer by content rather than an arbitrary URL makes the registration process considerably more complex. You can't get increased intelligence out of the registered descriptor(s) without putting considerably more intelligence into the registration process. Garbage-in garbage-out emphatically applies here. Furthermore, 'registration' becomes an ongoing process: Whenever you add new content, you must update or add to your registered 'content address.'

"Before you can even start the registration process, your P2P community must agree on a language for registration and searching. A vocabulary of descriptors and relations must be defined. But there are far too many specialized domains to expect a single term list or 'language' to capture all of human knowledge. It isn't solely a matter of abstruse technical areas. Every area, even a domain as familiar to the general public as movies or sports, has its own significant terminology. (A 'hit' has a quite different meaning in the movie domain than in the baseball domain.) Just considering what terms are useful descriptors, and what those descriptors mean, requires focus on a particular domain.

"Furthermore, it is not enough to generate a mere list of terms, a lexicon, for a given domain. Within any domain, the terms have a structure. There are generic relations like class-subclass (a wild pitch is a *kind* of baseball error), the part-subpart relationship (a scene or a score is a *part* of a movie). Then, there are domain-specific relations, e.g., film-cast, employer-employee. If the lexicon of a given domain is organized into a logical semantic structure, the result is commonly called an 'ontology.'

"Hence, what we really need for effective content addressing is the development of ontologies by domain. The ontologies for some domains might be developed by 'professional' experts, from industry, academia, or governmental 'experts.' Even then, consensus perhaps with public review would be required. On the other hand, many domain ontologies could and would be developed by 'fans,' enthusiastic 'amateurs' of the domain (who may actually be the real 'experts').

"Registered ontologies would then be available both to peer creators, who want to know how they can best describe their content, and for peer users, who want to know what questions they can meaningfully ask. Naturally, the peer who is an 'expert' offering content in one domain will be a user requesting content in another (or even the same) domain. Software agents, serving these peers, would not need to be specialized to a given domain. Instead, a general-purpose agent, given, e.g., a movie domain request, would access the movie domain ontology, and then search peers registered and constructed in accordance with that ontology.

"Many ontologies would incorporate generic ontologies such as 'time,' and 'money.' Many ontologies would be variations or specializations of others, e.g., movies and 'live' theater.

"Ontologies would embody constraints on descriptors. It is meaningful and important to be able to compute the difference between two dates: I'm looking for a movie that came out about six months after X.' On the other hand, who wants to multiply two dates together?

"Finally, it should be noted that content addressing, while it is certainly a vehicle for improving information access, is also potentially a vehicle for censorship (and for subjective judgment). The descriptor 'pornography' illustrates the potential problem. Wrongly applied to a peer's content, it may serve to filter out legitimate information, or (alternatively) to lure customers erroneously."

-- Ed Greengrass,
U.S. Department of Defense
with contributions by Dana Moore, BBN Technologies

INSTANT MESSAGING

As we suggest elsewhere in the book, instant messaging (IM) plays an important part in the understanding of many things P2P: how P2P applications handle naming and addressing; what architecture they use; how they are disseminated and virally spread; and what their immediate and enduring appeal suggests about the future direction of computers and networks (more about communications and less about "computing"). Further, computers have grown architecturally to support a wide range of user applications and experiences:

▼ **Communicating by voice as well as with text**   Most IM clients now enable voice communications during a session.

■ **Sharing immersive experiences**   When combined with other technologies, real-time chatting can transport a user to a virtual world, like the ActiveWorlds chat environments shown in Figures 4-8 and 4-9. Teachers and students can co-navigate a slide show in an extended classroom. Collaborators can coedit a text, as we have done in writing this book. People can engage in multiplayer games and explorations.

■ **Sending secure messages**   Users can send messages resistant to external snooping and can transfer files in most IM applications, securely and privately, which is very useful for those trapped in a totalitarian society.

■ **Bridging the human-to-agent gap**   Some of the toughest agent problems involve how software agents will integrate unobtrusively into everyday user experience. The primary questions revolve around how agents evince a presence, how responsive or intrusive they ought to be, and how they can present helpful suggestions.[11] Projects such as AliceBot (www.alicebot.net) demonstrate the potential of IM for exploring the dialog between humans and automata.

▲ **Bridging the human-to-device gap**   At a more mundane level, research projects and production efforts are under way in every major networking company to conjoin XML, IM, and smart devices and switches. Beyond turning lights off and on from a distance, or talking to our cyber-butlers, the combination of XML and IM is seen by many designers as the person-to-system and system-to-system architecture of first resort, especially where interaction with legacy systems is involved. A Hewlett-Packard research initiative called *CoolTown,* which seeks to make places and environments smarter, is working to enable users to call up a Powerpoint presentation from the PC at their distant office and beam it to the handy projector in the room. Thinking of Powerpoint as a "legacy" application might seem strange, but in the P2P-enabled future, all applications that do not bundle P2P capabilities for sharing and collaboration may rightly be deemed legacy applications.

---

11   The annoying Microsoft Office Assistants that infested the company's Office products for a number of years provide enough evidence as to why human-to-cyber relations can be a hot-button issue for most users. The Office products also are an excellent example of an eager assistant done the wrong way.

Figure 4-8.   A P2P Virtual Chat World Based on the Film, "Casablanca"

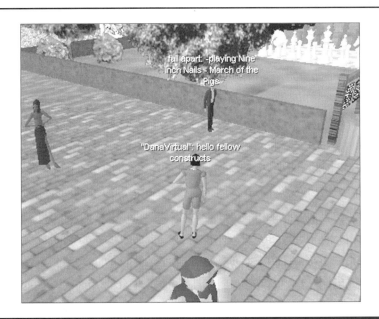

Figure 4-9.   A P2P Virtual Chat World Based on ActiveWorlds 3-D Rendering

Such applications need to be fairly sophisticated to resolve names. This section discusses how P2P IM addresses the naming of things and people, manages addressing, and forms a foundation for future applications. The discussion focuses on Jabber[12] as an example of how an architecture works, but we could have chosen other architectures as well. Having read the previous section on mediated P2P architectures, you will likely recognize how similar Jabber is architecturally to Napster, for example.

Instant Messaging: Just a New Kind of E-Mail?

The heart of the IM experience, regardless of the type of application to which it's applied, is immediacy. Conversion of Internet addresses to personal namespaces must occur with dispatch and without any of the participants even giving it a second thought.

E-mail certainly helps mitigate the naming and addressing problem, and it *almost* makes the grade as a way to do instant messaging. These days, in the middle of a phone conversation, you can ask someone to e-mail a technical document, and within a minute or two, you have the material in hand (although "on-screen" might be a better way to think of it). That seems pretty immediate to most people, and in this particular case, it may even be indistinguishable from doing a file transfer over IM.

Then what's the difference? E-mail had an earlier and different design center that dictated certain conventions with respect to naming and addressing. The design of e-mail services assumed that:

▼ A potential mail recipient would not ever necessarily be close to a network connection.

■ It would take effort for the addressee to connect to the net.

▲ A service provider (an ISP today) would have to provide application-level in-the-network intelligence and resources.

Providing intelligence meant ensuring that a server would be able to accumulate your e-mail for you in a way that would make sense to your e-mail client software when you eventually collected it. Also, when you eventually interacted with your e-mail via your e-mail management software, providing intelligence meant ensuring that the server would understand your protocol and the set of commands you use to manage your mail. Providing resources meant ensuring that a server would have to retain your e-mail on its disk drives until you downloaded it, and ensuring that the server would act in concert with your e-mail application to transfer your e-mail from its disk drives to yours.

From a resource standpoint, an e-mail system is much more like a private city parking lot, where a reserved space is worth paying for and charging for. In contrast, an IM system is more like a highway system. The overheads involve keeping the roadway beneath you intact so that the vehicles riding on it (your short messages) run smoothly and are kept intact. The dynamics involved in opening a new downtown parking lot dictate reserving a lot

---

of space for potential parkers, and that space is expensive; space provided on an e-mail server in the net must follow essentially the same dynamics. Resources have to be reserved in case you want to use them, so they require more overhead.

From a naming and addressing standpoint, e-mail service tends to look like a rural post office. You drive or walk to a familiar address, and there's a certain mail slot for you. You pick up your mail, and in doing so, you clean out your slot so that it doesn't become overfull and cause the system to deal with something it wasn't designed to deal with: overuse of capacity. The bookkeeping of names and addresses is simple enough that it doesn't take special genius to become an e-mail service provider. Also, the design center is sufficiently simple and understandable to give the system value for both the service provider and its customers.

Certainly, e-mail is still the killer application that defines the baseline of utility for the Internet. While e-mail is demonstrably P2P, forcing it to become a P2P conversational tool stretches it to the breaking point. E-mail is sometimes used as a vehicle for person-to-application tasks, but it's not usually structured enough to allow for automated handling or for dialog between applications.

To understand e-mail being used this way, think in terms of subscribing to a listserver (a listserver publishes content, threaded discussions, and the like to a community of subscribers). When you subscribe to a listserver, it is only smart enough to read your e-mail address and perhaps look in the e-mail's subject field for a simple command such as subscribe or unsubscribe. Because the address and subject fields are among the only structured parts of an e-mail message, these are the only things the listserver knows how to parse or tease out of the message itself. For an application to be able to *understand* the contents of a message, it must have greater structure. Later, you will learn about the importance of structured information for P2P. Structured information has as long and interesting a history as naming and addressing.

E-mail is not really a good way to think of the instant messaging model. Even if we removed any latency at all to minimize the store and forward time, and even if each conversational piece reached its intended recipient without delay, the e-mail experience still wouldn't be the same as instant messaging. The tiresome addressing would impede spontaneity. Also, people tend to "compose" e-mail rather than let the conversation flow in a stream of consciousness.

This way of thinking about e-mail isn't quite right, though. E-mail was meant for an earlier age in which ubiquitous connectivity was a lot less common. IM assumes a reliable bidirectional connection stream, where "instant" really does mean instant.

Instant Messaging Architecture

As previously suggested, e-mail and IM are similar architecturally. It's the user experience that's different. During an IM session, you need not perform explicit addressing steps or operate through e-mail handling software, but what goes on behind the scenes is quite similar.

In a system like Jabber, peers are connected to a mediating server. In Figure 4-10, one of the server machines is a departmental class machine (Jabber Server A), but it needn't

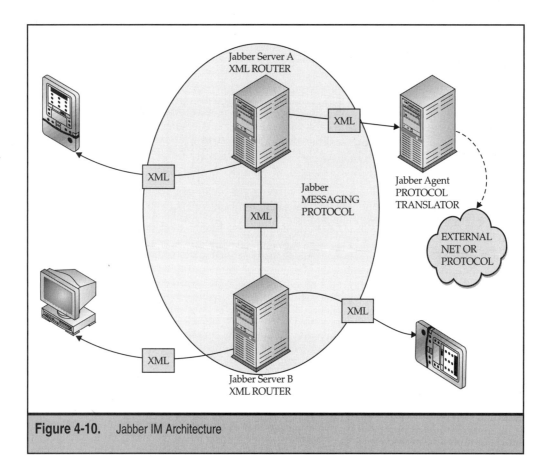

Figure 4-10. Jabber IM Architecture

be. Quite often the server machines are set up on home computers—modest places at the edge of the network where unused cycles can be found (the authors use lowly 233MHz PCs as our Jabber server on our home networks). As is common in P2P, a machine can be a servant, performing both as server and client, by simply including server capability.

With many IM systems, as with e-mail systems, the routing is directed from node to node until reaching the server closest to the recipient, which then delivers the message through a socket or HTTP connection. Servers are responsible to negotiate the delivery and receipt of their client's data with other servers (or with other networks—as Figure 4-10 suggests, Jabber can operate with Yahoo Messenger, and Microsoft Messenger) using whatever protocol is available. The actual underlying protocols may vary because of firewall issues, as we discussed previously.

The connections on the interior of the network (inside the ellipse labeled "JABBER MESSAGING PROTOCOL") are all point-to-point connections; that is, they know only about the machine(s) to which they are directly connected. A server within Jabber keeps an internal table of dynamic DNS addresses for the server. By convention, a user ID is in the form joe.doorstop@foo.com. Interior servers can resolve the portion of the address following the at sign (@), which in this case is foo.com. Then the interior servers deliver the message to the correct server or *servent*. For convenience, client users will often specify an alias for the server in their machine's hosts file.[13] Thus, a user will see a login screen such as that shown in Figure 4-11.

After establishing a conversation with their servers, machines on the network's edge can establish real-time conversations with any other peer. Notice in Figure 4-10 the heavy use of XML as a message-structuring mechanism. The figure shows XML used as the structured messages move between every part of the IM system. For example, Figure 4-10 even shows wireless mobile devices connected as peers.

XML is immediately useful as a way for Jabber to construct pathways between traditional IM services. Contemplating XML in the role of creating a better way for applications to talk to other applications and for applications to talk with people is also intriguing. We won't discuss these contemplations now, reserving the entire discussion of XML and its role of providing structure and even meaning to P2P conversations. We do, however, want to tantalize you with Figure 4-12, which we hope will fire up your interest and imagination for future chapters in which you will learn more about XML, software agents, and their role in P2P.

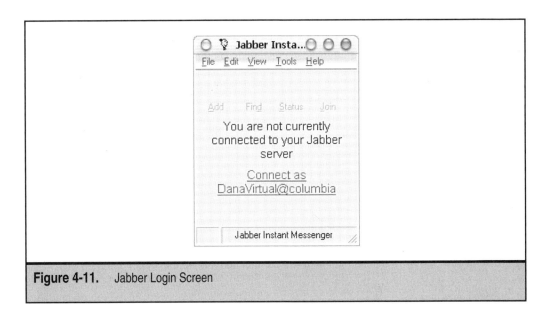

Figure 4-11.   Jabber Login Screen

---

13   The hosts file is usually squirreled away in some arcane location; Windows 2000 puts it in the directory *<root*-drive>:\windows\System32\drivers\etc. The file's format is trivial, consisting simply of a series of entries in the following format: *<IP-ADDRESS > <ALIAS-NAME>*

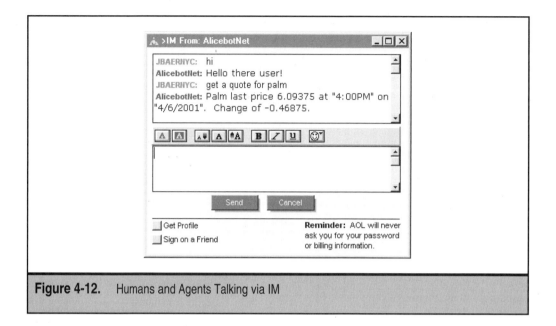

Figure 4-12.   Humans and Agents Talking via IM

If you realize that only one of the participants in the conversation shown in Figure 4-12 is a human being, you may begin to get a sense of the real potential in both P2P and IM to create person-to-application and application-to-application dialogs. Technology is not yet at a point where people are beginning to operate their X10-enabled garage door openers remotely with mobile devices. But is technology very far from a time when users will be able to delegate that task to an *eager assistant*, a cyber butler who performs that function with its non-human peer (the garage door opener) on the user's behalf?

Clearly, there is no requirement that the peers in P2P must both be human, and there is no requirement that IM participants must be human either. While P2P is not some magic way for machines to pass the Turing Test,[14] it may be the right conceptual framework for taking the first steps toward human-to-machine dialogs. The coming epochs in the human-to-machine dialog won't be so much about applications trying to pass Turing, but rather that it won't matter.

---

14   The Turing Test is meant to determine whether a computer program has intelligence. Quoting Turing, the original imitation game can be described as follows: *The new form of the problem can be described in terms of a game which we call the "imitation game." It is played with three people, a man (A), a woman (B), and an interrogator (C) who may be of either sex. The interrogator stays in a room apart from the other two. The object of the game for the interrogator is to determine which of the other two is the man and which is the woman. He knows them by labels X and Y, and at the end of the game he says either "X is A and Y is B" or "X is B and Y is A." The interrogator is allowed to put questions to A and B.*

Roaming Mobility:Part 1

Though it is not commonly acknowledged, IM derives conceptually from Short Message Service (SMS), which allows people to send and receive short written messages (up to 160 characters) using their GSM (Global System for Mobile Communications) telephones. In terms of the architectural mechanics, however, although name and address resolution in IM owes its heritage to Internet addressing, the SMS addressing scheme derives from the European cellular phone industry.[15]

To orchestrate the addressing and naming of message recipients, all GSM networks have a Message Center, which is responsible for managing the messages (in addition to handling all the voice traffic on the network). When you send a text message to another user, the message is routed to the Message Center, which determines the recipient's location. The Message Center adds to the message the date, time, and number of the sender and sends the message to the recipient. If the recipient's telephone is not active, the Message Center stores the message and then sends it when the recipient reconnects to the network. Thus the GSM system is similar to a mediated P2P architecture (or to an e-mail server).

From a user's perspective, using SMS is best described as "painful." A user selects "write message" from the soft key menu of his or her mobile phone. Then the user types in the message, using the keypad of the telephone.[16] He or she then retrieves the recipient's number from the phone's contact database, or enters it from memory. Finally, the user selects "send" from the soft key menu. Planned mobile phones from Nokia, Motorola, and others recognize that this experience is less than optimal for building a roaming P2P culture, and their newest phones (which they call *terminals*) reflect this growing understanding from P2P instant messaging. Figure 4-13 shows an example of a mobile terminal.

If the ongoing evolution of mobile P2P naming, addressing, and messaging owes something to PC-based IM, the reverse is also true:[17]

▼ Mobile P2P made it clear that messaging could be asynchronous and did not have to involve making a synchronous connection to the other person as in a telephone conversation.

■ It inspired designers to think in terms of logical sessions, where long gaps could punctuate the actual conversation (as anyone who has observed a teen-ager's IM will understand).

■ SMS helped designers understand that an ongoing dialog with one or several people could be maintained and messages from various people could arrive at your phone or pager interleaved.

---

15   In 1999, there were over 200 million SMS enabled cellular phone users, with Germany leading the pack. In 2001, over 2 billion SMS messages are expected to be transmitted over the (largely) European GSM mobile phone system.

16   Using the telephone keypad to type such a message is very labor-intensive; for example, typing in the phrase "Hello, World!" requires over 150 key pushes. You've got to really *want* to communicate to put yourself through this process.

17   In a probable tribute to its roots in the paging and SMS world, Yahoo Messenger, one of the most popular IM clients, was originally called Yahoo Pager.

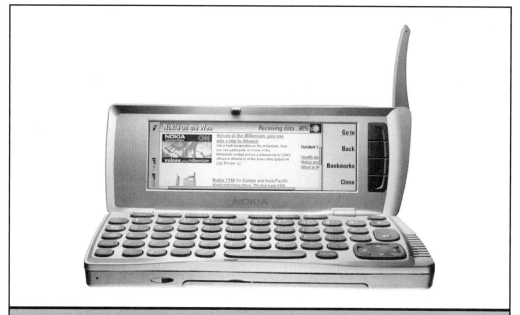

Figure 4-13.   Nokia 9220, a Mobile Terminal

▲   SMS helped us understand that addressing should be a simple push-button operation, and that the hierarchy of communications has a place for short, conversational utterances that need not even be grammatical, or even consist of words, for that matter. Anyone who communicates via IM can attest to this, as conversations are full of emoticons (smiley and frowning faces) and abbreviations for almost everything.

SUMMARY

In this chapter, you began by exploring the naming of things and addressing of resources in ancient days and worked your way up the evolutionary ladder to learning how roaming P2P users are addressed. Where once news of a baby's arrival had to be transcribed onto a clay tablet and delivered, today you can communicate such news with an instant message to a cell phone (or to all the cell phone users in your peer community). Arriving at this point as been a long, but fascinating, journey.

The mobile P2P experience has many more facets than just the addressing aspects that this chapter has covered. The software agent's role in P2P may suggest how we will design all software in the near future. Upcoming chapters will cover more fully both the mobile P2P experience and the emerging roles of software agents. The next chapter explains the elements, roles, and responsibilities in a P2P architecture.

CHAPTER 5

Supporting P2P: Architecture Matters

Architecture is a big concept encompassing all the supporting requirements that move a P2P solution from a novelty to a necessity—from a fair-weather friend to a tried and true one. Novelties need not be secure or robust; they are merely *interesting*. Our goal is to enable you to create dependable solutions. Anything less will never truly contribute to your important business or personal goals. Architecture is about dependability. Your architecture directly determines the solution's ultimate viability. Without an effective architecture, your solution will be unstable, undependable, and ultimately unused.

Let's first define the term *architecture*. We take a traditional approach to ease our way into an often vague topic. *Merriam-Webster's Collegiate Dictionary* defines architecture in three major ways:

Architecture
1: the art or science of building; *specifically*: the art or practice of designing and building structures and especially habitable ones
2 a: formation or construction as or as if as the result of conscious act <the *architecture* of the garden> **b:** a unifying or coherent form or structure <the novel lacks *architecture*>
3: the manner in which the components of a computer or computer system are organized and integrated

The first definition offers some interesting insights. Architecture is both an art and science. Although some computing architectural issues are well defined with clear paths, some are not. Artsy areas require someone's creativity. Some love this area and others hate it. But whether you are assembling a business solution from existing products or creating one yourself, good architecture demands some level of creativity. The first definition also makes a strong reference to a *habitable* structure. This refreshing word captures the essence of a successful architecture. A habitable P2P solution feels good over time. You don't want to gawk and move on (as with the merely *interesting* solution). You want to stay and even possibly live there. *Design* is another key word. The second definition embellishes design further by making it a *conscious* act. Some systems clearly were designed almost unconsciously as an ad-hoc act of coding. They are the *interesting* solutions, not the used ones.

Architecture is a clear, conscious act of will and discipline. Good architecture pays equal attention to both dazzling user features *and* mundane features like security. Developers gravitate toward the dazzling features at the expense of little seen or reward architectural features. Now you know why so many developers avoid it. Architecture addresses the *whole* problem not just the immediate, surface functionality. Architecture gives you the real solution and addresses the complex issues that aren't always directly associated with the desired functionality.

All solutions have an architecture, whether you notice its existence or not. The key factor is whether the architecture is appropriate for your solution. If you *design* the architecture, it will most likely be appropriate. If you don't, the architecture just *happens* and your solution is unlikely to fulfill its potential. In most cases, architecture just happens, which often leads over time to disastrous results. The potential disasters include compromised sensitive information, failure to accommodate a large number of users, and a host of other ugly side effects that undermine your system's usefulness.

You need not implement all the architecture requirements that this chapter discusses, nor do you need to be burdened with implementing all the architecture features at once. Instead, you should implement architectural features as the need arises. The key difference is that you are *prepared*. It is often stated that 10 minutes of planning saves an hour of work. The careful design of an architecture is the 10 minutes that saves you hours of headaches. Let's illustrate this with an example gleaned from our real-life travails.

We were faced with developing a real-time electronic message-delivery system that required, with absolute certainty, the receipt and delivery of each electronic message. Our architectural approach incorporated multiple parallel activities to achieve efficiencies. Our architecture also considered and managed security and failures at every point.

We were in direct competition with another group. Our competitors went after the direct functionality path of just delivering messages. They were planning to build the architectural features of security and availability later. Almost immediately they needed significant hardware upgrades: "The requirements are just too demanding for this size box." In contrast, our solution worked on the original hardware. The last update we received was that our competitors were still ironing out the security and failure requirements.

Retrofitting architecture features like security and failure management is extremely difficult and often intractable. Many good ideas simply litter your hard drive because their developers failed to address these indirect requirements. Clearly architecture requires some additional work, but for a serious solution, the investment is well worth the extra effort.

Why is architecture so often shortchanged? The answer is simple: Architecture rarely results in a cool feature; it only *supports* the cool features. Architecture is thus like the technical people who work in motion pictures. Their names appear on the endless list of credits that roll at the end of the movie, but the audience rarely remembers any names except for those of the two or three stars. But those supporting people enable the stars to shine and directly contribute to the movie's success. Architecture works similarly behind the scenes. Without a well-thought-out architecture, the headline features are often unprepared for any unusual requests (which are guaranteed to occur eventually). Movies bomb under such circumstances, whereas computers crash.

As users' tolerance for system frailties continues to decline, how many crashes and errors can you expect them to tolerate until they remove and forget a faulty program? Architecture can never eliminate all problems—nothing is perfect. But it does help turn an *interesting* solution into a real solution—one that is dependable and therefore one that is used. This chapter outlines architecture requirements that your solutions need to consider to achieve these pragmatic goals.

WHERE DO YOU START WITH ARCHITECTURE?

Rather than presenting a long list of architectural features or a lengthy treatise on architectural philosophy, this section deals directly with the results of good architectural components and works backward. This way you always understand the benefit that each architectural element provides.

We have struggled for years to get across architecture in a fun, direct way. To have a little fun, we have empowered an architectural team to lead your way through the architecture solutions. Similar to the behind-the-scenes crew for a movie production, our team is largely unseen and unrecognized by the user but is essential to a solution's adoption and continued success. The architecture team guides you through the various benefits that architecture delivers for P2P solutions. The team members are a friendly bunch and, like the background movie crew, they give the solutions that you select or build the potential for stardom.

Table 5-1 introduces the architecture team. The team consists of seven players. Their goal is clear from the beginning: a system that truly works.

	Role	Description
	Accountant	The accountant focuses on the cost and value of the P2P assets. The assets are the various components—hardware, software, and data—that constitute your solution. Like all assets, your solution's assets have real, immediate value and an eroding value as things change and evolve. Some solutions depreciate rapidly. Such solutions are like junk food: They are satisfying to consume, but they exact long-term costs. True assets are more flexible and retain much of their value for years. The longer an asset holds its value, the greater its true worth. The accountant must make the difficult decision of balancing short-term fixes with long-term investments in the solution. The accountant must also establish policies that protect the investment made in solutions.
	User Advocate	The user advocate looks over your shoulder as you design your solution, to represent the user's point of view. Users need the solution to be usable. Often this need becomes lost in a whirlwind of menu options, pop-up boxes, and mouse menus. The user advocate reminds you of your true goals and constrains your wild interfaces to focus on efficiently and easily satisfying the user's need. Another focus is quality. Users don't deal well with unexpected failures and crashes. Unfortunately, quality often gets shortchanged in the rush to get a solution into the user's hands. In Chapters 2 and 3, your P2P tour revealed some of these quality inadequacies. The user advocate is quite passionate about quality and usability.
	Security Guard	Any real team needs a tough security guard. After all, the team needs to protect many different assets. The security guard protects the integrity of the solution and any user information. This is a tricky job that had two major fronts. First, *system security* protects the basic hardware and software. Second, *user security* protects and insulates the various users from each other. The security guard is key in establishing system trust. Without trust, a system will never be truly valuable or useful.

Table 5-1. The Architecture Team

	Role	Description
	Inspector	The inspector's role has several major aspects. The inspector keeps your solution within specifications. Specs include standards that allow exchanging information with complementary systems today *and* tomorrow. Without a watchful inspector, solutions can quickly drift away from useful standards. This hubris of independence can make it difficult or impossible for your solution to receive value from other systems and also unnecessarily erodes the life of the system. The inspector is also concerned with making sure that the system can connect to already existing sources of information. Such a system is often called a *legacy system*. Integrating legacy systems and information with your solution can establish system value quickly.
	Administrator	The administrator is responsible for the overall, long-term operations of the solution. This team member constantly monitors the system looking for early warning signs of trouble or looking for ways to improve the system. The administrator also must manage disasters and plan for partial or total failures. The administrator operates the 911 for the system and must be ready to restore full operability quickly and protect all the system resources. As a side job, the administrator also makes monitoring, repairing, and recovering easier.
	Pilot	The job of pilot is often seen as glamorous, but in this case, the job is mostly like that of a long-haul freight pilot rather than that of a pilot who flies chartered jets to Bermuda. The pilot focuses on transporting your solution to additional arenas. In computing lingo, this task is referred to as *portability*. The pilot must take your solution to new platforms and new computing environments. Also, the pilot must manage the turbulence in moving the solution from one environment to the next. Keep in mind that a solution may move to other platforms today *and* tomorrow. Although the former may not be a concern, the latter is guaranteed in the dynamic, ever-changing computing world.
	Training Coach	The coach focuses on the solution's overall flexibility and distribution. If your solution is inflexible or brittle, the harshness of user or environment demands will literally break it over time. If the various components of a solution are not properly balanced, many activities will be inefficient and may fail to accommodate growing demands. Developers often rush solutions into the user's hands without heeding the coach's preaching. Such solutions may seem *interesting* initially, but lack the stamina to play a long-term role. Ultimately the coach must keep your system in shape, alive, and ready to service its users and handle current and future demands.

Table 5-1.   The Architecture Team *(continued)*

The architecture team brings together your allies in constructing a solution that works. Listen to them. They are supporting your goals and ask for little of your spotlight.

Now that the team has been introduced, let's put them to work. Each team member demonstrates his or her value and role in attacking specific architectural challenges. The team follows up each section with an acid test in which the team asks you questions to help determine your specific needs.

PUTTING THE ARCHITECTURE TEAM TO WORK

The team details P2P architecture pragmatically. We won't spoil all of the team's surprises, but here is the game plan. The team assumes you have nailed down the basic functional requirements for your P2P system. This is the functionality that the user sees and interacts with such as file sharing. These functions were highlighted in our city and jungle tour. The team's job is to go beyond user functionality and deal with those troubling issues that are often ignored at the system's and user's expense. The architecture team first outlines the need to secure your peer and the various dimensions of security. Once the peer is secure, make sure that authorized users can access your solution.

Next, make sure that the authorized user has a jolly good time using the system. Then make sure that the system can handle lots of authorized users by examining how the demands are distributed across your P2P resources. Your system also needs to remember and store valuable facts about your users that you garner through the various exchanges they have with your solution. The information constitutes the user's context. This context customizes and simplifies future user exchanges, for your system knows something about them. You don't want to seem forgetful and keep asking the same questions. Finally, you need to establish a good home for the solution and keep it gracefully incorporating new features and attributes.

SECURING YOUR PEER (FEATURING THE SECURITY GUARD)

The security guard is often the first person you meet when you enter a facility these days. This should also be the case for P2P solutions. Security is the first step in establishing trust. Trust is a higher-level system attribute that depends on a multitude of responsibilities, including information management. A electronic commerce site may protect your credit card number but also pass your purchase information to third parties. In this case, the information is secure but the site is not trustworthy. Security is the first step in establishing trust with the user and the owners of the P2P solution. An insecure system is inherently untrustworthy, but unfortunately a secure system isn't always trusted. The system earns the trust of its users and owners by handling sensitive information and other security facets well.

Your security guard manages two distinct types of security you must consider for your system: system security and user security. System security deals with halting anonymous, unwanted infiltration of your hardware and software. User security deals with separating the various users, their capabilities, and their information correctly.

The security guard outlines the first type, system security. The guard begins with a firewall. P2P by its very nature is a networked solution. A P2P solution enables access from anyone connected to the P2P network. If this network is the Internet, almost anyone can access the solution. You need broad powers to block the preponderance of users because, quite frankly, not all of them are likely to be your users; some may be quite malicious or mischievous. Your first line of defense consists of a broad fence to protect the hardware and software. The best term to use is a firewall, although this term can encompass many implementation types that Chapter 6 explores.

A firewall's job is to block unwelcome access broadly with defined electronic gates. These defined firewall gates carefully scrutinize the visiting traffic looking for unwelcome or unusual occurrences. This scrutiny can be anything from a cursory, high-level examination to a bit-by-bit examination. Your security requirements depend on two criteria: the value of the data and the likelihood of a malicious user having network access. Usually the value is low and thus simple protection is all that is required. P2P, by its distributed nature, typically doesn't place all its eggs in one basket and therefore you probably don't need super-tight corporate-level security.

The broad protection of a firewall keeps out most of the bad network traffic. It forms a fence that you can monitor. This is much more efficient than checking every access point on your computer. Imagine a building with thousands of apartments. In each apartment are several windows, and you need to check each window for a lock each day. This repetitive task would be no fun and ultimately you would miss an unlocked window.

Your computer is much like the building, and your computer's many applications are like the building's windows. You can be assured that over time one of those applications will let its guard down and leave its access open. A firewall requirement makes this repetitive searching for open windows unnecessary. However, the security guard quickly points out that this broad security requirement has its vulnerabilities. A firewall does not scrutinize many details of each communication entrance and exit. Such details require additional security.

The improved system security comes from deeper levels of scrutiny—more analogous to the strip search previously mentioned. You can construct firewall security that recognizes and eliminates inappropriate network addresses, protocols, or connection requests. However, with each probe, you pay a price. During a security alert at an airport, either everything slows down or additional security resources need be added quickly. Computers work similarly. The deeper you probe looking for trouble, the more resources must be dedicated to the chore. You must carefully decide the depth of examination you need. Each additional level exacts a cost in additional hardware and software.

All types of firewall understand only generic issues such as destination addresses and protocols. Not truly *understanding* the specific P2P exchange can hamper the firewall's effectiveness. Thus the firewall is similar to a guard stationed in front of a building. The guard remains unaware of specific exchanges between the various building occupants and must rely on following simple, generic rules. A specific visitor may be acceptable today but not tomorrow. You could customize a security guard with myriad special requests.

For example, you can tell the guard to admit a user after-hours only if he or she intends to go to a specific destination. You would follow up this order with a similar request the next day and then the next. If these rules tend to propagate, you lose track of why they are there in the first place and they tend to pile up. You are then reluctant to remove them for you no longer know what they do. This creates a firewall full of holes and eventually the guard simply lets everyone through due to failure to close an unnecessary hole. This approach thus makes Swiss cheese out of a security policy. You just re-created the thousand open windows in the building example, except that they are now holes in your firewall.

Beware of slicing up your own security policies. Simple policies are simple to implement and administer. Complex policies tie up valuable resources and expose you to a higher risk. Complexity breeds confusion that eventually leads to mistakes.

You can also take firewall security a step further by having multiple firewalls. Prisons take a similar approach using rows and rows of barbwire fences. This slight variation allows you to separate your semiprecious resources from your precious ones. A typical configuration exposes the semiprecious system behind one firewall. This system is commonly referred to as the demilitarized zone (DMZ). The next firewall allows requests only from the resources contained within the DMZ and not from the general Internet. This configuration does indeed tighten up security at the expense of a more complex networking arrangement and multiple peer computers. Remember the complexity rule.

Up to this point, the security guard insisted on constructing a broad fence to keep out the riffraff. Next, the security guard must deal with the users whom the system does admit. The guard must take on a new role and direct (sometimes forcibly) the approved users to locations approved for that particular user. This process forms user security, which is based on a context between the user and system functionality. For example, some users can delete files, whereas others cannot; some users can explore your photographs, while others cannot. User security starts with two main objectives: authentication and authorization.

Authentication verifies that the user is who he or she claims to be. Authentication implementations are responsible for the litany of user IDs and passwords, which you'll learn more about later. There is no perfect implementation. The token of authentication, whether it is a password or something else, is presented to the security guard. He or she validates the token. If the token passes muster, the guard grants the user access. However, the access is constrained by the next job of user security: authorization.

Authorization provides a cross-tabulation of the token and what the token enables the user to do within the protected system. This authorization is organized around resource capabilities and resource information. For example, two of your P2P users may be able to read and write their schedule information but not each other's information. An effective authentication and authorization guard guarantees that the correct users can do the correct activities with appropriate information. Such a guard bars both illegal users and legal users from doing illegal things (relative to their authorization). A good security guard can make things very easy for other parts of your P2P solution. They can depend on only dealing with validated users *and* performing valid operations.

The security guard's job is not yet done. Although operations are typically trusted within their firewall domain, most operations require reaching out to folks outside the firewall into the unknown. Lurkers wishing to spy or alter the communications come in and out of your domain. The security guard offers several additional services to prevent this evil. The services all depend upon encryption. An effective encryption of a communication makes it difficult for the wrong user to understand a message and easy for the right user to understand. This balance is not always easy to achieve.

Encryption ensures that the communication is not read but it does not ensure that it was not tampered with or even that it originated from its alleged source. The electronic world follows our normal traditions. The security guard provides a valid electronic signature coupled with an electronic seal. These combine to assure the user that he or she is reading what the actual writer intended.

Systems also require a security specialist to guard against computer viruses. Any electronic communication may contain a virus. A virus can take many forms. Executable communications are particularly suspect. If any part of the communication directly or indirectly guides system execution, it may contain a virus. Unfortunately, this is true for almost every communication. As you will see in the next chapter, we outsource this complex position. Several implementations exist that focus on virus security.

Another specific need that the security guard provides is nonrepudiation. Nonrepudiation ensures that you can verify that communication you receive is actually from the identified sender and not from an imposter. Nonrepudiation is important for highly trusted communications such as financial transactions.

The security guard stands with quiet assurance. This team member has provided you the requirements for effective security. You need the broad-brush protection provided by a firewall system and the specific needs of user security for authentication, authorization, privacy, and nonrepudiation.

The Security Guard's Security Acid Test

The security guard asks the following questions:

▼ Do your P2P solutions manage sensitive information about yourself and others?

■ Do you want to maintain your configuration of software and hardware?

■ Do you want to establish trust between your users?

▲ Do you suspect that someone will attempt to break into your system?

The bottom line here is that security is essential to any worthwhile solution. If any of your answers to the preceding questions are no, reread this section. The security guard is a necessary expense in protecting your computing assets and the users who access those resources. Security needs consideration from the onset of your project. You need not implement every security feature immediately but you must plan for its eventual adoption. Security, like many other architectural features, is very difficult (sometimes impossible) to retrofit.

MAKING YOUR PEER ALMOST ALWAYS AVAILABLE (FEATURING THE TRAINING COACH)

Now that you have a secure P2P solution, let's make sure that when the security guard admits a valid user, your system's functionality is ready to serve that user. This is another step in establishing system trust. Even if you completely trust a system to keep your information secure, that system still is of little value if you cannot trust that it will be available when you need the information. You need to establish a P2P system that is potentially available 24 hours a day, seven days a week.

This brings another team player front and center: the training coach. The training coach keeps the system running despite failures and required maintenance. The general geek term is *availability*. Availability is the degree that your system's functionality is ready to serve all legitimate users. Theoretically, you can never achieve 100 percent availability, but you can get close. Today's computers are highly reliable, but not all components are equal in maintaining availability. Your job is not to point fingers or place blame but rather isolate the problem areas and compensate for them.

The coach first points out that like security, availability is a balancing act. You can make your system as available as you want, but each improvement in availability comes at a price.

The first lesson is eliminating or compensating for all single points of failure. When your system attempts to fulfill a user request, a long chain of computing events must occur, such as disk reads, network connections, and processor executions. If a link in that chain fails, the entire request is at risk. Today's complex systems have forged a rather long chain. Attempting to compensate by duplicating each link in a solution is a rather daunting task. You need not attempt to do so anyway, for some areas are extremely reliable. The Internet, the bedrock of P2P, was created and thrives on an extensive list of tried and true technologies.

Redundancy

You address availability by grouping the many links in your P2P solution into four large components. These logical groupings consist of the computer itself (hardware), the P2P applications, the P2P applications' corresponding data, and the communication network. Each of these components in turn has hundreds of subcomponents. However, grouping these components provides a practical level for managing single points of failure. This practical level aggregates hundreds of components into a few manageable ones.

You have two choices in managing single points of failure: You can maintain several inexpensive redundant components, or you can purchase a single expensive, but extremely reliable, component. The former just places eggs everywhere. The latter is analogous to placing all your eggs in one basket that you then must watch very carefully. Surprisingly, using inexpensive, relatively unreliable components placed in a highly available architecture actually achieves higher reliability than using one extremely reliable component.

Friendships easily demonstrate this principle. You may have one very reliable friend who always seems to be there when you need him. Of course, due to illness or other obligations, sometimes this good friend is not available. You also may have a group of 10 friends that you go out with every Friday. Of course, on any given Friday, one or more of them is likely to be unavailable. However, *all* 10 being unavailable is extremely unlikely. Although individuals within the group are less reliable than others, the group as a whole is much more reliable.

You achieve availability similarly. A highly reliable solution must maintain redundant components. The redundant components maintain awareness of one another and recognize when one is no longer working properly. When one component discovers a failure, it takes over for the failed component transparently to the user. This is referred to as *failover*. When the primary component fails, the secondary one steps in.

Let's look at statistics to see how this magic occurs. Consider a sample of high-level components: a computer, a P2P application, P2P data, and a communication network. For simplicity, suppose that the availability is 90 percent for each component—that is, 90 percent of the time, each component is fully operational. You need all four components, so you need to multiply each: $0.90 \times 0.90 \times 0.90 \times 0.90 = 0.66$. This would mean that the entire system would be available only 66 percent of the time. On average, your users' requests would fail one-third of the time.

Each dependent component that you add, such as an additional computer or application, continues to decrease overall availability. Redundancy reverses this downward trend. Using the same numbers, if you maintain one component, its availability is 90 percent. If you add a redundant component, what happens to that component's availability? Since the solution maintains a redundant component, the solution fails only if both the original component and the redundant component fail. To calculate the resulting availability, you reverse the previous logic.

What is the likelihood of both systems failing? This would be 0.10×0.10, since each component fails 10 percent of the time. This equals 0.01, or 1 percent. Thus by adding the redundant component, you have increased the system's availability from 90 percent to 99 percent. Adding another redundant box improves the availability to 99.9 percent. Each redundant component increases the solution's costs, and its marginal value to improve availability decreases. This is a perfect illustration of the law of diminishing returns. If you add a redundant component to each of your four solution components, availability would increase to 96 percent. Luckily, computing components maintain much higher levels of availability, and some are extremely reliable, especially hardware. Your solution must identify the most vulnerable components and establish a backup or redundant component.

Loose Coupling

So far this section has dealt with complete failure. We looked at your solution in a binary fashion: It was either operational or not. You can also design a system to offer partial functionality by effectively managing a partial failure. Such a design produces a system that is not overly dependent on each component. The technical name for this design is *loose coupling*, a term that was used extensively in the 1960s.

Loose coupling is an architectural feature that minimizes dependencies across system components. The Internet is loosely coupled. If your browser crashes while perusing Amazon.com, Amazon.com does not go down. Thus loose coupling is a secret to the Internet's success. The Internet would not be viable if it depended on all of its components working properly. Your solutions should follow a similar architectural goal. For example, suppose that your data component is currently not operational; your system can still do any operation that does not depend on the data component. This approach is especially important as your solution grows in complexity by incorporating multiple computers, applications, and the like. Consider your system a little Internet.

One of the most difficult areas in which to address redundancy is your P2P data. The main reason is the dynamic nature of most systems' data. Your application itself probably changes infrequently. You or your vendor offers a new release at the most every couple of months. If you offered redundancy at the application level, you would need to copy the updated application to the redundant location just a couple times a year. Hardware and network configurations change even less frequently.

Data, unfortunately, do not operate on the same schedule. Data often represent the information currency of your application. This currency is being exchanged constantly. These exchanges form a certain state at any given time. State represents a context of current operations. State tracking can often get very granular. The best example is the shopping cart. The state of the shopping cart changes with each item that the user places in the cart.

Many critical data areas exist. These include user IDs, passwords, and filenames. This information is critical to the overall operation of your system. Your solution needs to identify the level of redundancy and the frequency at which the data are made redundant across the system. You could decide that transient information such as a shopping cart is not redundant—that is, if a data component fails, all current shopping cart contents are lost. You may choose to maintain redundant copies of only the most critical information, such as user IDs and passwords. The level of redundancy that your system requires determines the frequency of the redundant copy. If your system requires redundancy at the lowest level, you must expend significant resources to keep all components in sync. If not, you might only need to copy information as frequently as necessary to resemble application redundancy. Databases offer a service to keep the data in sync all the time. This service is referred to as *replication.* Replication keeps multiple databases working in concert by continually updating each other.

Whether to synchronize or replicate information is an important architecture decision. You may not need to implement this feature immediately, but it is important to consider the overall design and not box yourself into a corner that ultimately constrains your solution.

Redundancy at the system level offers another possibility: load balancing. Load balancing distributes the incoming requests to *all* the redundant systems. Backup systems are not just warm standbys in such a system. They are active participants in handling system requests. This keeps *all* of your systems offering services to your users. Load balancing creates two benefits: an instant failover if a system fails and improved performance when all systems are running normally. In addition, you just add more identical systems to improve both reliability and performance—a very nice combination.

Typically, you achieve load balancing with a separate hardware system that stands between requests and your systems. Several vendors offer special hardware that merges multiple systems into one virtual system. Your users see one system rather than an active system and its associated backup. Load balancing algorithms can be very simple or very complex. The simple algorithms, which constitute most of the current implementations, offer a simple round robin approach.

This approach sends each request to the next system in line. If you have two systems, the algorithm would just alternate requests from one system to the next. The simplicity creates several problems if your users' requests vary considerably in terms of system demands. The round robin approach might just by chance keep giving the hard requests to the same system and the simple requests to the other system. Such a distribution would create an inconsistent system response time. More sophisticated algorithms examine current system load or the nature of the request prior to selecting a given system. The variability of your requests determines the necessity for simple or complex load balancing requirements.

Backup and Recovery

Now the coach reappears to make one last plea. Despite the best architecture with the most redundant components configured with load balancing, failure is still possible. In the real world, you must consider the possibility of complete and total system destruction. Two steps deal with this situation: backup and recovery.

System backups save the overall configuration and information on a medium outside of the computer. This could be a zip disk, CD, or another computer on your network. The important requirement is that the entire state is recorded and stored elsewhere. Although you can reconstitute the various applications, the state can be another story. Most applications require specific customization information and depend on certain other components to be present in specific locations.

This state represents the entire context of your computing solution. It is built bit by bit with each program installation, and many personal computer owners fail to recognize the total effort it requires over the many months of installing the various applications. The volatility and importance of the data determine the backup frequency. Many computer users fail to back up at all and each day roll the dice. The daily gamble is usually a safe one, but eventually you will have a complete system failure.

Many problems can cause a catastrophic failure. The most obvious is a hardware failure such as a disk crash. Another less obvious possibility is a defective software module. This could occur, for example, when first loading a new software application.

Chapter 6 investigates backup solutions in more detail, but a brief introduction is in order for this section. There are two types of backups. One is a complete backup, where every bit of information is stored. The other is an incremental backup, which stores only files altered since the last full backup or a given date. The incremental backup is much faster and goes right to the heart of the matter by recording only the most recently changed information.

Recovery consists of the steps that fully restore the system using the backup information. You can restore the system only to the state of the last backup. If the last time you backed up was last week, then the machine's recovery will step back in time a week. All the information entered in the current week is lost. But all the information, applications, and such from before are fully restored.

Backup and recovery are prudent steps that few take. If your solution is critical to you or your associates, backup and recovery provide insurance against the worst case. Although you probably don't expect to have an auto accident today, you probably have auto insurance; have the similar regard for your hard work in your P2P solution. After all, no one likes to hear the coach say "I told you so."

The coach summarizes the availability issues. Redundancy compensates for the propensity of component failures, be they hardware or software. Redundancy abides by the law of diminishing returns. The first redundant component increases availability much more than the second. You must decide which level of redundancy is appropriate. You can start your solution without redundancy at all but design for the possibility as the solution evolves. The second lesson is designing loosely coupled architecture. This allows your system to continue operating through a partial failure and is critical as your solution grows to incorporate many components.

Loosely coupled approaches keep your solution marching forward. The third lesson deals with the reality of any system: they *will* fail. Backup and recovery strategies prevent you from paying the ultimate price of losing all data and information. Storage media are cheap, and you can perform backups during off-hours, so you have no excuse not to do them regularly. The coach will certainly get on you if you fail to do so.

The Training Coach's Availability Acid Test

The training coach ends his session with the following questions:

- ▼ Do your users require the system to be available at all times?
- ■ Does your system contain information that is hard to reproduce?
- ■ How often does your system receive sensitive information? (This determines the frequency of backups.)
- ▲ How fast does your system need to be up and running after a catastrophic failure? (This determines the needs for rapid recoverability.)

The bottom line is that often we neglect the real value of data that are present in our systems and thus fail to plan adequately for the availability and the recoverability of the system. This is especially true with personal computers. How many of your associates regularly back up their systems or detail recoverability strategies over a beer? The recognition of these requirements moves your solution from a fickle, unreliable one to a dependable one. Again, your goal is to build real solutions, not just *interesting* ones.

Availability and recoverability, while not always appreciated, definitely work toward that end.

MAKING YOUR PEER EASY TO USE, ADMINISTER, AND MAINTAIN (FEATURING THE USER ADVOCATE AND THE ADMINISTRATOR)

Now you have met the security guard and the coach. Together they provided a solution that is secure and available. The next step is making your solution easy to use, administer, and maintain. For this purpose, we introduce two additional team players: the user advocate and the administrator. They both deal with the usability of the system but from different perspectives. The user advocate is responsible for easing the path to a P2P user's goals. The administrator, on the other hand, is responsible for tuning and adjusting the system. Your solution should make both jobs as easy as possible.

First let's meet the user advocate. The user advocate's focus on the architecture team is usability. Usability simply refers to the ease of addressing user goals. It deals with arranging the tasks in a clear, intuitive way that smoothes the path in what can be complex operations. The user advocate eliminates any unnecessary or confusing steps required for a user to reach his or her goals. This is not an easy job, for the steps deal directly with the user interface and its operations.

A system must walk a careful line between power and flexibility. These interests typically oppose each other. For example, you could design a word processor that automatically constructs a formal letter from a user's input or you could design a word processor that constructs hundreds of different types of documents. The former, called the *letter writer,* offers tremendous power as long as you only want to write a letter. The latter offers tremendous flexibility but requires you to navigate through lots of menus and format properties to set up your perfect letter. This balance of flexibility and power presents a tough challenge for any solution. Many implementers try to have it both ways by offering loads of menus but also straightforward wizards. In any event, most user interfaces are much too complex and cumbersome because they want to be all things to all people.

The user advocate cringes at such discussions. To maintain sanity, the user advocate focuses on one thing: the user's goals. If you don't know them, then you tend to offer even more options and gradually drift toward enhancing flexibility at the expense of power.

Ultimately the user is responsible for what your solution actually achieves. If the user becomes befuddled, frustrated, or just plain mad, your system will suffer terribly despite the best of intentions. You must first understand the user's goals. Without user goals in mind, you can do little to design power into your solution. Second, you must clearly optimize those goals within your solution. If the user needs to print out a report, your system should not require 17 mouse clicks to perform this simple task. So what requirements help build a system that is usable?

There are many good rules of thumb for interfaces. The user advocate outlines major ones:

▼ **Appropriate, Graceful Disclosure**   The system should not disclose more than it has to, and as the system is asked to do more, it gracefully presents the user with addition interaction devices like response text boxes. A system should not besiege the user with lots of paths via pop-up windows, menus, status bars, and right-mouse clicks, to name but few. The palm pilot interface has a wonderful way of gracefully disclosing complex instructions. Simple tasks are presented in a simple straightforward manor whereas complex tasks, such as establishing a repeating appointment, require additional screens.

■ **Goal-Oriented Widgets**   The interface widgets should guide the user toward his or her goals and not away from them. Many systems try to be everything to everybody and therefore fail to offer clear paths to the user's goals.

■ **Focused Presentation**   A landscaping course will teach you that an effective landscape design cannot have multiple specimen plants and trees. A specimen plant is one that draws your attention. If a landscape is littered with specimen plants, the eye is constantly pulled in multiple directions. An interface does this with animation, blinking, red fonts, and such. It should focus a user's attention at one point, not multiple ones.

■ **Familiarity**   An interface should leverage a user's previous computing experience. This is what has made the Web browser and many Microsoft products so successful (although their interfaces break many of our other rules). Familiarity enables quick use.

■ **Simple But Not Simplistic**   A simple interface helps the user get the job done with minimal effort. In other words, simplicity is productive. A simplistic interface, one that pompously steals power away from users (since they are so stupid) in the name of simplicity, is patronizing and insulting to users. Microsoft's paper clip held the patronizing, simplistic award for many years. Finally, Microsoft has retired this feature.

■ **Always Accessible Help**   Help in many forms should always be available on any screen and for any action. Help should be available in multiple forms such as a help guide, an index list, or a help wizard. Your system should always offer a quick, easy way to find and use help.

■ **Ancillary Noise Reduction**   This is a critical goal of an interface. You should hide or possibly eliminate anything nonessential to the direct task. A P2P solution requires many low-level settings and commands such as network or operating system configurations. Most users do not jump for joy on seeing a network setup box. The more these underlying complexities are hidden, the more successful the solution. For example, many of the successful P2P solutions explored in the early chapters completely remove the network settings from the configuration. Networking is complex and usually ancillary to the user's goals. Does the user want to set up a network or share a file with a friend?

- ■ **Reinforcement Without Redundancy** A user should know when he or she has performed the correct action without being annoyed with pop-up boxes, musical notes, and the like.

- ▲ **Recognition That You Are Not Your User**   If anything ruins interfaces, it is this mistake. The designer or implementer is not the user. Do not make any assumptions as to wording or sequence. What appears clear in a design session can completely befuddle the eventual user. It is amazing how words are understood differently by the user or how a sequence of events that appears so intuitive to the designer can be so confusing to the user.

Those are the user advocate's rules of thumb. As with all rules, there are always exceptions. The preceding make good default rules unless you can make a good case to supercede them.

Perhaps the most important rule is never to try to make your interface all things to all people. The old animated film *The Point* said very eloquently, "To point in all directions is not to point at all." Such a lack of focus undermines the guidance that your solution can provide. It confuses options with power.

Ultimately, users judge an interface on one criterion: Did the user achieve his or her objectives? This is referred to as usability testing.

The user advocate now is rather smug, for few solutions meet all these rules. But consider them when selecting a product or designing your own solution. The user advocate actually reigns supreme, for ultimately it is the user who gets things done with your solution. The easier that the user accomplishes his or her goals, the more successful your system.

One more area assists you in usability. Now the administrator steps forward. Regardless of how much your solutions adhere to the user advocate's rules of thumb or how extensively you conduct usability testing, your solution will always be less than perfect. You have two choices with this guaranteed result: You can defend your approach or you can adapt. The former is simply immature. The latter requires the administrator.

In addition to performing other tasks, the administrator measures the system. The team member then analyzes the metrics to see good and bad patterns of usage. For example, the administrator may find that a feature is never used. Is this because it is difficult or just not needed? The administrator continues to dig until an approach is found to address this deficiency. The administrator's refinements not only adjust to correct initial missteps but also keep your solution in step with the system's evolution. Your solution should be dynamic, as the world in which it will be used is dynamic. If your solution stays in step with the world's changes, its value will continue to increase.

Both the user advocate and the administrator have made their points. Usability is paramount to user success. The architecture must always remember to focus on the user. Without users, a solution gets very lonely.

The Making Your Peer Easy to Use, Administer, and Maintain Acid Test

The user advocate poses the following review questions:

▼ **Does your system have users?** This seemingly simple question is not completely rhetorical. Some P2P solutions that later chapters explore are just machine-to-machine, but even these solutions have a hidden user: the coder.

■ **What interfaces are your solution's users familiar with?** These interfaces may be inferior, but if the users are familiar with them, don't let your solution's interface veer too far.

▲ **How comfortable with computer complexity are your users?** Some like lots of options and greater control, others just want to get the job done.

DISTRIBUTING THE PEER WORKLOAD (FEATURING THE COACH)

The coach now makes an important return. Your solution has to accomplish many tasks to please your demanding and fickle user. The more tasks the system has to perform, the less the user should have to do. However, this isn't always the case. Don't ever confuse action with results.

The combination of tasks contained in your P2P solution can quickly add up. Many of these tasks have dependencies. For example, a task may await a user response or a hard disk read. If you order your tasks sequentially, the list quickly adds up to a long wait. In addition, users like to control the computing flow. They determine the order of events, not the computing solution. Ultimately, your solution cannot exceed the abilities of the system in terms of memory, processor speed, and network bandwidth or test the patience of its users.

An effective solution distributes its load and allows parallel activities. Effective distribution enables small systems to accomplish large tasks. Poor distribution can make even large computers crawl. How do you distribute the load? Fortunately, P2P is a marvel of computing distribution. The first step is to have a powerful local architecture that allows parallel events.

The coach's second task takes you one level up to the machine level. This level consists of three major resources: memory that enables short- and long-term persistence, a processor that enables services, and the network that enables communication. All three resources are limited. But the magic of P2P can expand this finite pool to tap into the edge of the Internet of your fellow peers. In some cases, it is wise also to include servers that act as hubs for peer solutions.

Distribution allows the solution to interact with and tap into resources outside of the local computer system. This powerful technique is at the root of the P2P and Internet success. But you cannot achieve distribution by merely hooking up some Ethernet cable. First, let's consider the major high-level types of distribution requirements and their implications.

Four Forms for Solution Distribution

Four major types of P2P distribution are available: independent peer, dependent peer, broker server, or centralized server. This section examines the key advantages and disadvantages, and takes a peek at corresponding instant messaging architectures, some with actual implementations. Don't consider one better than another. Rather, consider what each offers to address your problem. Solutions swing from completely decentralized to fully centralized.

Independent Peer

The first choice, independent peer, is a true peer-to-peer configuration. Every P2P system is completely identical and able to make *and* perform all requests. All systems within the solution must have both the power and the knowledge to meet every user's expectations at any time. This presents a slight problem: If all systems are identical, you don't need any other participants. A stand-alone solution would be just fine. But one item is missing: *you*. You and your fellow participants create a unique entry in the system. Thus each system offers identical services, but each represents unique users.

This architecture works well for small, well-defined tasks. If the system's use can be contained to such tasks, it is highly available to the group at large. If the P2P system demands CPU-intensive operations or large memory requirements, the system demands these resources from each participant in the solution. In addition, new solution functionality requires upgrading every participant's environment. This type of architecture is excellent for small group activities with low system demands. Everyone downloads the one version and off they go. This type of system is also very scalable.

Let's examine an instant messaging system based on independent peer. You launch your instant messaging program. All your addresses are stored in your system. It reaches out to each address to see whether your buddy is present. Your buddy is present and you begin to chat. What happens as your buddy list grows? How does someone find you in the first place? Although easy to set up, such an independent peer solution can make many basic functions, such as addressing, quite challenging. This type of instant messaging is found in various quick chat programs on the Web. For example, a simple client, like an applet, might converse with a web site. The chat is true peer-to-peer, but the addressing is actually handled by a third party—the web site.

Dependent Peer

You can compensate for the drawbacks of the independent peer by, strangely enough, advancing the architecture into dependent peer. This distribution maintains a fully P2P solution, but as in George Orwell's *Animal Farm*, "some participants are more equal than others." One or more machines take on a senior role and provide coordination services. Thus your P2P solution *depends* on the senior participants. You can select the senior participants in various ways, but ultimately a slight hierarchy forms.

This slight adjustment makes many solutions easier while still maintaining a mostly equal architecture. The senior systems offer services and store information beyond the normal participant's capacity. Thus only senior participants need to have the storage and service requirements for such chores. The normal participant need not care. Thus, this system is open to a participant with fewer resources but there is a price to be paid. The senior system *must be* available. Your dependent peer solution thus depends on some systems more than others.

A slight alteration of this architecture involves specialized peers. In this altered architecture, all peers are equal, but are not identical; they each have a different focus. This allows one set of peers to work on one part of a solution while other peers work on another portion. This architecture requires some centralization to determine assignments and coordinate activities. The overall solution depends on many peers. This approach decomposes a complex problem solvable only by a supercomputer to one of simpler problems that a set of peers tackles together.

A chat system based on dependent peer architecture nominates one or more participants as a hub for addresses and presence information. These hubs form a notification network when addresses and associated information change. This network reduces the number of updates, for it forms more of a hub and spoke distribution instead of a point-to-point distribution. Figure 5-1 illustrates the dedicated peer, or hub and spoke.

If peer 1 wants to find descriptive information, it connects to its dedicated peer 6. The dedicated peer 6 need only receive updates from its local group, which consists of peers 1 through 5 and its dedicated peer 12. The dedicated peer aggregates peer information and thus most descriptive information is only one hop away. This architecture improves performance but imposes the dedicated peer's vulnerability on your system. Your system now depends on a specific peer. If that specific peer fails, your system fails. Solutions compensate by forming a backup dedicate peer that your system seeks out on a failure. Also since the dedicated peer reflects only other peers' information, it may contain information that is no longer correct. Any changes within a given peer take time to propagate to the dedicated peer.

Let's contrast this hub and spoke distribution with point-to-point information distribution. As shown in Figure 5-2, each peer is equal in this distribution. Therefore, to search for descriptive information, the user must query each machine. As the number of participants grows, the system becomes unwieldy and slow. However, the information is more accurate since you are getting it directly from the source and the system does not depend on any particular peer. If a single peer fails, that peer just won't enter into the search for information.

With a dedicated peer, you connect with the short list of senior participants, looking for your buddies. This senior server delivers the current state of your buddies. You select one of them and initiate a direct chat session. The senior server only assists in the chat connection. The actual chat remains peer-to-peer.

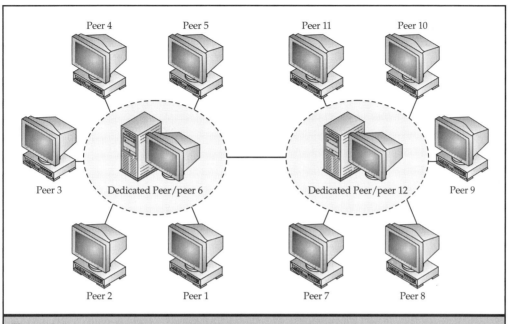

Figure 5-1. Dedicated Peer, or Hub and Spoke

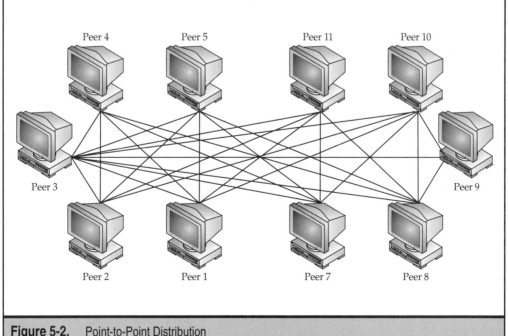

Figure 5-2. Point-to-Point Distribution

Broker Server

The next choice moves the senior participants into a dedicated server. The server maintains no direct peer-to-peer role. It only offers services to unite peers, acting as a peer broker server. The role is much like that of a real estate broker. A real estate broker brings a home seller and home buyer together. A peer broker server brings two peers together, acting as a catalyst to the emerging peer relationship.

This formal server role has several advantages. Your solution need not go in search of a senior participant nor volunteer as one. You can size this broker server to handle the resources for the role and you do not risk latching onto an underpowered peer. However, the solution does have a major drawback: If the broker server is unavailable, no new peer relationships can be formed. This drawback creates a new type of system vulnerability. It also exposes the system to legal action since there is a formal server—the Napster dilemma.

Napster was at the hub of all the alleged music theft. Shut down Napster, argue its critics, and you shut down its theft. Other more distributed systems such as Gnutella do not have the same weakness and are still going strong. Shutting down a senior participant in the dependent peer architecture would inconvenience the direct users of that senior participant only until the peer locates another senior participant. The broker system is highly optimized. It allows the broker to do what is does best: storing and coordinating descriptive information yet still allowing direct peer-to-peer exchanges.

A chat system based on this type of architecture maintains a connection with a server to store address information and presence information. You search the broker server for information about your buddies. The broker returns the state and address of each of your buddies. You select one and start chatting directly peer-to-peer with the supplied address. The system removes the broker from future exchanges until you require updated status information. If the broker fails, it would not affect your existing exchanges. This architecture has some limitations if you wish to engage in a group chat. The broker removes itself from actual chats. If your chat includes five people, for example, each participant must send his or her comments and responses to five systems.

Centralized Server

You can fix this problem easily by using a fully centralized server, which is the final type of distribution. Fully centralized architectures change the broker into an autocratic, domineering ruler (not always bad in the computer world). The fully centralized solution locates *all* services and information at the centralized server. The actual users maintain no real software; typically, they need just a browser. If you need to add to update the functionality, you only need to update the central server. Your system's users instantly access the central server and obtain the new functionality. The system requires the absolute minimum from the users since all the real power (and requirements) resides at the centralized server. Ironically, this approach is both very vulnerable and very available. The vulnerability comes directly from the reliance on a single server. The availability comes from absolutely no reliance on any user.

Let's examine a chat system based on a centralized architecture. You would connect with the well-known centralized server. The server would present you with your buddy list information. You would select an available buddy and send your chat information to the centralized server, *not* to your buddy. The server would then transmit the information to your buddy. Notice a key privacy issue: Every conversation goes through a centralized server. This makes the conversation easy to monitor. It also makes it easy to provide unique services, such as chats with hundreds of participants. Each peer only needs a connection to the centralized server. Scalability is determined solely by the server's capabilities in terms of the processor, memory, disk space, and network bandwidth.

Comparison of the Distribution Types

Table 5-2 summarizes the key differences between the distribution types.

Moving left to right in the table's columns, the architectures range from fully decentralized to fully centralized. Along this path, the architectural factors change. The decentralized approach depends more on the peer; the centralized approach depends more on the server.

Architectural Factor	Independent Peer	Dependent Peer	Broker Server	Centralized Server
Example	Chat applets	Gnutella	Yahoo!	Jabber
Scalability Determinant	Peer	Peer	Server and peer	Server
User Maintenance	High	High	Medium	Low
User Resource Needs	High	Medium	Medium	Low
Overall Availability	High	Medium	Medium	Low
User Startup Costs	High	High	Medium	Low
Privacy	High	Medium	Medium	Low

Table 5-2.   Distribution Architecture Summary

Dealing with Sometimes-Disconnected Peers

The coach then points out a troubling fact with distributed approaches: Sometimes the participants are just not available. Their systems may be turned off or not connected to the network. Your solution must choose to support these sometimes-available peers. A peer could be a laptop currently in flight to San Francisco or one that just hung up on America Online (AOL). Your P2P solution could choose to ignore such peers and not allow them to participate. However, in today's world, this would eliminate most of your fellow peers. Only isolated solutions could assume always-on connectivity. Even then, machines still occasionally fail. Your solution must consider how to deal with a sometimes-disconnected peer.

Dealing with the sometimes-disconnected peer requires your solution to store information intended for the missing peer and then update the peer when he or she connects. You have to decide where to store the information and when to update the peer. This often causes an ugly problem of distributed computing: the existence of two versions of information.

Suppose that your group is collaborating on a document. While you are all connected, there is one definitive version. Then one of your participants disconnects in the middle of your effort. Your system must note this departure and remember to update the version on the missing peer when he or she rejoins the effort in the future. While the missing peer remains disconnected, two independent versions of the document exist: the one the main group is working on, and the version that was current when the participant disconnected. If the system updates the wrong version, it might destroy or corrupt the work. Your system must handle such cases.

Such situations can get even uglier. The system must synchronize the correct version with everyone that connects. Synchronizations are low-level bit-for-bit copies of the information. The low level approach can create problems that result in chaos. For example, John once had a disaster with a Palm Pilot (a good example of sometimes-disconnected peer). Something went seriously wrong with the synchronization. It failed to recognize identical entries on both my computer and the Palm Pilot. This caused the software to duplicate, on each synchronization, all records. He discovered this problem after the software made four copies of everything. Then the ugliness really started. He tried to remove the records on his computer, but they reappeared from the Palm Pilot after each synchronization. He finally had to remove each one separately on each synchronized device. This is not a fun task on a Palm Pilot, where you have to delete many records individually.

Synchronization deals with, in computer lingo, *edge cases*. Edge cases are special incidents that rarely happen. For example, at any moment the synchronization may fail. What occurs with the partially transferred information? Does a future synchronization pick up where it left off or start all over again? These cases often take 80 percent or more of the product development effort. You should consider solutions that adequately deal with these occurrences because eventually they do happen. This is especially true in the P2P world, where a successful system could quickly grow to millions of users. Poor handling of edge cases will keep your phones ringing and your mailbox full of messages from disgruntled users.

The Training Coach's Distribution Acid Test

Are you using the *2* in *P2P?* Distribution is a fact of life with a peer-to-peer solution. You simply have no way to avoid the issues with distribution. You need to design an architecture that properly distributes the functionality across many systems.

The real question is which required form your solution should take:

▼ **Does your peer contain lots of state information, such as addresses, filenames, and so on?**   If so, a more centralized approach may help.

▲ **Is your peer solution self-contained and simple?**   A fully distributed approach may fit the bill.

REMEMBERING IMPORTANT INFORMATION: A TRUE SIGN OF P2P INTELLIGENCE (FEATURING THE ACCOUNTANT)

This section introduces the accountant for the first time. This team member watches and protects your assets. Information is one of the most critical assets of P2P solutions. Most systems relegate a significant role to information. The accountant insists on adequate storage, protection, and use of the information. Your information needs depend on several informational dimensions:

▼ **Sensitivity**   The system information may include very sensitive information that the system should share only with approved users. Your P2P system must protect the information from unauthorized users.

■ **Magnitude**   The system may need to handle small or large amounts of information. As the amount of information grows, basic information functions such as searching and storing become quite challenging.

■ **Multiple Users**   P2P systems maintain much of their value by have multiple users share and interact with your information. Multiple users create quite a bit of information management challenges, especially if one or more of the users can update the information. Multiple updates can create "racing" situations that accidentally and unknowingly lead to the destruction of information. For example, two of your system's users, Jonathon and Susan, are both working on the next day's presentation. By chance they both send an update for page 3. Which one wins? Jonathon was the fastest on the keyboard and pressed ENTER first. Your system dutifully updates page 3 with Jonathon's information. But right behind it, Susan's request arrives, which your system quickly processes and uses to replace Jonathon's page. Jonathon's page is completely lost. Ironically, the last user to submit information wins and the first one across the finish line loses. This racing situation is evident in several of the P2P sharing products that earlier chapters explored. There are programmatic ways to recognize that multiple changes have occurred. These methods at least warn you that your submission may overwrite your associate's work, but they don't help the system decide which information it should or should not transfer into a merged version. This task falls to you.

■ **Information Robustness**   Your system's information may represent hours of a user's work. If the system loses that information, many hours of work are lost. Your system may protect this information in two ways. An information and recovery requirement enables your system to recover information in the event of a catastrophic loss such as occurs with a disk crash. In addition, you may want to audit changes to understand how your information changed over time. This process can catch errors that your program or its users have made.

■ **Information Services**   Information services consist of the methods that your users use to interact with your system's information. Information services can start simply by saving and retrieving information such as saving your address. These functions quickly extend to searching to find other addresses. They can also grow to enable new combinations of the information such as producing all addresses from New Jersey. Often these services harvest additional value from the basic information by establishing new combinations.

■ **Lack of Corruption**   This covers two major areas: data consistency and data integrity. Information must remain consistent and accurate to be truly useful. A phone number must contain digits and an e-mail address an *at* sign (@). A useful, high-quality system does not allow inconsistent information to be entered or presented. Integrity, on the other hand, ensures that system information is properly protected and cannot be purposely or accidentally altered without the correct user privileges. Protection against information corruption makes your system's information dependable and hence your system dependable. The more protection against corruption, the more formality that surfaces via various system rules. You need to determine the optimal trade-off between these two concerns. For example, you may require a zip code in your solution. You can check whether a user enters all digits, the proper number of digits, a valid zip code, or a zip code that agrees with an entered city. Each level of checking requires more complex rules and additional system resources but provides a higher likelihood of accurate, useful information. The importance to your system of accurate information determines the level of checking that you should implement.

▲ **Flexibility**   Information can arrive in many formats. Your system may support a few well-defined formats or be open to any format. The overall information requirements must consider flexibility.

These seven traits form the basic requirements for P2P information storage. The degree of importance of each determines your solution to these information challenges.

Files and File Systems

You can require your system to store information in various formats. The simplest format is files—just plain files. This format seems like an easy solution at first, but is fraught with hidden difficulties that are revealed as your solution grows. First, files are dependent on the file system and hence the operating system on which they reside. File systems are different on each operating system, so information contained in files is not always easy to move from one system to another. They also have strange limitations, such as the file-name length, characters, and extensions (such as .doc or .ppt). Your solutions must work with the limitations of the various operating systems that your solution supports. In addition, filename conventions cannot force consistency and integrity. You might receive a file named "Jingle Jangle – The Archies.mp3" and find out to your horror it is a Britney Spears song or even a spreadsheet. Filenames are never more than a convention. They guarantee nothing.

Sheer magnitude quickly affects file systems. As your file collection grows, you are forced to add dimensions to the files. These dimensions are often called directories. Thus, you can store your Archies song in an oldies directory and the Brittany Spears song in the modern directory. Directory naming allows only one dimension and is subject to the same looseness as filenames. The Archies file cannot be both in the oldies and bubblegum directories.[1] You must make a choice and *remember* that choice.

That is only the beginning of file difficulties. Have you ever lost a file? You know that it is somewhere among the 10,000 files on the C drive, but where? You instigate an exhaustive and time-consuming search on some indirect indicator or keyword and cross your fingers. This is never a fun experience. Your search often results in finding the desired file, but the process can be quite time consuming depending on the number of files searched.

Files have one major advantage: They are easy to create. You can jump-start your solution with files, but don't lose sight of the larger requirements. All this risk without a clear reward concerns the accountant. This team member seeks better protection of your information.

Databases

The next step in information protection is to use some form of a database. A database is merely a more formal organization of your information that is designed to manage and protect that information. The database maintains complete control over the information that it stores. To store and extract information, you must make a call to the database. Databases have their own language, typically Standard Query Language (SQL).

Databases make demands but offer much better control of key information. They offer an extensive array of services that far exceed services offered in file systems. These include efficient storage, auditing, user security, and controlled multi-user access. The

---

1   UNIX systems do allow linking to multiple directories. But the file really resides in only one directory.

more that your solution depends on storing and maintaining information, the more your solution will require a database.

The accountant points out that although most database programs are commercial products such as Microsoft Access or Oracle, an operating system may contain internal database software that a solution can also use. An example of such an internal database program is the Microsoft Windows Operating System Registry. The registry offers an inferior subset of database services, but all Windows applications share these services. Thus if you wish to share information with other Windows applications or store startup and configuration information, the Windows registry could be a wise choice. Just keep in mind that these operating system databases are not for general-purpose storage.

Comparison of Information Storage Choices

Table 5-3 compares the two major choices, files and databases, by contrasting the features.

Table 5-3 clearly points out the advantages and disadvantages of information storage requirements. Files are simple to set up and very flexible but offer only simple services.

Information Criteria	Files	Databases
Sensitivity	File systems offer only spotty file protection that is limited to an entire file. You cannot protect parts of a file from a user.	Databases provide extensive protection down to a very granular level.
Magnitude	File systems can handle large amounts of information, but file naming and directory creation become cumbersome.	Databases can handle and store efficiently enormous amounts of data, although the capabilities of individual databases vary.
Multiple Users	File systems do not handle multiple users at all.	Multiple users can safely update information simultaneously.
Information Robustness	File systems often contain backup systems, but they must be set up.	Databases can be set to back up all changes automatically and restore quickly.
Information Services	The services of file systems are simple and limited to reading and writing information. They impose no restrictions on the information, and thus do not maintain data integrity.	Databases provide extensive services that ensure consistency and integrity.

Table 5-3.   Information Requirements Contrast

Information Criteria	Files	Databases
Integrity	None.	Extensive.
Flexibility	Unlimited.	Constrained.
Ease of Creation	Simple.	Complex.

Table 5-3.   Information Requirements Contrast *(continued)*

Databases are much more complex but offer superior management and control over critical information.

The Accountant's Information Management Acid Test

The accountant suggests that you ask yourself the following questions regarding your solution's information:

▼ Does your system store critical, sensitive information?

■ Do multiple users update the same information?

■ Does your system require rapid recoverability in case of a catastrophic failure?

■ Would a recombination of your information be of value to your system's users?

■ Does your information have multiple, undefined formats?

▲ Does your system require users to construct information storage constantly?

Databases offer the most control, but also demand the most control. The more important that flexibility and ease of creation are to you, the more file storage makes sense for your solution.

BEING A GOOD PEER BY ADHERING TO STANDARDS (FEATURING THE INSPECTOR)

The inspector examines the standards requirements. The computer industry is rife with standards. There are existing standards for almost all types of exchanges and processing choices. Why are they so important? Why should you care about addressing standards in your solutions?

The inspector is quick to point out the many advantages:

▼ **Faster Creation and Deployment**   Few systems stand alone on their own hardware, connectors, and communication systems. There is a good reason for this. Systems depend on a multitude of operations to work. If you had to design and build your system from scratch, you would be at it for quite a while. Instead, solution designers build on others' work that implements standards.

■ **Longer System Life**   Standards extend your system life in several ways (which the accountant greatly appreciates). They are constantly improving. If it supports the standards, your system benefits from these advancements with little or no effort. In addition, related technologies, such as operating systems, do not usually break a standard when they advance. Instead, they continue to support the standard, thus ensuring that your solution continues to work.

■ **System Synergy**   Standards enable disparate systems to cooperate. This cooperation can form a new aggregated solution that is actually many times more powerful than the two solutions separately. The Internet itself is a prime example of different operating systems and different browsers working together with a common standard. Your systems may eventually cooperate with other solutions that have not yet even been imagined.

■ **Better Support**   Standards come with a multitude of support mechanisms. If you have a problem with a standard's related issues, thousands of mechanisms may come to your rescue. The more popular the standard, the more aid you receive. If you decide on bucking the trend and create your own standards, you are out in the cold if problems arise.

■ **Higher Quality**   Standards significantly reduce edge case blindness. Edge cases, discussed earlier, represent all the strange events that your robust P2P solution must handle. These cases cover an ever-growing list of unusual but possible happenings. A solution designer's main focus is on the actual functionality of the system. Designers don't focus on the long list of exceptions, many of which are quite esoteric. This edge case blindness produces low quality as the edge cases surface. Edge cases spring to life as soon as the system is released to a multitude of users, but it's quite unlikely that your system will be the first to experience a particular new edge case. Most likely, the edge case has already affected another system, which the standard has then addressed, most likely by releasing an update. Thus, if your solution follows a standard, you can simply update your solution rather than repair a serious defect. Security provides many good examples of how updates are used to manage edge cases. We are constantly barraged with security warnings and fixes. Usually you need only implement the fix rather than deal directly with the security defect itself.

▲ **Good Peer**   Finally, the whole team encourages you to be a good peer. Standards make you compatible with other peers without an extensive and often prohibitive negotiation, and this compatibility forms the basis of good relationships. Your system will need to overcome a host of hurdles if you have incompatibilities due to standards.

Standards are no panacea. They also impose distinct disadvantages. You will need to consider both the advantages and disadvantages before adopting a particular standard for your solution. The following summarizes the disadvantages:

▼ **Inhibition of Innovation**   Unfortunately, sometimes the standards bureaucracy stifles innovation in order to gain agreement across the many constituents.

■ **Lack of Customization**   Standards, by their very nature, are not customizable. If your solution requires a high degree of customization, standards will often get in your way rather than assist you.

▲ **Overall Expense**   Sometimes a standard covers many areas that do not affect your solution. This unneeded coverage can incur performance issues and the like.

The advantages and disadvantages are clear. But what exactly is a standard?

Two types of standards exist today. The *official* standard emerges out of an independent standards body that theoretically is not driven by special interests. These standard bodies usually consist of representatives from all interested parties. These representatives trudge through every possibility to arrive at a fair and exemplary standard. This approach, although somewhat fair, can lead to a lethargic bureaucracy. This stifles innovation rather than promotes it.

Another standard type steps into the vacuum created by sheer urgency: the *de facto* standard. The *de facto* standard typically consists of a vendor's approach that has become very popular. The Windows operating system is a primary example of successful *de facto* standard. A *de facto* standard emerges when a determined vendor that perceives a need for innovation promotes its standards for wider adoption. Many Internet companies sought such adoption in the Internet boom by giving away anything such as discount coupons to achieve dominance through its particular standard. The browser itself was caught in this vortex of innovation.

Which standard type is better—official or *de facto*? The official standard contains the least bias and correspondingly the least innovation, but is likely to be the most comprehensive. Extensible Markup Language (XML) is an example of a successful official standard. (You learn more about XML shortly.) Distributed Computing Environment (DCE) is an unsuccessful example. (For this reason, this book doesn't cover DCE at all.)

Many good standards die due to lack of clear profit motive. Official standards often lack vested interest and hence a profit motive. *De facto* standards contain the most innovation but they are tied to the success of their originating vendor. In addition, a *de facto* standard may intentionally or unintentionally leave out major features to strengthen the vendor's market position. You may not discover these limitations until it is too late. So neither type of standard is without risk.

Standards exist across the board in every computing area. So which ones are important to your P2P solution? First let's examine how your solution uses standards. Your solutions use standards in two ways. The first way is the actual construction of the solution—the internal parts. If your solution adheres to standards, the construction often goes quicker. Many of the required pieces you need to assemble are literally off the shelf (or off the download button). Of course, nothing stops your competitors from doing the same thing. So you acquire components that are necessary and build the ones that differentiate your solution.

The second way your solution uses standards is to connect to complementary systems or external standards. The external standards form the connection methods to these complementary systems, which can create new combinations that form more powerful solutions. Marketing commentary often refers to this feature as *system openness*. An open system may understand a multitude of protocols and formats but internally may use only one standard or no standards at all. The more the standards your system supports, the more your solution can be combined with others to form a larger solution for the user today and in the future.

The key standards of P2P are those that interact with other components and involve exchanging information and services. The chapters ahead delve into specific standards and their benefits. Effective standard selection drives the ultimate success of your system, for it enlarges your possible combination set and extends the life of your system. The last point is an important one to the accountant. Standards march on with the advancements of computing world. If your solution is based on a standard, your solution marches in step with minimum investment.

We separate standard adherence into two major categories: internal and external. The internal standards are the ones that contribute to the inner workings of your system. The external standards are those that easily exchange information and services with other complementary systems. Let's look at the key areas to focus on for requirements in both areas.

The key internal standards of P2P solutions all surround rapid construction of a robust solution. These are most important to system developers, but less important to P2P solution designers who seek off-the-shelf solutions. The key internal standards are as follows:

▼ **The Computer Language** The computer language forms the instructions to the computer. Many computer languages exist, but only a few are considered major. Computer languages struggle with a simple principle: The more flexible, the more complex. Thus, less flexible languages like Visual Basic offer simple development to a constrained set of problems. More flexible languages like C++ or Java offer more complex development but tackle tougher problems.

■ **The Computing and Programming Environment** A computer language exists in a sea of services and components. A comprehensive, powerful environment may even make up for a weak language. A standard environment that achieves some level of success offers an ever-growing list of powerful services and components that you can easily integrate into your solution.

▲ **Information Storage**   A solution's success often depends on its ability to store and retrieve information reliably. A storage standard helps ensure that your solution achieves this objective. As with the computing environment, successful information storage standards offer an ever-growing list of valuable information services.

The key external standards for P2P all focus on transferring information and services over a network:

▼ **Communication**   These standards simply enable you to move data from one place to another. Communication standards do not dictate the data type but ensure that the data move correctly without errors. Communication standards may also include compression standards to squeeze the most out of the available bandwidth.

■ **Protocols**   Protocols form the rules for exchanging data. Systems need to acknowledge each other's communication and respond to successful and unsuccessful transfers. The systems must perform these tasks according to very specific rules of engagement; otherwise, electronic chaos would ensue. Protocols are analogous to a Federal Express shipment. Federal Express cares little of the contents of a package but maintains specific protocols to move the package from its origin to its destination.

■ **Data Formats**   Data formats form the language of the exchange. They represent the payload of the information exchange. Standard data formats enable two systems to exchange information easily without requiring a detailed knowledge of the other system.

▲ **Naming**   Communication depends on the ability to find each P2P solution component consistently. If peers don't agree on naming conventions and services, they are voices screaming to the unknown. (Chapter 4 fully explored naming.)

Often standards combine to offer a complete interaction package that handles everything from basic communication to specific data formats. The chapters ahead illustrate specific implementations and their use in your solutions. For now, these categories identify the critical areas that we delve into later.

Standards simplify integration across a host of diverse technologies, solutions, and platforms, but they are not all compatible with one another.

Dealing with Disagreeable Peers

Disagreeable peers are the technologies and solutions that you would like to integrate into your overall solution but which lack the standards that your solution supports. They make integration much trickier.

Disagreeable peers usually don't start out that way. They normally begin as solutions that rushed to fill a need prior to the existence of any standard or to address a need that was so unique that it required a proprietary solution. Over time, these solutions grew to take on a significant role in the computing world. Such systems are known as *legacy systems.*

Despite the inherent incompatibilities of legacy systems, you may still want to add their functionality to your larger solution. You can apply an integration approach to incorporate these disagreeable peers into your solution if you place additional integration requirements on your overall solution. Typically, your solution requires an additional layer that translates between your system standards and the legacy systems. This layer essentially isolates your solution from the legacy solution. Over time, a replacement for a legacy system can replace the translation layer without major system changes. Thus the translation layer enables a graceful transition from a legacy system to its replacement.

Standards "Extensions"

As stated previously, standards offer a wonderful shortcut to integrating and developing a solution. However, they offer little benefit for a vendor to create and manage a standard. Standards can help improve a solution's performance and support, but adhering too closely to a standard can make it challenging for the vendor to differentiate its solution from others.

To address such problems, standard *extensions* are invented. Extensions use an existing standard as a springboard directly into proprietary features. These extensions bring new power and innovation to an existing standard, but at a high price: The new features do not immediately become part of the standard. Sometimes the standard may incorporate them later, but their addition is not guaranteed.

In the meantime, your solution has to make a choice: whether to stick with the standard and its limitations or to adopt a vendor's extensions and deal with the resulting incompatibilities. The vendor may not intend to incorporate the feature into the standard, to help ensure that the vendor's innovation remains unique to the vendor's solution. This technique creates a vendor *lock-in*—that is, if your solution uses an extension that will never become part of the standard, your solution is *locked in* to that vendor. A lock-in is not necessarily a bad thing unless you are unaware of it. Just make sure that you make an informed decision before you choose to rely on proprietary extensions and don't fool yourself into thinking that they are part of the standard. Your decision may impact the evolution of your solution as this lock-in continues to hold your solution captive for better or worse.

Standards Summary

The inspector has made his point. Standards benefit your solution in many ways that affect both the solution's construction and its association with related systems. Standards are dynamic. They evolve and splinter through vendor extensions. Taking advantage of standards is often a good idea, but you must keep your eye on their dynamics.

The Inspector's Standards Acid Test

This is another easy test area:

▼ Does your solution require interaction with other systems?

▲ Does your solution require extensive building blocks to establish communication, storage, and the like?

Standards are truly a big win for any P2P solution. Just be aware of their frailties and you will do just fine.

ESTABLISHING A HOME FOR YOUR PEER (FEATURING THE PILOT)

The pilot's job is to land your solution properly in a computing environment and enable its safe movement to other environments. This is commonly referred to as *system portability*. A portable system moves easily from one environment to another.

Portability has two dimensions: You can move your system to a different existing computing environment or move your system to the next version of the current computing environment. The easier your solution moves to different computing environments, the greater your system's portability. The importance of portability depends on the type of computing environments that your system's users have today *and* tomorrow.

A computing environment consists of all the tools and resources at your solution's beck and call. Computing environments typically are operating systems. An operating system controls system resources such as memory, the processor, and the network. Your solution obtains resources by making requests to the operating system.

In the P2P world, the operating system of choice is obviously the one that your peers are using. This is usually a variant of the Windows operating system. This simple choice belies some of the difficulties. A multitude of Windows operating systems exists, each with its own unique features. The Windows operating system has evolved quite rapidly and maintains a professional/business version and a home version. Fortunately, the various Windows versions overlap quite a bit. Thus many operating system requests behave similarly, but not all of them. If your requirements mandate the use of the Windows operating system, keep in mind that your choice represents more than one operating system.

Windows is not the only peer operating system. A major competitor, unfortunately a distant one, is the Macintosh Operating system. It is powerful and well established in certain fields such as education and graphic arts. It maintains only a small market share compared to Windows, but its users remain very loyal. You may need to consider this group in your requirements.

Another more unusual but viable choice is the Linux operating system. Linux, a part of the open source movement discussed earlier, is a full-blown UNIX operating system with rich development tools and applications. My Linux machine has been running unabated for many months despite my best attempts to crash it, and it runs very efficiently on machines that would make a Windows application crawl. Linux is a powerful operating system that anyone can run. It offers many applications and runs on almost all hardware platforms. You may have few peers running Linux, but it has other advantages that we'll discuss later.

We carefully defined a computing environment to include but not be limited to just operating systems. Many computing environments exist *above* the operating system, forming an additional, isolated computing environment. These higher-level computing environments offer additional power or focus. They also promise to isolate your solutions from the particularities of a specific operating system such as Windows or Linux.

The most notable higher-level environment is the one for the Java language, the Java Virtual Machine (JVM). The JVM is the computing environment that executes Java programs. The JVM forms an additional layer between your Java instructions and the operating system. This layer allows your Java solution to run anywhere that a JVM exists. JVMs exist in many environments, from the smallest hardware environment to the largest. A Java solution moves quite easily across operating systems big and small.

Java is not the only higher-level computing environment. Databases offer stored procedures that run program instructions on the same type of database but on different operating systems. If your solution requires extensive data manipulation, you need to consider database stored procedures. The Internet has created several focused environments to allow programs to move across platforms regardless of the operating system. These environments typically exist as a browser plug-in such as Macromedia Flash. Flash, for example, forms a powerful computing environment that is independent from any operating system. Upcoming chapters examine specific technologies.

So now that you have choices, which do you pick and for what purpose? The main question is, what is your users' computing environment? This becomes your primary driver for requirements. But several key questions remain.

Do you build directly on the operating system or do you use a higher-level technology such as Flash or Java? The answer depends on several issues. The first is your need for portability. Portability, as discussed earlier, is the ease of moving your solution from one computing environment to another. At first glance, the need for portability seems unlikely in the P2P world of common platforms. But have you run the same operating system since you started computing? Are all your friends using the same one? Do they have the same upgrade path as you?

The answer to these questions is probably no. Your solution will have to run in multiple platforms or at least will have to migrate to them in the future. Portability determines the ease of this transition. Participation alone is a key driver of success of P2P solutions. The more computing platforms that support your solution, the more participation. Portability is a key determinant of participation and, hence, success.

Performance is another key issue. Typically, the closer your solution gets to the actual resources of the processor and disk, the faster and more efficiently your solution runs (albeit minimizing the computing instructions and resources in the way also paves the way to efficiency). Higher-level technologies impose additional layers that have the positive effect of insulating you from the operating system but also have the negative effect of requiring additional processing instructions.

Luckily, not all instructions require high performance. In fact, most solutions have a very small set of performance-constrained instructions. Some environments handle multiple tasks better than others. Thus the environment that you choose clearly can be a bottleneck in offering your peer resource to multiple users or users who enjoy multitasking.

The type of power contained within the various computing environments is also an important consideration. Some environments offer rapid development, others offer powerful network functionality, while still others have tremendous breadth. Upcoming chapters examine in detail several environments to help drive your selection. Just keep in mind that no computing environment is perfect for all solutions. Beware of sale pitches that make such a statement.

One final concern that the pilot points out is the distributed needs of your solution. Sometimes using a peer just isn't enough or isn't efficient. Your P2P solution may just need a server. You haven't yet seen how to implement a full P2P architecture, but we have alluded to the need, in some cases, of a centralized server. Different platforms display different levels of comfort with such a role, and your solution must be aware of their limitations in a server role.

Multiple users connected in various ways can dramatically increase the load of any system. Some computing platforms scale well to handle the multi-user load, others are less successful. You must consider this carefully in assigning a computing environment to handle a multitude of users. Microsoft Windows is not designed to handle multiple users simultaneously. The operating system offers few controls to assist and manage performance. Essentially, Windows pushes a single-user machine uncomfortably into a multi-user role. Linux, on the other hand, is built to handle and easily manage many simultaneous users. High-level refers to computing environments above the operating system level such as Flash or Java.

Table 5-4 summarizes the features and assesses the various platforms.

Avoiding Turbulence

So far this chapter has discussed requirements for moving your solution into different computing environments. Another type of move is likely to affect your solution: evolution. Your solution must be able to handle change as it moves forward into the future. This future environment will contain new standards, new platforms, new complementary peer solutions, as well as a great increase in computer power. In a sense, your solution moves to a new solution environment. Your ever-changing, demanding users also will place new demands based on changes all around them. Most of these changes are difficult to foresee. How will your system react?

Criteria	Windows	Linux	Macintosh	High-Level
Hardware Portability	Limited to hardware supporting Windows	Open to almost all hardware platforms	Limited to hardware supporting Macintosh	Specific to technology but usually provides extensive support for hardware platforms
Performance	Good	Excellent	Good	Fair
Power	Good	Excellent	Good	Excellent
Flexibility	Good	Excellent	Fair	Limited to the focus area
Multi-User Capabilities	Fair	Excellent	Fair	Very dependent on specific technology

Table 5-4.   Computing Environments Summary

Flexibility becomes a key requirement in today's rapid cycle of innovation. The chapters ahead delve into implementations that provide this needed flexibility. Flexibility is a design attitude. Your solution must seriously take on the Boy Scouts' motto, "Be prepared." You can't be prepared for every possible outcome, but many are straightforward and predictable. You need to prepare your solution for more users, more data storage, more interfaces, and so on.

A pilot would not be doing his or her job without steering around this solution turbulence. *Solution turbulence* is the need to change your solution based on a reaction to changes in the computing environment or the computing world. Ideally, your solution would not need to change regardless of how the world changes. Unfortunately, you must design your solution to fly smoothest through these often-unseen future obstacles. The following are rules of thumb for avoiding turbulence:

▼ **Fly High** The further you remove your solution from low-level details, the less likely low-level changes will demand changes to your solution.

■ **Fly by the Rules** Many computing environments clearly outline actions that you should not take within the environment. Many of these actions can affect particularly volatile areas of the system that your solution should not use in any way.

■ **Prepare for a Landing** As you develop a solution, note the areas that are the most likely to change and isolate them from the rest of your solution.

▲ **Keep Your Radio on** Make sure you listen to the industry as it moves forward. This way you can most gracefully move your solution forward.

One final note brings together the pilot, the accountant, and the user advocate: Portability is proportional to the solution's operation life. A solution that is more portable will have a longer life than one that is less portable. Also, portability is proportional to quality. If your solution runs on more computing platforms, it is less likely to run into specific platform difficulties. Hence portability offers some real benefits to the overall team and is a strongly encouraged architectural requirement.

The Pilot's Portability Acid Test

Here are some key questions about piloting your solution:

▼ Will your solution run on different hardware platforms and/or operating systems? Which ones?

■ Will your solution stick around to run on future operating systems and future solutions environments?

▲ Will you be able to adjust your solution to changes in the computing environment?

ARCHITECTURE APPROACH

This discussion of architecture should not conclude without mentioning some requirements for actually *establishing* an effective architecture. Architectures don't just happen. All of these architectural considerations may overwhelm your simple goals. Many systems lack even basic architecture, and this deficiency clearly diminished the system's value.

Correspondingly, many architectures are developed simply to demonstrate pure theory. Sometimes these architecture endeavors take a life of their own, an existence separate from the goals of the solution. Vested interests keep these efforts alive despite any use in real solutions. Such instances are so common that many architectural efforts are tainted from the start. You must strike a careful balance between architectural goals and the direct solution goals. You have to decide how much attention the star features get and what remains for the architecture supporting cast.

If you focus only on the star features, your solution will never reach its full potential. If you focus on just the architectural supporting cast, you really don't have a solution at all.

So, here are some rules for establishing and maintaining this important balance:

▼ **Architecture Is Important**   Repeat this mantra often. You will need it during the dark moments where you want to take a quick but unwise shortcut to deliver system functionality at the expense of architecture. Never forget the indirect role that architecture plays in securing a high-quality solution.

■ **Architecture Earns Its Way; Never Give It a Theoretical Free Ride**   One of the biggest mistakes you can make is to include architectural features that originate from theory and not from practical need. Make sure that your solution needs each feature in the supporting cast. You can even start to build the solution without a key architectural feature until you clearly see the need for it. Be warned: Following this rule requires an objective view that is often lost in the urgency of delivery.

■ **Design Big; Build Small**   Design is a paper exercise. It does not require mounds of code or large integration efforts. The design holds the key to the majority of architecture requirements. You should always design your system to meet architecture requirements, then build small pieces that you need today. This demonstrates that you are prepared to meet the requirements, but saves you from investing your efforts in meeting them until your solution actually calls for you to do so.

■ **Build Your Architecture Incrementally and Iteratively**   This rule translates into building what you need now, but keeps in mind your design and your solution's future. These small increments allow iterative corrections before your solution drifts too far from its intended goals. This drift gets more costly, eventually resulting in delays to make necessary corrections. As a simple example, suppose that you and a friend walk along lines that are just a few angle degrees apart. You both initially start out just a few inches apart. But with each passing day of your walk, the small degree adds up to ever-increasing distances. Eventually, the small degree of separation grows to many miles. Incremental and iterative deployment can help you minimize this separation.

▲ **Ensure That Incorporation and Evolution Occur Gracefully**   You need not implement all architectural features at your solution's inception. Architecture can unfold as the value of the solution becomes more critical. This allows you to address the functionality that you need to deliver immediately and to make the solution robust for the longer term. The secret comes in design. Architecture really is design. Design does not always require implementation, but rather makes room for it. When the need for an architectural feature becomes apparent, you can then incorporate it. Without the design, you end up hacking a quick fix that directly undermines your architecture and its goals.

SUMMARY

The team members have now finished their job. They have taken you through the benefits of placing architecture requirements on your P2P solution. The team's driving goal is to move your solution beyond the *merely interesting* phase into the truly useful phase. A truly useful solution is trusted, robust, and available.

The team's game plan begins by establishing a secure environment—one where you allow the right users in the right places and disallow the wrong users. The next step is to make your system always available and ready to serve legitimate users. Then the team worked on making the user and administration experience simple, direct, and efficient.

Next the team attacked performance constraints through the construction of hardware components that support your performance needs. Then the team went to work on storing information so as to remember events across multiple interactions with your users. Next, they outlined the importance and pitfalls of computing standards that enable you to construct your system and integrate with other systems easily. Finally, the team considered the computing environment of your system and worked to minimize the difficulties in moving to a new computing environment.

The team hopes that you have taken the architectural requirements to heart. These requirements impact any system you select, build on, or design. Their impact is subtle but very real. The team deserves a rest now, so it's time to move on.

The upcoming chapters reflect back on these requirements. You first look at off-the-shelf solutions that maintain their own balance of features and architectural requirements. You need to weigh the architectural implications of each solution. Then you look at customized solutions that demand some architectural design.

CHAPTER 6

Getting P2P Enabled

Now that you have explored the requirements behind successful P2P solutions, in this chapter you begin establishing practical implementations. This part of the book goes beyond the theory to provide detailed instructions to enable the full potential of P2P.

To enable P2P, you first need to address three key requirements: getting connected, getting secure, and getting known. This chapter addresses these requirements in that order. These establish the foundation of any successful P2P effort.

First, you get connected. Your connection to the Internet sets the stage for all of P2P. You need to consider several alternatives, each with corresponding advantages and disadvantages. There are also two dimensions to cover: the wide area network (WAN) for your connection to the Internet, and the local area network (LAN) for your local computers (if you are lucky enough to have more than one computer). This chapter focuses on the WAN. After all, P2P is somewhat powerless without the Internet, although current technology enables powerful LAN approaches too.

Next, you get secure. An unprotected connection to the Internet is not a solution that you would grow to depend on with sensitive information and trustworthy functionality. As you now know, connecting to the broad expanses of the Internet exposes you to all the good and the bad. You need to filter out the bad the best you can while maintaining easy passage for the good. Security is first founded on broad protection methods including establishing a firewall and protecting against viruses. Firewalls and virus protection come in several varieties including hardware and software versions. This chapter distinguishes between them, noting the advantages and disadvantages. You also need to establish practical policies that make these tools truly effective.

The final step to enabling P2P is getting known. You need to give yourself an address—one that is easy to remember and that works with many existing tools. If you are connected to the Internet, you have at least an IP address. No one likes providing low-level IP addresses, which may change without any notice. (How many can you remember?) You need to associate an easily remembered name that maps the IP address. This chapter explores ways to associate a URL with your IP address. Even if your IP address is constantly changing, you can associate a URL with an IP address by using dial-up access or the DHCP service discussed previously. This chapter also explores several techniques to establish a URL for both fixed and variable IP addresses.

For each of the three steps, this chapter will present specific practical, real-world examples and describe the tools that make the solutions possible. These examples do not demonstrate the only approach or even the best approach—just approaches that work and that illustrate the general steps that you need to take regardless of your specific implementation.

Now, let's get connected, secure, and known. Let P2P begin.

GETTING CONNECTED

Getting connected is where P2P really begins and ends. This critical step affects all your P2P efforts. This section guides you through two types of connections: that for the Internet and that for your nearby computers. The first is usually referred to as the wide area network (WAN). The second is the local area network (LAN). First this section covers your WAN connection, because this connection enables all peers to unite via the Internet. But we will not neglect the power of your local peers.

Getting connected builds on what you have already learned about networking in previous chapters. This process goes beyond just obtaining an IP address and a network connection. You also must obtain many services, such as the DNS. These services also maintain IP addresses and possibly a URL reference. This section describes the role for each of these critical pieces of information.

Connecting Your WAN

The WAN brings your system into the P2P world—a world with millions of potential peers. Your basic WAN goal establishes a connection with an Internet service provider (ISP). Your ISP is your access point into the Internet. The quality of your ISP will directly affect your solution's success. Selecting a poor ISP will haunt your every P2P attempt. Choosing an excellent one will advance each of your solutions. A multitude of ISPs and associated technologies is available. Which one is right for you?

Choosing the Right ISP

Let's establish ISP criteria to help distinguish between the alternatives. Then you can explore and contrast the various alternatives.

The WAN or ISP criteria are as follows:

▼ **Bandwidth**   ISP vendors exist on a foundation technology such as dialup modems, satellites, or cable television that determines their potential bandwidth. The bandwidth determines the speed of information to and from the Internet. Transfers of large files, video, or music are painfully slow over limited bandwidth. Bandwidth varies among ISP vendors by orders of magnitude. Bandwidth can also vary in each direction. Some vendors purposely limit outgoing transfers from your peer to be significantly lower bit rate than incoming transfers.

■ **Reliability**   Reliability covers many factors that contribute to the answer to one question: Can you depend on the connection? No ISP offers 100 percent reliability, but some are much better than others. Reliability includes the ability to connect to the net when you want. You may be blocked because of network congestion or a busy signal.

- **Geographical Availability**   Unfortunately, few peers have universal access to all ISPs. In many cases, your geographical location determines your choices, and in many locations, those choices are quite limited.

- **Cost**   Cost is always a consideration. ISPs typically charge a monthly fee. Most major ISPs price their services similarly. However, small differences quickly add up over many months. Some ISPs offer various packages that may better meet your specific needs.

- **Quality**   Quality goes beyond basic reliability to measure an ISP's ability to deliver consistently *as promised*. This covers consistent response time regardless of time of day or load from your fellow peers. Quality includes Internet services such as e-mail. Another key factor is the ISP's attention to customer support. Some ISPs offer phone support 24 hours, seven days a week, with a minimum hold time. Others don't even provide phone support. This support is critical if the service goes down. Without someone to whom you can address your networking problem, you are on your own; you won't know if the problem is with your system or with the ISP. Such a lack of support is very frustrating and time-consuming.

- **Remote Access**   Some ISPs enable you to connect to them from locations beyond your base location. If you travel and depend on e-mail, remote access can be a vital distinguishing feature.

- **Fixed IP Address**   ISPs assign addresses based on different schemes. The schemes fall into two categories: a fixed IP address or a variable address. The variable address uses an automatic address assignment service, DHCP. A fixed IP address can be attached directly to a URL through registration in a DNS. The fixed address could also be referenced directly in links. A fixed address is easier for both good and bad peers to find. A variable address escapes this two-edged sword. Each time you connect, the ISP assigns a currently available address. However, this book will describe some workarounds that can assign a fixed name to the variable address.

- **Always On**   An ISP connection can remain always on and therefore always available. Typically, this is a peer goal. A dial-up connection via a modem, for example, is not always on—you must initiate a call to create the connection.

- **Constraints**   ISPs often establish "acceptable use policies." These policies attempt to limit the types of activities that you can perform through your connection to the ISP. Typically, they do not allow Internet services such as an FTP or Web (HTTP) service. P2P pokes so many holes into these policies that they are often unenforceable. What exactly is a file transfer via your instant messaging programming? How about music sharing? Be warned that some ISPs are much stricter than others and actively probe your activities.

- ■ **Service Offerings**   An ISP offers other services in addition to basic connectivity to the Internet. The services offered include DNS (essential), e-mail (practically essential), web hosting (simply useless), DHCP (often a necessary evil), and newsgroups.

- ■ **Viability**   Vendors come and go. This is especially true in the unproven technologies and corresponding business models used by many ISPs. When your ISP fails, you are not only inconvenienced, but along with its exit goes your e-mail address and a whole lot more. Lately, viability has become a very serious problem.

- ▲ **Authentication**   Vendors need to know that the computer that connects to the Internet is the one that the bill payer wants to connect. The vendors have various schemes to give them some assurance. This control also allows the ISP to cut you off if the bill goes unpaid or if the ISP detects suspicious behavior.

Selecting the Right ISP Technology

The alternatives exist on two levels—types of technology and specific vendors. Unfortunately, as in the mobile phone industry, the two are intertwined. You cannot pick a technology and then pick a vendor. For better or worse, they go together. Things are starting to change in this area, but for the most part the marriage remains inseparable.

The following are the major types of technology:

- ▼ **Dial-Up**   Dial-up is the traditional way to connect. Your computer modem dials up a modem bank and begins an electronic exchange. Dial-up connections are slow and cumbersome, not to mention noisy. Who likes waiting for the various squeaks and whistles to subside? In its favor, dial-up is highly reliable due to the inherent redundancy and time-tested technology. Providers include EarthLink, AT&T Worldnet, America Online, CompuServe, and MSN.

- ■ **Cable Modem**   The up and coming home-based solution to high-speed Internet access, cable modem is usually referred to as broadband. Cable modem rides on top of your existing cable installation. Cable is installed in most parts of the country, although not all installations can meet the demands of broadband Internet. Cable modem connections suffer from the newness of the technology and the lack of redundancy. If your cable connection breaks, you have no recourse. When cable is good, it is very, very, good; when cable is bad, it is very, very bad. Providers include Comcast, AT&T, and Sprint.

- ■ **Digital Subscriber Line (DSL)**   Cable's rival for the broadband market, DSL, offers a contrasting choice for broadband Internet. It also suffers from its youth. It is built upon the theoretically more dependable wiring of the network, but our practical experience doesn't lend much weight to the theory. Some implementations place additional connection burdens that impair "always on" potential. They force you to make a connection with a login and password. Providers of DSL include Verizon and Sprint.

- ■ **Satellite** Another broadband alternative is satellite. Satellites offer coverage in locations that DSL or cable may not. Like the other broadband alternatives, satellite is a new technology that still has some bugs to work out. Satellite service costs are often much higher, and it also requires the entire satellite setup. A slew of environmental factors can also affect quality. Providers include OptiStream and StarBand.

- ▲ **Ground Wireless** Ground wireless uses technology similar to that of mobile phones. A wonderful idea that is often cost prohibitive, ground wireless also fails to deliver true broadband. Several providers in this area have recently failed, most notably Ricochet.

Table 6-1 contrasts the alternatives with the criteria.

As Table 6-1 indicates, some factors are highly dependent on the specific vendor. Various publications and web sites such as www.cnet.com rate ISPs. If you are lucky, your locale may have a choice of broadband providers. If you're not lucky at all, you may just have to accept a dial-up provider. In any case, none of your P2P solutions are dependent on one provider or another. Your solution's quality will vary according to the speed and quality of the provider, but the solution will work with any provider.

Choosing a Primary and Secondary ISPs

You should definitely select a primary ISP and a backup. A dependable P2P solution cannot rely on only one route to the Internet. Often at critical times, your primary ISP will fail. If you have only one ISP, a failure means no e-mail, no web surfing, and no P2P. You should, as a minimum, choose a broadband ISP as your primary Internet connection and a dial-up ISP as the backup Internet connection. Our primary connection is a cable modem. Our secondary connection is a low-hour usage of a dial-up ISP. Both have failed, but never simultaneously.

Requesting the Right Information of Your ISP

After selecting your ISP, you need specific information from your ISP to achieve your P2P freedom. Understanding this task requires that you delve into arcane network jargon, but this understanding is essential to control your Internet destiny. Many ISP vendors want to load their own software on your computer rather than just give you a connection to the Internet. At first, this seems easiest. You load their CD and, voilá: instant Internet. Such an ISP effectively traps the open standard of the Internet into its own program. You remain tied to the ISP's program and cannot break free into other exciting P2P stuff. If the ISP provides the right information, the vendor does not need to load any software or change any settings. They need not touch your machine at all. Our recommendation is to maintain your computer and let the ISP maintain the connection. A degree of separation is a good thing.

What is the right information to request of the ISP? It is all network-related. Don't let this scare you. The information is straightforward and truly enables P2P. So hold on to your network cards.

ISP Feature	Dial-Up	Cable Modem	DSL	Satellite	Ground Wireless
Bandwidth	Poor	Good – excellent	Good	Good	Fair
Reliability	Excellent	Fair	Fair	Fair	Poor
Availability	Everywhere	Good	Must be close to local phone switching office[1]	Good	Poor
Cost	Low	Medium	Medium	High	Very high
Quality	Varies	Varies	Varies	Varies	Varies
Remote access	Available from any phone, but may be long distance	Limited to your cable connection	Limited to your DSL connection	Limited to your satellite dish	Available only in major markets typically large metropolitan areas
Fixed address	Never	Sometimes	Sometimes	Never	Never
Always on	No	Yes	Depends on provider	Depends on provider	No
Constraints	Vary	Vary	Vary	Vary	Vary
Service offerings	Vary	Vary	Vary	Vary	Vary
Technology viability	Excellent	Good	Good	Fair	Poor
Vendor viability	Usually established	Still early	Still early	Still early	Poor
Authentication	Login and password	Reverse IP address lookup	Login and password	Login and password	Login and password

[1]You need to call your local phone service provider to determine if you are within the range of distance eligible for high-speed DSL.

Table 6-1.   Comparison of Technology Alternatives

The first important piece of information is the addressing assignment method used by your selected ISP. The ISP either assigns you a fixed IP address or a variable one via requests placed to the DHCP service. Using DHCP is straightforward. You just inform your system to use DHCP to acquire a network address and it provides an available one each time that you connect to the Internet. The other option is a fixed IP address. A fixed IP address requires setting the address manually. A fixed IP address also demands two other key information elements. The first is the IP address of the network gateway. The gateway handles any IP address not found in the local network. The gateway forwards requests beyond the direct network. Without a gateway, your system is trapped within the ISP's local network—not a fun place, usually.

The final addressing element is the network subnet mask. This subnet mask is a scheme to expand the number of network endpoints. Your system will not work properly without the correct subnet mask. A typical subnet mask is 255.255.255.0. This mask eliminates all the local address components in an IP address except the last address. Thus 192.168.1.7 reduces to 7. This subnet mask also enables up to 256 addresses, for you can set the last field anywhere from 0 to 255. Figure 6-1 shows the network settings for both situations in the Windows 2000 operating system.

The next piece of information is the IP addresses of your DNS services. Remember that the DNS turns your URL (for example, www.p2pcosmos.com) into a useful IP address. An ISP offers two possibilities here: List one or more DNS IP addresses that you set in your network, or enable automatic download of the DNS via DHCP. An ISP should always have more than one DNS. A single DNS presents a critical single point of failure. Your system just marches through the list of DNS address until it finds a successful translation from URL to IP address. The lower panel shown in Figure 6-1 also illustrates the network settings for DNS.

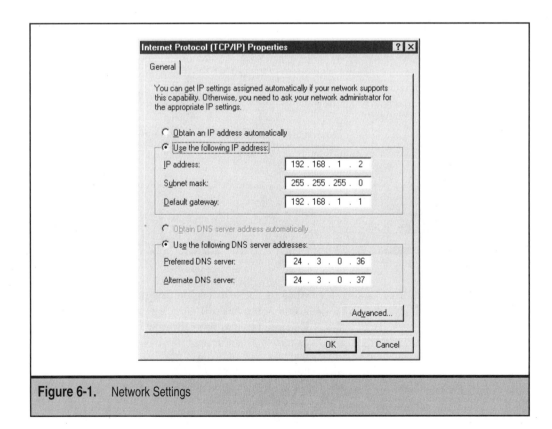

Figure 6-1. Network Settings

The next piece of information regards authentication. Authentication proves that you, the paying customer, are the person you claim to be. Different technologies demand different approaches. The traditional method requires a login and password. The ISP provides you with the login and password. You dutifully enter the information on demand. Dial-ups use this method exclusively. Surprisingly, so do some DSL providers. Broadband, always-on connections implement various schemes beyond login and password. The one favored is a reverse lookup. The network gateway examines the IP address and/or the machine name to verify that it originates from a paying customer and not an interloper. You need to determine how the ISP verifies identity. This may require logging in or setting your system to a given name. If you configure this setting incorrectly, the network will refuse to transmit your requests and appears like a network failure. Figure 6-2 shows a screen in which you set the network name for your machine.

The final pieces of necessary information surround the various services provided by ISPs. These include mail servers and news servers. Mail servers require two URLs. One URL receives incoming e-mail. This is commonly known as the Post Office Protocol 3 (POP3) server. Incoming mail usually has an independent security system and requires an additional login and password. The second mail URL enables you to send outgoing mail. This is commonly known as Simple Mail Transfer Protocol (SMTP). SMTP does not

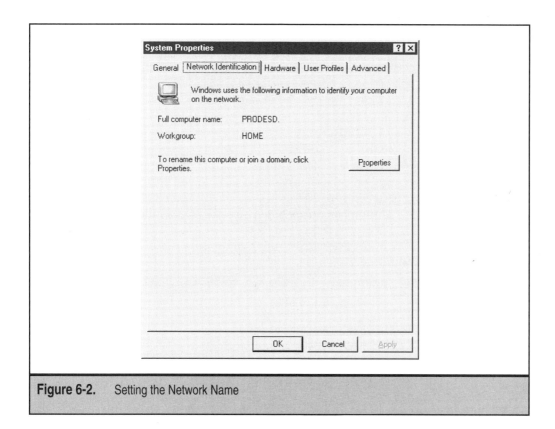

Figure 6-2.   Setting the Network Name

require authorization via a login. Thus, ISPs must watch SMTP activity to see whether any of their customers abuse the SMTP server by sending thousands of e-mails.

Such abuse not only creates spam for all of the recipients but also significantly degrades the performance of the SMTP server. An ISP often restricts the use SMTP services to IP addresses that the ISP administers (that is, the addresses of the ISP's customers). This prevents non-customers from using the SMTP server to send their e-mail. POP3 and SMTP services are distinct services that each use different standard ports—110 and 25, respectively. The mail services can exist on the same machine or different machines. This is why there are URL entries for each service.

A key area to consider when selecting an ISP is the ability to obtain these services when you are outside their coverage area. You may want to obtain your e-mail from a computer connected to the Internet via a different ISP. Such a setup might be useful, for example, when you are attending a conference that sets aside connected computers for its attendees. A cable provider might enable remote access (without connecting via your cable connection) to the POP3 server but not the SMTP server. This not only requires setting up an e-mail client such as Microsoft Outlook but also has the awkward effect of disabling you from replying to e-mails. Other ISP vendors offer a web interface into your e-mail. A web interface disallows direct access to the SMTP server and thus allows you to send mail despite being outside of your ISP's coverage area. You can access the web interface from any computer connected to the Internet, and if you enter the correct password, the interface allows the full access to your e-mail.

Two other services are worth mentioning: news and ping. A news server allows access to the various newsgroups. These newsgroups offer a treasure trove of information. The site www.dejanews.com offers a web interface for searching newsgroups. This site can help you narrow down the thousands of newsgroups to the useful ones for your particular concerns. A URL identifies the ISP's news server.

A ping service allows you to determine network connectivity quickly. You could ping a computer continuously to notify you instantly when it encounters problems, or you could ping on demand whenever you suspect problems. You can ping computers using either their URL or their IP address. If you are having e-mail troubles, you can ping the e-mail machine to determine whether it is operational. This test ensures that the network connection is working between your peer and your e-mail server. It does not guarantee that the e-mail service is running. If you are having trouble translating addresses, you can ping your DNS servers.

Making an ISP Checklist

The following checklist summarizes the information that you need to obtain regarding your ISP:

▼ Addressing method (fixed or DHCP)

■ If the addressing method is fixed, IP address, gateway IP address, and IP subnet mask

■ DNS addressing method (fixed or DHCP)

- If you choose a fixed address, a list of DNS IP addresses
- Authentication method (login or machine name)
- If you choose the login method, the login and password
- If you choose the machine name method, the required name
- Incoming e-mail server URL (POP3)
- Outgoing e-mail server URL (SMTP)
- News server URL (NNTP)
- ▲ If you are using a dial-up ISP, the complete phone list containing local and remote numbers (the latter provides coverage for possible trips away from home)

If you have a complete list, you are now ready to populate your network settings and connect.

Connecting Your LAN

More and more peer locations contain more than one computer. These computers can form their own network to share each other's resources. Software and hardware tools allow you to form a subnetwork quickly that contains your entire set of P2P resources. The subnetwork or LAN can allow higher privileges and greater trust among its local network members while preserving a level of distrust of the larger Internet. These privileges can include sharing resources such as printers, cameras, disk drives, and the Internet. You can also allow controlled exchanges between the LAN and the WAN.

This section looks at three types of connections to help you in your quest to connect locally: a direct connection with a proxy server, a hub connection with a proxy server, and a network router connection. In the process, you'll learn about several network devices and the proxy software application.

A Direct Connection with a Proxy Server

The first network solution connects the computers directly. The network card of one computer connects directly to another computer's network card. Obviously, this technique is limited to two computers, but some networks only consist of two computers. This direct connection requires a special network connecting cord that reverses some leads. This cord is called a network crossover cable. It is usually color-coded to indicate that it is not a normal network cable. This cable connects the two computers.

Now that you have created your own network, what IP address should you set in your computers? An address range has been set aside for LAN environments. The address range locks down the first two IP address numbers and allows you to select the last two. The first two IP addresses are 192.168. It is a convention not to use these addresses anywhere within the broader Internet. They are reserved for subnets. This preserves the address range for everyone LAN environment without conflicting with the WAN/Internet environment. Sticking to these guidelines, you should use 192.168.1.1

and 192.168.1.2. This convention, once learned, is also easy to remember, for it is consistent across all LANs.

To interact with both the LAN and the WAN/Internet connection, you need a software and hardware arrangement that enables a controlled bridging of the two networks. The arrangement includes a proxy software application and another network card connected to the Internet. The proxy application receives requests via one network connection and redirects them to the other network connection. Thus, the proxy switches back and forth between the LAN to WAN connection. The proxy acts as a go-between for the LAN and the WAN. For example, suppose your LAN consists of two computers (and associated network cards) that are set to the IP addresses 192.168.1.1 and 192.168.1.2. The first computer has an additional network card configured to the IP address 67.16.246.162. The proxy moves communication exchanges from the 192.168.1 network (LAN) to the 67.16.246 network (WAN). Figure 6-3 illustrates the direct connection LAN.

The next example uses a simple, straightforward proxy by nycsoftware called, appropriately, Easy Proxy. The computer that is not directly connected to the Internet sets the proxy setting of network applications like a browser to the IP address of the Internet-connected computer and the port dictated by the proxy. Figure 6-4 illustrates the Easy Proxy application.

The Easy Proxy application indicates the proxy settings for the browser on the other machine. The application tells the browser to redirect requests to IP address 192.168.1.1 on port 1080. Figure 6-5 shows the setting in Internet Explorer.

The proxy settings redirect all Internet requests to go to 192.168.1.1 on port 1080 rather than to the direct address of the Web site on port 80. Direct attempts to connect with the Internet would fail because the machine is not directly connected to the Internet; rather, it is directly connected to the LAN.

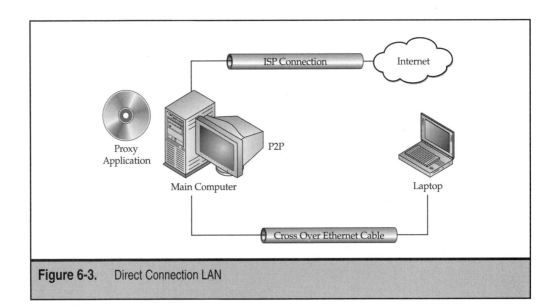

Figure 6-3. Direct Connection LAN

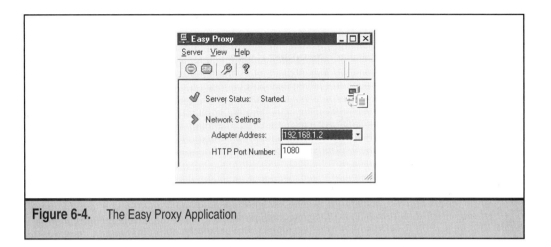

Figure 6-4.   The Easy Proxy Application

A Hub Connection with a Proxy Server

A direct connection works adequately in a laptop situation, but is quickly quite limiting. The next step is to add a hub hardware component. A hub is basically a local network extension cord. You plug each computer's network cable directly into the hub. You can purchase hubs with various numbers of connections depending on your needs. You can also string hubs together to grow your capabilities gradually. A hub adds no real intelligence to

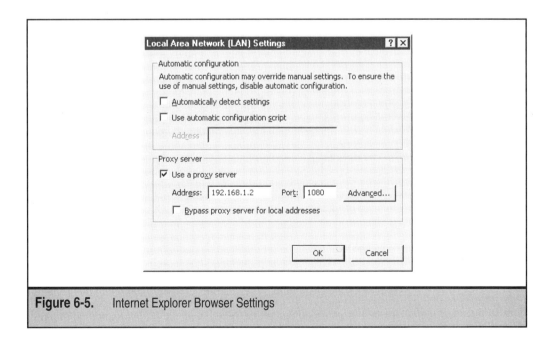

Figure 6-5.   Internet Explorer Browser Settings

the network. It simply allows multiple connections of locally networked computers. The hub only extends your LAN. You cannot just plug in the Internet connection using a hub.

The Internet connection exists on another network. You still need the proxy to allow your LAN to cross over into the WAN/Internet. This is just as well, because the hub offers no protection and therefore would be unable to isolate the local network from the Internet. One of your computers remains connected to both the LAN and the WAN via two network cards, as in the previous example, and uses a proxy application to handle the controlled exchange between the two networks. Figure 6-6 illustrates a hub network with the associated proxy application.

A Network Router Connection

The next network configuration adds a network router. A network router is a hardware component that combines the services of a proxy server, two network cards, and a hub all in one hardware component. Similar to the role of the proxy and the required two network cards, the role of the router is to represent all the machines connected to any computer outside of the router's domain. The router becomes the machine that is connected to the Internet. This is a very important concept. Your network settings—such as the IP address and gateway IP address—transfer to the router. The router performs the translations between your LAN and WAN. Figure 6-7 illustrates the initial setup for the Linksys Internet router.

Figure 6-7 shows the familiar fields, discussed earlier, including the host name, the IP address, subnet mask, gateway IP address, and the settings for your DNS addresses. These

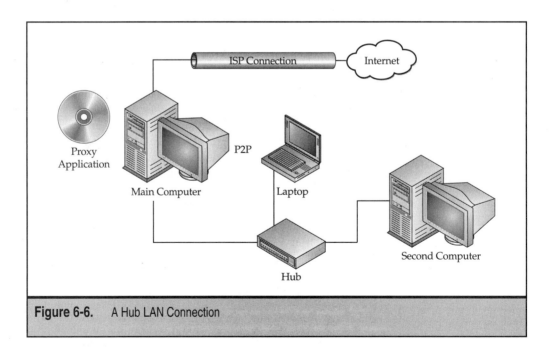

Figure 6-6.   A Hub LAN Connection

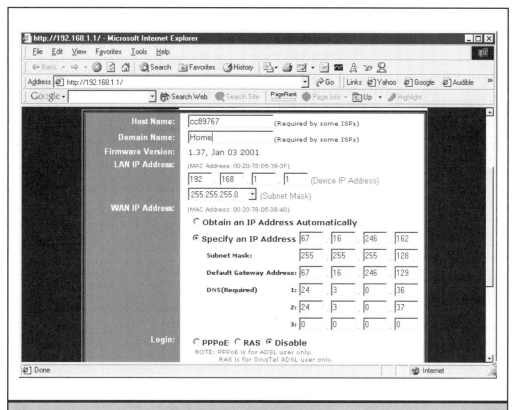

Figure 6-7. Linksys Internet Router Setup

settings become the settings for the router. The router itself actually has two IP addresses. One is the external WAN IP address, which is assigned by the ISP. The other is the internal LAN IP address, which is assigned according to your LAN needs. In Figure 6-7, the external IP address is set to 67.16.246.162. Figure 6-13 also shows the internal router address set to 192.168.1.1. Internet users would use the external address and local users would use the internal address. You are free to create your own addressing scheme for the connected computers. Your scheme might, for example, have the router assign the address via DHCP. The Linksys router contains a web server that responds to LAN requests to the internal address. Routers can also offer external access via the ISP-provided address.

Typically, routers control access via a login and password. If you use a router, make sure you change this password from the default provided by the manufacturer. Also, you should generally avoid enabling remote or external access to the router. If someone breaks into the router, that hacker controls your network configuration and can wreak network chaos.

The router examines each incoming packet and performs a lookup to determine which of the connected computers should receive the packet. The router acts like an old-fashioned switchboard. As with the proxy, this scheme has the additional benefit of hiding the underlying network from prying packets. Unlike the proxy application, a router is a separate hardware component. The router offloads the processing requirements from the main Internet computer. It also no longer requires a "main" computer connected to the Internet that the other computers traverse. The proxy approach discussed previously creates problems any time the main computer is not working. In addition, none of your computers needs to have two network cards since the router tackles the network transfer. Figure 6-8 illustrates a router network.

Combination Schemes

As you might expect, you can combine all of these schemes to create a complex network. Figure 6-9 illustrates a router network expanded by the use of multiple hubs. With our collection of computers and network connection devices, our network has grown to resemble Figure 6-9.

Wireless Network Capability

A nice addition to your network is wireless network capability. You can achieve this through hardware that implements the 802.11b or WiFi standard. It creates a wireless access point that plugs into the hubs or routers already discussed. The WiFi component sends the wireless network to a receiving wireless network card. This requires the wireless access point component as well as a wireless network card so that you can receive peer computers. You are not limited to one wireless device.

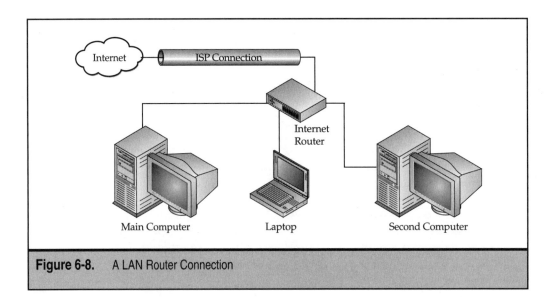

Figure 6-8. A LAN Router Connection

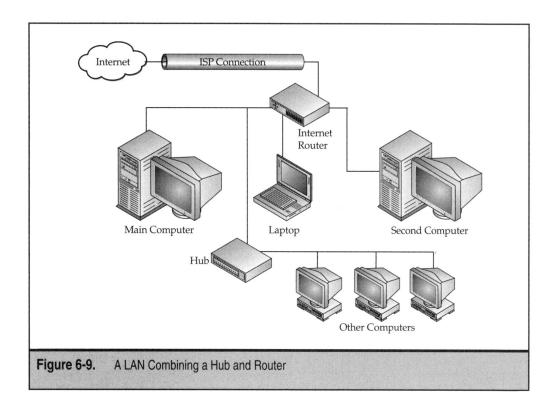

Figure 6-9.   A LAN Combining a Hub and Router

Your network can grow up to the LAN limitations, which are typically 256. Thus you are able to connect up to 256 different address. This is more than ample for the typical home environments and also is sufficient for many business environments. Wireless set-ups free you to establish new network locations without costly and time-consuming wiring. You are also free to work on your patio on a beautiful summer day. Figure 6-10 illustrates the combo network with a wireless addition. WiFi is limited to a slower rate than directly wired networking. This is not a factor with the Internet, because Wifi is still significantly faster than current broadband. However, the slower rate would impact local network transfers.

A Comprehensive Network

As a summary and a wonderful network setup, we now put a comprehensive network all together. Our network environment includes a broadband and dial-up ISP combined with a local area network consisting of a router, hub, and WiFi wireless access point. This setup enables a any computer in the local network to leverage all the computing resources within the local network and offers a shared, common pathway to the Internet. The common pathway offers two methods to avoid a single point of failure. Figure 6-11 illustrates this ultimate P2P network.

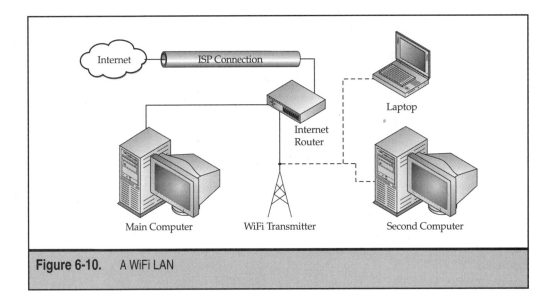

Figure 6-10.   A WiFi LAN

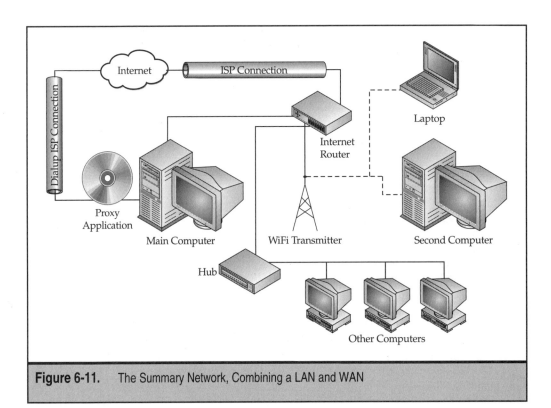

Figure 6-11.   The Summary Network, Combining a LAN and WAN

Getting connected offers many P2P benefits. You can share information, hardware resources, and connections. But you must protect yourself from all the potential problems out in the big, wild Internet. The connection may allow unscrupulous folks to examine or alter your P2P world.

GETTING SECURE

Now that all your computers are connected to the Internet, you need to make your peer world secure—very secure. Getting secure expands on the previous network setup and requires some additional delving into networks and their operations.

Luckily, all of your troubling traffic enters via your Internet connection from your ISP. You can also use the following approach to protect exchanges between computers on a LAN, but we hope your local situation is not so troubling. The LAN, being your local computing environment, is usually a trusted environment where protection is not necessary. You need to place a guard at that single point of entry. Your security guard examines the traffic for overall acceptance. This security cannot delve into every possibility but rather sticks to simple but effective rules. The security guard typically has two sets of rules:

▼ **Watch any requests, especially *incoming* requests**   Outgoing requests are ones that your machine initiates. These outgoing requests are mostly actions you directed. With the complexity of today's computing environment, however, this is not always the case. Incoming requests are those that originate somewhere out in the network. Your peer didn't initiate them. Incoming requests, by their nature, are more suspect, although not all of them are bad. They seek out a friendly listener application on your peer. P2P opens resources to outside peers via applications that listen for these inbound requests. The security system allows only inbound requests that you have generally approved. Security applications usually come configured to allow all typical legitimate exchanges such as an outgoing Web site request.

▲ **Allow communication only on specified port numbers or special protocols**   All network applications use ports to distinguish among the many applications running on your machine. They register this port number with the operating system network software. The network software examines the port number contained in the network exchange, then passes the number on to the application listening on the given port. If no application is listening, the software discards the packet. The security implementation can block any port number exchanged with the Internet that has not been specifically approved. Many network applications are intended only for the local network. They share sensitive resources such as disk drives. Security must disallow any remote access from the Internet on these sensitive ports. This type of protection is essential. Modern network setups have dozens of network applications. See the next section for a peek at the multitude of network applications. Some network applications do not rely on ports at all. They use special protocols. Ping, the program to test network connectivity, uses Internet Control Message Protocol (ICMP). You can also set security to block these protocols.

Security protection focuses on incoming requests on certain ports. These are typically the most suspicious requests.

How Many Network Listeners Do You Have?

How many listeners does your peer have? To find out, try running the following commands.

For Windows and UNIX operating systems, the command *netstat* reveals all. First, let's see an example of current connections on my peer:

```
C:\>netstat

Active Connections

  Proto  Local Address          Foreign Address         State
  TCP    PRODESD:netbios-ssn    DELL200PRO:2762         ESTABLISHED
  TCP    PRODESD:1081           columbia:netbios-ssn    ESTABLISHED
  TCP    PRODESD:1089           cs16.msg.yahoo.com:smtp ESTABLISHED
  TCP    PRODESD:1098           columbia:5222           ESTABLISHED
  TCP    PRODESD:1104           unknown.Level3.net:2492 ESTABLISHED
  TCP    PRODESD:2088           DELL200PRO:netbios-ssn  ESTABLISHED
  TCP    PRODESD:2430           unknown.Level3.net:2492 ESTABLISHED
  TCP    PRODESD:2629           216.129.199.160:1214    ESTABLISHED
  TCP    PRODESD:2664           cc722871-a.mtpls1.sc.home.com:1214   ESTABLISHED
  TCP    PRODESD:2671           cc722871-a.mtpls1.sc.home.com:1214   ESTABLISHED
  TCP    PRODESD:2962           www.google.com:http     CLOSE_WAIT
  TCP    PRODESD:2975           www.google.com:http     CLOSE_WAIT
  TCP    PRODESD:2984           slip-32-101-128-226.mn.us.prserv.net:1214   ESTABLISHED


  TCP    PRODESD:3071           www.google.com:http     CLOSE_WAIT
  TCP    PRODESD:3125           cc302778-b.wlgrv1.pa.home.com:1214   TIME_WAIT
  TCP    PRODESD:3128           cc302778-b.wlgrv1.pa.home.com:1214   ESTABLISHED
  TCP    PRODESD:3131           host177056.arnet.net.ar:1214   TIME_WAIT
  TCP    PRODESD:4749           www.google.com:http     CLOSE_WAIT

C:\>
```

This command provides only the active connections. The next command lists all connections:

```
C:\>netstat -a
Active Connections
  Proto  Local Address          Foreign Address         State
  TCP    PRODESD:echo           PRODESD:0              LISTENING
  TCP    PRODESD:discard        PRODESD:0              LISTENING
  TCP    PRODESD:daytime        PRODESD:0              LISTENING
  TCP    PRODESD:qotd           PRODESD:0              LISTENING
```

TCP	PRODESD:chargen	PRODESD:0	LISTENING
TCP	PRODESD:ftp	PRODESD:0	LISTENING
TCP	PRODESD:smtp	PRODESD:0	LISTENING
TCP	PRODESD:finger	PRODESD:0	LISTENING
TCP	PRODESD:106	PRODESD:0	LISTENING
TCP	PRODESD:pop3	PRODESD:0	LISTENING
TCP	PRODESD:epmap	PRODESD:0	LISTENING
TCP	PRODESD:imap	PRODESD:0	LISTENING
TCP	PRODESD:https	PRODESD:0	LISTENING
TCP	PRODESD:microsoft-ds	PRODESD:0	LISTENING
TCP	PRODESD:1025	PRODESD:0	LISTENING
TCP	PRODESD:1026	PRODESD:0	LISTENING
TCP	PRODESD:1033	PRODESD:0	LISTENING
TCP	PRODESD:1040	PRODESD:0	LISTENING
TCP	PRODESD:1043	PRODESD:0	LISTENING
TCP	PRODESD:1089	PRODESD:0	LISTENING
TCP	PRODESD:1098	PRODESD:0	LISTENING
TCP	PRODESD:1104	PRODESD:0	LISTENING
TCP	PRODESD:1214	PRODESD:0	LISTENING
TCP	PRODESD:ms-sql-s	PRODESD:0	LISTENING
TCP	PRODESD:1755	PRODESD:0	LISTENING
TCP	PRODESD:1801	PRODESD:0	LISTENING
TCP	PRODESD:2430	PRODESD:0	LISTENING
TCP	PRODESD:2492	PRODESD:0	LISTENING
TCP	PRODESD:2629	PRODESD:0	LISTENING
TCP	PRODESD:2664	PRODESD:0	LISTENING
TCP	PRODESD:2671	PRODESD:0	LISTENING
TCP	PRODESD:2962	PRODESD:0	LISTENING
TCP	PRODESD:2975	PRODESD:0	LISTENING
TCP	PRODESD:2984	PRODESD:0	LISTENING
TCP	PRODESD:3050	PRODESD:0	LISTENING
TCP	PRODESD:3071	PRODESD:0	LISTENING
TCP	PRODESD:3128	PRODESD:0	LISTENING
TCP	PRODESD:3372	PRODESD:0	LISTENING
TCP	PRODESD:3389	PRODESD:0	LISTENING
TCP	PRODESD:3849	PRODESD:0	LISTENING
TCP	PRODESD:4749	PRODESD:0	LISTENING
TCP	PRODESD:6666	PRODESD:0	LISTENING
TCP	PRODESD:7007	PRODESD:0	LISTENING
TCP	PRODESD:7778	PRODESD:0	LISTENING
TCP	PRODESD:8020	PRODESD:0	LISTENING
TCP	PRODESD:8025	PRODESD:0	LISTENING
TCP	PRODESD:8080	PRODESD:0	LISTENING
TCP	PRODESD:8888	PRODESD:0	LISTENING
TCP	PRODESD:9000	PRODESD:0	LISTENING
TCP	PRODESD:9078	PRODESD:0	LISTENING
TCP	PRODESD:netbios-ssn	PRODESD:0	LISTENING
TCP	PRODESD:netbios-ssn	DELL200PRO:2762	ESTABLISHED
TCP	PRODESD:1036	PRODESD:0	LISTENING
TCP	PRODESD:1081	PRODESD:0	LISTENING

```
TCP    PRODESD:1081        columbia:netbios-ssn    ESTABLISHED
TCP    PRODESD:1089        cs16.msg.yahoo.com:smtp  ESTABLISHED
TCP    PRODESD:1098        columbia:5222           ESTABLISHED
TCP    PRODESD:1104        unknown.Level3.net:2492  ESTABLISHED
TCP    PRODESD:2088        PRODESD:0               LISTENING
TCP    PRODESD:2088        DELL200PRO:netbios-ssn  ESTABLISHED
TCP    PRODESD:2103        PRODESD:0               LISTENING
TCP    PRODESD:2105        PRODESD:0               LISTENING
TCP    PRODESD:2107        PRODESD:0               LISTENING
TCP    PRODESD:2430        unknown.Level3.net:2492  ESTABLISHED
TCP    PRODESD:2629        216.129.199.160:1214    ESTABLISHED
TCP    PRODESD:2664        cc722871-a.mtpls1.sc.home.com:1214   ESTABLISHED
TCP    PRODESD:2671        cc722871-a.mtpls1.sc.home.com:1214   ESTABLISHED
TCP    PRODESD:2962        www.google.com:http     CLOSE_WAIT
TCP    PRODESD:2975        www.google.com:http     CLOSE_WAIT
TCP    PRODESD:2984        slip-32-101-128-226.mn.us.prserv.net:1214   ESTABLLISHED


TCP    PRODESD:3071        www.google.com:http     CLOSE_WAIT
TCP    PRODESD:3128        cc302778-b.wlgrv1.pa.home.com:1214   ESTABLISHED
TCP    PRODESD:3131        host177056.arnet.net.ar:1214   TIME_WAIT
TCP    PRODESD:4749        www.google.com:http     CLOSE_WAIT
UDP    PRODESD:echo        *:*
UDP    PRODESD:discard     *:*
UDP    PRODESD:daytime     *:*
UDP    PRODESD:qotd        *:*
UDP    PRODESD:chargen     *:*
UDP    PRODESD:epmap       *:*
UDP    PRODESD:snmptrap    *:*
UDP    PRODESD:microsoft-ds *:*
UDP    PRODESD:1034        *:*
UDP    PRODESD:1035        *:*
UDP    PRODESD:1042        *:*
UDP    PRODESD:1084        *:*
UDP    PRODESD:1123        *:*
UDP    PRODESD:1211        *:*
UDP    PRODESD:1755        *:*
UDP    PRODESD:3456        *:*
UDP    PRODESD:3527        *:*
UDP    PRODESD:38037       *:*
UDP    PRODESD:1177        *:*
UDP    PRODESD:1350        *:*
UDP    PRODESD:2508        *:*
UDP    PRODESD:2656        *:*
UDP    PRODESD:2707        *:*
UDP    PRODESD:2820        *:*
UDP    PRODESD:2901        *:*
UDP    PRODESD:3292        *:*
```

```
UDP      PRODESD:netbios-ns      *:*
UDP      PRODESD:netbios-dgm     *:*
UDP      PRODESD:isakmp          *:*

C:\>
```

As this section indicates, a typical computer has a multitude of network activity. Many of these network application listeners should not be exposed to the Internet. They share sensitive resources including printers and files. These are fine, in fact essential, for the local network. Rather than make a rule to block each one, you must tell the security guard which ports are acceptable. By default, a security guard blocks incoming request on all ports. This works out quite well for P2P solutions, which have assigned ports. These specific ports are identified to the security guard for safe passage. All other ports are blocked.

The basic job of system security is to block incoming requests on all ports except the ones noted. The security guard can also go further in the examination of the ports and allow only certain protocols or certain IP addresses.

Implementing System Security

You have two choices with which to address system security: a software solution or a hardware solution. Both have their advantages and disadvantages. The software solution requires no additional wiring but takes a slice of your computer's performance. It also fully exposes your computer to the Internet. A hardware solution isolates protection in a specific box but requires additional wiring. Both solutions work similarly. They stand guard between the Internet connection and your subnet. You establish rules to guide exchanges. You can enter rules to allow or disallow Internet communication based on the remote IP address, the local IP address, the port number, and/or the type of protocol. Typically, a default set of rules is already installed and you adjust them to you particular needs.

The software solution consists of a proxy or firewall software application that stands between your Internet connection and the rest of your system. Since the proxy is already intercepting Internet communication, it is relatively easy for the vendor to add security features. The Easy Proxy application, discussed earlier, does not have this capability, but more sophisticated applications, such as Deerfield's Wingate, have this blocking capability. A software firewall is a stand-alone application. Its sole purpose is to guard your Internet connection. If you only have one computer, you do not need a proxy; the straightforward firewall does the job.

The new tools are quite user-friendly and do not require extensive networking skills. Figure 6-12 illustrates Norton's Personal Firewall application. This application warns you when questionable Internet communication events occur. You can then agree to establish a rule to allow or disallow all similar future exchanges. You can also just enable the specific transfer in question. Figure 6-13 shows a warning screen that the application generates when Groove accesses the Internet.

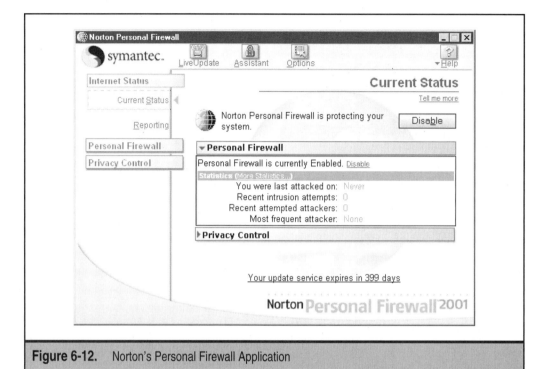

Figure 6-12. Norton's Personal Firewall Application

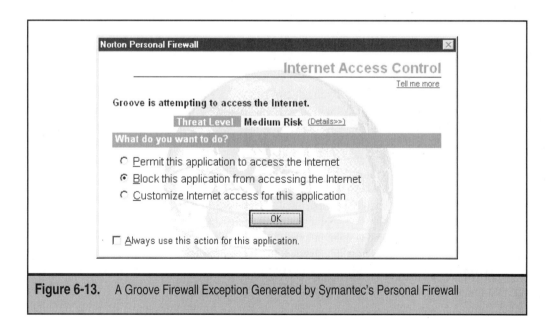

Figure 6-13. A Groove Firewall Exception Generated by Symantec's Personal Firewall

So do you use a software proxy or firewall? A firewall protects one machine. A software proxy protects multiple machines and shares the Internet connection. The determinant is whether you have a single computer or multiple computers.

Another option is using a hardware firewall. These hardware firewalls often combine with a router to give you functionality similar to a software proxy application. The hardware eliminates your need to burden one of your computers with an additional software application as well as your need to use two network cards. Each computer connects to the hardware firewall/router. You then establish communication rules inside the device. Typically, you connect via a simple URL web request to the hardware's internal web server.

The protection provided by the router works in two directions: outgoing requests and incoming requests. You can prevent a computer from accessing specific Internet addresses and/or ports. You can also restrict incoming requests based on the address and/or port number.

The Linksys box discussed earlier prevents outgoing requests through filtering. The settings in Figure 6-14 would disallow computers with IP addresses in the range of

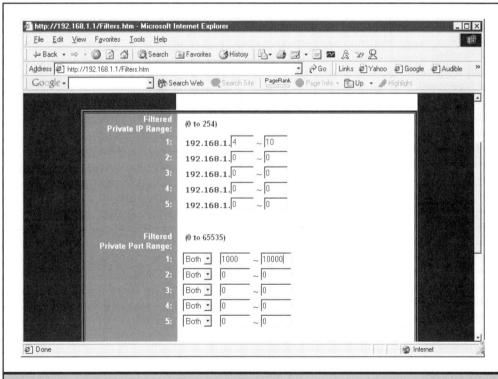

Figure 6-14. Linksys's Outgoing Internet Filter Screen

192.168.1.4 to 192.168.1.10 from accessing any exchanges on ports 1000 to 10000. This allows a high level of control on direct peer activity. Most peers do not use this option and remain open to rogue programs resident on your LAN. You should consider blocking all outgoing ports unless you specify that a port can send requests.

The other direction, incoming requests, usually poses the real danger. The incoming requests represent your offerings to the P2P world. You cannot simply abandon all ports and limit your P2P world to the LAN. Instead, you forward ports to specific computers in your network that offer that service. Figure 6-15 illustrates the ports that I forward for my P2P services. It starts to get quite complex. I have to track the reason for each port in a database. For example, port 9078 is my Microsoft IIS Web server and port 5222 is the instant messaging Jabber server.

Port forwarding allows you to specify which ports are acceptable. These are the ports you watch carefully. The firewall silently discards incoming requests from other ports. These requests never reach your computers.

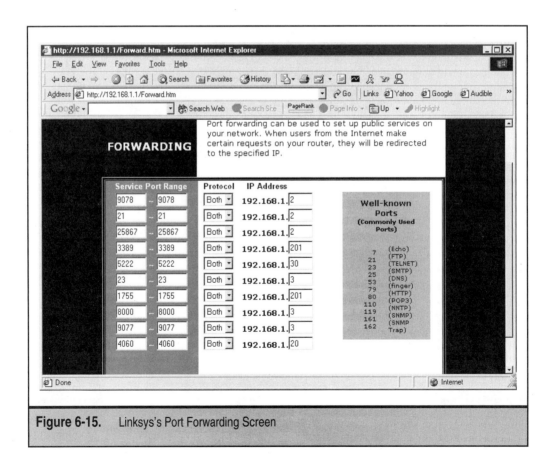

Figure 6-15.   Linksys's Port Forwarding Screen

Monitoring Your Security

Security requires some vigilance. You may need to adjust security based on what is happening to your Internet connection. A recent virus attacked Microsoft IIS Web servers by implanting a program that sought out other IIS servers in hopes of propagating the virus. Monitoring revealed a sharp upswing in port 80 requests. I installed the patch and moved the port of my web server to the current 9078. I am still receiving port 80 requests from infected servers months after the incident. Port 80 requests no longer bother my web server because the firewall stops them.

Firewalls and proxies come with reporting facilities to allow the monitoring of network activity. They can record every single network exchange. This quickly buries the essential information. There are tools that sift through the mound of information looking for specific pieces of information. You need to focus primarily on incoming requests. Figure 6-16 shows an incoming report provided by the Linksys router.

As Figure 6-16 clearly indicates, the IIS virus is alive and kicking. Most of the requests originate from other ISP members connected to my ISP. This is indicated from the IP ad-

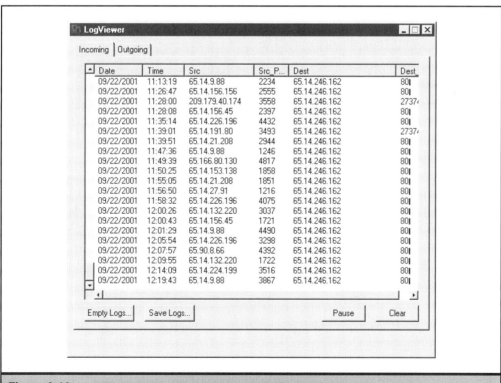

Figure 6-16.   Linksys Incoming Request Firewall Report

dresses. They are attempting to connect to a port 80 listener. Since port 80 is blocked, the request stops at the firewall.

In addition, the report enables you to examine the outbound requests. This gives you control over outgoing requests. The report also includes the URL rather than just the IP address. This report also identifies the machine that originated the request on the local network.

These reports allow you to refine your security policies with regard to incoming request and outgoing requests. Although relatively crude, the reports are adequate for most peer situations. You can purchase fancier software if the need warrants.

Protecting Against Viruses

Your peer couldn't be fully secure without protection from computer viruses. These evildoers obtain access to your computer through deceptive means that evade the restrictions imposed by simple firewall rules. Although they gain entry through a variety of means, they all have to transfer into your computer from outside. They could travel via the Internet, but they also could travel via a floppy disk or a local network connection. Therefore, firewalls are not sufficient to protect against virus protection. You need software that watches all doorways into your computer for the nasty buggers.

Viruses, by their very nature, mutate as fixes are identified and installed. They also grow as new applications' and operating systems' defects surface. Each could have potential holes that allow a virus to thrive.

The solution is to acquire a virus software application *and* its corresponding subscription of updates. The updates are essential to protect against the new types and mutations of existing ones.

You can protect against viruses in three ways: on-demand, scheduled, or event-driven virus checking. On-demand is exactly that: You run the virus check whenever you feel that it is necessary. Scheduled checks run at a regular interval and time. This allows you to run virus checking at a time when other applications do not need the computer's resources. Virus checking taxes your computer's resources, as the software has to check every file. It is a good idea to run the software after business hours. The third option runs virus checking whenever an exchange takes place that could potentially introduce a virus. This is the most secure scheme, but it requires checking every transmission. This level of checking can impact performance, but it provides a very high level of security.

You now have built a firewall to guard your system against improper incoming or outgoing requests, and have installed virus protection software to inoculate your system against viruses. You are now ready to broadcast your entry to the P2P world. Let's give you a real electronic address.

GETTING KNOWN

You are connected and secure—or at least your computer is. It is time to raise the world's awareness of your P2P offering and make it easy to find. Addressing your P2P system, like naming as discussed earlier, is a tricky and challenging problem. The network world offers many address books. Many of these electronic address services are specialized for specific applications such as instant messaging or music sharing. This section sidesteps these application-specific issues and leaves them for later. First, you aim at the big naming electronic directory—the DNS. The DNS is universally accepted to tackle the job of translating a URL to an IP address. It is independent from any entanglements with specific applications. The DNS system is highly distributed, scalable, and available.

The DNS system reserves a name that represents *any* resource across the entire Internet. DNS is not without its drawbacks. First, this name is so valuable that it costs money. This cost is a logical deterrent to the typical P2P developer. However, there are no cost alternatives that gain your entry into the DNS system. The second major deterrent is that DNS works with static, fixed IP addresses. Many P2P connections do not have fixed IP addresses. Dial-up users never have fixed IP addresses, and many broadband providers use DHCP to administer IP addresses. Here too, there are alternatives. You can actually create a dedicated URL for a variable IP address that costs nothing. This may not be the best choice for all P2P solutions, but it is available if you need it.

Getting Known with a Fixed IP Address

Getting known with a fixed IP address is straightforward and easy. The stability of a fixed IP address aligns well with the basic operation of the DNS.

The most logical first step would be to ask your ISP vendor to register your chosen .com name and associate it with your fixed IP address. However, an ISP would not want you running an addressable service such as a Web site. Fearing the impact to bandwidth, your ISP would push you toward business-level agreements with corresponding high prices. So even if you had a fixed IP address, you would still be out of luck. Fortunately, however, several vendors have successfully jumped in to fill this P2P void.

We entered several .com names associated with our fixed IP addresses by using www.register.com. Register.com charges $30 a year for each name. (There is no way around acquiring a direct .com name without some fee.) We registered p2pcosmos.com for the $30 fee. This gives us the right to set the associated IP addresses. We set the primary address for p2pcosmos.com to the ISP-supplied fixed IP address. The register.com service also offers some other goodies. You can set additional IP addresses with names adjacent to the main name. For example, we added ebmagic.p2pcosmos.com to point to a different IP address. You could establish an entire network of computers with URLs under the main name. This, of course, requires a fixed IP address for each machine. Figure 6-17 shows the current IP assignments for our URL, p2pcosmos.com.

We could add an additional IP address, delete an existing one, or edit an existing one. This simple interface enables you to be your own DNS manager from anywhere in the world. This is much easier than the direct manipulation of a DNS server. Register.com is a major empowerment for a peer user to enter the DNS world. The cost to entry, however, is prohibitive to most peers, for you need a fixed IP address and, of course, $30.

If you are lucky enough to have a fixed IP address, select a name and try it out. Just be ready to buy on the spot and have several acceptable names. Then associate the name

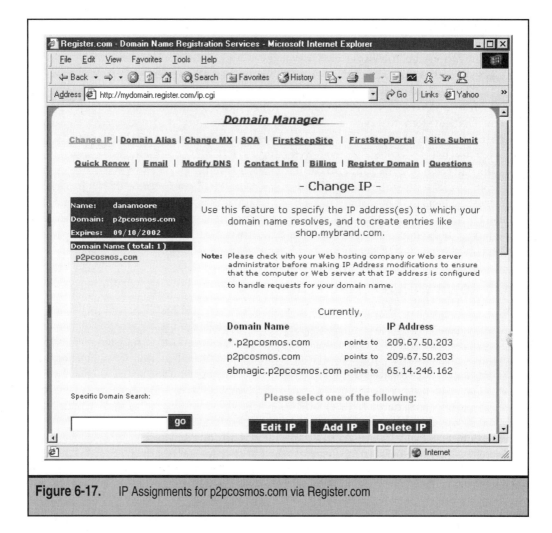

Figure 6-17.   IP Assignments for p2pcosmos.com via Register.com

with your IP address. In 24 hours, you will have an electronic global address. You will also have a user-friendly method to administer your slice of that address space. However, if your ISP connection fails and you switch to your backup ISP, your purchased URL does not track to your new IP identity. So even a fixed IP address can sometimes have a variable IP address. So even a fixed IP address may be interested in a URL that allows a variable address.

Getting Known with a Variable IP Address

You now move on the more challenging addressing problem: getting known when your IP address keeps changing. The basic DNS apparatus abandons you when it comes to solving this problem. Individual applications such as instant messaging handle this in a straightforward manner. Each time you log in, you pass along your current IP address. Unfortunately, DNS provides a mechanism to distribute to the many DNS servers throughout the world a fixed IP address for a given URL translation.

Let's step back a bit and examine how DNS works. DNS servers exist as a hierarchy that forms a widely distributed database of address information. The top DNS machines handle the rightmost extension, such as .com or .org. When you request a translation to a DNS, the DNS provides either the IP address of the destination or the IP address of the *next DNS* in the hierarchy. This technique limits each DNS server to managing only a subset of the entire Internet URL mapping and results in a highly scalable and robust architecture.

Let's follow a translation of collaboration.p2pcosmos.com. The request first travels to your ISP's DNS server. Initially, the ISP's DNS requests a translation at the start of the hierarchy: *.com.* This translation then returns the DNS for *p2pcosmos.* The ISP's DNS then makes a request to the p2pcosmos DNS. This request then returns either another DNS or the actual IP address of *collaboration.* This simple and robust architecture allows multiple DNS servers to cooperate to store and access address information. Each domain specified in a URL offers an opportunity for another DNS.

DNS is an open, standard protocol. It does not depend on any implementation details such as the operating system or database type. DNS depends only on a response and request protocol. Therefore, the next DNS in line could offer *dynamic* addresses instead of static ones. It could look up *variable* addresses and respond with the standard DNS protocol. To make this work properly, your computer supplies the variable address to this DNS whenever it changes. Several vendors have stepped up to this challenge and provide a complete solution: dynamic DNS (DDNS).

DDNS requires two operations: a dynamic lookup of an address and a dynamic supply of the changing address. To demonstrate this process, let's experiment with the site dns2go.com, which provides a complete DDNS solution (and then some). Your first step is to create a domain name. If you desire a domain name such as *yourname.com* directly under a the first-level domain *.com*, you must first visit a domain controller for .com such as registrars.com and pay for it. Otherwise, you can select one underneath dns2go.com. If you select one under dns2go.com, your URL must contain *dns2go.com* (such as *yourname.dns2go.com*).[1] Figure 6-18 illustrates the name selection.

After registering, you need to download the domain controller's client. This client monitors your Internet connection and reports back your IP address. This IP address is then used to update the DNS2Go DNS. Figure 6-19 shows the client application.

The client allows you to specify the IP address or have the client discover it on its own. The discovery process runs into trouble if your peer exists on a subnet, as discussed earlier. The DNS2Go DNS then forwards your supplied IP address to anyone who makes a request on your URL. The DNS2Go client contacts the DNS2Go server on fixed intervals indicating your IP address. This keeps your dynamic IP address consistently tied to the URL. The DNS2Go service allows you to set the interval or accept the default of every minute. Your setting depends on the likelihood of your address changing. A dial-up user should use the default.

---

1   2DNS2Go offers several other domain names.

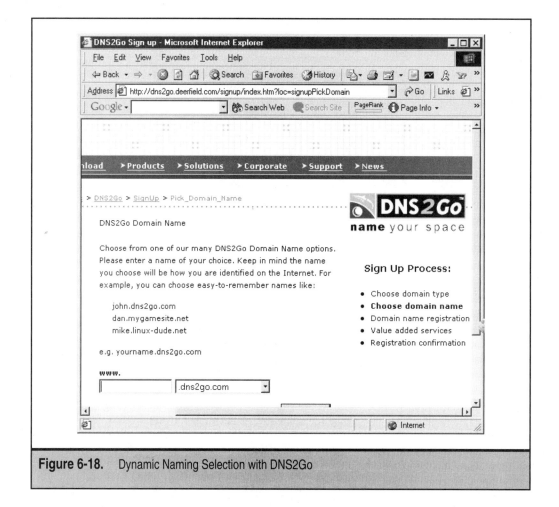

Figure 6-18. Dynamic Naming Selection with DNS2Go

The DNS2Go DNS offers two interesting services to augment the dynamic translation service. The first service extra allows port redirects on web requests. The other sends requests to a different URL if your machine is not currently operating.

Port redirection is a subtle but powerful feature. Web requests default to port 80. The URL www.yahoo.com finds an IP address from a DNS. The ultimate request must also contain a port number to reach the web server for www.yahoo.com. Rather than have everyone remember yet another number, the Internet has standardized ports for many activities. Web sites are standardized on port 80. Thus, port 80 is automatically filled in for you when you enter a web site URL at your browser. If you wish to host a web server on your peer, the logical port to use is 80. Your requesters can then use the default port. But recall that many ISPs do not want you running a Web site. Some ISPs probe port 80 on their client IP addresses to see whether you are adhering to their policy.

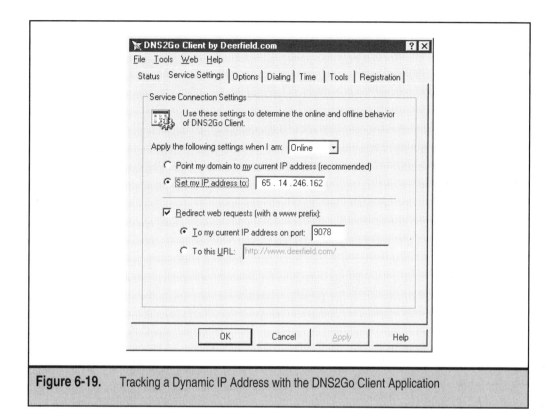

Figure 6-19.   Tracking a Dynamic IP Address with the DNS2Go Client Application

You now have a new problem: You must tell everyone the strange port number and force everyone's request to insert the port number (for example, http://p2pcosmos.com:7654). This situation quickly becomes complicated as your friends do the same thing for the same reason. The DNS2Go service allows you to redirect port 80 requests to any port you specify. This allows users to use the default and then be redirected to whatever port you specified without them ever having any knowledge of the port. This extra level of indirection also allows you to change the port without any notification. You might want to make such a change if you discover that another application needs the port you selected.

The second major feature is the ability to send requests to a different URL if your machine is not current operating. This is demonstrated in Figure 6-20.

If a request comes in for http://p2pcosmos.dns2go.com and the translated IP address does not respond, the request transparently transfers to http://www.ebmagic.dns2go.com.

This service creates high availability for your peers. If you have two peer servers running, each backs up the other. If one is down, DNS2Go redirects it to the other, and vice versa. This model extends to as many backups servers as necessary. The service achieves the high availability that your solution demands in a simple, cost-effective (free) fashion. Of course, this approach will make your solution dependent on DNS2Go.

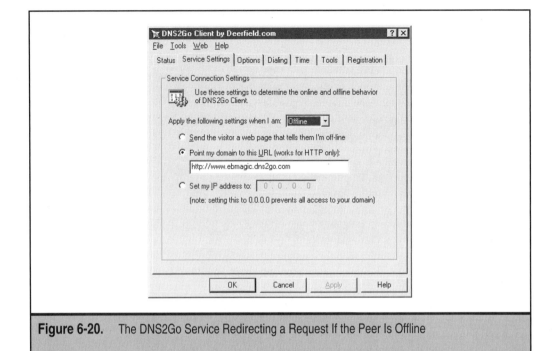

Figure 6-20.   The DNS2Go Service Redirecting a Request If the Peer Is Offline

Associating your IP address with a friendly URL format is straightforward and easily referenced by the many Internet services that allow URL entries. Unfortunately, the URL is not so universal. The major reason is its inability prior to DDNS to handle dynamic addressing. Many specific services maintain their own addressing with all the ugliness discussed in prior sections. DNS is a pure naming service. It maintains no bias toward the use of the address. You are free to use your URL for any Internet service, including your P2P services. You can easily extend your solution to multiple URLs with their own hierarchy.

The new services that allow you to control your DNS settings make it unnecessary to become a DNS protocol expert. Their web interfaces are intuitive and user-friendly. This allows you to set your fixed IP address. Luckily, the services also extend to P2P users who do not have the luxury of a fixed IP address due to the wonders of dial-ups and DHCP. A dynamic IP address does require an application to be resident on your peer to update the DNS dynamically. But all of this is attainable. You are now electronically known.

SUMMARY

This chapter covered the three key steps that provide a firm foundation for P2P solutions: getting connected, getting secure, and getting known. You might be tempted to skip to the "good stuff" in the upcoming chapters, but you would do so at your own risk. Sooner or later, you need to address these three steps.

P2P without Internet connectivity is simply not P2P. There are many choices to establish connectivity involving different technologies and reputations. This chapter outlined the key factors, including bandwidth, availability, cost, and quality. Every peer has choices among potential providers, if only among dial-up providers. Soon more and more peers should have access not only to broadband but to several broadband providers.

Many suppliers, through their quest to simplify *or* to control your network experience fully, make it difficult to obtain the necessary technical network parameters. These parameters include your IP address, gateway address, DNS addresses, among others. These parameters are essential to let loose your P2P networked solutions. Vendors prefer that you to load their own software and corral you as a web consumer. This chapter fully explored the key technical parameters to achieve your P2P network freedom.

This chapter also covered local connectivity to reflect the growing trend for peers to have multiple computers and devices. The local network has its own challenges and rewards. You can set up a subnet isolated from the larger Internet to share files, printers, and even your Internet connection. The latter requires special software, such as a proxy, or special hardware, such as a router to bridge the local and wider world of the LAN and WAN, respectfully. This bridge allows you to control formally what goes back and forth between the two networks.

Thus, the first step handles the details of selecting an Internet connection provider (ISP) and extracting the necessary information so you are not entangled in the ISP's view of the Internet. You also learned ways to develop and expand your local network to allow all your peers to share the richness of network resources. You are now connected.

The second step is to get secure. Your connection opens you to the wonders *and* dangers of sharing a network with the world. P2P cannot reach its potential unless each peer feels safe and secure. You can monitor and intercept any suspicious traffic being exchanged with the Internet. This chapter explored several techniques to guard against trouble. The first line of defense checks communication as it crosses the boundary into your peer or your peer local network. Options include hardware and software solutions. The software solutions either extend the software proxy used to provide Internet connectivity to your LAN, or isolate the application in a software firewall. Hardware solutions extend the router similarly to the software proxy. In either case, communication exchanges examine each transfer for several conditions, including the request origination (incoming or outgoing), the IP addresses, port number, and the protocol. Combinations of these conditions form the rules that guide your security. Be especially watchful of incoming requests. They attempt to break into a too trusting application or a poorly secured one.[2]

Monitoring your security is essential to the peer's overall well-being. Tools exist that allow you to determine what is going in and out of your system. This information helps you fine-tune your security as things change in your system and in others.

Security doesn't stop at your Internet entrance. Communications that pass through the firewall checks can still damage your peer and its associated network. Virus protec-

---

[2]   Security is often compromised because of a poor security policy rather than a faulty security system. Many break-ins happen when users fail to change default passwords or employ easy-to-guess passwords.

tion examines the new arrivals for a host of different attacks. Viruses lurk in executable code. Many years ago, viruses weren't too much of a problem since exchanging executable code was rare and usually very purposeful. Today, almost all communication has the potential to execute within your peer. Viruses have found their way into almost every executable hole, and unfortunately there are quite a few such holes.

Vigilance is the only answer. You need virus protection software that provides regular updates regarding the latest forms of attack. One advantage of the Internet's popularity is that problems are unlikely to hit you first; if your system is attacked, most likely many others have also been, and consequently a fix will already have been developed. So make sure your virus solution receives regular updates and is on constant watch. Viruses are especially likely in the P2P world for two reasons: the sheer number of peers and the relative naiveté of most peer owners. Stay alert.

The final building block in your P2P foundation is an electronic name, specifically a URL. The URL provides a standard, easily translated name for your peer and peer network. It offers a path to your system from many standard application interfaces such as browsers, e-mail clients, and ftp clients. You can decide to incorporate this naming convention into your solutions and thus avoid duplicating the naming system via your own naming convention and associated lookup mechanism. URL naming does have some disadvantages. Since you are competing with a very large naming service, many first-level names are taken. But if you exercise a little creativity, plenty of effective, fun names are left. Once you have established your high-level name (such as *name.com*) you are completely free to use any name under your first-level name (such as. *secondname.name.com*).

The URL naming service, DNS, has never been inclusive to the peer world. ISP vendors do not want anyone to find your machine. Also, many peer IP addresses change with each connection to the Internet. In addition, a URL can cost money—on a continual basis. This has caused a balkanization of peer naming, with each new application creating its own namespace. This balkanization occurs across the board with the popular instant messaging applications. Despite its flaws, instant messaging naming is simple and free.

You have now built a strong P2P foundation. You are optimally connected to the Internet. The connection is secure against invaders and viruses. Your site maintains an easy-to-remember and use URL. You are on the map for anyone who cares to visit you. Now let's make your peer something worth visiting. The visit may come from across the world or just from your office when you are checking in from work.

The strong foundation that you have established in this chapter is essential to future P2P accomplishments. Each P2P solution that you go on to use or build requires this solid foundation. You can choose to build it deliberately as laid out in this chapter or let its pieces gradually fall into place as you build a P2P solution. It is your choice. But either way, you must build the foundation.

The chapters ahead build upon this foundation. Let's begin building the fun stuff!

CHAPTER 7

Getting Together: P2P Collaboration

This chapter discusses the applications that are P2P's bread and butter—those applications that enhance collaborative efforts. The fundamental need for people to cooperate, share, and communicate has never been greater. The reality is that no one geographic area, no single pile of brick and mortar can attract and contain all the talented people and other resources needed to achieve results in modern multifaceted projects, from software applications, to marketing campaigns, to Hollywood films. Talent and resources exist anywhere and everywhere, and gaining the competitive edge requires a symphony of people, technology, and organizations.

WHY IS COLLABORATION A CRITICAL TOOL?

The distributed character of work environments both encourages and demands net-based collaboration tools. The Defense Advanced Research Project Agency (DARPA) UltraLog project is spread over two large BBN Technologies labs and 12 contributing universities and corporations, scattered geographically from Sandia National Labs in New Mexico to the University of West Florida. With collaborators so widely dispersed, can traditional collaboration tools such as e-mail and telephone conversations suffice? E-mail is problematic as a lively forum for debate and discussion, or even for disseminating information.

Even a listserver (a server that multicasts e-mail items to a set of subscribers) has problems. The problems involve separating categories of e-mail, keeping up with separate threads of conversation, providing immediacy (which e-mail has never guaranteed), making special arrangements with the IT department to provide external secure access to the corporate e-mail system (most of these systems are incredibly byzantine and force you to split your e-mail universe into a set of parallel worlds).

What are your options?

▼ Tell your Outlook client to forward everything to your web mail client, so that you can deal with it on your own timeline, thereby creating duplicate e-mail that you will have to un-duplicate later.

■ Forget about your corporate e-mail client, and route everything to a web mail account that you create just for this list.

■ Create separate e-mail accounts for each listserver to which you subscribe. Of course, you are likely to forget the user ID, the password, or both for some of these accounts, or forget that they exist at all.

■ Try to encourage the listserver publisher to create a usenet or netnews style newsgroup.

▲ Not bother trying to collaborate at all. Even if you do one or more of these things, you will lose some of the instantaneous nature of the collaborative experience. You will have to make a prodigious effort to move from one e-mail or netnews client to another to stay abreast of the content and remember the discussion thread(s).

Telephony is just as bad, if not worse. Nothing of the conversation gets recorded for posterity, and the etiquette required demands that you commit a large amount of synchronous time to the effort, thus preventing multitasking or complete responses. Group teleconferences have their etiquette and interaction problems as well. Turn taking ("Can I say something now? Or do I wait for the alpha male of the conversation to speak next?"), attribution ("Was that Bill or Joe that just spoke? Their voices are so similar"), and multiple threads ("What Alice just said reminded me of another important issue, but it is out of scope in the current loud and impassioned debate between Fred and Susan, so I will just forget about it") are issues that force social dimensions into the fore.

If you think of your own collaboration situation and needs, you probability will come to the realization that a good collaboration space has several common attributes.[1] Among these are:

▼ A common worldview for all the participants. For example, if a group of engineers is adding comments to a Powerpoint document in real time, the engineers should be able to see everyone's input without significant time lags. If a group of marketers is brain-surfing in real time on a list of strategies, the group output should reflect each person's input.

■ Persistent journaling of all work and discussions. Persistent links.

■ Presence information: Who's online? Who's got documents open from the group publishing area? Who's doing what at this moment?

■ Instant messaging.

■ Voice and text chat.

■ File sharing.

▲ Picture and media sharing.

THE GROOVE EXPERIENCE

At least a few of out-of-the-box solutions might be adequate to illustrate the utility of P2P collaboration, but a pair—Groove and Magi—stand out as having a number of the more critical features. Let's tour the user experience of using one of these collaboration tools, Groove, to understand how a good collaboration operates to enable its users.

Installing Groove

When you first download and install Groove from www.groove.net, the software prompts you to create an account. With the account, you receive a set of mediated P2P services,

---

1   Your list may differ from ours, but you should see a great deal of overlap.

including a relay server and a public user registry. Thus far, you haven't done anything really interesting. The installation executable runs a standard Windows InstallShield.[2]

Notice the Multiple Computers button in the top-right corner of the Create Account screen. You can install any space you create on a multitude of computers, thereby making the actual computer you use to interact with collaborators a matter of your own convenience. If you are on a PC at the office, then that's where you interact; if you are in a comfy nook at your local Starbucks, telecommuting with your RF-modem (or Starbucks' recently announced cyber cafe services), you can interact from there as well.

After you've created an account, the wizard takes you to the home screen shown in Figure 7-1, where you can manage your identity information, creating a contact card with

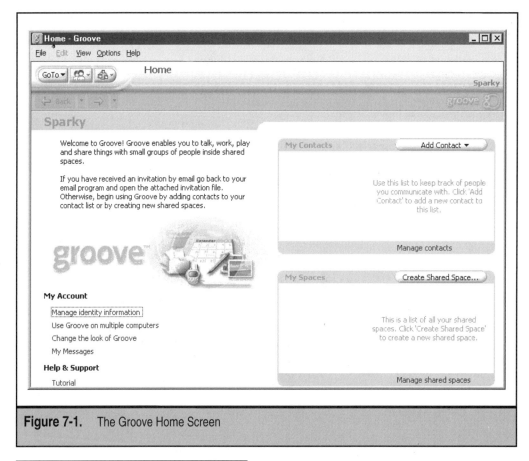

Figure 7-1.   The Groove Home Screen

---

2   You need a Pentium (233MHz or higher) processor with at least 64MB of system RAM. Groove initially takes up at least 40MB of hard disk storage, but will expand to *much* higher requirements as you add replicated files via synchronization. You should be able to run at a 16-color display resolution of 800 [ts] 600. Because Groove supports voice chat as well as text chat, you should connect a microphone and have a sound card if you want to use these features.

as much or as little information as you wish (the default is no information at all). You can create new identities to keep your life as compartmentalized as you want. The Change the Look of Groove option enables you to apply one of several "skins" or graphic overlays to the Groove client on *this* computer or on the multiple computers for *this* account. On the right side of the screen is a button labeled Create a Shared Space. Click this button to see the real fun begin.

You can choose to install individual tools or choose a collection of tools well suited to certain types of spaces. For this example, we chose a shared "standard" project space (shown in Figure 7-2) that already has a number of built-in tools.

The wizard then takes you to the next screen (Figure 7-3), where you choose a name for the space (one that will be relevant and meaningful to the collaboration group), and specify not to invite other users at this time.

When you click Finish, the space shown in Figure 7-4 appears. If you dismiss the Overview window pane at screen's right by pressing the Hide Overview button in the bottom-right corner, you can gain more screen real estate. There's nothing of importance in this space as yet, because the real power of a collaborative space comes from the contributions of the collaborators.

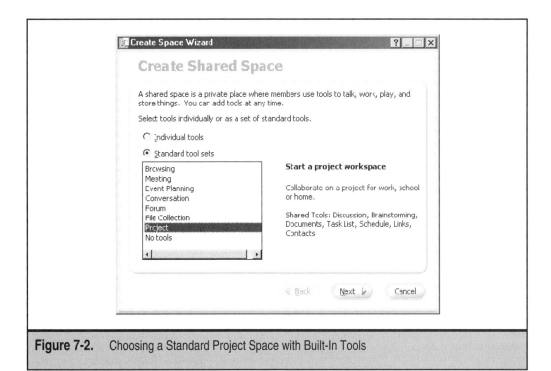

Figure 7-2. Choosing a Standard Project Space with Built-In Tools

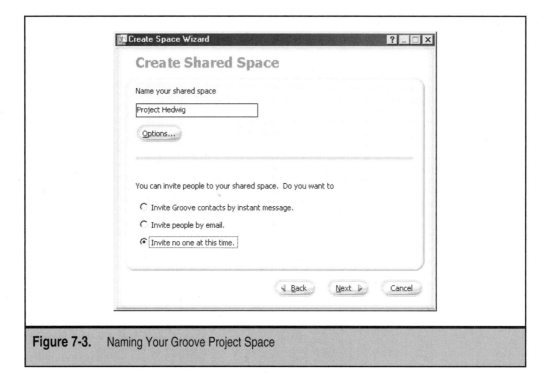

Figure 7-3. Naming Your Groove Project Space

Exploring a Groove Space

Let's tour an older and more established space to see what a month or so of collaboration yields in terms of content. Figure 7-5 shows a view of the Discussion pane of a space. The left pane displays the presence information for the participants in the space. The first two participants are shown as being online and currently interacting with tools in the space. Below them, two participants are shown as being online but not having interacted with tools in the space for some elapsed time.

If you hover over a particular name, a box pops up that indicates the person's access level to the space, and what he or she is currently doing within the space. For example, as shown in Figure 7-6, the first name in the space, Dana, is the nominal manager of the space, and the box indicates that Dana is currently engaged with the discussion and chat tools. Each tab near the bottom of the screen tells you how many people are in a particular tool at the moment. In this case, one user is in the threaded discussion tool, and one in the documents tool.

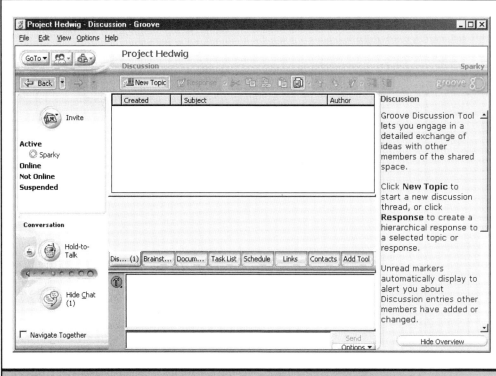

Figure 7-4.   A Groove User's View of a Space with Tools and a Help Panel

Mining Presence

Another user can infer from the presence information revealed that the best way (or at least an easy way) to contact the user might be via the chat window at the bottom of the screen. This is because the user apparently has a Groove window up, front and center, and is actively engaged in using the tool. Thus the user is likely to observe readily any new input in the chat window at the bottom of the space, or will be within hearing distance of a voice message using the voice chat/broadcast tool at the lower left.

On the other hand, the third person in the participant roster appears to be away from the keyboard. He or she might be at lunch or gone for the day, so perhaps the best way to contact this user would be to create a message that will be stored and later

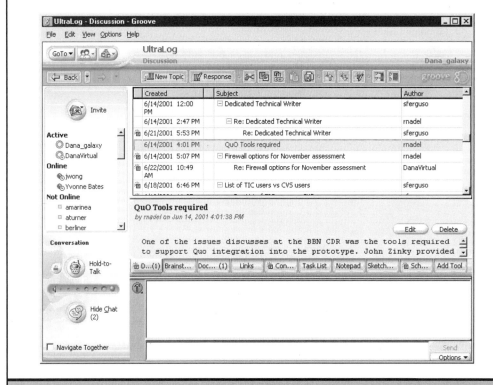

Figure 7-5.   A Groove Space with Lively User Interaction

forwarded to him or her. (This would be much like sending an e-mail, except that you don't need to switch contexts into an e-mail tool.) Figure 7-7 shows contact information for the participants in the space. This information may vary, depending of the user's need for privacy or for controlling the level of availability a person wishes to reveal to the group. The information is somewhat interactive; you can use several buttons to the right of the card to establish contact with the person identified by the card.

Currently, the interaction is limited to sending messages or chatting, but in the future you may be able to access contact information from mobile phone or other on-the-go devices. Future collaboration modes will be able to use a number of different non-desktop devices and interaction modes. Once you establish a strong software architecture for collaboration, many possibilities emerge.

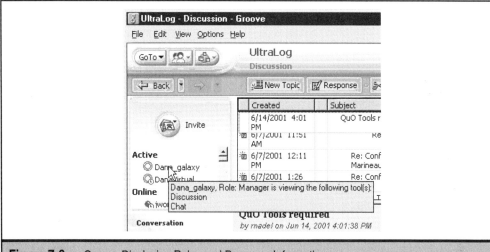

Figure 7-6.   Groove Displaying Roles and Presence Information

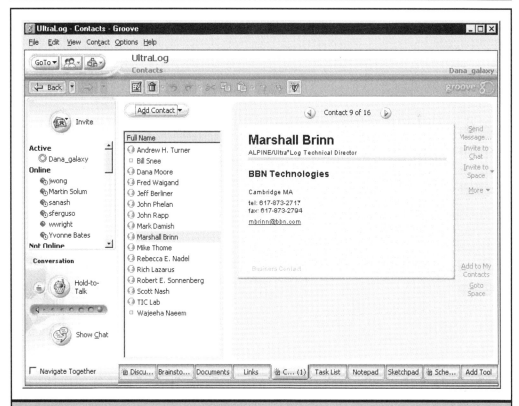

Figure 7-7.   Managing Contact Using Groove

Staying Alert

Groove and many other P2P collaboration solutions intend to enable users to gather presence information from mobile devices on behalf of the group, and forward messages or status changes to the on-the-go user.[3] Such "virtual butler" services and additional capabilities—running interference for you, filtering messages, preparing information summaries, and performing contextual searches—are regarded as an essential part of the next generation of P2P collaboration spaces. Groove currently bundles a few crude alert and notification capabilities as a part of its user experience.

Sharing Documents

Document sharing with Groove is very easy to understand: You simply treat the space as though it were just another drive on your PC. As Figure 7-8 shows, the look and feel are identical to a Windows Explorer experience. Groove effectively allows you to treat the repository as a part of your local file system, even though something significantly better than a local file system, or even a LAN-based file system, is working behind the scenes.

In fact, the local copy of the files in the document tool *is* kept on your hard drive, but it's a hidden file in a hidden directory. The only time you might notice this is if, for example, you perform a Save As command from Microsoft Word. In this case, the file dialog box displays a funny-looking directory tree.

However, if you simply double-click on files from the Groove space and let Windows' File Association feature figure out the right application to launch, if you simply drag and drop the files to the application, or if you use the Add Files button shown at the top of the Figure 7-8, the file synchronization mechanisms are all transparent to you. Groove faithfully replicates the files to all users in your shared space.[4]

It would be easy to look at Groove's nifty synchronization of shared files and miss a subtle but important point: Groove is designed around the concept of replication rather than synchronization. The software doesn't look for new files that it can copy to all users. Rather, Groove replicates everything you do in the shared space to every other machine in the shared space.

Whereas synchronization usually involves manually making a decision to bring multiple devices into line with each other, and a hard and fast rule set about which device holds the "real picture" of the truth, replication faithfully and automatically records every change made on any device out to all the other devices. To understand the difference,

---

3   Magi, which this chapter also discusses, already facilitates browsing back into your space from an Internet-enabled phone; however, P2P vendors still don't offer the capability to send communications to the mobile user. Also, bearing in mind the potential side effects of never being able to escape from work, an individual obviously wants to be able to turn this capability on or off selectively.

4   Upcoming versions of Groove may elect to keep exceptionally large files on a central in-the-flow server for you and your space-mates, rather than doing a full copy. In this case, Groove copies only the "meta-information" (name, size, modification date, and so on) directly to each space, and then copies the actual file on demand.

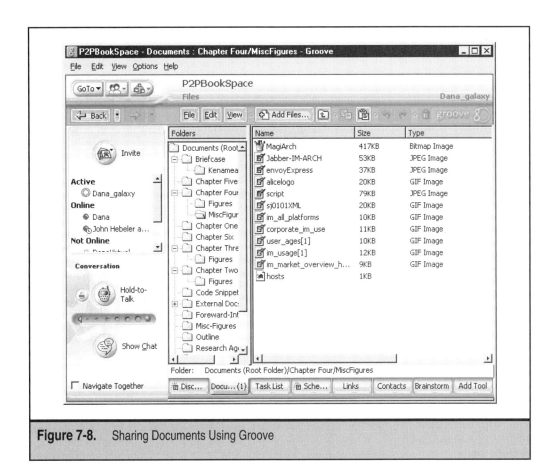

Figure 7-8.   Sharing Documents Using Groove

imagine a group of people who each have a handheld calculator. One of the people says, "I am pressing 2." In response, everyone else presses 2. It doesn't matter that some folks have Texas Instruments calculators, and others have a Hewlett-Packard. Each person is simply doing in his or her local context whatever is necessary to make his or her calculator 's view of the world consistent with those of everyone else.

Now, if someone else presses the plus key (+) and yells, "Now everyone press plus," then this ad hoc, human-based replication system ensures that each calculator is brought up to date. If the community then presses the 2 and = keys in response to anyone in the community initiating these actions, all calculators achieve a consistent result. This effect may be most clearly observed in certain tools such as the shared sketchpad, but it's the design center for all of Groove's tools.

There is no sense of ever needing to synchronize anything with Groove. In contrast, consider the design center for Palm computers, PocketPCs, and other handhelds. They hold your data in isolation until you periodically decide that you should upload a snapshot of their data to your PC, at which time the data on your PC (also existing in isolation) is brought up to date with your handheld. There is a distinct sense of your information existing in two different places and you having to act as the information coordinator. With Groove there is only a sense of sharing a simultaneous view of the same information.

A consideration regarding Groove worthy of mention is the intended size of the community of collaborators. While Groove could potentially handle the mechanics of replication to an arbitrarily large community, in practice most collaboration communities tend to encompass no more than a couple dozen people. The reasons for this are both technical and perceptible and also social and subtle. If you extend the calculator replication example to a stadium with hundreds or thousands of people in it, the scenario wouldn't work so well.

For one thing, it would be much more difficult to orchestrate technically. Some people would be out of earshot, and would need to have the instruction repeated, resulting in more latency in the shared experience. People distant from the person yelling out the instruction might lag so far behind the group that by the time they completed the button-pressing sequence, its significance might be lost on them. Arbitrarily long sequences might begin arriving out of order due to the repetition of instructions. Some people might hear "press 2" twice, and some not at all. There are some tough technical details to work out.

Also, sheer size dampens the motivation to interact. If you've ever attended a lecture or presentation with six people in attendance and then attended one with 600 people in attendance, you know that the level of interactivity in the small group is far greater than in the larger group. The rule in shared spaces is, "Small is beautiful."

Finally, there is the matter of taking turns in large groups. If several people are working on a document together, how does the group decide who should have a go at editing the document next? How does the group decide what text to keep and what to discard; or which viewpoints are germane and which are not? How does the group keep the document from reading as though it was written by an unorganized horde? Paralysis by consensus occurs in groups both large and small, but the larger the group, the more pronounced the effect.

For example, in Figure 7-9, Groove has highlighted new discussion items that have been added since the user last looked (which are circled in the figure), and is highlighting tools where content has been added or changed (highlighted in the figure with boxes over the bar at the bottom). The little alert icon is sufficiently visual to be informative, but not annoying.

Tooling Along

One of the more interesting capabilities in Groove and other P2P collaboration tools is to add a new tool to the space. In the past, when you bought an off-the-shelf tool from a traditional software vendor, the relationship generally ended there. If the software had bugs or you wanted new features, you often waited until the next release. Netscape and a few other vendors ushered in a new era with the ability to add plug-ins to the existing browser and thereby create a new capability in an existing tool.

They added hooks so that a software developer could extend the range of the tool without having to understand the totality of the tool's software design. P2P tools like

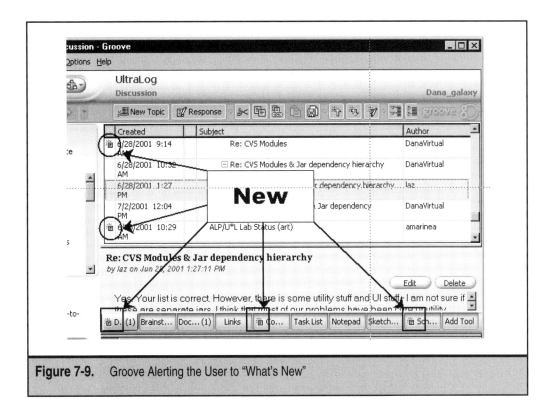

Figure 7-9.   Groove Alerting the User to "What's New"

Groove, Magi, and Kenamea strongly support the ability either to create very sophisticated plug-ins that tap the core capabilities of the tool, or at the very least to add scripting capability to the tool. You will learn how to write your own tool in an upcoming chapter. This section describes how to add one of the ready-made tools available from the Add Tool menu (see Figure 7-10).

If the permissions assigned to your role (manager, for example) allow it, you can add new tools to a shared space. If you click the Add Tool button (always the rightmost tab, shown in Figure 7-10), Groove displays the list of all currently available tools. You can select one or more tools or tool sets (groups of tools that perform a suite of functions) and add them. When offline collaborators return to the space, the tool is downloaded with their permission.

Maintaining Your Identity

When you first install Groove, you create an account for yourself and declare an identity, which by default is the same name as the account itself (refer back to Figure 7-1, where we created an identity called *Sparky*). An *account* is conceptually a bit different from an *identity* in Groove-speak. Whereas an identity is simply a display name by which you want to

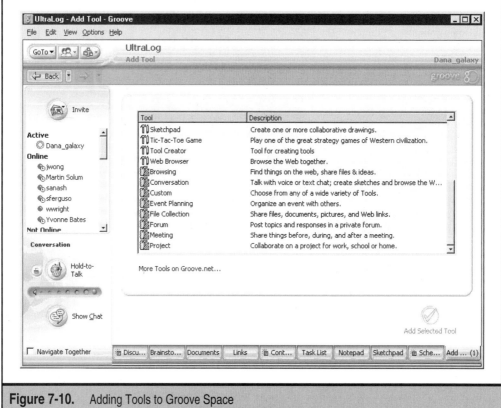

Figure 7-10.   Adding Tools to Groove Space

be recognized in one or more spaces, an account is a file object held on your computer that contains the following information in an encrypted format:[5]

▼ All your Groove identities

■ The computer systems on which you run *this* Groove account

■ A roster of the other members of shared spaces of which you're a member

▲ Names of the shared spaces of which you're a member

If you plan to use Groove on more than one computer (at a minimum, you will probably want to access the same files, contacts, and discussions at work and at home), you

---

5   Whenever you log in to your Groove space on a particular machine, you log in by the account name you used to create the space. Your password is the decryption key for your account information.

should use the same account on multiple computers. (Groove provides a facility for doing this on your account's home page.) This scheme will work better than creating a new account on each PC. This way you can immediately resume activities in any shared space in which you're a member, treating a particular computer as a convenient access point rather than an essential part of operating a tool.[6]

Figure 7-11 shows the management screen on user DanaVirtual's Groove account home page. To populate a new machine, the user has selected 9 of 10 of the shared spaces in which the user is a member. The left panel shows the update status of replicating the spaces. For example, the space Groove Opportunities-BNN is ready for use, and the space DAML Military Users is in the process of being replicated on this machine.

In the scenario shown in Figure 7-12, user DanaVirtual is sharing an account among three computers—SENIORSOFTY, EMPATH, and Ul134. The screen shows the status of

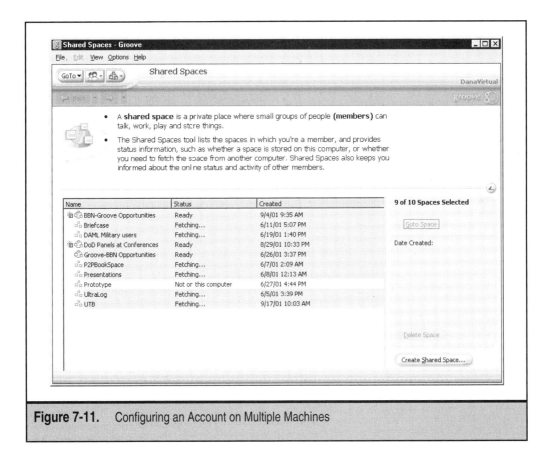

Figure 7-11.   Configuring an Account on Multiple Machines

---

6   Remember that a fundamental premise of P2P computing is to free people from having to keep a specific tool on a specific PC.

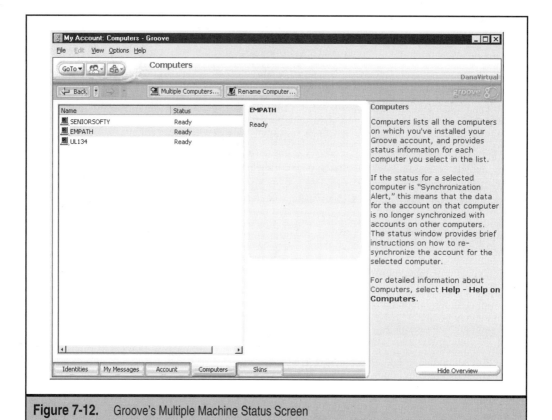

Figure 7-12. Groove's Multiple Machine Status Screen

the three machines on which the account DanaVirtual is resident. All machines are currently online and ready, so any changes made on any of the machines by user DanaVirtual are being replicated to all the other machines.

An account can contain many identities, but the reverse is not true. That is, an identity cannot be shared across accounts. Therefore, if you create a second account (which forces you to declare a unique identity) on another machine, and then you want to participate in the shared spaces of which you're a member as an identity from the first account, you will have to invite yourself to the shared space as your second identity from the second account. Further, if you join a shared space in this second identity, you then just confuse the other members of the space. Thus you should spread the same account across multiple computers. That way, even if you get "right-sized" out of a job in the next dot-com implosion, losing your cubicle and your laptop, you will still have your valuable information at home.

A Groove identity is the "display name" that appears in shared spaces of which you are a member. Groove makes sure that these identities are firewalled from one another, so that if you are Striker 45 in the Maryland Soccer Club space, the other members never know that you are Engineer Bill in the Big Software Co. space. Given that a single account can contain several identities, why would you want different identities in different spaces?

One reason is that you might want to limit the degree of exposure or availability that you offer to friends on your soccer team as opposed to work collaborators. For another, people tend to segment their lives into roles that they play out in very separate realms, now more than ever. As Sherry Turkle points out in her excellent book *Life on the Screen: Identity in the Age of the Internet* (Simon & Schuster, 1997), "What matters most now is the ability to adapt, and change—to new jobs, new career directions, new gender roles, new technologies." Being able to partition identities helps us safeguard our sanity and control demands on our time. Therefore, identity creation and maintenance are important parts of any shared space user experience.

Summarizing Groove

Groove has designed and delivered a well-conceived approach to solving group collaboration. Microsoft's equity investment of $51 million in Groove (October 2001) is clearly an endorsement of both P2P collaboration in general and Groove's approach in specific. Groove's concept is not the only approach to collaboration, however, as you will see in the next section, which introduces Magi, an open source collaboration suite.

THE MAGI EXPERIENCE

Groove has dominated mindshare (the power of an idea to dominate the thinking of forward thinkers) for a variety of reasons, including the scale of Groove's effort, its founder's track record, its numerous partners, and the size of Groove's ambitions. However, other efforts are in some ways less limited and perhaps more extensible. Groove is weak in its support for mobile users, so let's look at Magi, another collaboration tool that offers stronger mobile support. Before touching upon mobility, let's begin by exploring the out-of-the-box user experience just as you did with Groove.

Gift of (the) Magi

Magi grew from a research project at the University of California–Irvine. Magi's development was partly funded by DARPA, and is based on open source and Internet standards such as Java, a compact version of the Apache Web server, and Web-based Distributed Authoring and Versioning (WebDAV), the emerging standard in Web-based collaboration. Given its roots in the open source community, Magi is less wedded to a specific operating system (such as Windows) than Groove.

Magi is different from Groove in many ways, not the least of which is its user experience. Because Magi is largely Web-based, its user experience is rather more like using the Web than using a "standard" Windows client interface. Although Groove can and does render a lot of its content using HTML and JavaScript, it still has more of a Windows application feel to it.

Further, Magi's design center is much more about providing access than moving and replicating data, as is the case with Groove. Documents remain in place (as with the traditional Web server and client model), and the place at which work takes place is free to move about as necessary. Magi can provide server-based persistence of metadata for a user if specified. Centralization of metadata is a cheaper, performs less bandwidth-heavy operation than information collection, and enables the user to access offline data. Even if one of the machines on your buddy list or one of the peer machines holding your multiple presences is offline, a snapshot of the data on that machine is available from a Magi server.

Let's look at a few of the reasons that Magi and similar architectures are needed. Consider the problem of enterprise data. It's tough for the modern corporation to centralize enterprise data. Access strategies put in place by well-meaning but plodding IT departments are either burdened by a confusing muddle of exceptions to firewall rules and access privileges or so tight as to prevent the collection of internal and external resources necessary for a modern workforce. From IT's point of view, knowing when to prevent access is extremely difficult or, at times, impossible. Further, an estimated 70 percent of enterprise data are not located in a centralized server or database. Instead, data are on the desktops, laptops, home PCs, PocketPCs, palm devices, mobile phones, RIM Blackberries, and the coming generation of JavaPhones.

IT cannot possibly respond to the constantly changing and evolving nature of "enterprise data." Rather, IT should concentrate on exploiting strategies such as Magi, which leave information in place. ERP systems with large centralized databases at their heart are expensive to use, maintain, and access (especially remotely), and they fail to keep pace with the dynamic nature of essential corporate data.

Additionally, consider that the PC ushered in an era where the essence of human nature was respected and elevated. It is human nature to want your data close at hand and under *your* control. It's human nature to be aggravated at the draconian requirements of systems that require explicit synchronization and don't support convenient access. It's not that uncommon these days for people to work long hours, whenever and wherever the opportunity presents itself. Modern work life is not that easily compartmentalized. There's overlap between "work hours" and "off-duty hours." It's advantageous under these circumstances, to want *no barriers* between your available devices and network connections and the content required to accomplish work. Magi's design respects and supports the modern work paradigm.

Magi, in changing the model by embedding a Web server in each client, thus implementing a *servent* architecture as described in Chapter 3, allows every device controlled by a user to generate HTTP to every other device and absorb HTTP from every other device. Magi makes use of open source components such as the Apache HTTP server and plug-ins, and standards such as Java, XML, HTML, HDML (Handheld Device Markup Language), SMS (Short Messaging Service), WebDAV (Web Distributed Authoring and Versioning), and WML (Wireless Markup Language). By making its core code openly available, Magi strives for platform and OS neutrality while encouraging development and extension.

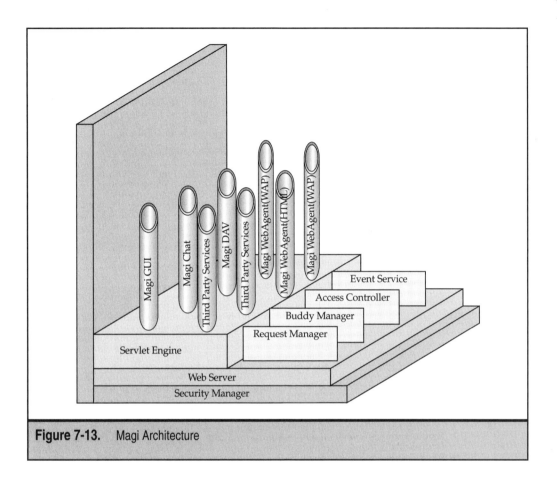

Figure 7-13. Magi Architecture

Figure 7-13 depicts the architecture for Magi Express, the freely downloadable P2P collaboration engine. The web server bundled with Magi Express operates with the Java servlet engine to provide external access to folders on a given machine's hard drive. The servlet engine also provides an interface to resident Magi system services such as the Request Manager, Buddy Manager, Access Controller, and Event Service. In addition, the servlet engine provides a plug-in API for GUI generation, authoring and versioning, and future third-party plug-ins. Underlying other architectural elements is a security manager, which controls access, authorization, and authentication for external users, including the owner of the account. The security manager enables external users to access their information remotely.

Installing Magi

Downloading and installing Magi from its web site (www.endeavors.com) require a familiar process. The installer program asks the user either to install or choose a previously installed JVM (Java Virtual Machine). The user chooses to use a previously installed JVM, but the installer will conveniently download a JVM if it's unable to find one on hard disk.

The installation of a JVM is a matter of little consequence on Linux and Macintosh OSes and on some current Windows machines. But given Microsoft's decision to exclude Java support from its operating systems, beginning with XP, it becomes a matter of inconvenience at the very least and a potential threat to open source software projects, many of which rely on the platform-neutral Java language. Magi makes it fairly painless to grab a Java run-time environment from the Internet. Perhaps other future Java-dependent efforts will merely do as Magi has done, and optionally bundle Java.

Next Magi will request a document root directory as shown in Figure 7-14. In this directory, Magi will create the following subfolders:

- ▼ **Private Folder**   Contains documents and links for you alone.
- ■ **Inbox Folder**   Where your buddies can drop files. Only you can retrieve files from or see the contents of the Inbox folder.
- ■ **Outbox Folder**   Acts as a queue for outgoing files and messages. It lets you see which files and messages are waiting to be sent to their destination(s). For example, when you drop a file on a buddy, Magi will copy the file to your Outbox, where the file will await availability of transport to your buddy's machine. If you or your buddy is not connected, then the document will remain in the Outbox until a complete connectivity path can be established.
- ■ **Shared Folder**   Allows your buddies to access its contents with full privileges. Your buddies (but not the world in general) can read, write to, copy, move, or delete the contents of the Shared folder.
- ■ **Public Folder**   Allows anyone, whether a buddy or not, to view and read any of its contents.
- ■ **Services Folder**   Maintains information about Magi-mediated services (for example, Magi Chat) to which you've subscribed.
- ▲ **Purchases Folder**   For purchase information where Magi has mediated the transaction on your behalf. This set of services is still in the planning stages as this book is being written, but could potentially become a new way of doing secure online commerce.

This arrangement of privileged and leveled access is quite reasonable and models the way that people tend to think. There will always be documents and media that you don't mind the world seeing (like the picture of your tournament-winning spike at last year's coed volleyball tournament), as well as documents that only your work team should be allowed to see (like the chapters for your next book) and documents to which only you want access (like your private journal or your legally acquired MP3s). Magi also allows you to create other folders and assign access permissions to them so that your buddies or groups of buddies can access them. You can thus securely share content and information in the way that you want. Any new folders you create will inherit the permissions of their parent folders.

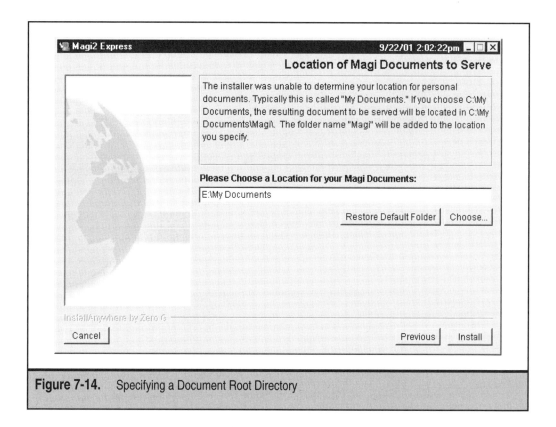

Figure 7-14.   Specifying a Document Root Directory

The file system transparency provided by Magi is based on WebDAV, an architecture for accessing remote resources (such as files and folders) across a network as if they were local. Web folders are an implementation of WebDAV supported by Magi. Unlike typical server-hosted Web pages, which only let you view or download files, web folders allow you to view, modify, and even upload files to the web folder, provided you have appropriate access privileges. WebDAV also allows multiple users to work on the same content by keeping track of file locking and versioning.

Many application vendors (including Microsoft, Adobe, and Macromedia) have integrated WebDAV into their applications (such as Microsoft Office XP) to facilitate file sharing and remote collaboration. The Magi architecture supports WebDAV-compliant applications, thus enabling you to create collaborative workspaces, hosted by your always-connected desktop.

Note that the actual Magi Express Server files for configuration and other information are located in a folder (usually C:\PROGRAM FILES\MAGI SERVER) that is not visible to the outside world under any circumstances. Thus no one other than a user with direct access to the machine (presumably the machine's owner) can make administrative changes.

The final step in the installation transports you to a registration Web site, shown in Figure 7-15, where you are required to supply data so that your machine can be registered with Magi's dynamic DNS. Magi uses a server in the connectivity flow to allow access to variably connected PCs (via a DHCP server, for example). A significant point on the registration page is "Step 3: Describe your device." Here you want to make sure to use a name with some significance (the fixed choices are names such as Office, Home, and Laptop). This name will be appended to the user name you've chosen and will become a part of the URL for your machine. Thus, choosing Home for the user name DanaMoore results in the following URL:http://p2pcosmos.com/Magi/MagiServer/DanaMoore'Home.

Each of Dana Moore's machines will be uniquely identified by the portion of the URL following the tick mark ('). Accessing a machine on a home or office LAN, where addresses may not be fixed, takes a bit of network engineering (but nothing too difficult). For instructions on using Magi on a LAN where addresses are assigned by a NAT (Network Address Translation) router, see the following section.

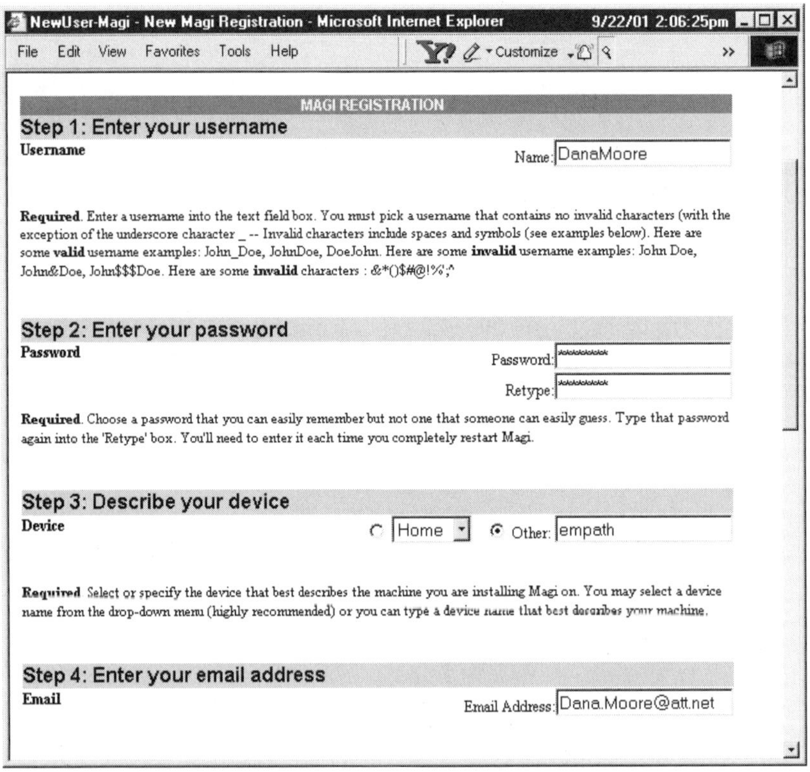

Figure 7-15. Magi's User Registration Site

Using Magi with a NAT'd LAN

This section was written by Dana Moore, BBN Technologies, and Mark Friedman, Cruxus, Ltd.

Magi often is installed on a home or office LAN where hosts have floating IP addresses—for example, on a home LAN with a DSL connection to the Internet. Both of the authors have multiple Linux and Windows machines in their home labs, hubbed by a multiport Ethernet router that assigns nonroutable IP addresses to the member machines and then uses Network Address Translation to route incoming packets to the correct machine on the LAN. In addition, both authors use a wireless access bridge to route to machines using wireless LAN protocol (802.11B) cards.

One of the authors (the smart one) has cable modem and therefore a fixed IP address, as is the cable providers' custom. The other author (the good-looking one) has a DSL line that disconnects frequently, and every time the line reconnects, it gets a new IP address from a pool of available addresses. In either case, the IP address visible to the outside world is the IP address given to the Ethernet hub rather than any of the actual machines on the LAN. Getting Magi to route properly under these circumstances requires a bit of home-brewed configuration magic. The authors thank Mark Friedman at Cruxus, Ltd., for contributing a succinct explanation of the appropriate workaround.

First, locate your Magi.properties file and change the MyURL parameter in it. At some point, Endeavors will make it possible to change this parameter from within Magi, but for now you will have to take the following steps.

Assuming you are on a Windows box and used the default install locations, the "business end" of your Magi server is in a folder in the Program Files directory. The folder should be called Magi Server. Then look for the conf subfolder of the Magi folder. In this subfolder, you should find your user profile folder. For example, the appropriate path on my machine is:

C:\Program Files\Magi Server\webapps\Magi\WEB-INF\conf\DanaMoore-Epiphyte.

In a similarly named directory, you should find your Magi.properties file. You need to edit the file to tell the MXDNS (Magi Dynamic DNS Service) to find your Magi Server at the WAN address of your router/proxy server. That should forward any HTTP requests to ports 80 through 88 to the IP of your NAT'd machines.

To do this, first make sure Magi is shut down, then open the Magi.properties file and find the string MyURL. You will need to repeat the search a few times to get down to the block you are looking for. It is near the middle of the props file and it will look like this:

```
1. #
2. #
3. # Parameter: MyURL
4. #
5. # Description:
6. #
7. # This is the callback URL to your MagiServer. If for some reason Magi
8. # Server cannot discover its URL, this parameter must be set. Otherwise,
9. # the system will default into firewall mode (cannot call back).
10. #
```

```
11. #If you are behind a proxy or firewall, you should manually assign the
12. # URL. For example, setting:
13. #
14. # MyURL=http://gateway.domain.com/username/Magi/MagiServer
15. #
16. # will force Magi DNS to update with this URL.
17. #
18. # A port mapping will need to be entered into the proxy configuration
19. # by your network admin. For example:
20. #
21. # http://gateway.domain.com/username/Magi/EventService
22. #
23. # — gateway.domain.com is either a IP number or actual
24. # registered domain name for a public accessible Network
25. # node.
26. # — username needs to be identified with the private network
27. # IP number.
28. #
29. # Default:
30. #
31. # None
32. #
33. # Example:
34. #
35. # MyURL=http://gateway.endeavors.com/ahitomi/Magi/MagiServer
36. #
37. /Magi/MagiServer
```

You want to replace the /Magi/MagiServer with this:

MyURL= http://*yourrouterIPaddress*/Magi/MagiServer

Save the changes to the properties file and then launch Magi. Now when you hit the MXDNS, you should see your WAN (external) IP address displayed. At work, you might need permission to use the IP address of the proxy/router, depending on policy. At home, you're the boss.

Exploring the Magi User Experience

Major elements of the Magi user interface are very browser-like in their implementation, thus the experience should not be unfamiliar to millions of browser users. The main view shows one of these elements:

▼ The menus provide access to all available Magi commands.

■ Located below the menus, the toolbar includes frequently used tool buttons and the URL Address window.

■ At the left side, the Explorer tab contains controls that allow you to access Magi buddies, groups, and services and indicates the presence of buddies on your roster.

■ The Buddies tab displays a list of all your buddies and allows you to navigate through their Magi folders as though the folders were local to your desktop.

■ The Groups tab displays all your Magi groups and allows you to add and delete buddies to and from the group. You must choose Buddies/New Group to create a group.

▲ The Services tab displays the services currently available to you through Magi. In the free version (Magi Express), these services are limited to creating and subscribing/unsubscribing to a chat (Magi Channel), and creating short messages (Magi Message Box). Finally, you can monitor uploading and downloading on your machine (Magi Transfer Monitor) using a tool evocative of the Napster transfer monitor.

Figure 7-16 shows the contents of user DanaMoore's Public folder on machine Epiphyte. Any of the links in the folder are directly browsable. The left panel lists the

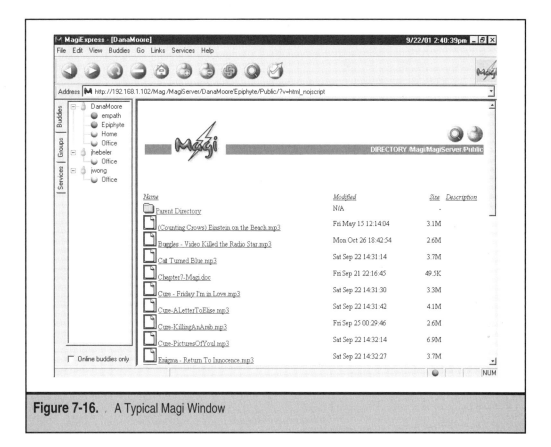

Figure 7-16.   A Typical Magi Window

presence information for the user's buddies and other machines. You learn about presence in the section "Indicating Presence," later in this chapter.

Chat

Chatting is reminiscent of IRC (Internet Relay Chat) and other unmoderated chat programs. The Chat window's title bar displays the name of the selected channel. The Magi user names of the current chatters are displayed along with the total number of chatters. The chat stream scrolls through a text area at the top of the window. If you want to do your own recreational typing (that is, add to the conversation), simply type your comments in the text field at the bottom of the window and then click the Send button.

Messaging

Messaging enables you to deliver a message to a buddy who isn't online or is away from the keyboard for a moment. Ultimately, Magi will make it possible to route a short message through to a user's mobile device (such as a pager, Blackberry, connected PDA, or wireless phone) which will offer significant advantages to using Magi. Whether this will be a part of the cost-free Express bundle or the Enterprise bundle is not known at this writing. It's certainly the kind of revenue-bearing service hook that turns open source-ware into genuine profit generators, and offers genuinely compelling services to end users.

Although we haven't talked at all yet about the business side of making P2P pay off, this is a good place to point out that often the simplest pieces of a P2P architecture are the ones that pay the freight for the rest of the product or service. Generally, this is because they fill a genuine need not otherwise addressed. In the case of messaging, a market remains unaddressed for a seamless way of getting to a user on the go without having to look up a pager or mobile number. The software agent community is currently researching how an agent assistant in the P2P system might help you to decide how and where to place most effectively a message to a user—the user's phone, an instant messaging client such as Yahoo Messenger, a Blackberry, or a PocketPC—based on the user's presence information.

Buddying Up

Since Magi is a collaboration tool, the first thing you will want to do is locate the devices of buddies, including your *own* additional devices. In response, the Magi DNS server returns the four devices for the user, shown in Figure 7-17.

After clicking the OK button, the user can see the status of all of his or her buddies' devices, as shown in Figure 7-18. Clicking on any of the names in the buddy list displays the device status of all buddies. Note that for DanaMoore the list includes both home and office machines, but the other two devices, empath and Epiphyte, are both lumped in the "Other" category. This is mildly confusing, and probably should motivate you to select one of the other categories (Home, Office, and so on) to describe your various presences.

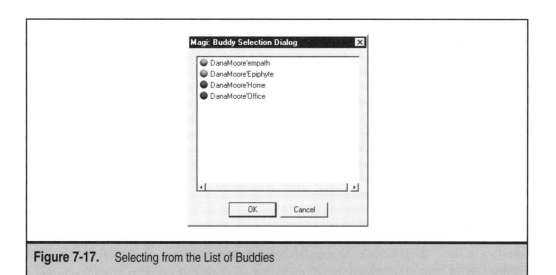

Figure 7-17.   Selecting from the List of Buddies

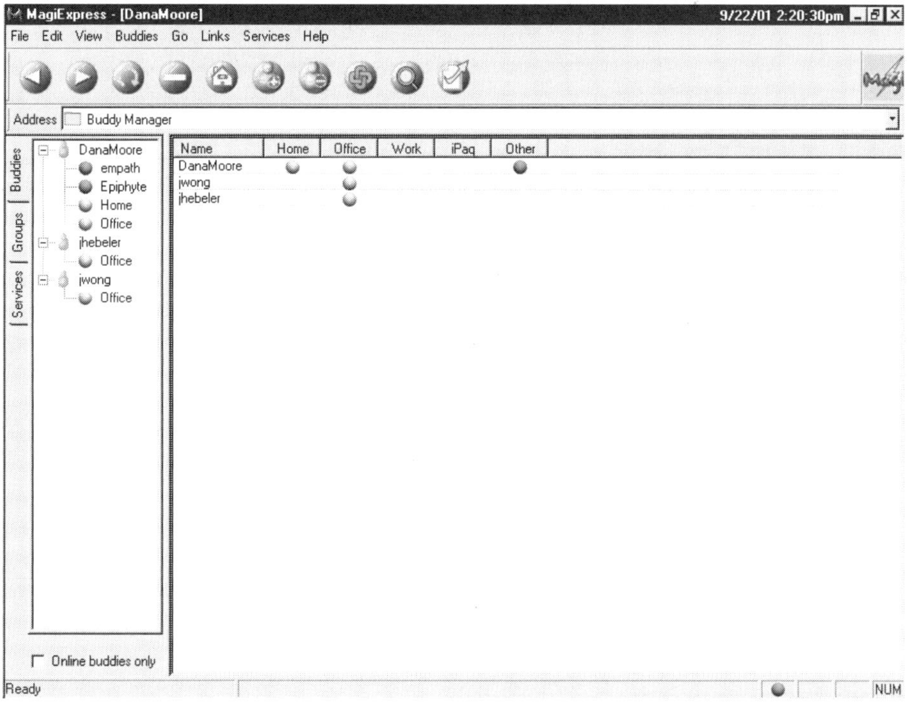

Figure 7-18.   Magi's Buddy Status View

Indicating Presence

Colored spheres in the buddy list indicate each buddy's Magi status:

- ▼ **Green**   Indicates that the buddy is online.
- ■ **Yellow**   Indicates that the buddy has been online in the last 24 hours.
- ■ **Red**   Means that the buddy has been offline for more than 24 hours or has never logged on to your server. This may also mean you are not on that user's buddy list.
- ▲ **Gray**   Indicates a connection problem and/or that the buddy does not have you listed on his or her buddy list.

Letting the mouse pointer linger over a sphere will display the time that the buddy logged on or the time that he or she logged off. As depicted in Figure 7-18, the user can see the state of the four machines over which his Magi account is active (empath, Epiphyte, Home, and Office) and the status of his buddies' devices (jhebeler and jwong).

Sharing Folders and Establishing Collaboration Groups

Magi takes a slightly different approach to sharing than does Groove. In Groove, admission to a space implies full participation in the space and all tools in the space. With Magi, you give leveled access to content by forming a group, then inserting into the group folder any content that the group shares. The group's folder automatically becomes a subfolder of Shared. Members of that group automatically have read and write access to that folder but no other subfolder of Shared. So, for example, if user DanaMoore on device Office has a group called Marketing and another called Engineering, the actual URL for the Marketing group folder would be:

```
http://mxdns.magisoft.net/Magi/Dir/DanaMoore´Office/Shared/Marketing
```

The actual URL for the Engineering group folder would be:

```
http://mxdns.magisoft.net/Magi/Dir/DanaMoore´Office/Shared/Engineering
```

The Marketing group would be able to see its content but not the Engineering group's, and vice versa. Further, although a buddy in a group would be able to browse into this URL with a normal web browser, he or she (or you, if you were logging in remotely via a browser) would need to log in. When you use the Magi client, on the other hand, you or your buddies don't need to log in, since WebDAV (built into Magi) monitors who you are, what permissions you have on a device, and what web folders are on the device. Since browsers don't utilize WebDAV, Magi forces a user to authenticate any connection other than those to the Public folder.

You can use Magi as a web-publishing tool, but it doesn't force you to use HTML as the only permissible displayable document format. Typically, before P2P tools such as Magi, if you wanted to serve up the digital photos, you would have to buy a web editor (or find a free one) and lay out the images appropriately on a web page. With Magi, just dropping files in the right place is all you really need to do. Just remember, if you put pages in your Public folder, anyone can browse to those pages. If you put them in your Shared folder, only your buddies can access them. If you put them in a group folder, only the members of the group can access them. Thus, you can use Magi to serve up documents or web pages to your family, your friends, your office, or the world. Even if you don't know how to create a web page, Magi lets you share files, pictures, and other documents with other people who are either using Magi or a web browser (including a WAP browser on a mobile phone).

You can create HTML-based web pages and send them using Magi to provide dynamic DNS, and your own PC(s) to be the web server(s). To do this, create your web pages and put them in a subfolder of the Public folder that represents the content. Then direct users to your Magi server. They can either go to the Magi Directory Service at http://mxdns.Magisoft.net/Magi/Dir/ and look up and select your Magi buddy name, or you can give them the URL of your Magi server. This URL follows the format of *buddyname´devicename* prefixed by the address of the Magi Directory Service. For example, Figure 7-19 shows a browser view of the Public folder at the following address:

```
http:// mxdns.Magisoft.net/Magi/Dir/DanaMoore'empath/Public
```

The address shown in the address text box is as follows:

```
http://192.168.1.100/Magi/MagiServer/DanaMoore'empath/Public/
```

This is because the Magi Directory Service has redirected to the device empath, NAT'd on a LAN at an address (192.168.1.100) not normally routable from outside the LAN. This capability is a pretty neat trick, and given the price of Magi Express (free), well worth it.[7]

If you're beginning to see the cool factor in Magi, you're only just beginning to scratch the surface, though, as you'll learn in the next section.

Using Mobile Magi

Browsing a Magi-enabled space like your home or work PC from another tethered device (that is, another PC) is certainly a productivity enhancer, but what about all the time you spend on the road or between campus locations, or simply in a colleague's office? Magi can render normal HTML and WML (Wireless Markup Language) or HDML (Handheld Device Markup Language), which are two strategies for rendering content to handheld devices.

---

[7]   To direct buddies to your Shared folder, substitute /Shared/ for /Public/,
as follows: http://mxdns.magisoft.net/Magi/Dir/*yourname´yourdevice*/Shared/
Also note that address components are case-sensitive and spaces in filenames must
be substituted with the underscore character (_). It's just one of those little "gotchas"
of URL addressing.

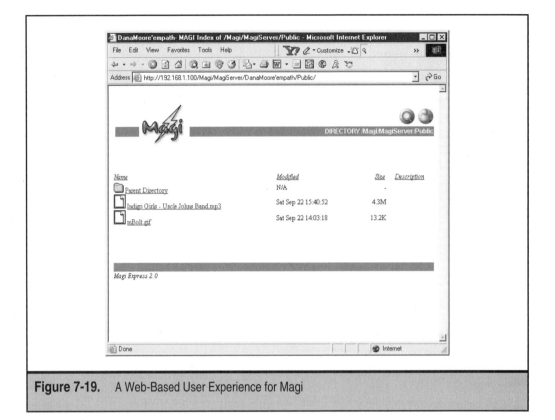

Figure 7-19.   A Web-Based User Experience for Magi

Nokia and third parties in its sphere of influence support WML vigorously. HDML is the "big dog" in the U.S. market. Openwave's followers currently serve more than half of all mobile subscribers globally and include AT&T Wireless, Verizon Wireless, Sprint PCS, and Nextel, as well as Japan's KDDI and British Telecom's Genie. Openwave's browser software is embedded in more than 70 percent of all Internet-enabled phones.

Magi's common design center is specifically mobile phones, but other wirelessly connected devices (such as the Palm line of handhelds) can render WML via third-party WML browsers such as the 4thPass KBrowser. Of the two markup languages, WML is more powerful, since it can employ on-device scripting, thus reducing the number of trips for new information across the narrow bandwidth of the wireless infrastructure. Which of the two competing standards will ultimately control more market share is open to conjecture, but there are currently a lot of disaffected WML developers, and in any case the compelling applications are slow in emerging. P2P applications such as Magi will help mobile applications become more useful and offer a more seamless user experience.

Consider that of all the information you're likely to want while mobile, the personal information rather than stale sports scores or instant financial updates is what you're likely to want to access and perhaps pay for. Suppose that you're at an extremely important meeting with a customer. Which of the following situations is likely to be more critical to you?

▼   Your laptop refuses to boot. Unfortunately, your Powerpoint presentation is stuck on the laptop.

▲   Your IBM shares are up two points and D.C. United just lost another soccer match.

Unless you're a day trader (in which case you should be hunkered over a PC making trades, not at a customer meeting) or a sports addict (in which case, you should seek professional help), the loss of your critical presentation might be slightly more important. In any case, Magi gives you the choice of remote browsing capabilities both from any PC and from a Web-enabled phone.

However, when you're on the go, the device you're most likely to have at hand is a mobile phone. Using it to browse your private information, e-mail, messages, and file system is both an exhilarating and often exasperating experience. The experience is exhilarating because it's almost certainly something you've not experienced before, and exasperating because the limitations of a telephone keypad and a skimpy four- or five-line display don't provide the smoothest user experience.

Oddly, many otherwise intelligent designers don't seem to understand the essential difference between a desktop and a mobile device, and instead insist on attempting to capture the fullness of a web experience served to a browser on a desktop machine. Designing for a mobile experience must take into account the limited processing power of the device and the context of the user. The context of the mobile user is that he or she is on the move, has limited bandwidth, and can do only a limited number of manipulations with desktop-resident content. These manipulations include searching metadata about the content, sending the content from its current location, and viewing summary data about the content (such as size, name, and type) or possibly a few words that might convey the gist of the document.

Consider the difficulty of trying to do anything beyond this:

▼   Any kind of web access from a mobile phone requires an explicit mode switch from voice mode to data mode.

■   The mobile device, with its limited memory and processing power, has very little ability to contain sufficient business logic to help a mobile user in the middle of a commute.

■   The limited display space plays havoc with menus, forcing them to be hierarchical and deeply nested. This also makes it awkward to switch to another item of equal priority.

▲   The voice user interface, the interface of choice for a telephony device, is still immature and relies on processing power in the net rather than on the device.

Accessing Magi via a Remote WAP Phone

Despite these limitations, Magi competently enables the mobile user to access the Magi space via a WAP (Wireless Application Protocol) mobile phone.

As we've suggested, what's most important for a user experience with a handheld device is not to try to replicate the experience of the World Wide Web on a PC. Rather, it is most important to use the Internet appropriately to give a user a consistent experience of remotely accessing his or her information. Thus, while interacting via a mobile phone, you should recognize folders and their contents so that you can accomplish the types of manipulations previously mentioned.

Magi enables this cognitively consistent experience by transcoding the HTML-based user presentation into the equivalent WML for presentation on a handset, and this gives a user a good feel of remotely accessing his or her information. Compare the views of the same content space in Figure 7-20 (showing the Magi PC client and the WAP phone views[8]), and you can better understand the idea of cognitive consistency. Clearly, the figures present views of the same data space; the only difference is that each is rendered to take best advantage of the capabilities of the available device. The Magi server on Epiphyte rendered each view optimally, because the server was able to understand how the data were being accessed.

WML is much like HTML in the sense that it tags data for presentation. It uses the metaphor of a card deck as shown in Figure 7-21. In the following listing, the code between the <card> </card> pair shown on lines 7 and 43 contains the presentation, internal navigation, and control logic. In some details, WML is trivially different from HTML. For example, fewer fonts are available (eight normal and eight bold fonts), and image links are not supported; images must be in WBMP (wireless bitmap) format. Note that there are some larger differences too.

```
 1. <?xml version="1.0"?>
 2. <!DOCTYPE wml PUBLIC "-//WAPFORUM//DTD WML 1.1//EN" "http://www.wapforum.org/DTD/wml_1.1.xml">
 3. <wml>
 4. <head>
 5. <meta http-equiv="Cache-Control" content="max-age=0"/>
 6. </head>
 7. <card id="intro" title="DanaMoore&apos;Epiphyte">
 8. <p align="center">
 9. <big><b>Magi WAP Server</b></big>
10. </p>
11. <p>
12. <b>Directory /Magi/MagiServer</b>
13. </p>
14. <p>Files &amp; Options:
```

---

8   The WAP phone emulator shown in Figure 7-20 is available to developers from openwave.com. In browser mode, the emulator behaves exactly as a real WAP phone would. *The Magi Express User Guide* goes into some detail about how to set up phones using Verizon and Sprint Wireless to access your Magi devices.

```
15. <select name="file" value="noact" title="File Listing &amp; Options">
16. <option value="Inbox" onpick="Inbox/?v=wml">Inbox</option>
17. <option value="Outbox" onpick="Outbox/?v=wml">Outbox</option>
18. <option value="Private" onpick="Private/?v=wml">Private</option>
19. <option value="Public" onpick="Public/?v=wml">Public</option>
20. <option value="Purchase" onpick="Purchase/?v=wml">Purchase</option>
21. <option value="Services" onpick="Services/?v=wml">Services</option>
22. <option value="Shared" onpick="Shared/?v=wml">Shared</option>
23. <!—
24. <option value="next" onpick="?v=wml&amp;O=A&amp;PN=1&amp;PS=10">Next Page</option>
25. —>
26. <!—
27. <option value="prev" onpick="?v=wml&amp;O=A&amp;PN=1&amp;PS=10">Previous Page</option>
28. —>
29. <optgroup title="Sorting File">
30. <option value="name" onpick="?v=wml&amp;S=name&amp;O=D&amp;PN=1&amp;PS=10">Sort by Name (D)</option>
31. <option value="date" onpick="?v=wml&amp;S=mod&amp;O=D&amp;PN=1&amp;PS=10">Sort by Date (D)</option>
32. </optgroup>
33. <optgroup title="Buddies Mgmt.">
34. <option value="Add" onpick="?c=B&amp;a=A&amp;v=wml">Add A Buddy</option>
35. <option value="Remove" onpick="?c=B&amp;a=R&amp;v=wml">Remove A Buddy</option>
36. </optgroup>
37. <optgroup title="Short Message Service">
38. <option value="Message" onpick="?c=B&amp;a=M&amp;v=wml">Compose Message</option>
39. <option value="MsgList" onpick="?c=B&amp;a=M&amp;s=L&amp;v=wml">Inbox Messages</option>
40. </optgroup>
41. </select>
42. </p>
43. </card>
44. </wml>
```

The <select> </select> pair on lines 15 and 41 is typically what you might see in a form on an HTML page. The tags identify a pick list of the subfolders available to the authorized user (who was required to log in to receive this WML). The <option> </option> tags in lines 16 through 22 specify that depending on the option chosen, the user will append to the originating URL the string in the onpick parameter, and this string will be submitted to the Java servlet behind the URL.

That servlet is the Magi client behind the Magi web server on your PC. So, if you scroll down to the Shared menu item, as shown in Figure 7-20, and press the OK soft key, you will pass the following string to the Unwired Planet cellular gateway:

```
"http://mxdns.Magisoft.net/Magi/Dir/DanaMoore'empath/Shared/?v=wml"
```

In turn, the gateway will create an HTTP request to your PC (or in this particular case, *my* PC). The final part of the parameter, ?v=wml, tells the servlet to transcode its output to WML.

Figure 7-20. An HTML Rendering of a Data Space (left)
A WML Rendering of the Same Data Space (right)

Figure 7-21. A WML Card Deck for a Mobile Magi User Experience

All of this may seem rather like a complex dance, but in fact it works quite well, as you can see from Figure 7-21. The information shown on the phone is precisely the same information shown in Figure 7-22. Only the device context has changed. This is what we mean by a cognitively consistent experience: Only the presentation of the data differs from device to device; if you delete a file using the phone, it will also disappear from every other view.

You might wonder whether the experience is truly consistent—that is, whether you can do precisely the same things on the mobile phone that you can do on the desktop. In fact, you can't *quite* do the same things. Since most mobile phones do not have a native MP3 player, for example, you can't *render* the file (that is, you can't play the music from the file). If the file were a Powerpoint presentation, you couldn't show it on the phone either. However, neither of these tasks is something that you would truly want to do on a handset anyway.

What you probably *would* want to do is hinted at in Figure 7-23. Scrolling through the options we see that we can choose View, Send, Email, and (scrolling down further) Fax, Print, Delete, and Move. If you actually choose View, you just get a message from your Magi stating, "File: Buggles - Video Killed the Radio Stars.mp3 File-type: unknown is *not* viewable." If you had chosen something more prosaic, such as a text file, then the WML rendering engine would have been able to format it for viewing on the device. Choosing Delete would actually operate via WebDAV to delete the file.

In summary, compared to the poor and in some cases nonexistent mobile capabilities supported by most commercial applications, Magi delivers an impressive set of capabilities. Magi also supports an appropriate set of capabilities to PocketPC and Palm OS devices as well. Since support for other devices is not a part of Magi Express, they are beyond the scope of this chapter.

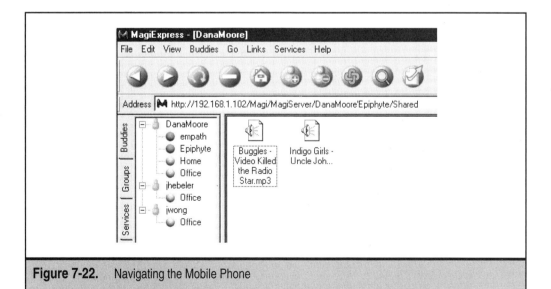

Figure 7-22.   Navigating the Mobile Phone

Figure 7-23.   Manipulating Your Magi Desktop Client via a Mobile Phone

Searching in a Magi Peer Group

The search space most familiar to many Internet users and the only one freely available is the World Wide Web. In fact, recall that Tim Berners-Lee's initial motivation for creating the Web was to create an open space to facilitate collaborative publishing among colleagues in the high-energy physics community. To achieve this level of operating system transparency, searchability, and interoperability at the document level, users would have to pay a price:

▼ There would be a single document format, HTML (thus no heterogeneous documents); anything you wanted to share would have to be explicitly and intentionally converted.

■ There would be a single protocol (HTTP) for browsing and retrieving data.

■ Special rules would have to apply to anything you wished to publish; you could include only certain directories in a web presence. Anything you wanted to make public would have to be specifically mentioned in the setup of a Web site, and any additions or modifications would have to be done with painstaking attention from you or your IT surrogate.

■ Security would be (essentially) single level, and very few ISPs would allow you to implement any security whatsoever. Thus, either your corporate or campus IT management or you (in the case of the proportionately few individuals having the constant connectivity and bandwidth and the time to host a web site) would have to set up security painstakingly at the document or folder level.

▲ Searchability would have to be based on keywords that you as the author or caretaker for published material would have to supply. In many cases, indices based on document meta-information can be extremely misleading, as some American Internet newbies eager to dash off a letter to their government may have discovered. When typing in "white house" into a search engine, one of the sites to which they may find themselves directed is www.whitehouse.com, an adult content site (rather than whitehouse.gov, the *real* White House site). You certainly can't blame the automated indexers—the adult site offers the information. Crawlers and indexers simply report what they find.[9]

```
...
1. <META NAME="Author" CONTENT="white house">
2. <META NAME="Classification" CONTENT="white house, whitehouse, the
white house">
3. <META NAME="Description" CONTENT="White House is where Your House
meets the other White House. This White House is a heckuva lot more fun
than the other White House!">
4. <META NAME="Keywords" CONTENT="white house, whitehouse, the white
house, sex">
...
```

Web publishing, as it was originally conceived, was never meant to be effortless or for the fainthearted, and the Web in general certainly neither achieved the goals nor maintained the direction that Berners-Lee set out for it.

Generally, although you can take the multiple steps necessary to prepare the output of these processors for web presentation and read-only access, the process is time-consuming and requires significant planning and execution. What you really want to have is a flavor of personal peer publishing that enables you to access your documents remotely without forethought or specific publishing steps required.

Most of the interesting things that non-Web-guru types want to publish for their own remote access and for their peer collaboration group are the documents they create on their hard disks with productivity tools. These tools include document processors (such as MS Word, StarOffice Writer, Koffice, and KWord), presentation processors (including Powerpoint and StarOffice Impress), and analyzer/calculation processors (such as MS Excel and StarOffice Calc). In particular, corporate intranets and information spaces are populated by a diverse assortment of document types. In the corporation, a mix of Word,

---

9   This particular case is so notorious that most indices will have manually corrected the problem
     by the time that this book is in print.

Excel, and Powerpoint, HTML, PDF, Framemaker, and Illustrator, among others, is the rule, not the exception. Traditional search engines index only HTML and ASCII text files, ignoring other document types. As a result, normal search engines fail to index several important classes of documents on an intranet.

Thus, even though personal peer publishing is a tough proposition, the flip side, searching and finding document spaces using current technology, is equally limiting. Finding something on the Internet that is not in "proper" World Wide Web format (HTML) can be frustrating for a variety of reasons, including the reasons discussed here and in Chapter 4. Beyond these well-known reasons, there are also problems caused by the logistics of connectivity (namely the intermittent connectivity of devices with dynamic IP addresses) and of the growth of post-PC device types.

As a wider array of devices emerges in SmartPhones and PDAs with broad range of power reserves, bandwidth, and processing characteristics, and memory footprints, the meaning of *client* shifts significantly. If post-PC edge appliances are meant to be searchable for their content, then their resources and formats must also be considered. A complete capability will include device-dependent search services, the use of proxies, and consideration of the frequency of change of information. Given these constraints, let's look at how Magi takes into account this growth in information-bearing gear.

Magi's Searching Approach

Magi also has taken additional aspects of distributed search, distributed trust, and variable connectivity into account in its thoughtful approach to the design of a distributed search system, and this approach pervades the design of Magi.

Consider, for example, the problem of variable connectivity and how it would frustrate a normal search engine. Magi designed its search and indexing in such a way that if a host became disconnected, indexing would restart precisely where it left off. As an earlier chapter pointed out, good P2P design assumes that variable connectivity is the norm. Next, there's the problem of dynamic IP addresses. As we've pointed out numerous times, good P2P design assumes that no IP address is fixed and unchanging. Magi's search service can cope with desktops or devices changing IP addresses and not index the same device multiple times. Magi's dynamic DNS, which maintains a mapping between a user's devices and their IP addresses, is used to provide "named" machines rather independent of their location. Indexing of a laptop can be done while it is on the network at the office, but the search result may return a live pointer to the file while it is logged on from home.

Also, device context is an issue. In a Magi network, a host may run in different contexts at different times. Consider a situation in which a company laptop migrates between an office environment, a home network, and an offsite conference room. In each case, a local Magi search service may query the node for its resources and services, yet the node will reveal only those resources appropriate to its context. You can accomplish this by using an automated Access.xml file and a strong authentication PKI system with symmetric keys. Additionally, all file crawling and transfers are done over SSL.

Further, consider the issues of computing and energy consumption with respect to non-PC devices. In a Magi network, hosts execute on devices with a wide range of capabilities. These devices may range from a PC workstation, to a Palm Pilot or a PocketPC, to a RIM Blackberry, or even a WAP phone, each of which offers significantly different processing power, communication bandwidth, and power requirements, and may have only intermittent access to the network. Most search engines index a site without regard to such characteristics, and thus can easily exhaust a device's limited resources. Magi's search service can determine and respect a device's unique characteristics, and avoid crippling the device during indexing.[10]

Finally, if a device is offline, Magi's search service can retrieve a copy of it from its cache. Caching can serve as a backup for corporate knowledge that might normally be lost. Caching enables limited bandwidth devices to redirect resource requests to Magi's cache, either because the cached copy is known to be up to date or because a certain degree of staleness can be tolerated.

In short, Magi's designers have wisely decided that searching is fundamental to successful P2P collaboration. Accordingly, they have designed much of their architecture on the principle that searching replaces synchronization, that content ought to remain in place near the tools of its creation, and that connectivity between islands of content is essential to collaboration.

Magi's Search Components

Magi search has three components that, when combined, are a significant leap beyond current Web-based capacities. Figure 7-24 shows Slither, Quarry, and Squirrel, Magi's search components.

Magi's Slither locates and logs to your Magi host a description of your devices. With this information, Magi can tune its output to reflect the capabilities of specific access devices.

```
1. <?xml version="1.0" encoding="UTF-8"?>
2. <!DOCTYPE device SYSTEM "http://www.endeavors.org/device-1.0.dtd">
3. <device name="Dana's Palm Pilot"
 class="PalmPilot" GUID="0x0983123210939292020292">
4. <memory>
t5. <physical>8192</physical>
6. <total>8192</total>
7. <flash>4096</flash>
8. </memory>
9. <bandwidth>600</bandwidth>
10.</device>
```

---

10   The fact that Magi can index a non-PC device *at all* is remarkable. The fact that the characteristics of the device are considered *in addition to this capability* is even more striking.

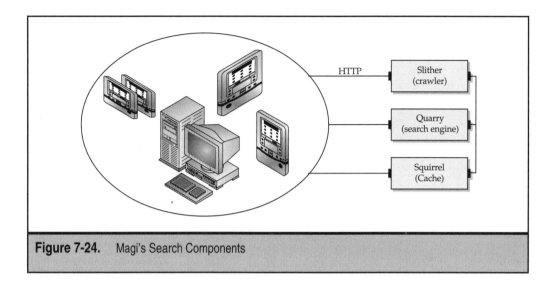

Figure 7-24.   Magi's Search Components

The GUID (unique ID) shown on line 3 allows Magi's dynamic DNS server to address the Palm Pilot, even though it may exhibit variable connectivity. The Slither search engine locates and fetches resources from a device and records them to the file devices.xml in its installation directory. Then, using this file, Magi adjusts its output to reflect a device's bandwidth, processing power, and memory. Magi can asynchronously track when device resources change and can detect new data content on the device.

Squirrel, Magi's data caching implementaion enables you to retrieve a cached copy of a disconnected Magi peer as a backup for corporate knowledge and index a variety of popular document types, including those generated by the pervasive Microsoft Office tool suite.

Magi's third search component, Quarry, provides a web-based search mechanism for the public folders of all Magi end users, indexing a variety of document types and metadata. Quarry even indexes special resources (device and service descriptions) and accepts updates directly from devices such as WAP-enabled phones, Palm devices, and devices such as the PocketPC,[11] which can display HTML directly. Magi uses of pluggable components (shown as the cylindrical shapes in Figure 7-18) to implement its GUI, chat engine, and third-party software such as the search engine. (Currently Magi uses AltaVista as the component, but others are possible.)

Using Quarry is much like using other web crawlers except that all Magi users share the same search space and the search is not limited to HTML-formatted documents. Magi allows open searches of all Public folders (and subfolders of Public) for all members and permits searches of the Shared folder for others on your buddy list. In this way, Magi

---

11   Since PocketPC devices include a compact version of Microsoft's Internet Explorer, they
operate well within the web experience promoted by Magi as being a sensible way to design
a user experience.

asserts a reasonable measure of access control to limit exposure of your file space to the outside world. In Figure 7-25, the user has asked for all the .gif files, and Quarry has returned a list of all available .gif files.

Clicking on any of the links displays a Web page and makes the appropriate file available for viewing or downloading. Obviously, you can use this same technique to remotely access your own collection of legally acquired and legally ripped MP3s. For example, Figure 7-26 shows that user DanaMoore, using machine empath, is accessing his Magi Shared folder, which is physically resident on machine Epiphyte (via the URLhttp://192.168.1.102/Magi/MagiServer/DanaMoore'Epiphyte/Shared). From the machine empath, DanaMoore has chosen to listen to a legally acquired copy of the Buggles' *Video Killed the Radio Star*.

In response, the Magi web server on machine Epiphyte will serve up the file to machine empath. Since the user has configured his browser to render MP3s via Windows Media Player, the song will render just as if it were being served from a local hard drive.

Of course, in this case, the user has the supreme satisfaction that he is doing nothing illegal, and (if the user is a U.S. citizen) is operating perfectly within the boundaries of the

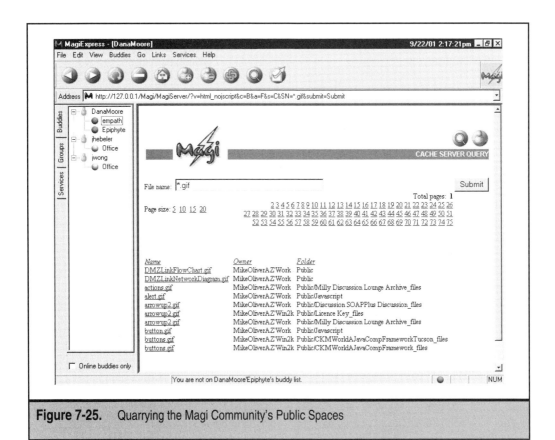

Figure 7-25.   Quarrying the Magi Community's Public Spaces

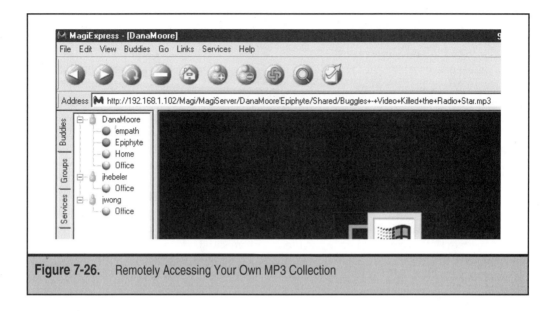

Figure 7-26.   Remotely Accessing Your Own MP3 Collection

Home Recording Act. Because there is a central server involved, as in the case of Napster, Magi as a corporate entity would presumably have the same responsibility as Napster to monitor "illegal" metadata descriptions of content residing on private machines. One big difference is that private data remain private and that anonymous access to an individual's private data is restricted to the user's Public folder. Also, since Magi is not primarily a music-sharing service and is not (at this writing) as well known as Napster, it is not likely to be a highly visible target for litigious entities such as the Record Industry Association of America (RIAA).

The access-controlled sharing done by the user remotely accessing his or her own folders, or by buddies accessing folders in a closed group, is much less likely to be externally monitored by an entity like the RIA. What *might* be illegal is copying MP3s from your Shared folder into your Public folder, as illustrated in Figure 7-21 and thus making MP3s available to anyone.[12]

Working with Metadata Rather Than Actual Data

One of the exceptional features of Magi's browser-based approach is that, unlike with Groove—whose philosophy is complete replication of the entire space, including all the documents contained within the space—the browser view with Magi displays only

---

12   This was done for illustration purposes while on a private, nonroutable LAN, and then quickly
      undone before the space was put back online. All the MP3s shown in the illustration were
      legally acquired and ripped by one of the authors. Therefore, no laws were challenged or
      circumvented. We wanted to demonstrate that while sharing music collection in this way is
      possible, there might be legal considerations.

metadata for documents. Therefore, if you were using a system with only a low-speed modem, you might prefer to forego the agony of trying to stream one of the multimegabyte music files. One oft-heard complaint about Groove is that the hidden files automatically replicated onto your system consume many megabytes of space, especially as Groove does document versioning in the background. In Magi's case, a file is transferred only if you request it.

The transfer monitor reports status of all files being downloaded. The file will reside physically in the Public folder in Magi's home directory, which you specified during Magi setup. The other advantage of offering up metadata rather than the actual data is that Magi supports the use of many kinds of devices, and clearly capabilities vary from device to device, as we touched upon earlier.

Summarizing Magi

Magi, like Groove, provides a number of critical solutions for successful collaborative computing. Magi's open source philosophy may well bring the tool the sort of success that others (such as Linux, Java, and SOAP) have had in gathering a community of stakeholders concerned about their longevity and success. Whether Magi is a "here today, gone tomorrow" phenomenon or a long-term success matters little. Its approach to design and enabling collaboration is well worth studying, and its open source approach assures that Magi will leave a legacy.

SUMMARY

Collaboration spaces provide closer connections among individuals, flexible and secure interaction among businesses, and (in some cases) a platform for building peer applications. Collaboration spaces accomplish the following:

▼ Help individuals strengthen ad hoc connections without having to make ad hoc arrangements with less coordinated tools like the telephone

■ Facilitate communication and collaboration

■ Enable users to communicate via the Internet without the need for a central server

▲ Provide a persistent "memory" (via threaded discussions, synchronized document repositories, and automatically saved chat logs) for a project and the people working together on it

CHAPTER 8

Getting Entertained: P2P Music and Video

N ow that we covered the serious side of P2P—collaboration—let's move on to P2P's fun side: entertainment. Clearly P2P established its roots in entertainment with the huge success of Napster. P2P has since moved on and offers a vast array of entertainment choices to create and share among friends or with the world at large.

This chapter focuses on two areas of P2P entertainment: music and video, or simply multimedia. The P2P multimedia world leverages three primary tool abilities: to play multimedia from your computer, to create multimedia on your computer, and to share the multimedia. All three steps are essential. Music and video each have their separate tools with similar approaches. The personal computer offers tools to create, manipulate, and manage music and video information. P2P offers the tools to share this exciting world. This chapter covers detailed instructions for P2P music and video. Let the fun begin.

MUSIC

P2P offers an exciting world of music. It potentially offers you access to everyone's music collection. P2P also allows you to access *your* music collection from anywhere. Imagine having your own Internet radio station originating from your peer computer, playing *your* music just the way you like it. We cannot easily express the sheer joy in enjoying limitless amounts of our favorite music whether it originates from our machine, our friends' machines, or a fellow peer out in Internet P2P space. Much of this book was written listening to P2P music. It kept us going through the many edits, exploration investigations, and writing sessions. You, too, can experience this.

This chapter takes you through the steps required to take full advantage of P2P music. This starts with obtaining music files from existing P2P shared music networks or creating them yourself. You then learn how to play the music on your peer. Finally, you create a P2P radio station that consists of your music broadcasted onto the Internet. Your radio station could remain private for you to enjoy when away or to share with your friends or the world.

This section details three specific steps with music files. Step one obtains existing music, creates new music, and shares the music. In step two, you play the music files through a player. Finally, step three broadcasts your music files.

Getting Music

All P2P music starts with a simple computer object: the computer file. Music starts on a peer as a given file type. The music file consists of digital information bits that represent audible frequencies. Conceptually, these bits are no different from information bits representing a document or a graphic. Whereas chapter1.doc contains instructions to Microsoft Word to display and manage a specific document, song.mp3 contains instructions for a music player application to play a specific song. In the case of music files, the bits represent music.

Music's representation as a file is a key P2P concept. The music files can take advantage of all the tools that organize and transport files from one computer to another. This simple secret produces much of the magic for P2P music.

Music files come in various formats and quality levels. Each format has its own encoding technique. This technique is similar to that used in electronic documents. The same document could be stored in Microsoft Word's format and Corel WordPerfect's format. Music files have three major formats: Wave (wav), Windows Media Audio (wma), and MPEG Layer 3 (MP3). The mnemonic in parentheses is the commonly used file extension. On the other hand, music file quality is analogous to electronic graphic storage. You can store a graphic at a detailed level in a large file or less detailed level in a small file. In either case, the graphic files maintain the same conceptual information but at different quality levels. Music files have a wide range of quality levels, from AM radio quality to CD quality. The quality levels and length of the music determine the actual size of the music file.

Wave files are traditional sampling files without any real compression. Microsoft originally created the wave format. Wave files simply sample the volume of the signal and record its corresponding digital value. Because they do not employ any compression, wave files are large—one minute equals approximately 10MB. A typical wave file for a four-minute song is over 40MB. The second format is Microsoft's new format, WMA. This format significantly improves on wave files, reducing one minute to less than 1MB. WMA is a Microsoft proprietary format. Depending on your perspective, WMA users are either held hostage to Microsoft's whims or the lucky recipients of the best, most efficient music file format. The newest WMA players have built-in security to disallow piracy and such.

The third format is MP3. The MP3 format has not achieved quite the same level of compression as the WMA format, but it is very close. One MP3 minute equals about 1MB. The MP3 format is independent from Microsoft's control, or anyone else's for that matter. The open standard of the MP3 format has escaped the large business shackles to flourish in the P2P world. The thriving format is supported by dozens of players on every major platform. Many users have MP3 storage in excess of 20GB of music on their personal computer. Playing just 1GB of MP3 files would last over 16 hours. With P2P, you can tap into this vast reservoir.

The other major characteristic of music files is quality. Each of the three formats uses a technique that digitally samples an analog signal (that's the music). Without getting into the math, suffice it to say that you have sampling options. You can sample very frequently and produce a larger, higher-quality file, or you can sample less frequently and produce a smaller, lower-quality file. Lower sampling may be very appropriate for certain situations such as transmission over low bandwidth connections, storage in a limited memory portable device, or storage of speech-only audio. The higher the sampling rate, the higher quality the sound, but keep in mind the law of diminishing returns. Generally, a sampling rate that produces a bandwidth of 160-128 kilobits per second (Kbps) produces CD quality sound. A sample at 96Kbps produces "near CD sound" (whatever that is) and 64Kbps produces FM-quality sound. Your own ears and your bandwidth requirements determine the best sampling rate.

Before moving from the topic of formats, keep in mind a final note on quality: Compression has its price. Compression squeezes out pieces of music information that are *considered* gratuitous. Ideally, this eliminates sounds that you don't care about, such as silence suppression and sounds masked by louder sounds. The deleted choices are not always correct and are subject to quite a bit of debate among the compression experts.

Modern music such as country, rock, and pop is already so electronically altered that compression largely goes unnoticed (could even unintentionally make it sound better). Classical music, which is much less subject to electronic manipulation, can suffer. Ultimately your own ears must be the judge of the compression techniques.

Some listeners are very sensitive to these compression tricks. Others remain oblivious, even with extensive levels of compression. For many listening situations, such as listening to background music while searching for more music, lower-quality audio is not a critical issue anyway. But remain aware of these techniques before you abandon your familiar digital CDs or even your analog vinyl records. Music remains precious, every note and every bit.

Of the three major file types, the MP3 format is the most flexible and ubiquitous. Changing the sampling rate can alter the quality within each of the formats significantly and the quality is proportional to the file size for the same duration.

Now that you have the necessary background on music files, let's get some music files. Getting music covers three areas: finding existing music files, creating your own music files, and finally sharing those files.

Finding Music

To obtain music files, you have two choices: You can search various P2P storage areas (a peer's hard drive and your own) using the many P2P file-searching tools, or you can create the files yourself.

There are many examples of file-sharing P2P application tools. Typically, the level of participation determines the success of these tools. The higher the participation, the more musical choices the P2P application offers to you. You explored several file-sharing applications in previous chapters. And, of course, P2P emerged on the granddaddy P2P application of them all, Napster.

We choose the Morpheus application to obtain music. Morpheus is part of a larger music initiative under way at www.musiccity.com. This file-sharing application has a large and growing number of participants in addition to some powerful technical features. You can share many types of files with Morpheus, including files containing music, video, images, documents, and software. This section focuses on finding music files with Morpheus.

Morpheus uses the dependent peer architecture discussed previously. Appropriate peers are selected for a more senior role that coordinates some P2P activity. The architecture does not depend on any one of these more senior peers. Morpheus can switch to another senior peer quickly. The really impressive advancement with Morpheus is that you can receive pieces of the file from several peers at once. Morpheus breaks up the large file transfers into smaller blocks. If multiple peers share the same file, they combine to send you the file faster. Morpheus instructs each participating sending peer to provide only pieces of the file. Sending peers can combine their network bandwidth to increase the download speed rapidly up to the total bandwidth that you maintain.

This type of file decomposition lends itself to another powerful feature. The transfer operation automatically recovers from any interruption. If either the sending peers or your receiving peer stop operating, Morpheus simply marks the current transfer progress point and, when it is possible, the application resumes the transfer right where it left off. Sending systems that stop participating can be dynamically replaced with another participating system containing the same file. This feature has one weakness: It depends on an exact match of the filename and other criteria such as sampling quality. Many files contain the same information but under a different name.

You first need to download and install Morpheus. You can find Morpheus at www.musiccity.com. Figure 8-1 illustrates the basic search screen that highlights Morpheus's search capabilities.

To search for music, you select the Audio option button. Morpheus then offers some additional searching criteria. You usually need to focus on two areas: the quality of the format (sampling rate), and the quality of the network. Morpheus eliminates the network criteria since the application automatically combines multiple senders, providing you with the best overall network throughput. Morpheus does allow you to select the format quality. We typically ask for music recorded at 128Kbps or more. Note that Morpheus doesn't allow you to search on the format type, such as MP3. Such a search is largely unnecessary due to the preponderance of MP3, but you need to watch for matched files that are not saved in your desired format.

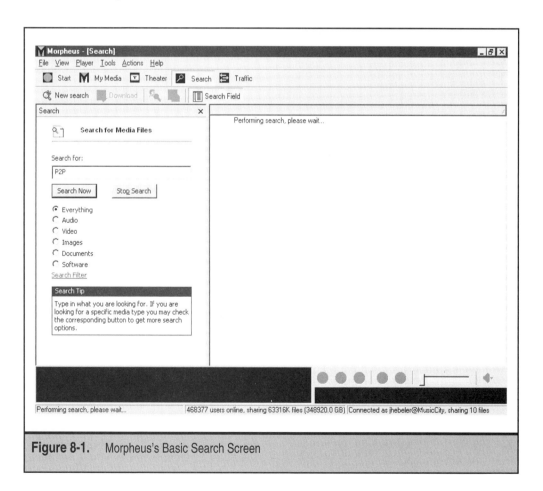

Figure 8-1.   Morpheus's Basic Search Screen

If the search is successful, the returned matches appear in the large window on the right. You merely double-click on the desired song, and Morpheus issues a transfer request to the appropriate peers. The progress of each transfer is tracked under the Traffic tab. The Traffic tab is a bidirectional transfer *dashboard* that provides a summary of all transfer progress and activity. In turn, Morpheus offers your freshly downloaded files to fulfill other users' requests. The screen lists the state of each requested transfer. If a request is under way, a progress bar indicates the percentage of the transfer completed. Many requests fail due to the dynamics of P2P computing. The current set of selected peers containing your selection may not succeed in transferring the file because of the many networks in between and because of peer fickleness.

Persistence pays. Morpheus is tenacious; some peer out there will eventually come to your aid. You and Morpheus simply need to hang in there. In addition, many files, as explained earlier, do not have a fixed format. Your desired song may come under several titles. When the titles are different, Morpheus cannot implement the feature of combining file transfers from multiple senders since the file name is different. So you may need to try several titles and see which is the first one that initiates an actual transfer.

The actual transfers are under your control. Selecting Tools | Options allows you to change any of the default control settings. The traffic settings allow you to establish the download directory to receive your files (and correspondingly the files you share with others) and throttle the bandwidth for both your requests and those requests that your system is receiving. Setting the number of simultaneous uploads and downloads indirectly determines your bandwidth utilization. You can even choose not to share any files at all.

The amount of simultaneous requests you should set depends on the overall bandwidth provided by your ISP. If your ISP has a small amount of bandwidth, set the transfer to one or two. Since the bandwidth is distributed among the simultaneous activities, selecting too many transfers causes each individual transfer to become very slow. The longer the download takes, the more likely it will fail due to the many unknown factors that arise over time with the network and the participating peers.

In addition to the Morpheus application, the P2P world offers many other file-sharing programs. They all allow simple searching and downloading. The key to your success is the level of P2P participation. All the P2P file-sharing applications tend to minimize all the technical jargon and allow you to get right down to finding your music. This simplicity often hides the fact that you *automatically* share your files too. The magic of Napster is that it made your files accessible without requiring anything from you. You became an automatic publisher. If you don't want to share files with others, you must find the appropriate options and disable this feature. You also may want to move files from the shared directory to decrease the level of sharing.

Security is not that flexible in Morpheus and similar file-sharing applications. If you choose to share, you open up your sharing directory and all its contents to the world. You cannot selectively choose users and their abilities; *everyone* has *full* read access to your shared directory. Keep this in mind as you move files on your system. You do not want to place an important file in the shared directory accidentally. With the magical magnification of P2P, the file could quickly spread across the world, never to be contained. Once it is out, you cannot pull it back. Any file resident in a shared directory is available to *everyone* participating in the application.

In all fairness, tight security works against the goals of a generic sharing application like Morpheus, so its security weaknesses are understandable. If you require selective security, allowing only designated users to access your files, choose the tools discussed in Chapter 7 such as Groove. These tools offer highly selective security appropriate for sharing sensitive information, including music files, among a trusted group.

Creating Music

Morpheus and similar P2P applications allow you to tap into the musical vastness of P2P. What if you want to create the music file yourself? You can convert original sounds and music to files and also convert your collection of albums and CDs. Many applications are available to convert original music or music on CDs.

To create music from CDs, you will explore two applications: Musicmatch Jukebox for creating MP3-formatted files, and Microsoft Media Player for creating WMA-formatted files.

Musicmatch is available at www.musicmatch.com. It is a full-feature player but also allows MP3 formats at up to 160Kbps. Many other applications that allow the creation of MP3-formatted files do not allow you to go above 96Kbps (near CD quality).

You begin creating MP3s by adding the recorder view from the View menu. If you now place your CD into the computer, the recorder view lists the CD's contents, including the song titles. The song titles come from an extensive peer-driven database referred to as CDDB (compact disk database). CDDB is a database service that incorporates contributions from fellow peers all over the world. You can check the recording settings by choosing OptionsSelect | Recorder | Settings. Figure 8-2 illustrates the recording options settings that enable you to select the format and its associated quality.

The recording settings enable you to specify the format and quality. You've already learned about the various formatting types and their sampling rates. Musicmatch allows MP3, Wave, and WMA file formats. A couple of other interesting options are available. You can set Musicmatch to record in digital mode or analog mode. This setting determines where in the stream of information flowing through your computer the application makes the recording. Digital recording is more accurate and faster. However, due to the differences in players and sound cards, you may need to choose an analog setting. Also, the recorder automatically falls back to analog recording if digital recording is not operating correctly.

The digital recording offers error correction. This feature slows down the time required for the actual recording but eliminates any clicks and pops created when seeking errors.

You must choose one final setting: the directory location that receives the newly created music files. You can find this location by clicking the Tracks Directory button. In this location, you set the desired directory and naming conventions for each file. You can choose various combinations of album title, artist name, and track name.

After choosing your settings, you need only select the desired songs in the View window and click the record button. The recorder view keeps you updated as the recording progresses. When the recording process is finished, you have just created your formatted music files.

Matchmaker Jukebox also enables you to record from other sources, including your microphone, the line-in jack from your sound card, or a combination of both. Your microphone

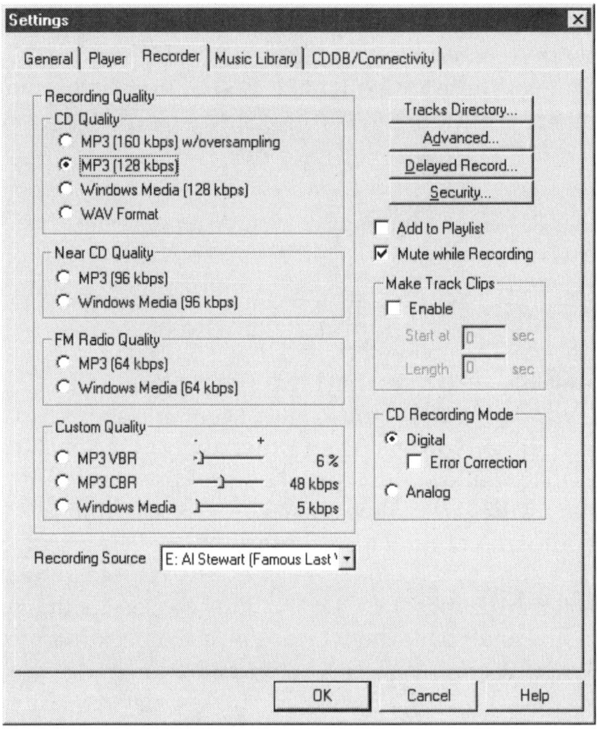

Figure 8-2. Musicmatch Jukebox Recording Settings

allows you to make live recordings from your classes and concerts. The line-in input allows you to connect any audio input source. You could record from your old tapes or albums, thus preserving them in a digital format. You simply select the source from the Recording Source control at the bottom of the Recorder tab.

Now you have a collection of music files. You can choose to play them in Musicmatch Jukebox. You can also share them with others by placing them in the Morpheus sharing directory. Everyone using the Morpheus application can then access them.

Microsoft also has an excellent conversion application. The multipurpose application Windows Media Player offers a quick, easy way to convert CDs to the WMA format. Future versions promise third-party plug-ins that can convert MP3 files, but the current version supports only the WMA format. Media Player comes standard with any new or recent computer, so you are saved from the download and installation processes. You simply load your CD and fire up the application. You select the CD Audio button from the controls aligned on the left side of the screen to display a complete track listing of the music.

The Copy Status column provides progress information when a recording is under way. It also remembers whether the song was copied earlier. Before you start recording, you must first examine the recording settings, which are located under the Options menu. Then click the CD Audio tab to see the settings shown in Figure 8-3.

In the Archive panel at the bottom part of the CD Audio tab, you can set the receiving directory to store the created files. In the Copying Settings panel, you can set the quality of the recording (that is, the sampling rate). This panel also has most of the same digital and error correcting options that Musicmatch Jukebox offers. The file format options are omitted, since Media Player only allows you to create WMA-formatted files.

After you adjust the settings appropriately, you are ready to begin recording. To do so, simply click *Copy Music* button. You can even record while you are listening. Again, you can share these newly created files by coping or moving these files to the Morpheus directory that you established earlier.

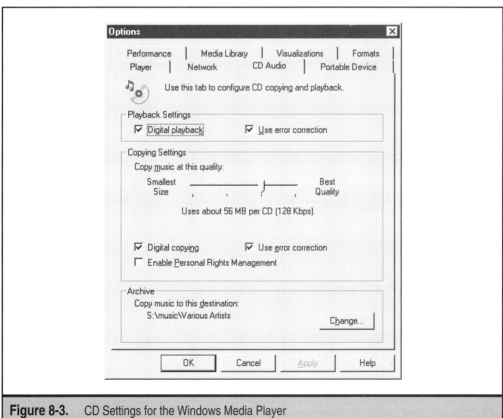

Figure 8-3.   CD Settings for the Windows Media Player

You now have two ways to create music files. Musicmatch Jukebox is very flexible, allowing all three types of formats and various quality levels. Microsoft's Media Player offers fast and easy conversion to WMA files. You can play the converted files in either application using the player features. You can also share with file-sharing applications such as Morpheus application, if you place the files in the appropriate directory.

Playing Music

This section examines some options for playing your newly created files. You have already explored two players, but haven't yet used their playing capabilities. Instead of focusing on the already discussed players, this section introduces a new one: the Nullsoft Winamp player. This application deserves attention for three reasons. First, it is an excellent player that supports all major music formats. Second, Winamp has a plug-in architecture that produces a P2P life of its own. Peers have contributed all kinds of improvements and new functionality. Third, the player forms an integral part in the establishment of your own P2P radio station, which you'll learn more about shortly.

You need to go to www.winamp.com to download the player. It works only with the Windows operating system. Make sure you get the full-feature version, which supports WMA files in addition to the other key formats. Figure 8-4 illustrates the basic player screen.

The Winamp player application consists of three windows. From the top to the bottom of Figure 8-4, they are the control panel (the main window), the equalizer, and the playlist editor. It also has a minibrowser view not shown in Figure 8-4. You'll learn about the minibrowser's value shortly.

The playlist editor lists the music for the Winamp player. Initially, it is empty. You can populate the playlist in several ways. The easiest is just to select the music files from a Windows directory window and then drag them directly to the playlist. You can also select the Add button to add a selection of files or an entire directory. The playlist reflects the sum total of all the files that you have instructed Winamp to play. If you want to use the playlist again, you need to save the playlist by selecting the List Options button (in the lower right of the screen) and selecting Save List. You can restore your saved list by entering it just like a music file. You should create some large list files that cover various categories or themes.

You are now ready to move on to the control panel. The control panel resembles CD or tape controls. The Shuffle button randomizes the playlist, and the curved arrow button enables you to set replay modes. If you have a long playlist, selecting the Shuffle button combined with the replay creates a steady flow of your music. Essentially, this selection creates a local radio station. Your selection is not P2P yet, for only your computer can access the musical stream. But it is the first step in establishing the P2P radio station.

The equalizer window is self-explanatory. You are free to adjust the frequency emphasis in the many bands provided. You can also save various settings. This window is useful for different listening situations such as listening through headphones.

Winamp has many fun extensions due to its flexible architecture. The first is skins. Skins enable you to adjust the overall look and feel of the application. There are hundreds of skins, ranging from futuristic to mundane. Many are based on popular characters or celebrities. You can change skins with a simple menu selection.

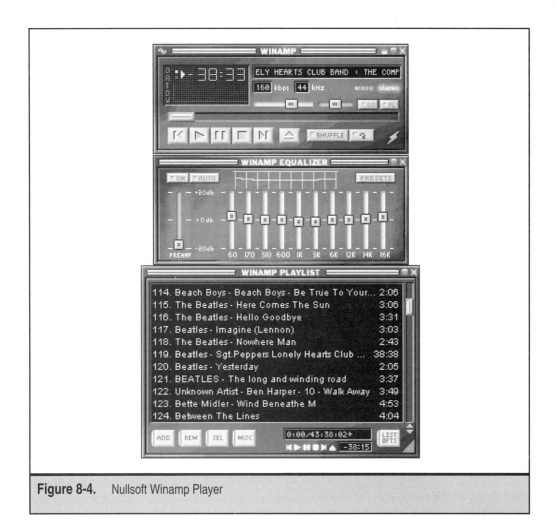

Figure 8-4.   Nullsoft Winamp Player

Another fun Winamp extension is the browser window. The browser behaves as a normal, albeit fixed-sized, browser. You can explore any Web site. The integrated browser window enables you to access the many Winamp extensions directly. These include visual music effects, digital music plug-ins, games, and information directly related to the song currently playing. We are not sure if this is a distraction to keep you in the Winamp world or a wonderful extension of a powerful player. Have some fun and decide for yourself.

The flexibility of Winamp and the player's large following show much promise for the future of the application. The next release promises advanced playlist features that self-organizes and assembles into a rich database of all your music as well as improved transfers to portable devices. Stay tuned to this exciting application.

Broadcasting P2P Music: Your P2P Radio Station

Now you have the foundation to create your P2P radio station. You can create music files in the various formats, share them with fellow peers, and play them back in several players. You just need to set up your broadcast capabilities. You now take the leap to establish a P2P broadcast station.

Before going directly into the implementation, you need to understand the basics of Internet broadcasting. Internet audio broadcasting transmits your music files as a buffered stream. This transmission is also referred to as *streaming*. You need an architecture that converts your selection of music files into a different format—a buffered stream.

The buffered stream technique solves two network problems. First of all, music files are large. If you have to download them first in order to play them, a large delay would be evident. Streaming allows you to play music almost instantly. Unfortunately, this causes the second problem. Internet bandwidth is not consistent. Streaming must adjust for these inconsistencies in order to deliver the music in a timely fashion.

The buffered stream makes up for the inconsistency in bandwidth for most peers. Let's demonstrate with an example. Your listener is connected to the Internet with bandwidth that averages 128Kbps. You want to stream music that was sampled at 128Kbps. This requires a steady transfer of 128Kbps. Due to the inconsistencies of the Internet, your listener's connection eventually falls below 128Kbps, and the remote P2P playback fails. Streaming adjusts for these inconsistencies. Streaming buffers the content by building up *extra* samples when the connection goes above 128Kbps. These extra samples fill in when the connection drops below 128Kbps. As long as the connection maintains at 128Kbps or above average over relatively short intervals, the approach works fine. The initial buildup of the buffer causes a startup delay when you begin listening to a stream. Streaming is an effective fix for the inconsistencies of today's Internet.

Now that you have the necessary background, let's put it to use. The P2P radio station requires two additional software components beyond the tools that create music files and play them back. The first software addition converts the output of a music player application into a stream. Your digital music makes an additional translation to a streaming source. The second software, the streaming server, assembles the streaming source into a port on your system that a remote listener can access. The streaming server can serve as many listeners as your bandwidth and processor capabilities allow. Figure 8-5 illustrates the overall architecture from music source to remote peer listener.

The streaming converter takes advantage of the plug-in capability of your Winamp player. You add a DSP plug-in that handles the conversion. You can find this plug-in, referred to as the SHOUTcast broadcasting plug-in, at www.shoutcast.com. The plug-in converts the song currently playing into a network-available stream. You first need to download and install the plug-in. The installation process automatically integrates the plug-in with your Winamp player.

Now you need to configure the streaming converter. Select Options | Preferences, then select DSP/Effect under Plug-ins heading. The newly added plug-in appears, entitled Nullsoft SHOUTcast Source DSP. Select the plug-in and click the Configure button. A four-tab window appears.

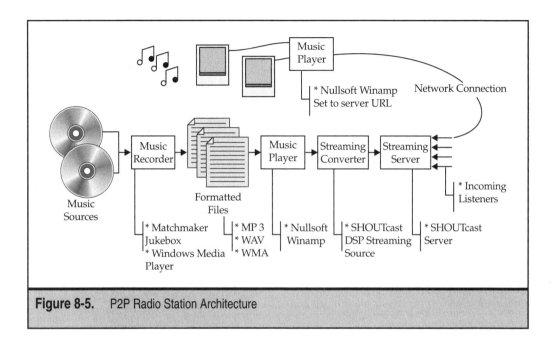

Figure 8-5.   P2P Radio Station Architecture

You now need to set up the input to the stream, the encoding of the stream, and the output of the stream. First, let's configure the input. You need to select Winamp as the input source. This selection establishes the current music generated from the Winamp player as the source of the stream. Click the Input tab to display the screen shown in Figure 8-6.

Next you click the Encoder tab to display the screen shown in Figure 8-7. You can set the encoder to your required broadcast quality level. This valuable feature alters the quality of the original source to best match your bandwidth requirements. You do not want to force your radio to play the bandwidth of the recorded song. Doing so can be a prohibitive problem if you have a huge collection of files with 128Kbps quality and you want to broadcast to listeners who do not have bandwidth of 128Kbps or above. A very safe, yet acceptable, level is either 56Kbps or 96Kbps.

The last step is to set up the output connection. Click the Output tab to display the screen shown in Figure 8-8. Here you configure the location of the streaming server. The server can run on any networked location. If the server is running on the local machine, you need only to enter *localhost*. If the server is running on a remote machine, you may enter its URL or IP address. You must also set up the port. Typically, the connection uses port 8000. There is also a field in which you enter a password. The streaming source must have permission to connect to the addressed streaming server. Winamp determines the permission by sending the streaming server a password. The password entered in the streaming converter must agree with the password for the streaming server. The other settings within this configuration establish the connection between the streaming converter and the streaming server. But first, you have to set up the streaming server.

Figure 8-6. SHOUTcast Streaming Converter Input Configuration

Figure 8-7. SHOUTcast Streaming Converter Encoding Configuration

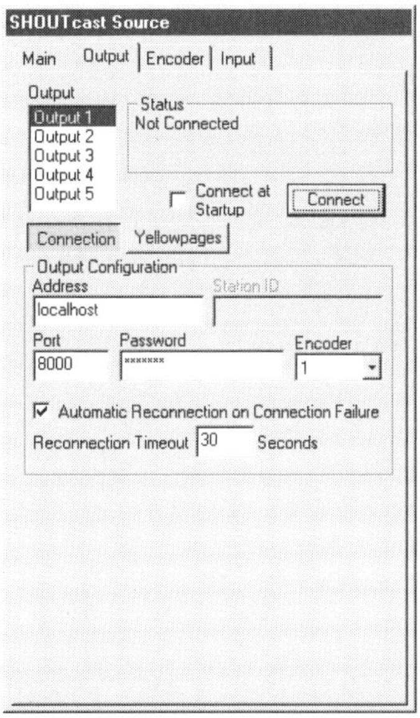

Figure 8-8.   SHOUTcast Streaming Converter Output Configuration

The streaming server is the SHOUTcast server. It receives the produced stream from the streaming converter and offers it to multiple networked listeners. The server controls and multiplies the stream for all your P2P listeners. You need to download and install the application. It is separate from Winamp and runs as an independent application. Let's get it started.

The server has not connected with your streaming converter, so it has nothing to offer to any listener. You need to set several configuration parameters. A word of caution here: The configuration interface is very basic and does not contain cute drop-down menus and buttons. Instead, it offers a straightforward text interface. It uses simple text files to drive its configuration. You edit the text configuration by clicking the Edit config option. It opens the Windows application Notepad to allow your edits. Be very careful not to delete or modify the text accidentally. This text file directly drives the SHOUTcast server. Before any changes in the file take effect, you must restart the SHOUTcast streaming server.

Luckily, only a few options require adjustment. Each setting is preceded with an explanatory paragraph. The most important is the password setting. The password value must agree with the settings in the streaming converter entered in the last section. You also need to check that the port agrees with the streaming converter. You can also select the maximum number of listeners. The correct setting depends on your bandwidth. You do not want to invite more listeners than your bandwidth can accommodate. If you are broadcasting a 128Kbps stream and you have a 512Kbps network connection, you can allow only four listeners. If you accept more than four, the server cannot operate correctly. A fun option to set is the TitleFormat. This gives your radio station a name that prints out in the listener's player.

The SHOUTcast server comes with a complete Web service. The URL for the Web service is http://*yourURL*:8000. Figure 8-9 illustrates the Web home page of your radio station.

The Web interface provides status, administration capabilities, and a listing of the last songs played. The interface also enables you to launch the player directly with the correct URL, so that you can control your streaming server from a remote location. You can even disallow a current listener. The interface also gives your listeners an easy steppingstone for obtaining the stream. They must have the Winamp player or a similar one installed.

Let's return to the Encoder tab shown in Figure 8-7. You now need to connect the streaming converter to the streaming server by clicking the Connect button. If the connection is successful, the upper-right corner indicates the amount of data transferred to the streaming server. You can also set the connection to reconnect on a failure and on the startup of Winamp automatically. This automatic reconnection works only with MP3-formatted files. Any other format does not translate into a stream.

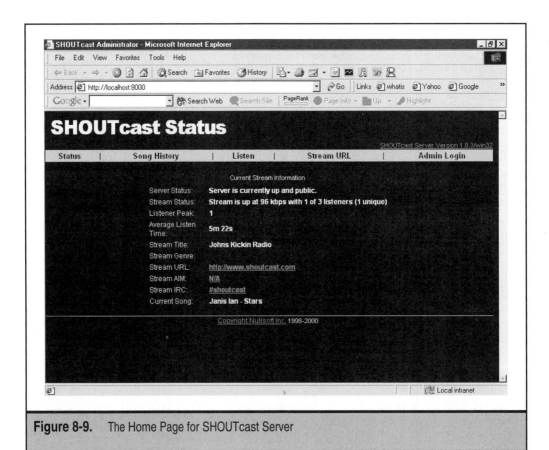

Figure 8-9.   The Home Page for SHOUTcast Server

Your listeners have two choices when tuning in to your radio station: They can use the Web interface already discussed, or they can set the URL directly in the player. In either case, it is the same URL—http://*yoursever*:8000. The remote player needs to support the MP3 streaming format. Clearly, Winamp supports this format, but other players do as well, including the player application freeamp, found at http://www.freeamp.org. In addition, freeamp supports the Linux operating system.

The streaming server offers another service of note. You can stream files *on-demand* directly from the streaming server. You must place the formatted MP3 files in the directory specified in the streaming server configuration file. You can reference each music file directly by entering the following URL: http://*yourserver*:8000/content/*songname*.pls.[1] You could create a Web page that lists all your songs within the directory and choose whichever ones you want. This ability is above and beyond the streaming from the streaming converter. The streaming server can do both simultaneously—streaming a continuous list of music and allowing on-demand selections.

Your P2P Radio Station's Hours of Operation

You now have an operating radio station that continuously plays the playlist set in the Winamp streaming source. Now you establish the hours of operation. A P2P radio station takes up significant computing resources including bandwidth, processor capacity, hard-disk seek time, and memory. You may not want or need a 24-hour, seven-day radio station. You might prefer to play your radio station during your lunch hour so that you can access it from work, for example.

How do you establish the window of time during which the radio station is active? You take advantage of a Windows 2000 or Windows XP feature that can start and stop applications automatically. Windows offers a *schedule tasks* setting in the control panel. Select the schedule tasks settings and click on Add Schedule Task. This starts up an easy-to-use wizard to determine the application name and such. The Scheduled Task Wizard first asks you to select the specific program.

The next window asks for the periodicity of running the program. This could be daily, weekly, monthly, every time you log on, or every time you start your computer. If you want your radio station to run every weekday at lunch, you would select daily. In the next window you would then select weekdays and the start time of 12 P.M. The next screen requests the user ID in order to run the program. This allows the program to run with the correct privileges even if you are not logged in while starting up the program. If everything has been successful so far, the wizard greets you with a summary window.

This process covers starting up the program. To shut it down, you must open the advanced properties window by selecting the *Open advanced properties for this task* check box. This brings up a new window containing several advanced configuration settings. You must set the maximum run time on the Settings tab. To cover a generous lunch break, you stop the task after running for two hours. Figure 8-10 demonstrates the two-hour setting.

---

1   Do not include the extension .mp3. Use .pls instead.

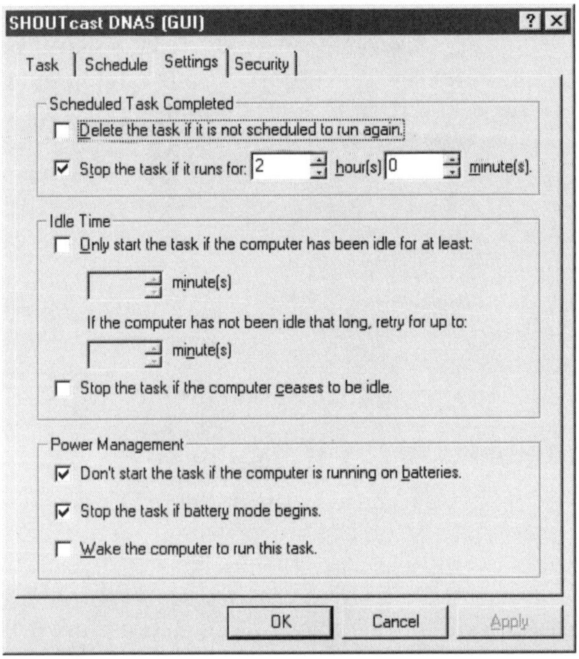

Figure 8-10. The Windows Scheduler Stop Time Window

If you do not set the end time, the program keeps running until the machine stops or the program fails.

To run your radio station, you need to schedule two tasks: running Winamp to generate the stream, and running the SHOUTcast streaming server to broadcast the stream to your listeners. You also need to set some additional configuration parameters in the Winamp plug-in. In the SHOUTcast server's Output tab, you must select Connect at Startup and Automatic Reconnection on Connection Failure (see Figure 8-8). These settings initiate the stream connection automatically and retry if an error is encountered.

One other setting is necessary. Your two scheduled programs now will start each weekday at 12 noon and run for two hours. However, Winamp does not automatically start playing. You must pass Winamp a parameter with your playlist. This parameter informs Winamp to start playing on startup. You can find this setting also among the advanced settings. The playlist is entered on the Tasks tab under the Run text box. Figure 8-11 illustrates the run-time parameters. You simply enter them directly into the text box.

Your radio station is now up and running during the hours that you have specified. Maybe you want the station only for your own needs, and want to set it for the lunch hour so that you can relax to your tunes wherever you are enjoying your lunch, or maybe you want to share it with your friends or even the world.

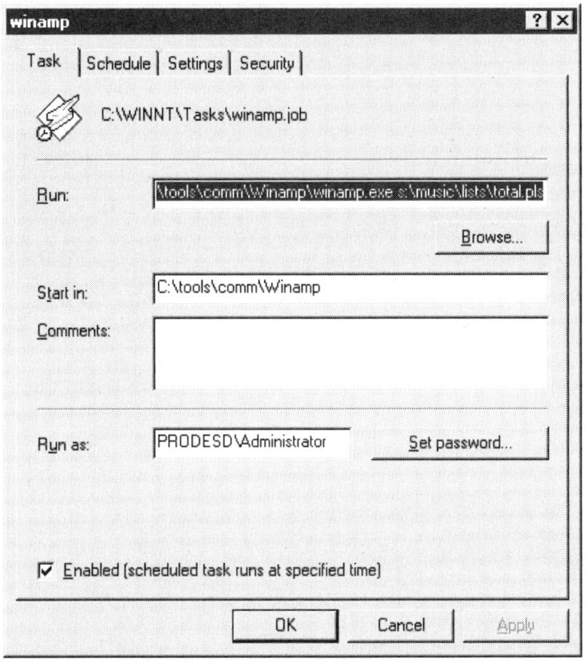

Figure 8-11. Windows Scheduler Run-Time Parameters

Note that this schedule technique is useful for any P2P service you offer. You can set the hours of availability for any service you want to offer. This provides you with complete control over the service's availability.

A P2P Expansion of Your Radio Station's Bandwidth

Your radio station audience is limited to your network's bandwidth. As discussed earlier, a 512Kbps bandwidth would be limited to four 128Kbps connections. How can you expand your radio station to a larger audience without bringing a T1 line to your computer? You actually have a simple option to expand your radio station in an unlimited fashion. Any of your listeners can act as a relay to use their bandwidth for connections. New listeners would not connect to you, but rather to your relay. Each new connection can also be a new relay. This relay process can go on forever—a true P2P accomplishment. This approach is a manual operation where each user must enter the repeated station and track its local P2P location. But an approach similar to that of the Chaincast product, explored in the Chapter 3 tour, could eventually automate the P2P distribution.

Getting Your Radio Station Known

Enabling you and others to locate your radio is the final step. You may or may not want your radio station to be known to others. You can name your computer as outlined in Chapter 6. This provides a URL that translates your current IP address into an easy-to-remember name. You can then distribute the URL and the selected port number. Your listeners simply enter the URL into their player and immediately begin listening, or enter the URL into their browser where they are greeted with information about your station and how to listen. In any case, they must have a compatible player on their machine, and the network connection must be adequate to handle the additional exchange.

You can also choose to register your radio station with the world. The SHOUTcast Web site (http://yp.shoutcast.com) offers a directory for all radio stations that are open to the public. The SHOUTcast configuration parameter, PublicServer, found in the SHOUTcast configuration file, can be set *always* to allow public registration or *never* to disallow public registration. You can also set up your station description by selecting the Yellowpages button in the Winamp player (see Figure 8-8).

Finding Other P2P Radio Stations

The SHOUTcast yellow pages offer a multitude of options for finding other P2P radio stations. These are live stations resulting from a registration from active SHOUTcast streaming servers. The SHOUTcast server provides regular updates to maintain an accurate picture of which P2P radio stations are active. You can search by bandwidth, genre, or a specific word. The upper-right corner provides status detailing the number of active radio stations and their associated number of listeners. Typically, there are thousands to choose from. Our radio station is entitled "John's Kickin' Radio." You may even find it working. It plays only classic rock. We did a search on *John,* and found our station as the fifth entry. It even lists the current song. You can also join a chat. Figure 8-12 details the response from the SHOUTcast yellow pages.

P2P radio stations broadcast directly from each peer. You can find a unique listening experience or create one of your own.

Music Summary

Music gave prominence and recognition to P2P. Sharing music all starts with converting music into standard file formats and then moving the files around. Compression techniques using formats such as Windows Media Format or MPEG Layer 3 combine with larger disk drives and broadband to provide an easy, affordable approach. P2P already offers many options to move files, such as the Morpheus application and others. You can also choose to stream your files in real time, thus creating your own online P2P radio station. P2P extends music's reach and your connection to your music files and those of peers.

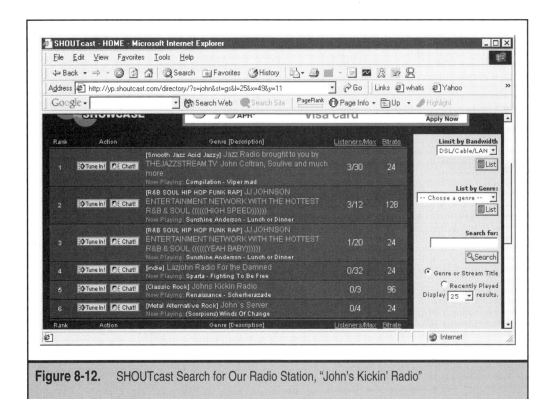

Figure 8-12.   SHOUTcast Search for Our Radio Station, "John's Kickin' Radio"

VIDEO

P2P video shares many similarities with music. The electronic video capture translates into regular files noted with a special file extension. The video files support standard formats. Each format allows quality variations that directly affect the files' size. There are few key differences. Video takes many more bits of information than music. This poses a couple of challenges for P2P. Good video requires significant bandwidth—bandwidth that often exceeds that of the typical P2P user. Video files are huge; just a short video often requires hundreds of megabytes. Additionally, the video software applications are not as mature as the music applications, and your choices are more limited. Still, there is lots of fun to be had with video.

Setup requires some creativity, for video is still finding its niche in the P2P world. The choices do not follow clear standards and they are often deficient in key areas. None of the video implementations has the maturity of the P2P music applications, but many useful video applications are available, and the field is evolving quickly.

You will follow a similar course with video as with music. First you will find existing videos, then create your own videos, play your videos, and broadcast them directly from your video camera or from prerecorded videos, effectively creating your own P2P television station.

Getting Video and Graphics

You can obtain video and graphic files with the same sharing applications as music. The Morpheus application discussed in the "Music" section also offers a wide selection of video and graphics. Video files are much larger and therefore are more difficult and frustrating to acquire. Because larger files are less likely to be multiplied among many peers, they usually are stored on fewer peers. The longer download time means that the connection must stay active much longer. The connection is susceptible to the same problems that music downloads have, such as peers turning off their computer or stopping the application, or the network simply becoming congested. The longer download time simply increases the likelihood that the overall download will fail.

Some of the advantages of Morpheus help make up for these frustrations, but the application's strengths are often still not enough. Morpheus, when possible, acquires the files from multiple peers simultaneously and remembers where a file transfer left off if it stops for any reason. Persistence is eventually rewarded, but acquiring video files does take longer than acquiring the smaller, more prevalent music files.

Another issue that detracts from P2P video is its low quality. Whereas music files achieve a close semblance to CD music quality, video is often not close even to the quality of standard videotapes, much less that of DVDs. Many videos offer a picture quality that is small and grainy. It is in many cases more a novelty than a viable form of entertainment. However, recent advancements are quickly closing the gap.

The major video fiasco of the Victoria's Secret online fashion show reveals the weaknesses of recent video Internet broadcasts. Often the viewers couldn't tell whether the video was showing a bra, a human being, or just a blurry white thing. And that was if they were lucky enough to obtain a connection to the overtaxed site. However, some of the new videos are finally taking advantage of larger bandwidths (greater than 300Kbps) and new compression techniques. These videos provide a peek into future possibilities and offer quality well beyond that of a grainy postage stamp. The trailer for the movie *Lord of the Rings: The Fellowship of the Rings* demonstrates the progress (see www.lordoftherings.net).

Still, some videos are worth a thousand words, and the medium is evolving rapidly as prices drop, bandwidth increases, and computing platforms become more video-friendly. Video is useful today and shows real promise for tomorrow.

Four types of video formats are the Audio Video Interleaved (avi) conforming to the Microsoft Windows Resource Interchange File Format (RIFF) specification, Apple's QuickTime format (mov), Windows Media Video, and the MPEG-3 (mpg or mpeg) format commonly referred to as *mpeg*. The latter format is not the same as MP3, which uses a different MPEG standard. There is also the emerging MPEG-4 standard, which promises very high-quality video. The video players such as Windows Media Player, Apple's QuickTime Player, and RealPlayer from RealNetworks play all the main formats. To play MPEG-4, you must download the decoder at www.divx.com. The site also contains a nice, simple player. If a player is unable to play a specific format, it searches for a plug-in module that can convert the format, then (if available) automatically installs it. So playback is straightforward and easy.

Each format offers a range of quality levels determined by the number of pixels, color depth, and the number of frames per second. The number of pixels directly determines the video size and its level of detail. The color settings determine the richness of color. The frames-per-second setting controls the smoothness of the video. The fewer frames per second, the more the video stutters and appears unnatural. The formatted file grows larger with any increase in the number of pixels, the level of detail, the depth of color, or the number of frames per second. Video contains a wide range of variables and correspondingly results in a wide range of file sizes.

In searching for videos, you will find many shorts and a few full-length features. The typical length of a video is a minute or two. Depending on the quality level, a minute of video may range from several megabytes to 40 or more megabytes. As you explore P2P video, you will quickly determine that offerings are not nearly as plentiful as for P2P music. However, feel free to use the Morpheus application to download some videos. It takes longer to find your desired video and much longer to download it. But if you are patient, Morpheus will eventually succeed.

Video is closely related to graphics that represent a single snapshot. The preferred graphical format for pictures is JPEG. The JPEG format compresses the graphics by eliminating unnecessary information contained in the graphic. Typical pictures are not large and rarely exceed 200KB, and less than half of that size still produces a high-quality picture. Since cameras are in reality rapid photograph takers, it is no surprise that the cameras can also generate snapshots.

Creating Video

Many tools are available that enable you to create your own videos. All the options involve a digital camera. Digital cameras vary widely in quality. The most common and inexpensive is the webcam, which is a small camera that sits upon you main computer or laptop. Webcams are inexpensive and provide low-quality video. Their limited abilities are a perfect match for the P2P world of today. High-quality digital video cameras have recently just emerged on the market. You can download the digital video and manipulate it. These high-quality videos are somewhat ahead of current P2P capabilities. We stick to the webcam for practical P2P applications.

A webcam can also generate pictures. The picture format is usually JPEG. It also has quality parameters that include the number of pixels and the color depth. Graphics deliver a single snapshot to a file. Video delivers a sequence of snapshots to a single file. That is the only real difference.

Any webcam package that you purchase usually includes software to generate video and photograph files. Rather than tie you to any specific webcam hardware, this section demonstrates the use of two software applications that are independent of any specific hardware: Microsoft's Windows Media Encoder and Surveyor's Webcam32 application.

The Windows Media Encoder is free and available directly from Microsoft. It can incorporate the input from a video camera and a microphone to create a video file encoded in Windows Media Video (wmv) format at various settings. It also can provide a video stream for your P2P television station.

The Windows Media Encoder starts by examining the connection to the camera and the microphone. If the encoder finds your hardware acceptable, it lets you establish a recording session. A session wizard helps you set up in sequence all the necessary configuration information. The wizard first asks you the type of selection— a live stream, a saved video, or a conversion of an existing video file to the wmv format. The latter is a useful translation tool, with only one caveat: You must convert the file to the Windows format.

You are going to make a saved video file, so you select the middle choice, "Capture audio or video from attached devices or computer screen." Next you select the specific devices for the recording. You can select your specific cameras and microphones. (You can have more than one of each, as you'll learn later.) You can also create a movie composed of screen sequences. This option is useful if you want to demonstrate the operation of an application. You simply record the screen flow as a movie. You can even insert your dialog box. The next wizard selection window details the output file. Keep in mind that the files can be quite large, so make sure you have plenty of space on the particular drive.

There are a few more configuration parameters. The next step requests the ultimate purpose of the file (see Figure 8-13). You can set the file to be optimal for a streaming server or a Web server. The former produces the best file for your purposes. The next step

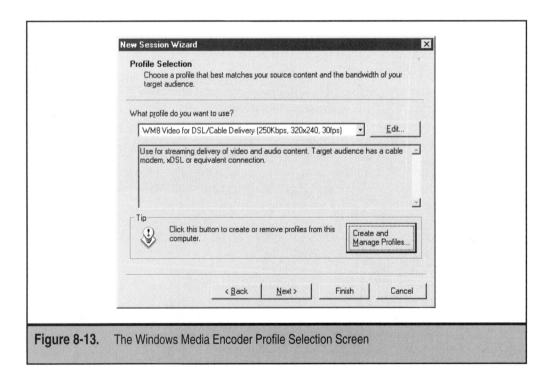

Figure 8-13. The Windows Media Encoder Profile Selection Screen

defines the quality level of the video. The application lists specific profiles that combine several of the quality factors. A nice balance of the various factors for broadband connections is the profile WM8 Video for DSL/Cable Delivery (250Kbps, 320 × 240 pixels, and 30 frames per second). If you do not find a profile that meets your specific needs, you can click the Create and Manage Profiles button. In the resulting screen, you can create any combination of quality factors you need and then save them as a new profile.

The last configuration screen contains metadata to describe the video. Your configuration is now finished. You are now ready to shoot your first video. You simply click the start button in the lower-right corner. The video continues until you click the stop button.

The file is automatically saved to the filename set in the configuration. You can play it back using the Windows Media Player. Your masterpiece is ready for sharing. If you wish to maintain private sharing, use the collaboration tools discussed in Chapter 7. Otherwise, you can offer the video to P2P-sharing applications such as Morpheus.

The other software webcam application is Surveyor's Webcam32. The Webcam32 application was our first exposure to the power of a webcam application. We explored the many functions until late in the night on several occasions. This application has a multitude of features beyond simple video recording. We are still having fun with it and discovering new possibilities.

Webcam32 operates more like your multimedia P2P control center than a straightforward recording tool. You can set it to do all kinds of video and graphic operations. In some ways, these capabilities make the application more powerful than Windows Media Encoder. You can set a graphic or video operation against an event you set. The event can either be time-based or motion-based. The latter option is an exciting way to monitor activity automatically—a motion detector.

You will examine these advanced features shortly. Let's first create a simple video file. As with Windows Media Encoder, you must first set the configuration. You start by choosing File | Preferences. You then select Capture, for you are going to capture graphic information into a file. Because you are creating a file, you select avi in the leftmost panel. This selection brings up the window displayed in Figure 8-14.

The AVI File name setting specifies the fully qualified filename of the capture's destination. Other settings give you complete control over the camera. In the Frame Interval control, you can set how often the camera takes a picture. In the Playback Frames/sec control, you can set how often the pictures are revealed to the viewer. The combination of these two controls specifies how condensed time is and how quickly the viewer sees the playback. For example, you may choose to take a picture every minute (Frame Interval = 60000) and view it at 10 frames per second. These settings create a timed video that presents a 10-minute period for each second viewed.

You may want to see the goings-on in your study throughout the day. Given the same settings, you could view an entire eight-hour day in about 48 seconds. The camera doesn't capture everything during the eight-hour day, for you take only one snapshot every minute. You can decide the threshold for the frame interval. The saved file can either be compressed or uncompressed. The uncompressed format creates huge files. Compression takes advantage of unnecessary and repeating patterns and serves most webcams extremely well. If you set up your camera to take continuous snapshots of the same view, compression can eliminate the redundant video information.

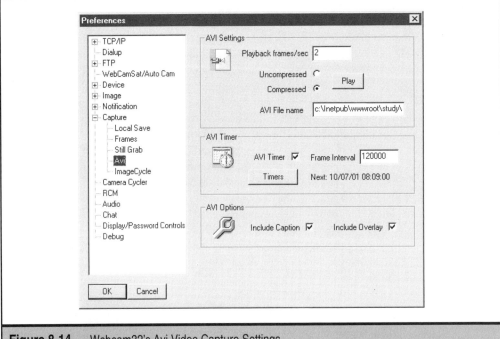

Figure 8-14. Webcam32's Avi Video Capture Settings

For a typical continuous view, compression shrinks the file size by multiple orders of magnitude. Let's set the application for real-time video of 15 frames per second and a matching frame interval of 67 (1,000 milliseconds divided by 15). You also need to set up the pixel size and color parameters found in the Preferences window under Device and Format menu selections. Then just click the OK button to set your configuration. You only need to click the stop sign to start recording—which is not necessarily intuitive. To stop recording, click the stop sign again. The avi file is now created in the directory that you specified. You can play it using Windows Media Player or the Webcam32 application.

This is only the start of Webcam32. Let's dig a little deeper into its video capabilities. You can combine the previously mentioned settings with a video motion detector. You may not be interested in seeing real-time pictures of your study desk chair, especially for eight hours. However, if you set the video as in the first example, which displayed eight hours in less than a minute, you would miss anything that happened within the one-minute interval between pictures. The solution combines two features of the Webcam32. You first configure the settings to take real-time pictures as previously described, with the frame interval set to 67 and the playback set to 15 frames per second. Then you add a new feature found in the Preferences dialog box. Simply click Image, then Video. Figure 8-15 shows this configuration window.

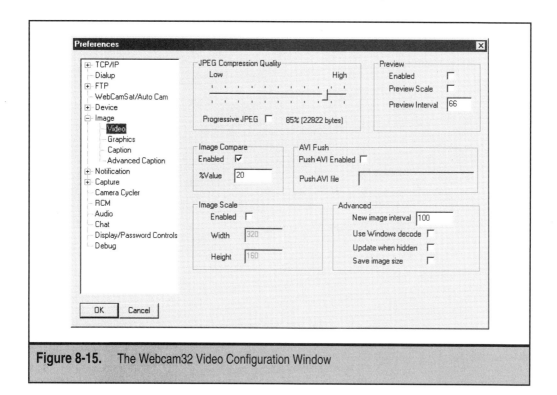

Figure 8-15.   The Webcam32 Video Configuration Window

If you select the Enabled option in the Image Compare panel, the picture is saved to the file *only* if the picture changes by the indicated percentage. The camera takes a picture and compares it to the last picture. If the image changes by the indicated amount, the application saves the picture. If there is not a change, the application doesn't save the picture, but uses it for the next comparison. A small percentage indicates little or no change in the picture. A large percentage suggests a major change in the picture. Thus, the application saves only significant activity in the image area. Thus if you set the camera for real-time but with an Image Compare threshold, you see only the events in front of the camera. The result is essentially a "highlights" video.

Another valuable feature allows you to schedule the camera to turn on and off automatically. This feature eliminates the need for the Windows scheduler. The camera then allows you to set up the picture-taking intervals, determine whether to save the picture based on changes, and have it automatically turn on and off.

We can't leave the topic of video without discussing some finishing touches. You can add pictures and text captions to the video. The pictures can add a visible mark to your video much like a television station placing its call letters or logo over the bottom corner of the screen. The text captions can contain time stamps to record the exact date and time of the picture. You insert these options using the same Preferences dialog box. Under Image, select Caption. The caption window shown in Figure 8-16 appears. You can type in

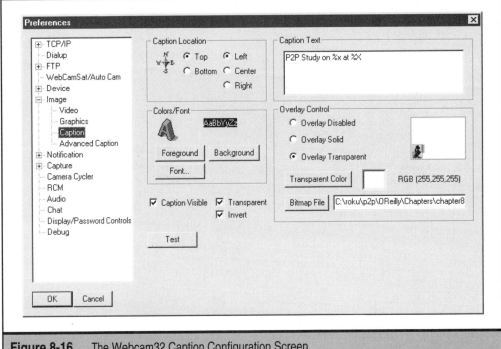

Figure 8-16. The Webcam32 Caption Configuration Screen

your text message and contain variable time information. You substitute the current date with %x, and the current time with %X. You need to make the caption visible; we recommend setting it to be transparent and inverted. The recommendations seamlessly merge the text into the video or graphic.

You simply type in your text message with the desired variables. Then you set the placement in the Caption Location panel. In addition, the *Advanced Caption* window enables finer tuning of the caption location if the basic location is not sufficient.

The video features all cross over to graphics capabilities. You can schedule the generation of a JPEG. Snapshots have the advantage of being instantly viewable. In contrast, a video file is not available until the video recording completes.

You now have two methods to create video files. The Microsoft Media Encoder is easy to use and also allows conversions. The application limits you to Microsoft's formats. The Webcam32 offers the powerful creation of videos driven by timing events or motion detection. You can now share these files through a general access application such as Morpheus or a private sharing tool such as Groove.

Before you start broadcasting your newly created videos, let's explore a tool that manipulates the videos. Apple's QuickTime Pro allows you to perform simple edits such as cutting and pasting. It is not free, but the price is very reasonable. In addition, QuickTime doesn't support the proprietary formats of Windows or RealNetworks. It does, however, support many other types, including the avi format created by the Webcam32 application. You can import and export files into many formats, not just the QuickTime format.

You can edit video either by importing the encoded file or simply by opening it and then exporting the file to the selected format. Once you have the video in the correct format, you can select portions of the video for editing. You can also set up video filters. QuickTime can also string together still images into a movie or slide show. This application thus provides a whole new way to create a video from existing videos or just graphics.

Broadcasting P2P Video: Your P2P TV Station

You now can create video files in various formats, share them with fellow peers, and play them back. You thus have the foundation to set up a TV broadcast facility. The P2P TV station works similarly to P2P radio stations, with several caveats. As stated earlier, P2P video is not as advanced as P2P audio, and therefore broadcast tools are not as straightforward. Many of the tools and applications for broadcasting video require serious computing horsepower and are quite expensive. In video, you have two clear choices: stored files or live. The former provides a list of videos that stream out to your audience. The latter connects to a live camera.

You have two choices for the architecture of your P2P TV station. First, you can set it up very similar to the radio station. This alternative follows the same architectural path with a video stream and a video-streaming server. Unfortunately, the video-streaming servers available today are either expensive, run only on business-level operating systems, or are not compatible with common streaming sources. The second alternative takes advantage of webcam software to create a simple broadcast stream. The following sections explore both alternatives.

The Traditional Approach to Video Streaming Servers

Video streaming as compared to video downloads offers even more benefits to P2P users. Video files are much bigger than audio files. No one wants to wait for a 60MB file to download.

Here you explore your first architecture alternative. The actual architecture is very similar to using the SHOUTcast plug-in in Winamp and the SHOUTcast streaming server. You must first create a video-streaming source and then connect it to a video-streaming server. You have three possibilities: Apple's open source Streaming Server, Windows Media services, and RealNetworks' RealServer. All have some limitations. The latter two have serious limitations for P2P applications but are interesting to explore anyway. In any case, their limitations may not affect your particular system.

Windows Media services are well integrated into the Windows operating system. You set up the Windows Media Encoder to be a broadcasting streaming source. You then start up Windows Media Server to coordinate the video stream with any subscribers. The Media Server creates a linkage file that you provide as the URL to represent the stream. The user merely references this URL to initiate a connection to the video stream. The video stream can be either recorded movies or a live video taken directly from your webcam. You can set up multiple linkage files to enable multiple video channels. There is one big catch with this solution (besides the fact that Windows Media services provide support for only Windows formats): the server only runs on the Window Server operation system. This is an expensive business-class server operating system and out of the price range (and needs) of a typical peer.

Each video channel resides on its own port. You set the port using the new session wizard within Windows Media Encoder. Figure 8-17 illustrates setting the port.

The Windows Media Administrator administers the video-streaming server and video-streaming encoder. It creates the linkage files that comprise a specific stream as a URL addressable from a browser. The streaming server acts like a Web server, so you don't need to add your own Web server.

After creating the linkage, you must start the encoder. This device generates the stream. The subscriber need only address the stream using the provided URL. The streaming server then connects the subscriber to the stream. The streaming server coordinates multiple subscribers to the same stream. The Windows implementation of video streaming follows the normal architecture of connecting a streaming source to a streaming server. All the tools come with the operating system. You only need to run the Windows Server operating system and stick to Windows encoding formats.

RealNetworks also has a complete streaming system. You set up the RealProducer to create video files encoded in the RealNetworks format. You can record directly from your video camera. You can also set your camera as a live feed. You then need to set the stream-

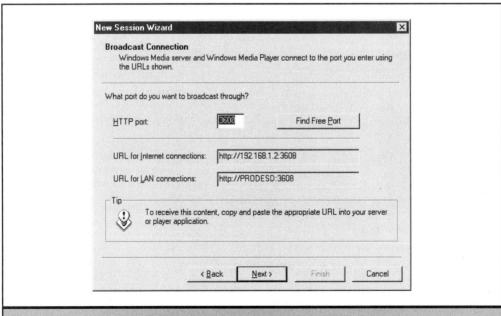

Figure 8-17. Setting the Port for Video Streaming with Windows Media Encoder

ing source port number. You then start the RealServer to serve the stream to any subscriber. Besides the limitation of the RealNetworks format, disadvantages include the fact that you have to pay for the server. The basic server is free for 12 months, but thereafter it costs thousands of dollars—well beyond the means or needs of your P2P world.

Apple comes to the rescue with sponsorship of an open source streaming server called *Darwin*. It is a little rough around the edges compared to the other two, but the price is right: It's free. You start up the Darwin server, then coordinate its activities via the Darwin streaming server administration tool. The administrator is written in Perl script, so you must have the Perl application installed. (This application is available for free from multiple sites, including www.perl.com.) The administrator connects on the standard port of 1200. Figure 8-18 illustrates the status screen of the streaming server administrator.

The screen indicates the overall status of the Darwin streaming server. The next step is to create a playlist of movies. This forms your streaming TV station. Choose Settings | Playlists Settings. This takes you to the playlist control window. Select Create New Playlist. This brings you to the Playlist: Create window (see Figure 8-19). Here you enter

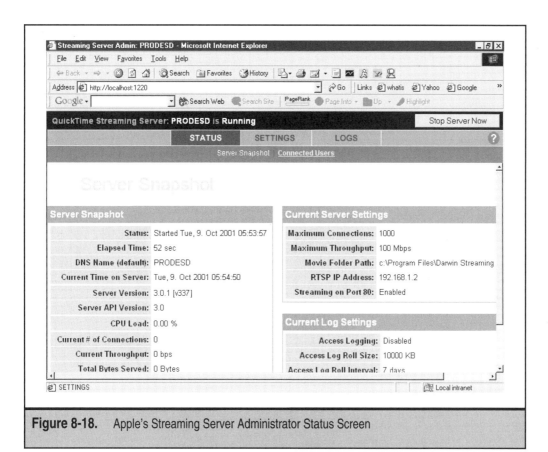

Figure 8-18. Apple's Streaming Server Administrator Status Screen

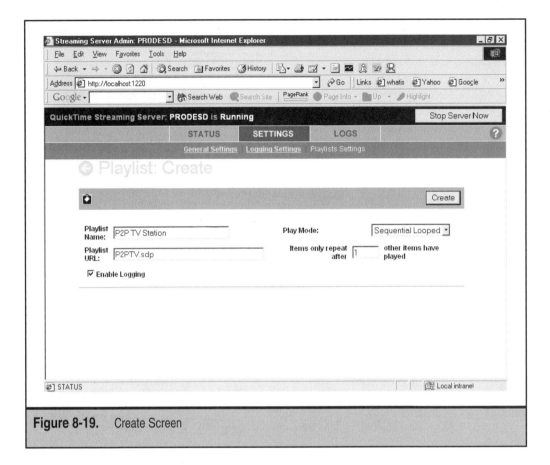

Figure 8-19.   Create Screen

the playlist name and the playlist URL. The URL is the reference name that your subscribers will use. You can also indicate the order that the movies play within the playlist. You can select a random order, a sequential order, or a sequential loop of the movies within the list. The latter will play continuously.

To create the playlist, click the Create button. The new window refreshes with the contents of the playlist. At this point, the playlist is empty. You use the link entitled Create Here to Add/Remove Items to the List. This takes you to a window that outlines the movies available for insertion into the playlist. The potential list is created from files within the directory that you set in the configuration file. You simply select the desired contents of the playlist and click Add to Playlist. The window refreshes, allowing you to delete the newly added entries. Select the back playlist arrow to return to the Playlist Status window. This new window lists all your playlists and their current status. The window may indicate that a playlist is either stopped or playing. If you select the play arrow next to the newly created playlist, the playlist starts playing. Your subscribers can then enter the URL to see the streaming video.

The streaming video is in the Real Time Streaming Protocol (rtsp) format. Subscribers use a video playback application that supports this protocol. Apple's QuickTime player supports the standard and is available for a free download. The user enters the URL: rtsp://machinename/P2PTV.sdp. QuickTime then buffers the stream and begins playing it. You now have a working P2P television station. The one serious limitation is that you must work with the QuickTime format.

This completes your exploration of the first alternative for your P2P TV station. This alternative echoed the architecture of your P2P radio station. You start with a streaming source located at an established port. The port connects to a streaming server that serves up to any subscriber. You explored three possible implementations of this approach. All three implementations have limitations:

▼ **Microsoft Streaming Services**   Microsoft offers a well-integrated suite of applications to form the P2P TV station. The Windows Media Encoder creates a stream from either a prerecorded source or a live source. The stream connects to the Windows Streaming Server, where it awaits a subscriber. The Windows Streaming Server is controlled and managed by the Windows Streaming Administrator. The tools are straightforward and easy to use. The Microsoft approach has two major limitations. First, the Windows Streaming Server runs only on the Windows Server operating system, which is quite expensive and typically not an appropriate operating system for a peer. Second, you also must use only Microsoft-supported formats. This limits the type of player that your subscribers can use.

■ **RealNetworks Streaming Services**   RealNetworks also offers a complete streaming package. You set up the stream from either a live or prerecorded source using the RealProducer. The stream connects to RealNetworks Streaming Server, where it awaits subscribers. You use various text files to configure and manage the RealNetworks Streaming Server. This approach also has two limitations. First, the RealNetworks Streaming Server is very costly. Second, RealNetworks solution requires that you use RealNetworks formats only. This means that the stream subscriber must use RealPlayer to play the stream.

▲ **Apple's Open Source Streaming Services**   Apple's package is complete and the price is right. A playlist broadcaster creates the stream. The stream connects the Darwin streaming server, where it serves subscribers. The Administration server controls the Darwin server. This server requires the installation of Perl. Although most techies already have Perl installed, the average user typically does not. The Apple solution currently requires QuickTime format. But the price and quality are right. As an added bonus, QuickTime Pro offers a world of possibilities for converting video formats, editing video, and adding special effects.

The Webcam Approach to Video Streaming Servers

The traditional approach doesn't quite achieve what you need, for a variety of possible reasons. The webcam software explored earlier has some wonderful extensions to offer interesting, albeit still incomplete, methods to create a P2P TV station.

The Webcam32 software actually contains a limited functionality Web server that understands the HTTP protocol. This server makes it possible to interact remotely with the camera and its video and pictures. This interaction includes placing pictures and video directly into a Web-accessible directory. To do this, you need a full function Web server; see the upcoming section, "P2P and Web Servers: The Aggregator."

The Webcam32 software offers several ways to view live content. It doesn't work with prerecorded video, although you can set up individual graphics files. The software works with either live video or a snapshot. This section focuses on video, as you are using the application to create your own P2P TV station. The Webcam32 software does not offer the sophistication of the Windows and RealNetwork encoders. The camera simply takes a snapshot and then sends it to a browser window. Then it takes another snapshot, and so on. The delays involved in creating a file and sending it make the Webcam32 video capabilities inferior to that of its competitors. But the Webcam32 software works simply and cheaply.

There are three ways to create live video with Webcam32: You can take advantage of Server Push technology resident only in Netscape's browser, you can create a Web page that contains JavaScript that keeps loading a new picture, or you can use a Java applet. This section doesn't cover the first option due to its browser limitation. JavaScript and Java applets work with any browser, and the Webcam32 software supplies a template Web page. These approaches, however, require the use of a Web server (see the upcoming section, "P2P and Web Servers: The Aggregator").

Let's set up the Java applet. You must open the Preferences window by choosing File | Preferences. In the Preferences window, select Features. This outlines the acceptable ways to transmit live video via the network. Select Applet Enabled. Next select Access. In the screen that appears, specify the port number to use to reach the Webcam32 network server. If you are using a firewall, you must make sure that the firewall allows exchanges over this port. If desired, you can alter the video settings to allow for large or small bandwidths. You need to set up a Web page to link a subscriber to the Webcam32 application. Start up your Web server and place the link file. This file will then be the reference file to access the camera.

```
<html>
<TITLE>My Streaming Webcam</TITLE>
<body BGCOLOR="black">
<CENTER>
<applet code="JavaCamPush.class"
codebase="http://192.168.1.2:25867/applet"
archive="JavaCamPush.jar"
width="352"
height="288">
 <param name="URL" value="http://192.168.1.2:25867">
 <param name="cabbase" value="JavaCamPush.cab">
</applet></TD></TR>
</TABLE>
</CENTER>
</body>
</html>
```

You need only substitute your IP address or URL and your port number. If you were to name this file camlink.html and set it up on a Web server running on port 80, the URL would be http://yoursite.com/camlink.html. You now have a bare-bones TV station.

Surveyor, the creator of Webcam32, has also started a Web site to register active webcams and allow others to find you. From the Preferences window, choose the WebCamSat/Auto Cam option. This enables you to log in and provide details about your camera location. You can set your live camera feed in a public area or private area requiring a password. This feature essentially provides a global name for a webcam and an easy way to look up the name. There are other ways to achieve the same objectives, as discussed previously.

The webcam provides a cheap, easy, low-quality video experience. However, for many simple purposes, it is a P2P wonder. You can have free videoconferences or just keep an eye on your house. The Webcam32 is a slightly different approach to video, but for many applications it works well.

The Webcam32 application has two other features of note. The software can switch between multiple cameras. You could hook up multiple cameras and switch between them just like a fancy security operation using the software. In addition, all of the cameras are available remotely. You could place cameras throughout your house and monitor everything, regardless of your location.

Another noteworthy feature is a remote-controlled pad on which your camera sits. This pad enables you to move your camera by remote control. If you place the camera in a weatherproof case, you can mount the camera and pad on your roof and be able to scan your entire yard from any browser. If you combine the two features—multiple cameras and remote controlled pads—you would have a James Bond house with the ability to see anywhere on the premises.

P2P and Web Servers: The P2P Aggregator

At first glance, a Web server and P2P seem to be at odds. Don't let this perception affect your solutions. It turns out that many of the P2P tools explored throughout this book essentially contain a Web server. Usually the Web server in question isn't a general-purpose one, but one that has a limited understanding of the HTTP protocol and possibly even HTML-formatted files. There is nothing stopping you from including a full feature, general purpose Web server in your P2P suite of solutions. Such an addition offers you a general-purpose method of moving files to others without worrying about the P2P client, because your peers already have the necessary client—their browser. Originally, the general-purpose Web server was the beauty of the Web, and it still remains a stalwart contributor to the Web's success.

One of the most outstanding Web servers is free, easy to use, and readily available. It also runs the vast majority of Web servers everywhere, so you are in good hands. It is the Apache Web server. Executable versions are available at http://httpd.apache.org/dist/httpd/binaries. You simply download the HTTP server for your particular operating system and platform. Apache supports almost every major platform. The Windows version automatically installs and sets up all basic operations. After installing Apache, you can immediately test the server by firing up your browser and entering your local address or just http://localhost.

Apache does not have a fancy administration Web interface. Instead, configuration text files drive the Apache configuration. The main configuration file, httpd.conf, is found in the conf directory off of the main Apache installation directory. There are plenty of comments to guide you through any modifications. For example, the parameter for the port is appropriately called *port*. Note that you do not have to run the HTTP service on port 80. You can choose any port that is available. You can also use DNS2Go (discussed in Chapter 6) to allow users to specify port 80 and still find your Web server on another port.

A general-purpose Web server allows you to create many linkage files to connect to your various P2P offerings. Your Web server main page could become P2P central for your offerings. You can set up your radio station and TV station links along with anything else that is interesting. You can also set up security to allow only selected peers. As a side benefit, you can allow access to specific video or audio files and even playlists. The Web server becomes the poor man's streaming server.

The Web server is not set up to handle lots of streaming connections, but the limits of P2P generally reduce the number of users anyway. After all, a Web server's primary job is to move files back and forth, and multimedia is ultimately just files. Don't be afraid to play in the traditional camp. Web servers are good things, and the Apache Web server is simply the best for P2P aggregation or a portal.

Video Summary

Video is still emerging as true Internet capability. Today's computing environment often lacks the processor horsepower or the network bandwidth to create a good video experience. Although none of the many available approaches will meet all your video needs, they still offer value. Table 8-1 summarizes the key differences between the approaches.

	MS Streaming	RealNetworks	Apple	Webcam32
Broadcast Quality	High	High	High	Low
Live Broadcast	Yes	Yes	Yes	Yes
Prerecorded Broadcast	Yes	Yes	Yes	No
Encoding Format	Windows	Real	Apple	AVI/JPEG
Platform	Windows	Many	Many	Windows

Table 8-1.   P2P TV Stations Implementation Comparisons

	MS Streaming	RealNetworks	Apple	Webcam32
Cost Factor	Must have Windows Server	Expensive	Free	Nominal
Setup	Complex	Complex	Complex	Easy
Web Registration Service	No	No	No	Yes

Table 8-1.   P2P TV Stations Implementation Comparisons *(continued)*

You have several options to run your P2P TV station. The easiest to set up is the webcam, but it also offers the lowest quality. The other solutions limit the formats that you can use and possibly the platform that the streaming services can run on.

The days of tuning in to many P2P TV broadcasts are not quite here. However, the ability to check in on your home surroundings or provide some fun videos for friends and family is already here. Video remains a space to watch as P2P gathers strength and video applications begin to serve the peer market better.

SUMMARY

This chapter explored two fantastic entertainment areas: music and video. The fun you can have with these technologies is boundless, as you can tap directly into the favorite music and video of millions of fellow peers. The many P2P advantages nicely address the problems of large files and thin pipes. In addition, P2P leverages the growing ability of peer applications to create and manage these encoded formats of music and video. You can create and manipulate all the various formats. You can generate files from original sources. Once you have the ability to create music and video, it is only a short P2P step to share, exchange, and enjoy these files via the many existing P2P file-sharing applications. The file-sharing applications are themselves advancing, coming up with new strategies to exploit the many P2P advantages. You can also share files privately using the applications discussed in Chapter 7 or using the audio or video tools directly.

Audio offers more mature solutions for P2P. The ability to create and exchange audio files, specifically MP3 files, was the start of P2P. This has led to tools that directly enable you to broadcast your own radio station that delivers high performance over limited bandwidths and average peer hardware systems. Through the P2P network, you can acquire your favorite music, then create your dream playlist and broadcast to yourself remotely, to your friends, or to the world.

Video is currently less mature for P2P and aimed more at the business arena. Businesses can easily afford the expensive systems and their associated bandwidth needs. But it is still possible through the open source network to set up a P2P TV station. Also, the inexpensive webcam offers an easy way to get many benefits of live video.

Audio and video combine to offer a rich network experience to connect two peers next door to each other or located around the world. The fun of finding that obscure song from a fellow computer user or seeing someone from far away in real time on your monitor would have been unthinkable a decade ago. At your fingertips is a world of P2P entertainment. Jump in and enjoy.

CHAPTER 9

Getting to Tomorrow: The Future of P2P

In this final chapter, we get to do something both exciting and dangerous. We are going to peer into future (no pun intended). We will examine current trends and economic, technical, and social conditions. The chapter will suggest what these conditions may portend for the P2P phenomenon. This exercise, while fun, can reveal both the authors' biases and the shortness of their vision. Additionally, external events and poor fundamental assumptions tend to prove a poor basis for conjecture. You need only think back to the last decade of the 20th century and the heady predictions of a "new economy," the "dot-com revolution," and the "virtuous spiral" of economics to know this to be true.

So many prognostications prove to be unfounded or off-target, or undone by some unforeseen factor, that it's risky business indeed to attempt to suggest what current developments may lead to. Even so, attempting the analysis is necessary, if only to perceive a rough outline of a possible set of futures. Certainly a few of our predictions will be in the ballpark. Consider that, although the 1939 World's Fair was dead wrong in many of its fine-grained predictions on the shape and scale of technological accomplishment, its coarse-resolution worldview of a society dominated by leisure and abundance granted by the use of technology was spot-on (see Figure 9-1). With this in mind, this chapter makes some observations and suggests potential impacts from these trends and influ-

Figure 9-1.   The Utopian-Minded World's Fair of 1939

ences. In any case, it will certainly be fun for us to get together in a convenient P2P space with our reader community and debate these trends and ideas.

HOME GATEWAYS

Before moving to the controversial, let's begin with something rather prosaic. We have talked at length about the flow of function, intelligence, and capability from big servers in the net to the PC in the office or home. In the early Web era, the PC had been relegated simply to supporting the browser experience; it was largely disruptive to the status quo ante. PCs grew up to be the equivalent of "server class" machines once found only in the middle of the net. However, general PCs are not ideally suited for the role of network server. Too powerful in some ways, not well optimized in others, the PC as we know it is a compromise of esoteric features. It certainly was never intended to be a network server, a router, or a firewall—swiftly shuttling packets, making routing decisions, or protecting against various attacks. As the home LAN becomes a less formidable concept for the average person, the home gateway—part router and firewall, part network and Web server, and part shared file system server—becomes a reasonable proposition.

Although both Cisco and 3COM backed off from an initial foray into purpose-specific home gateways with embedded operating systems and Web servers in 2000, eventually such systems may return to the marketplace to be the control center at the heart of the home. Such systems might be used to coordinate video and audio devices, information manipulation and workgroup collaboration devices (including the PC and PDAs), appliances, security systems, and home energy systems.

The home gateway might make the next iteration of devices such as the Audrey Internet appliance,[1] the Kerbango Internet radio (see Figure 9-2), and Compaq and Sony's Internet appliances (all of which disappeared from the market in 2000 and 2001) a more compelling possibility. Abortive attempts at handheld slates from at least three major vendors were never brought to market for essentially the same reason: the lack of a multifunction, multiprotocol processor.

GOING WIRELESS VIA LANS

Along with the gateway will come the next generation of wireless LANs. Whether they will be 802.11A (our favorite bet), Bluetooth, or something else may not be as important as the fact that they will surely come. Much of the existing housing in the developed

---

[1]   The Audrey was blessedly short-lived, not just because it was not useful without a PC on the same home LAN, but also because its user experience was shallow and its ergonomics (screen, keyboard, and wireless usability) were poor. Let's hope that the next generation of Internet appliances is more compelling to use.

Figure 9-2.   Kerbango Internet Radio

world was constructed prior to the Internet era; the idea of a home LAN would have seemed bizarre in the 1990s. HomePNA (Home Phoneline Networking Alliance) or power-line-based Ethernet networks might seem like a good solution for the home or small office, but ultimately Wi-Fi[2] solutions will prevail. For one thing, the average house doesn't have enough phone jacks to build a reasonable LAN for all the appliances likely to be Internet-enabled. For another, phone jacks were usually installed in locations ideal for conveniently conducting voice conversations. Additionally, mobile and cordless phones tend to make additional jacks unnecessary. Finally, Wi-Fi is cheap, doesn't require you to understand either computers or networks, and is promoted by both the computer and networking industries. For these reasons, Wi-Fi will predominate in the home.

An office building's cabling is often inflexibly placed, and every move of temporary walls, every rearrangement of personnel is made more complex by the need to drag CAT-5 cable along with the individual. More and more, businesses are turning to wireless access points for internetworking. Standard issue in many modern corporate settings is a laptop computer with a wireless card. The user is free to roam from office to office, across the company campus, or from company location to location. An employee can stow the laptop in a backpack at the end of the "official" workday. Arriving at home, people will naturally want the convenience of the same wireless LAN that they have at the office.[3]

Collaboration tools such as Groove and Magi reinforce the desire and the ability to move seamlessly from home to work and back again, without having to deal with arcane VPN arrangements. The notion of "working where it works for me" further promotes a Wi-Fi workplace. We don't insist that everyone will work this way. Just as a few black-smiths are still around long after the era of the horse, certain people will still work

---

2   The term *Wireless-Fidelity (Wi-Fi)* refers to a networking scheme that creates a wireless connection between a device and a network. The term can refer generally to one of a number of protocols. However, the term often specifically refers to 802.11B.

3   Wi-Fi made the writing of this book much more enjoyable. Sitting on the patio with a laptop and a cool drink is always preferable to hunching over a traditional PC in an airless, sunless space.

eight-to-five jobs, able to transition from work to social context at a crisply defined point in time, never moving from their appointed cubicles, always tethered to a desktop PC. Such people will continue to exist—but they probably won't be the readers of this book.

Outside the home, and the formally defined workplace, Wi-Fi enables P2P (as well as traditional Web browsing). Working with companies such as Wayport, MobileStar, and Airwave, hundreds of airports, hotels, and even restaurants are rolling out Wi-Fi access. In January 2001, Starbucks and Microsoft announced plans for the coffeehouse chain to begin offering Wi-Fi access for its patrons. Once a technology has become a Starbucks fixture, it can be said to be solidly mainstream.

GOING WIRELESS VIA MOBILE DEVICES

The previous section discussed the evolution of the LAN into a fully wireless experience. This section considers trends in the "real" wireless arena—mobile devices and users—which is closing in on a billion users, half of whom will have mobile devices capable of supporting the P2P experience. Mobile devices will be significant to the future of the P2P culture for a variety of reasons, which this chapter explores.

First of all, mobile equipment both from the PDA world and from the cellular world is evolving to offer more a more useful combination of features and packaging. Power budgets are continuing to grow, and the available CPU power is rising as well. In addition, bandwidth limitations will (eventually) vanish or at least become less of a limiting factor. The emergence of so-called 3G (Third Generation Wireless) in both Europe and the United States means sufficiently larger bandwidth. The motivation behind increasing bandwidth was originally to deliver higher-fidelity Web experiences to mobile handset users. With the implosion of the dot-com bubble, some of this motivation may dissipate, but we don't think so. Consider the unfilled needs in the mobile context, and you'll understand why the expansion of this space will, over time, make the dot-com boom look like pretty small stuff indeed.

DESIGNING FOR MOBILE P2P

Information needs and presentation requirements in the mobile context are different to those of the user at a desktop PC, and will continue to be different, simply because the user is on the go. More than likely, the user is traveling from place to place for a purpose. Therefore, the person is much less likely just to meander the Internet aimlessly. Current mobile Web-browsing capabilities for WAP phones, having no sense of what might be most important to a mobile user in the middle of a commute, merely seek to transcode a full Web-browsing experience into the confines of a small display device.

Current handhelds such as the PocketPC, whose design center is chiefly concerned with faithfully replicating the full PC experience onto a small form factor device, violate several of the rules of good design as espoused by Guy Haitani, designer of the Palm OS. The following sections discuss some of Haitani's more interesting rules, which future product designers, implementers, and buyers should bear in mind.

A Mountain Won't Fit in a Teacup

One of Haitani's design rules states, "Don't try to fit a mountain in a teacup." Instead, mine the diamonds from that mountain (i.e., on the PC *servent*,) and then put only those in the teacup. The buyer also should look beyond how glitzy devices appear in the show-room, and do a real utility analysis based on his or her needs in the mobile context. The combination of experiences that you want bundled for you should guide you in selecting one approach or product over another.

Consider a practical example: meeting management using a Palm device. Under Haitani's design rules, entering a simple meeting into the device should be straightfor-ward. Perhaps 80 percent of the time, this is sort of task that you'll need to do. Therefore, a single pen tap should be sufficient to enter a simple event. You tap next to a time slot and begin entering data. In no time, and with little effort, you have scheduled a single hour-long meeting (see Figure 9-3). For a more complex meeting activity, such as chang-ing meeting details or entering a note, you may first need to make a couple pen taps to un-cover these options.

Because you tend to do these kinds of tasks less frequently, they don't need to be front and center and available at all times. Therefore, the screen that displays them is hidden behind a couple pen taps. Occurring even less frequently are events that recur regularly, so options for managing those events are hidden yet behind another pen tap or so (see Figure 9-4). An interesting experiment that you can try at the purchase counter is to

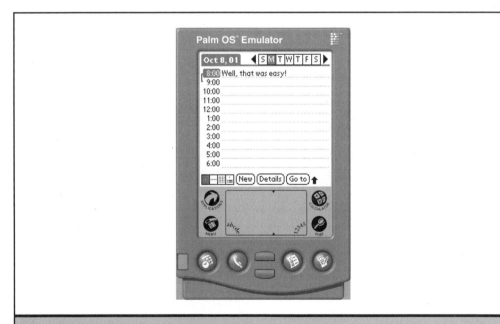

Figure 9-3.   Simple Event Management

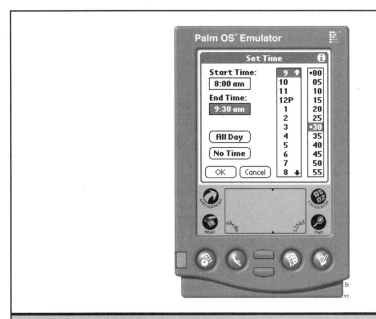

Figure 9-4.   More Complex Event Management

schedule an event first using a Palm device, and then using a PocketPC device. Which is easier? Which one will you want to use for event management a half dozen times per day, five or six times a week?

Product Simplicity Wins

A simple product that works well will succeed. A full-featured product that works poorly will fail. Don't design features into the product that are unlikely to be used, but which take up CPU cycles, power, storage space, and possibly network bandwidth (and therefore the time to achieve a desired result). Anyone who has tried to use one of the combination devices that bundles a PDA with a cell phone has experienced mindless design. Have you ever tried talking with someone to schedule an upcoming meeting, while attempting to consult the PDA calendar on the other side of the device?

In contrast, some collaboration capabilities are well thought out on data-only devices. Figure 9-5 shows the user experience for instant messaging via the PocketPC 2002 operating system. MSN Messenger works just like the desktop version. As Figure 9-5 depicts, a menu allows you send one of several (customizable) canned phrases with a stylus tap. For longer messages, you use Transcriber (a freeware handwriting recognition application available from Microsoft), a "Graffiti-like" recognizer or the standard character

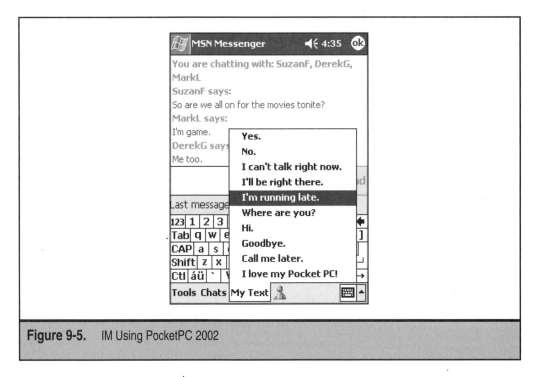

Figure 9-5. IM Using PocketPC 2002

recognizer, or the keyboard.[4] PocketPC also includes Windows Media Player 8, which now supports streaming video. This feature enables you to broadcast from your P2P TV Station, as Chapter 8 documented. The virtual keyboard is just fine for entering the kind of short messages you're likely to want to exchange on MSN Messenger or the equivalent. The user experience design is well tuned for the activity.

Figure 9-6 shows some of the work the authors codesigned into Roku. Roku is a P2P remote and mobile access user experience, similar to Magi as discussed in Chapter 7. Well tuned to the needs of the mobile user, Roku on a PocketPC[5] allowed you to handle your

---

4   A contrary view is that the multitude of input choices provides yet another example of the Microsoft "overkill" mindset, which tends to aggravate rather than delight many users. The authors' spouses and kids tend to dislike the fact that Microsoft applications typically offer three ways (menu, toolbar, or keyboard shortcut) to do a file management operation, and four ways (menu, toolbar, keyboard shortcut, or drag and drop) to perform an edit operation. They tell us that this design center is an assault on their productivity and ask why Microsoft can't design a *single* set of controls that is actually easier to use than any of the three or four offered. In contrast, the authors, being engineers and therefore part of the problem rather than the solution, don't see a problem, and think they would like to see even *more* nifty features, gizmos, and controls.

5   Roku, a mobile access and P2P engine developer in the early days of P2P, ceased operation in May 2001, partially as a result of the new millennium economic "downdraft." The authors, who were chief scientist and vice president of engineering, are currently using their many worthless stock options to wallpaper kitchens and family rooms.

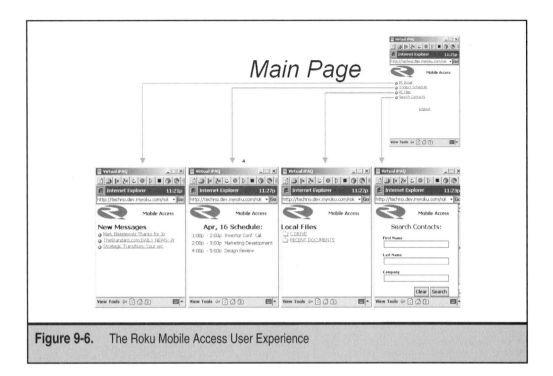

Figure 9-6.   The Roku Mobile Access User Experience

e-mail from several e-mail systems directly and seamlessly (as though they existed in a single e-mail space). It allowed you to interact directly with your Outlook calendaring system, to access and manipulate the documents on your PCs (that is, you could view summaries, picture thumbnails, faxes, and e-mail messages, as well as delete and rename documents). It also enabled you to search and get summaries for people, places, and things from the otherwise unorganized content of your desktop PCs. Roku could organize your multiple PCs into a consolidated and consistent view from any device capable of connecting to your PCs. The design center for Roku illustrates the point that a simple, consistent user experience is an exemplary starting point for any P2P product.

No Watch Cursor, No Modes

A watch cursor has no place on a handheld device. Haitani stresses that a PDA should have zippy performance in booting up and moving from one application to another. Scott MacNealy, Sun Microsystems CEO, points out that you never think in terms of "booting up" your cell phone. You just turn it on and use it. Why aren't all information edge appliances that easy to use and understand?

This dictum applies to all aspects of the mobile experience as well. Successful designs will reflect more deeply what should be presented to a mobile user and how long it may take to deliver meaningful content.

Maximize Predictability

Haitani suggests that there should be no explicit modalities and thus less complexity. That is, there should be no menu items like "Save." Everything you work on should be explicitly and instantly saved for you. You should be able to pick up right where you left off and not have to think in terms of moving from application to application. Rather, you should be able to think in terms of moving across a seamless expanse of information at will.

ADDITIONAL RULES FOR MOBILE P2P DESIGN

In addition to Haitani's maxims, several of our own design rules would help ensure the success of future products.

Maintain Contextual Consistency

Interaction with your data should have predictable results, regardless of the access device or method. When you delete an e-mail item on your device, that action should result in the e-mail being actually deleted, regardless of whether the e-mail client currently holding the information is Microsoft Outlook, Eudora, or a Web mail service. The "feel" of owning your data should not trap you into the specific metaphors of the tool, such as your PC, that you might use to create or interact with the data on some particular platform. Closely aligned with this concept is that of freeing your information from specific tools.

Untrap Information

In Figure 9-7, we illustrate a common experience that many of us have encountered time and time again. Potentially valuable information is back at the office on a desktop PC. You are in the car or on public transport armed with one or more wireless devices, heading for a meeting. Meanwhile, significant events and information are accumulating back on the good ol' PC and you have no way of knowing about these changes. Consider for example, that you're driving to a meeting with your telecommunications vendor. It would be really great to know that the vendor's closest rival just e-mailed you a cost proposal offering hefty discounts.

A mobile user often faces "information blackout" when trying to get to his or her data that are being held in any tools other than the one that holds proprietary access to the user's own data. The problem is that tools lock information so that it is not available for interfaces other than those for which the tool's maker intended the tool to work with. This concept is fine for the tool provider. The primary business objective of Microsoft (just to pick a vendor at random) is to create a continuing dependency on its specific tools. This is a fine objective for the vendor, but it is *not* a fine objective for you.

Currently, information that you need here and now is not available here and now, and even if you could find and access it somehow, the format would more often than not be unintelligible, and would be mismatched for whatever interface and display you happened to have handy. What you want instead is that your information be accessible from a device close at hand.

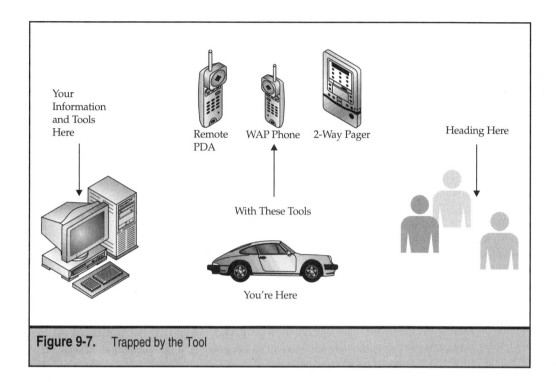

Your
Information
and Tools
Here

Remote
PDA

WAP Phone

2-Way Pager

Heading Here

With These Tools

You're Here

Figure 9-7.   Trapped by the Tool

To accomplish high transparency, vendors will have to move to an application neutral format. XML is a good choice because it currently is far more flexible and amenable to multi-application and multidevice access than proprietary formats. This is the reason that the StarOffice 6.0 suite of applications now uses XML for a data representation, and why others ought to as well. The financial gains from offering new services will outweigh the loss of proprietary advantage of trapping the user's data in the confines of a specific tool.

You would almost certainly want to buy your zippy new mobile summarization and searching software from Microsoft, because you know Microsoft's abilities as productivity tool producers. Certainly Microsoft's prodigious capabilities in producing this type of application would put the corporation well ahead of any competitor. Meanwhile, any tools that Microsoft chose not to produce would open markets for other vendors to fill in market and technology gaps. Aside from business concerns, you may wonder why Microsoft (or anyone else, for that matter) would have difficulty with the concept of separating tools and data as two different things. One answer is that separation of concerns, or *disintermediation*, though highly necessary in P2P implementation, is not necessarily trivial.

Disintermediate Tools

Disintermediation is the pulling apart of productivity tools into simpler components. The feature will be increasingly important in P2P. Vendors of tools and applications will either pull their tools apart voluntarily or have them pulled apart by others, because tools that are device-, time-, and place-restricted will not survive the transition to a P2P world. As you saw with Groove, it was necessary to pull apart the tight bindings between documents and the file system in order to share documents, ideas, and collaborative actions, and in order to replicate the contents of the space among machines.

However, disintermediation will go further than where Groove and Magi have gone thus far. Most applications are tightly bound in terms of their information model, the views they allow the user into the information model, and the business logic they apply (also called the application's *controller*). This triumvirate, called the Model-View-Controller paradigm for application design, does not generally allow an intermediary between the parts of an application.

An exception is the application that uses APIs (application programming interfaces) to allow external software to access the content of the application, to offer alternative views, or to apply alternative business logic to content. The exception will ultimately become the rule, however, because such use of APIs is necessary to enable desktop applications (which we can think of as legacy applications) to become P2P-enabled. New architectures such as Microsoft .Net will assure that this is so. The exception may be Microsoft's legacy applications. Currently, the APIs for Microsoft's productivity suite allow only limited scripting access to the applications, usually by VBScript, rather than the full access that Linux open source office productivity applications are providing.

Instead of retrofitting its applications for P2P access, Microsoft sees the future much differently. According to Microsoft's Web site, .Net will become "an operating system for the Internet," designed to replace the Internet's current "disjointed, disparate, fractured environment" with a common infrastructure with "one model of developing for it." The common infrastructure will be a proprietary platform that Microsoft owns and controls, just as Windows is today. P2P's fight for applications that allow disintermediation will apparently go forward without Microsoft's help.

P2P Is Not the Web

An obvious prediction (more an observation) is that bidirectional, distributed applications will steer the mobile P2P experience clear from slavishly reproducing the PC's Web experience of content consumption. *Content consumption* is the idea that the Web is another TV network, and that you are a generally passive "set of eyeballs" viewing that network. In some cases, certainly, the user will want to browse for information. Primarily, this browsing will be based on the user's current location. For example, the user might want to find a good Thai restaurant near his or her current location, or find out what movie is playing at a nearby theater.

Overall, however, throwing out the browsing and meandering metaphor in favor of a design centered on personal information will be a good first step. One cellular provider offers a Web browser that will allow you to access market news and find your favorite sports team's score. The device delivers short summaries of these data formatted for a mobile phone. As Chapter 7 pointed out, such information is not normally what a person feels is critical when on the go. Appropriate design must always consider what information

Right Information Means:	Right Time Means:	Right Place Means:
Contextual; the experience answers the questions who, what, when, where, why, and how	**Contextual**; your calendar has event sensitivity	**Contextual**; the experience relates to device at hand and your current location
Personalized	**Notification enabled applications**	**Uses what's here;** the experience is fully capable of leveraging the device that you are using, and is sensitive to the device's input support, display, and on-board applications
Correctly prioritized	**Guaranteed delivery**; time sensitivity	
Filtered		
Trusted	**Synchronized with related information**	
Secure		
Private		
Consistent across interface		

Table 9-1. Goals of Mobile P2P

is relevant and timely in situations where a mobile phone will be used. This goal generally entails providing the user data access when he or she cannot access the Internet via a personal computer.

Users of mobile services (whether P2P or not) are primarily interested in brief and quick information. Access to *relevant* transport schedules, *my* traffic, and *very local* weather information are good examples. In short, mobile P2P should offer the right information, at the right time, in the right place. An experience that fails to achieve all three goals fails in its entirety. Table 9-1 suggests that context has special significance in P2P.

Good designs will therefore start from a P2P design center and reflect the types of interactions that will comprise the P2P experience. These types of interactions will be primarily message-based. They will be person-to-person (as in instant messaging between two humans), person-to-system (as in searching or in instant messaging between a human and a software agent), and system-to-system (as in updating your peer with presence information from a shared buddy roster). Winning designs for the required infrastructure will achieve the goal of a seamless user experience and reflect what a mobile person actually wants to do.

A user on the go, in asking the question,[6] "Tell me about John Black," expects the experience shown in Table 9-2, which exhibits all of the interaction types previously delineated, and reflects the inherently message-oriented nature of P2P interaction.

---

6   The user will ask the question either via a voice user interface or, less optimally, via a keyboard. You'll learn more about this topic later in the chapter.

Message Type: Person-to-Person (P→P), Person-to-System (P→S), System-to-Person (S→P), or System-to-System (S→S)	Action or Goal
P→S	The request is transmitted to the user's hosting P2P PC.
S→S	An agent searches the content held in a particular device —on the PCs, handhelds, and any other information-bearing devices in the user's P2P space. This information might include e-mail, chat logs, Word documents, and buddy rosters. The agent prepares a summary of the data found. An appropriate summary might include the fact that John Black is currently active in a Groove space, or is accessible via Jabber (the agent gains this S→S knowledge by perusing buddy rosters). The summary might also state that you have a meeting with John at noon (S→S knowledge gained from your Outlook calendar). The agent might also report that John has sent you an e-mail with the subject line, "Meeting cancelled" (S→S knowledge gained from your Eudora client and with the content, "Reread the proposal I sent last week before we reschedule the meeting"). A summary also includes an eight-word synopsis of that MS Word document (S→S gained from your file system) authored by John.
1. P→S, and then S→P 2. P→S, S→S, and then S→P 3. P→P	You might take several actions in response to gaining this knowledge. These actions include instructing your agent to deliver a short acknowledgment to John via SMS, having your agent instruct an Internet-based TTS (text-to-speech) service to ring you back to read the document aloud to you (because you are on the road), or starting an IM session with John (after you safely pull your car off the road).*

*The authors can remember zooming down Route 66 in Northern Virginia's Internet Valley typing instant messages to one another on our mobile phones shortly after the introduction of Mobile Yahoo Messenger. While it was exciting and both of us emerged unscathed, communicating via instant messaging while driving is not a recommended activity for the rational or the sane.

Table 9-2. Message-Based Interaction

Searching Should Replace Synchronization

In the previous era, the PC was at the heart of the computing and (data) communication experience. Every other device that you used was a satellite of the PC. The PC was the locus of schedules and calendars, contact information, and e-mail, with your PDA acting as a little data clone. Microsoft's Outlook product wore the mantle of "official" keeper of all your information.

Never mind that most of your new contact information would probably enter your information realm via your Palm PC, and most of your new phone information via your cellular device. Never mind that synchronization was painful, always had to be carried out at the PC, always had to be remembered and scheduled, never was scaled, and never led to multiple realities. ("Let's see, is the phone number on the PC more current than the one on my Palm, or is it vice versa?") Never mind that even multiple Outlook instances can be synchronized with one another. Unsurprisingly, according to Palm's internal assessments, fully 80 percent of Palm users never synchronized their PDAs, despite the fact that synchronization to guard against data loss was a huge selling feature of the Palm.

In large measure, the rarity of synchronization reflects the isolation of multiple data sources for the same category of information. Jumping ahead a few years into the P2P collaboration era, in which tools such as Magi and its successors will arise, users will search for information that remains at the place of its creation rather than attempt to synchronize all information. Magi allows multiple, isolated data sources to be viewed as one virtual, trusted source. That's exactly what you want in any context, but especially the mobile context. You shouldn't care about where a bit of information is, or what its point of entry into your information space was. Rather, you should only be concerned that the information is available to you securely and privately at whatever point of access you're using.

If searching thus replaces synchronization, then data replication among repositories would become unnecessary. Especially since consistency is achievable at low cost, searching makes excellent sense, for the same reason that replication in Groove is an excellent way of spreading data across several devices, thus reducing the risk of data loss. In addition, local caching, close to the user, enhances performance.

Mobile Capabilities

Figure 9-8 plots the expected growth in mobile bandwidth over time. The table overlays the timeline with representative projects being rolled out right now at Nokia, Ericcson, Microsoft Research, Qualcomm, DARPA, and elsewhere. Market realities reflected in the dramatic growth of mobile capabilities include the following, even allowing for the potential slowing of the world economy:

▼ By 2002, there will be 100 million data-enabled mobile phones (that is, phones able to access the Internet).

■ By 2003, mobile connections will constitute 10 percent of the high-speed Internet market.

▲ By 2003, the number of wireless users will top 1 billion. Americans will spend over $60 billion.

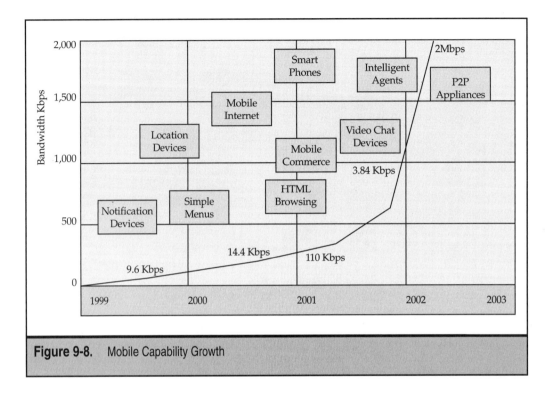

Figure 9-8.   Mobile Capability Growth

Figures 9-9 and 9-10 show Nokia's current vision of mobile handsets facilitating personal collaboration. The first thing you notice is the support for rich media. Not only is Nokia's handset a traditional voice grade machine for spoken interaction, but it's also capable of presenting text and video. Although the current vision doesn't demonstrate live video narrowcasting, adding such capability, at least to a primitive degree (perhaps 5–10 frame equivalents per second), won't put a huge dent in a 2 megabit per second bandwidth allocation. The technology should thus be able to present at least a "talking head."

The interesting twist will be that the norm, rather than the exception, will be that notifications from personal software agents will reside with the e-mail outpost on your home or office PC. Actually, notification will come from both PCs, regardless of the actual physical location of the information and content. Peer information spaces will become more consolidated, and software agents will commonly be capable of searching across the various pools of your content.

WHO WILL WIN THE MOBILE P2P PRIZE?

We have been asked many times which platform, and which design center, will win all the marbles—the mobile phone or the PDA. The cellular design center has always-on,

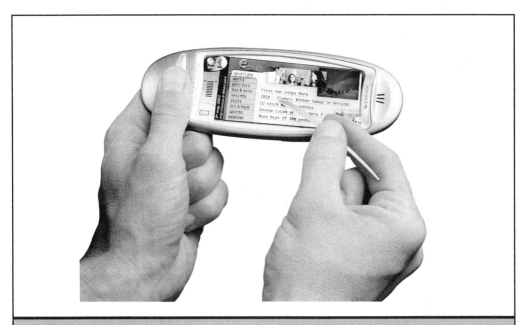

Figure 9-9.   Nokia Concept Phone (1)

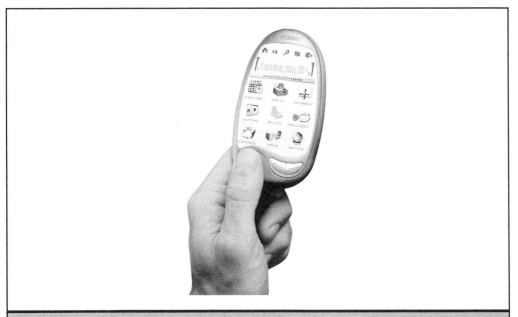

Figure 9-10.   Nokia Concept Phone (2)

always-available communications in its favor, but it is weak in its data-entry, persistence, synchronization, and software update capabilities. Perhaps the addition of Java-enabled or BREW (Binary Runtime Environment for Wireless) applications to data phones will help them handle information as well as PDAs do.

The PDA design center, on the other hand, offers strong data-entry, coordination, control, and on-the-go usability, with less limited battery life and power budget. In contrast to a mobile phone, a PDA is not capable of being an always-on and always-available device. This shouldn't present a huge problem, however—after all, P2P applications and platforms should be able to tolerate variable connectivity and periods of unavailability. However, this criterion is meant to apply in the aggregate, not necessarily to an individual and unique resource. That is to say, Napster worked because it provided significant redundancy in the aggregate content. If there had been an irreplaceable element, perhaps a song existing on only one machine, then Napster would have succeeded in the aggregate, while failing in the particular.

Thus, both design centers are flawed as fully capable peer devices. Both cellular and PDA designs are moving toward each other. PDAs such as the Palm and PocketPCs are evolving toward offering capabilities previously found only in full-fledged PCs. Particularly in multimedia—the playing of MP3s and snippets of video—PDAs are becoming interesting devices. In addition, the devices are beginning to boast expansion slots that allow a digital camera and even cell phone attachments to be plugged in. Cellular devices are a bit further behind in their attempts at combining voice and data capabilities, but Nokia is demonstrating devices such as those shown earlier in this chapter.

So which approach will take the market? Ultimately, both camps seek to achieve a market dominating combinations of features and packaging beyond what they are currently offering. There will be attractive, sensible, and successfully converged devices, as exemplified by the Motorola Accompli series (see Figure 9-11). Introduced in 2001, the Accompli uses an ear bud and microphone, has a full keyboard (not just the dreadful numeric phone keypad), and allows the user to use both data and voice functions simultaneously.

In the end, it may not matter which design center wins. Currently, however, neither is ready to become the device of choice for the P2P experience. For you as a consumer to emerge as a winner, the various industry factions will have decide on one design center to expand, putting aside any current allegiances for the good of the industry as a whole.

Consider, for example that less than 2 percent of the global population currently has PC access to the Internet. The other 98 percent of the world, never having experienced today's computers, is far more likely to opt for the coming wave of unobtrusive always-on, always-connected, low-power-consuming personal devices. Such potential users are the target market that will increasingly drive industrial design and new product development, making wireless devices the center of the P2P world in a post-PC era.

This may seem a Third World–centric view, but when you consider that electricity costs nearly 55 cents per kilowatt hour in Germany (rather than the 6 cents in the United States), talk of PCs being always on may seem ludicrous to Europeans. On the other hand, cellular penetration is very strong in Europe. Europe has adopted a single network stan-

Figure 9-11.   Motorola Accompli

dard, GSM (Global System for Mobile Communications), and its associated data transmission standard, GPRS (General Packet Radio Service). These standards are popular, result in reasonably priced service offerings, and support visual data and textual interfaces. Thus, the winner of the mobile P2P prize will ultimately be the global consumer.

THE ROLE OF VUI (VOICE USER INTERFACE) IN P2P

In the film *Star Trek IV: The Voyage Home*, the crew is transported back through time to the late 1980s to save the whales. The film includes a rather prescient scene in which Scotty, the engineer attempts to use a Macintosh computer. At first, he speaks to the Mac from across the room, and of course gets no response. Another character, this one a 1980s contemporary, notices Scotty's consternation, and advises him to "use the mouse" instead. Scotty walks over to the computer, picks up the mouse, and begins speaking into it, with predictably hilarious results. Scotty finally gives up talking to the mouse, notices a keyboard begins to type away, muttering under his breath, "A keyboard—how quaint."

Perhaps if Paramount made that film a few years from now, audiences might not perceive the intended humor in the presumption that the human voice should be a preferred interface to cyberspace. We are on the verge of the next real revolution in the Internet experience, one in which the very idea of tethering oneself to a keyboard and mouse and interacting with human and software peers and collaborators by gazing at a CRT will seem rather "quaint." Indeed, as we have previously suggested, the types of "interfaces" to computers that users now experience, especially with small mobile devices, will seem more like *barriers* than links to cyberspace.

Although Microsoft may not agree, shrinking a mammoth GUI to a palm-sized device is not a sensible proposition. Neither, for many of us, is pen computing, now in its third or fourth incarnation. What really may make sense is a small device that connects users to peer services front-ended by a VUI (voice user interface). Speech recognition continues to get better and better, but will not likely overtake the keyboard and mouse on the PC, especially in the noisy office setting. Although we currently laugh over recognition engines, which are unable to tell the difference in unconstrained grammars between "Recognize speech" and "Wreck a nice beach," we can look forward to voice-enabled P2P Web services in the mobile context using more restricted "menu" or "command" grammars.

Given thoughtful crafting of voice-enabled services and the continued growth of computing power in *servent* machines, your ability to interact with software should become extremely satisfying. Of course, to make the user experience believable and palatable, users will need intelligent software on the other side of the conversation, which creates an architectural connection between P2P and software agents, and that's the part of the near-future landscape that you'll visit next.

AGENTS AND P2P

"A software agent is a program that a person or organization vests with its authority, that can run unattended for a long time (e.g., a week), and that can meet and interact with other agents (or perhaps with other people)."

—*Jim White, agent visionary and designer of Telescript, the first mobile agent language*

This section suggests a future in which software agents, maligned in the 1990s for promising much and delivering little, play a significant role not only in enabling P2P, but also in playing a pivotal role in P2P.

What precisely is conjunction between software agents and P2P? Agents should occupy new and existing niches in cyberspace. You may not know a precise algorithmic or mathematical model for defining software agents[7]—certainly White's definition is more functional than explicit—but you probably have some notion of how an agent should behave in a P2P setting.

If you have read Neal Stephenson's novel *Snowcrash*, you have already been introduced to a conception of interaction with an agent of transcendent qualities. The Librarian character in the novel is *transcendent*. "He" is embodied with a gender and maintains a persona. He is *telepresent*—that is, he can appear anywhere you summon him, in a manifestation appropriate to the context. When the protagonist is in front of a screen, Librarian

---

7   We can't do that much better, despite having worked in agent technology since the early 1990s.
     The term *agent* covers a lot of ground, and a lot of media-hyped expectations.

is physically embodied and capable of complex gestures. When the hero has only audio capability, Librarian is more conversational. Librarian is always believable and empathetic.

Further, Librarian is autonomous and inherently mobile.

Like a Groove space spread over multiple machines, he has no fixed host association.

Finally, *Librarian* maintains knowledge of user preferences, is goal-oriented, and catalogs previous interactions. In short, Librarian is a perfect peer collaborator.

P2P Agents Are Not Tools

One way that agents contribute to P2P is by responding in a communication-centric, messaging-oriented way familiar to P2P users. Additionally, *agents* are different from *tools* (such as a word processor) in many ways, as depicted in Table 9-3.

Characteristics of Tools	Characteristics of Agents
Tools are essentially invisible and without reasoning or "personality." When you use a tool such as a presentation processor like Powerpoint, it doesn't reveal any of its inner structure. You must manage it directly.	Agents are assigned goals and tasks. In contrast to tools, you can assign a task to an agent, but you don't directly manage the agent. An agent is likely to have "personality" or appear to have reasoning capabilities. It exists in a setting of "managed chaos," in which you can create an agent and partially manage its life cycle. In this sense, agents fit perfectly into the P2P collaboration and searching milieu.
Tools are right at hand. For a tool to be useful, your senses must be able to perceive the response to any input to the tool.	Responsibility is delegated. For much of its functional utility, an agent may not operate right at hand. Actions performed by an agent may not necessarily produce any immediately perceivable output.
Tools are transparent. The feedback that they provide is normally directly visible (GUI) or audible (VUI).	Agents can provide ongoing dialog and reporting, but after a time, as trust grows, users find less need for transparency.

Table 9-3. Comparing Tools and Agents

Characteristics of Tools

Tools have no user model. Anyone can get hold of a copy of StarOffice and begin using it, without the application suite having to know anything about the user.

Tools are directly manipulated. They make their functionality available to the user via keyboard, mouse, and button interactions, and return the results of those interactions within milliseconds to seconds at most.

Characteristics of Agents

An agent collaborating in a P2P environment operates under a different design center. It must gain contextual information about its human creator to operate effectively. Is the user readily available to ask a question or offer clarification, or should the agent shift to a lower fidelity decision-making mode (or do nothing at all)? When an e-mail program receives an e-mail message marked "urgent," and an agent is watching the e-mail program, the agent will probably want to try to alert the user. Without a model of the user that says, "According to her Outlook calendar, she's in a meeting now; she told me to alert her on her mobile device," an agent won't operate very effectively. P2P agents therefore need to understand their users very well.

Agents are indirectly manipulated, and their interaction is deferred. For example, you might ask an agent peer for a summary via instant messenger and then receive a response some minutes (or hours) later. Because of the nature of the P2P asynchronous interaction model offered by IM and by P2P collaboration in general, a user does not expect or require a response in milliseconds. Many tasks (Web searching, for example) are actually far better delegated to a communication-centric agent that finds and summarizes answers (not URLs) over time.

Table 9-3.   Comparing Tools and Agents (*continued*)

Characteristics of Tools	Characteristics of Agents
Tools have a microtask design center. You perform one microtask after another (specifying font sizes and paragraph style, typing in test, drawing polygons, specifying line widths, and so on) until a macrotask (creating a document, spreadsheet, or presentation) is accomplished.	The user communicates with a peer, not a tool. You specify to the agent the macrotask (the *what*), not the method required to implement the task (the *how*).

Table 9-3.   Comparing Tools and Agents *(continued)*

In addition to operating differently than tools, agents can take many forms. Agents may be personified or invisible. They may be avatars that appear on a computer screen, or the ethereal voice behind a voice user interface. They may be mobile, or stay in one place. They may be capable of learning or guessing via "fuzzy logic." They may represent their human creators, protect their human creators from annoyances, or act as information filters. In P2P computing, these capabilities are all of great importance. This section presents a few other ways in which we predict that software agents will become integral to P2P.

Personification

Shopworn computer metaphors like "desktop," "folders," and "files" become less relevant to users' lives and needs in the P2P era. What people really want is to communicate with their information directly from whatever device is handy, without needing special tools like word processors or e-mail readers. Agents will facilitate a uniform interaction model, mediated by a software avatar that takes on the form most appropriate to the means at hand: an animated avatar for a graphics capable device; a presence at the other end of an IM conversation; and a VUI for mobile phones.

Personalization

To understand your context well enough to pursue your goals, software agents will need to reside close to information spaces. P2P is the best way to get closer to the locus of your online activities.

Representation

Agents will represent your interests while you are away from your computer or mobile device. Massachusetts Institute of Technology (MIT) Professor Pattie Maes, who first enumerated the fundamental design principles for software agents, suggests that many people may not be comfortable at first with having an agent act as their proxy. Over time, resistance should change to acceptance. Your personal, private agent—living behind your firewall on your P2P *servent*, able to browse the Web and the Internet on your behalf, and in touch with your *context* (discussed in the section, "*The Importance of Context in P2P*") —will become a valued companion and a useful advisor.

Figure 9-12 is a reminder that people are already comfortable with the idea of representing their presence information to their IM clients. In most cases, the IM software also generates state information as well. For example, if you've been away from the keyboard, or haven't engaged in a conversation for a certain number of minutes, the IM service may mark you as "idle" or "away." It's not much of a stretch to see that agents within a P2P *servent* will be able to understand and portray your presence information more accurately.

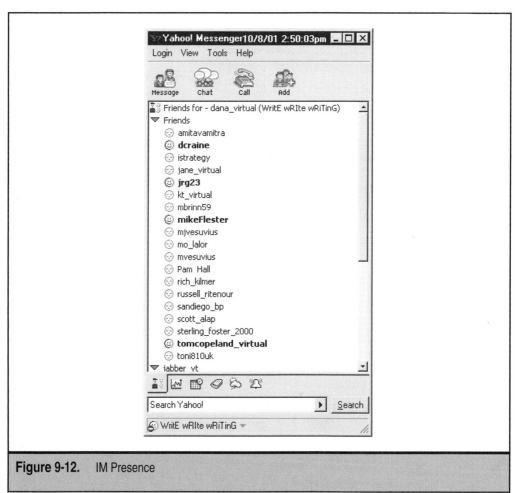

Figure 9-12. IM Presence

Notification

Documents don't need to notify a user. P2P, on the other hand, implicitly assumes a communication-centric model, and communications occur in real time, as events and not as documents. Software agents help moderate the impact of interruptions from these real time demands for your attention.

Mobility

Mobility enables agents to learn from resources that are outside the machine of origin, and bring results back "home" from other software or other software agents.

Learning

Agent frameworks can contain, acquire, and express knowledge. As expectations for P2P systems rise, agents are the best hope for systems that learn and retain user preferences, beliefs, desires, and intentions.

Deferred and Delegated Interaction

Direct interaction is more appropriate to tools such as word processors. Many tasks (Web searching, for example) would be far better delegated to a communication-centric agent that finds and summarizes answers (not URLs).

P2P systems give software agents a home base from which they can operate; they become the user's preferred way of interacting with his or her computers and other information resources. In exchange for gaining living space, software agents become a highly valued P2P collaborator.

Not only will agents be an "eager assistants," they will also be valid P2P endpoints in and of themselves. The open source Alicebot[8] artificial intelligence project, recognizing the applicability to P2P, is working on several P2P initiatives:

▼ AliceGroup super-bots that can answer any question by querying peers

■ An Alicebot-based search tool that, like Gnutella, enables users to query Alicebots manually and find those with the best answers

▲ An Alicebot-based P2P-U project involving universities that build Alicebots and then link them to one another via JXTA

A traditional agent researches and resolves "deep problems" of representation (depiction, presence, physical manifestation, and so on) and interaction (interruption, turn taking, the need for voice or gesture recognition, and such). Just as users now hold multiple IM conversations, they will be holding them in the near future as well, the only difference being that some of their conversational partners won't be quite human. They will

---

8   See www.alicebot.org. AliceBot is an attempt to construct an artificial person in software that is
     able to converse with you and perhaps help you find answers to questions posed in natural
     human language ("What is the weather in Annapolis, Maryland?").

appear to be knowledgeable in certain domains, and as AliceGroup agent-only groups form and share knowledge, they will appear to have even more general knowledge.

Agents will have more *specific* knowledge as well. Your P2P spaces will have access to increasing knowledge about the information most important to you (it has to be the most important, or it wouldn't be in your P2P spaces, right?). Also, a persistent profile of you will exist in your P2P spaces. It will have been populated by your numerous interactions with previous agents and saved onto your hard disk, and expressed in a universal agent language, such as DAML (DARPA Agent Markup Language) or AIML (Artificial Intelligence Markup Language). This profile will be the first thing that an agent sees whenever you summon it. For an additional view on the importance of agent markup languages to P2P, read the following section's article written by John Flynn.

In summary, software agent technologies find a congenial place in P2P, and P2P finds additional capabilities by employing software agents. Agents will be *big* in P2P's future.

Peer-to-Peer Computing and Agent Technology

BBN Technologies' John Flynn, a leading contributor to the development of DAML, wrote the following article, which examines the need for a structure for conversations amongst software agents. In this section, he talks about the need for a "semantic markup" language. Semantic markup is intended to provide capability to describe information in ways that facilitate the use of software programs to find or interpret it. Syntax gives a conversation structure, and semantics give a conversation meaning. For software agents to work effectively, information must have something beyond structure—the terms "criminal lawyer" and "civil engineer" appearing in free text may both be *structurally* correct depending on the sentence in which they appear, but may perhaps have *meaning* which is context dependent. John discusses the need to give explicit meaning to information.

"The World Wide Web is in a rapid process of evolution. The Web relies on Hypertext Markup Language (HTML) as a standard way to mark up Web pages for display via the Web browser of your choice. The Extensible Markup Language (XML) is also now being used to mark up information so that it can be directly processed by software applications. Now a new Web language is under development that provides the capability for semantic markup of information. This new Web language will also be directly readable by software agents that can be programmed to do various things with the information.

"The DARPA Agent Markup Language (DAML) and the European Union Ontology Inference Language (OIL) have been merged via a joint committee into a very powerful language for representing objects and their properties and relationships (ontologies). This new language is called DAML+OIL. It is being submitted to the World Wide Web Consortium (W3C) for consideration as the starting point for an eventual W3C recommendation as the standard language for the creation of Web-based ontologies in the semantic Web of the future.

"In a recent article in the journal *Nature*, Tim Berners-Lee and Jim Hendler described the semantic Web as follows:

The Web was designed as an information space, with the goal that it should be useful not only for human-human communication, but also that machines would be able to participate and help users communicate with each other. A major obstacle to this goal is the fact that most information on the Web is designed solely for human consumption. Computers are better at handling carefully structured and well-designed data, yet even where information is derived from a database with well-defined meanings, the implications of those data are not evident to a robot browsing the Web. More information on the Web needs to be in a form that the machine can "understand" rather than simply display.

"Software agents, or robots, will be able to read, understand, and process information across the Web that is marked up using the DAML+OIL language. These agents will be programmed to do a variety of different things to assist their human owners. There will be agents specifically designed to conduct information searches, perform data fusion, negotiate with other agents, provide multiple services, as well as many other things. These agents may operate in an environment quite different from the traditional Web client-server model.

"Information on the Web is provided to Web browsers via Web servers. Uniform Resource Identifiers (URIs) provide the pointers in Web-space that allow browsers to find which servers, and which Web page on a server, to access. The unique nature of HTML markup on Web servers and the rendering of HTML via Web browsers for humans to read, matches very naturally to a client-server environment. However, agents will not need Web browsers to filter the marked up information since they can understand and process it directly. This provides the opportunity for a new Web model in which agents, and the information they process, function in a peer-to-peer (P2P) environment.

"You will be able to put DAML+OIL marked up information in a sandbox (a restricted access area) on your computer that represents any information that you wish to share. Agents on your computer or others will be able to rapidly search large numbers of computers looking for information to process that satisfies their specific objectives. Agents may be used to dynamically create overlapping P2P communities based on subject matter. Agents may also be able to interact with other agents in this P2P environment, teaming to share information or processing, allowing them to achieve larger goals than they might be able to do alone. For example, my car-shopping agent will be able to interact and negotiate with multiple car-dealer agents to find the best possible deal without my direct involvement in the process.

"It is likely that once large amounts of information on the Web become machine readable, agents will perform functions that we can't even imagine today. The advent of smart agents will truly revolutionize the way we interact with the Web of the future. It is even conceivable that, over time, combinations of agents may interact in ways to modify their objectives so that humans may no longer be completely aware of what they are up to. Is the day of true machine intelligence just around the corner?"

THE IMPORTANCE OF CONTEXT IN P2P

We used the term *context* earlier in the chapter, suggesting in Figure 9-9 that context was of more than passing interest. Let's explore this idea further. In her book *Plans and Situated Actions: The problem of human-machine communication*, Xerox PARC sociologist Lucy Suchman describes an experiment in which a new copier is placed in a lab populated by a group of PARC scientists. She sets up a camera and then videotapes the scientists trying to use the machine with its various complex and arcane controls, often giving up in frustration, sometimes hitting and cursing the machine. She concludes that the main reason for the user frustration with the machine's software and user controls is that the users could not convey enough of their desired instructions to the machine, or put another way, the machine *did not have sufficient context* about the users' desires and intentions.

P2P software especially needs to understand a user's (or group's) context. Some of the future capabilities described in this chapter absolutely depend on it. Therefore, we boldly predict that context gathering and persistence will be an integral part of future P2P applications involving collaboration, notification, communication, presence detection, and commerce. We also contend that a P2P engine will be able to comprehend a user's context by building an information Web from the contact management tools (such as Microsoft Outlook, Palm PDA records, Netscape address books, and similar information managers), presence information from IM clients (such as Jabber and Yahoo! Messenger), e-mail stores, and (with a bit more difficulty) word processing documents.

In our estimation, and also in our experience having designed and built such software, that context engines involve some hard problems, but these are not insurmountably hard. The basic idea of context gathering is to build a Web relating the essential elements of people, places, and things meaningful to an individual:

▼ **Who**   What organizations is the person a member of? What other people in the individual's contact lists belong to the same organizations? Who is related to this person? Who is her spouse, her children?

■ **What**   What documents, folders, IM logs, e-mails, Web pages, pictures, and songs does the user maintain in her P2P spaces?

■ **When**   What reminders, meetings, e-mail content has relevant information about the meetings relevant to the user?

■ **Where**   What addresses, Internet hosts, and meeting locations are linked to the user?

■ **How**   What are the communication paths to this user and to the others in the P2P space? Which individuals in this person's collaboration space are currently known to be available and by what means?

▲ **Why**   What actions and goals is the user attempting to achieve through the others in her context Web?

Without a solid grounding in context, no software that seeks to be of personal service to an individual can do a credible job. Like the copier machine in Suchman's study, the machine will simply not know enough about the user's current environment to be of much real assistance. However, a solid context Web as a foundation makes possible software agents, consumer driven e-commerce, and improved notification. Context is fundamental to a number of crucial parts of P2P's future.

THE WEB SERVER IS EVERYWHERE

Certainly the trend toward turning the traditional client computer into what we have termed in this book a *servent* will continue unabated. This will almost certainly mean the ascendancy of HTML, XML, and HTTP, and the disappearance of the artificial division between what's "on my desktop" and what's "out there in cyberspace." In fact, the whole desktop metaphor may become obsolete with the disintermediation of the PC as a result of the proliferation of mobile devices and gateways, discussed later in this chapter.

These trends will lead more and more applications on more and more devices to embed a browser, with each application blithely ignoring the fact that other applications are doing the same thing. This seems like a recipe for disaster, or at the least, the suboptimization of the capabilities of the hosting environment. It would be better for application writers to adopt a common infrastructure for *servent*-to-*servent* communications. Additionally, there is not a good answer to over-the-net performance issues. XML, wordy to begin with, over HTTP is not a high-performance solution. Consider the prospect of transmitting binary data, Base-64 encoded and encrypted, over SSL via HTTP, and you'll understand what we mean by "not a high-performance solution."

HTTP will not soon go away, at least not within the foreseeable future. However, the front runner for HTTP's successor is likely to be BXXP at the transport layer or the Jabber application building layer.

WEB SERVICES

As we have said previously, P2P is a set of concepts. Web services will be the way in which these concepts will be implemented. Since all known P2P implementations include a Web server, Web services—supported by technologies such as CLR (Common Language Runtime, a binding layer for many programming and scripting languages, and part of the Microsoft .Net offering), SOAP (Simple Object Access Protocol, a World Wide Web Consortium standard), and WSDL (Web Services Description Language, also a World Wide Web Consortium standard)—will become unchallenged standards.

The interesting question, and one worthy of some educated guesses, is who will win all the marbles in Web services. Answering this question comes down to whether Microsoft and its Hailstorm strategy or a competing strategy from Sun Microsystems, tentatively being called the Liberty Alliance, will carry the hearts, minds, and—more important—wallets of online consumers.

First, Web services, although creating a huge amount of buzz as this book is being written, is hardly "ready for prime time." Serious problems have yet to be addressed. Among the problems are transaction capabilities (especially for more complex transactions that may span multiple parties and multiple days or months, as between multiple parties in a supply chain), dependency chains of novel technologies all working together smoothly, and perhaps most important, authentication and nonrepudiation.

Microsoft, Sun Microsystems, and AOL all have their approach to authentication. Behind each approach is the idea that you shouldn't have to present credentials to every Web service that you use. You should be able to use "single sign-on" to authenticate you to cyberspace, sort of like a passport allowing you entry into a foreign land (hence the name *Passport* for Microsoft's service architecture).

P2P folk won't want to use a single identity in cyberspace all the time anyway. As we talked about earlier in the book, people play many roles and therefore assume many identities in their everyday lives; they generally want to keep those identities safely firewalled from one another just to make their lives more manageable. You rarely want your volleyball league persona to be indistinguishable from your engineering director persona; that's why you established a volleyball e-mail account, spiker@my-junk-email-account.com, and a business account, joe.doorstop@bigcorporategiant.com.

However, let's suspend disbelief for a moment and assume that you can accept having a single identity in cyberspace. If you can believe the premise, then what Microsoft will do for you (as of this writing) is hold your identity information—name, credit card information, shipping address, and billing address—in a repository. Then, as you surf the Web, you won't have to reenter all that information again and again as you purchase merchandise. You will have "single-button" purchase power.

The stakes in being the provider for authentication resources are very high. For Microsoft, it means that it can build a family of services around the idea, and it can charge other companies for being the authenticating authority and support service provider. Microsoft is currently committing to accepting standards-conforming certificates from others to loosen the reins a bit. That means you could *conceivably* sign on in cyberspace using your Yahoo! Messenger ID or your AOL ID. This is a bit like charging for the beer but giving away the foam for free. To allow interoperation, Microsoft is committing to accepting authentication tokens that adhere to a standard for Web security called Kerberos, developed at MIT, to provide this single sign-on authentication service for multiple Web sites. Microsoft did not originally plan to use Kerberos, so it will have to revamp Passport now as well.

For Microsoft's cyberspace rival Sun Microsystems, this revamp buys time for the emergence of rival approaches, and this is something Sun very much wants to happen. They see Microsoft's attempt to gain an early lead with Passport as nothing less than an attempt to create a monopoly in an important new business area.

Therefore, while giving the nod to Microsoft for having captured initial mindshare, Sun feels that it's time to open things up completely, to allow anyone, not just Microsoft, to enter the authentication business. To be fair to Microsoft, we should point out that Sun's motivations are not entirely altruistic either. Certainly we can accuse Microsoft of wanting to maintain its hold on our desktop lives, and extend that hold to the rest of our electronic experiences, from the Web to the mobile phone. However, we must also point out that Sun is the supplier of many, if not most, of the servers that run the Internet. If Microsoft can be accused of attempting to create monopoly through software, Sun might be accused of doing the same via its preeminence in hardware.

Sun has therefore (hurriedly, just as we were going to press) formed a loose confederation of partners in something Sun tentatively calls the "Liberty Alliance," whose mission is to design, develop, use, and promote an open standard for authentication services. This development is exciting to those of us who get the point of open source, and embrace it in our career lives and philosophies.[9] Sun intends to quash Passport by not allowing Sun's many partners to adopt the Microsoft standard.

Who will win? Single-identity authentication is generally a good idea, but the proposals don't quite go far enough in solving users' real problems in cyberspace, which are more related to architecture that allows separation of concerns, and to the maintenance and bookkeeping that users need to maintain their multiple personae. No one outside of Groove really seems to understand these problems.

Users will find a single point of entry to cyberspace useful, but it's such a small step. After logging on to whatever device is useful for facilitating their movement from one port of call to another, users want to accomplish tasks that will involve some level of commerce and buying. In showing their "true selves" to a vendor, users want their own *personal* control—not *Microsoft's* control—over their exposure in cyberspace. Users really may want something like an anonymous cash system to limit their exposure (this probably is why single males rarely use their American Express cards to buy their *Playboy* magazines from the newsdealer, or why so few people opt to watch porno movies in their hotel rooms).

The effects and benefits of new authentication architectures will mean much more to big business than they will to the average consumer. Eventually, however, we will all find these services useful *as long as they do not put the power to identify us, to sell the collateral information that the services gain about us, to "target" us*, into the hands of someone whom we have no inherent reason to trust.

The authors use Groove conscientiously, and on a daily basis. Groove allows us to maintain a tidy separation of concerns, a better control over the various personae and roles we play, and do the bookkeeping of our lives. We are unlikely to ever want to return to our previously fractured state of disorganization. We are ready to trust Groove, Magi, or Kenamea because we can be sure that they know very little about us. They may know how to translate a name and a buddy roster into IP addresses, but only our cooperating peers know what we are sharing with one another. Only our machines and those of invited peers hold our multiple calendars; only our own machines orchestrate our ability to manage separation of concerns, to collaborate, or to provide Aunt Ethyl a place to publish a Magi space for the photos of her trip to Majorca.

Whoever wins all the marbles in the Web authentication space will have to understand that we don't want them to *own* us. Unfortunately, that concern may get swallowed up in the struggle that, for better or worse, Microsoft seems likely to win.

---

9   As this chapter was being written, Sun's StarOffice version 6.0 emerged. We abandoned our Windows machine (admittedly with some initial trepidation) to finish the chapter on Linux 7.1 using StarOffice, and did not find any reason to go back to Windows for any part of the effort, including working with the art of the chapter. Both Linux and StarOffice are excellent examples of open source excellence.

Creating a Personal Web Services Engine

In this next section, Richard Kilmer, CEO of InfoEther, a P2P company creating personal information management tools, explains the idea of the personal Web services engine, and how this idea transforms the experience of the Web.

"A PWS (Personal Web Services) Engine and supporting service infrastructure allows for individuals to be represented behind a Web services interface. Such a system would provide the ability for individuals to publish and subscribe to Web services in a peer-to-peer manner, creating a distributed workflow capability that does not suffer from single points of failure in the event of catastrophic emergencies.

Web services seek to transform the Internet from a sea of content into a sea of capability. The essence of Web services is to add a standard network-programming interface through which capabilities can be accessed on the Internet. The core of the emerging standard is the Simple Object Access Protocol (SOAP). SOAP establishes a common format to allow a system to call functions of another system across the Internet using XML. Layered on top of this protocol is the Web Services Description Language (WSDL). Whereas SOAP defines *how* to call a function on another computer, WSDL creates a method of *describing* what functions are available, their syntax, and semantics. Lastly, the Universal Description, Discovery, and Integration (UDDI) protocol completes the architecture by creating directories of services, by service class, available on the Internet.

"Coordination of activities between people currently relies on traditional (human-to-human) communications mechanisms including telephony, e-mail, instant messaging, and video conferencing. Using this model, people communicate human-readable messages to each other to manage activity coordination. These human-readable messages prevent computers from facilitating and logging activity coordination. Current groupware solutions only address computer-mediated coordinative problems in the group time/scheduling domain, and then only on an intranet scale, ignoring cross-corporation necessities of coordination. Groupware also suffers from a centralized computing model, which is susceptible to central points of attack and failure. Under normal coordinative load, the human-to-human communications model works, although with the advent of the Internet even "normal load" is becoming overwhelming in certain situations. This model completely breaks down, however, when dramatic increases in the number of coordinative activities occur, specifically in instances of catastrophic emergencies.

"Using Web services standards, a PWS Engine would execute in the context of personally managed computation devices, such as desktop PCs or mobile, wearable computers. Executing in this context allows the system to integrate with existing personal information sources, e-mail, files, and organizational systems. The system could provide a unified namespace in which all of these existing information and capabilities can be integrated, and user experiences that allow users to publish access to these unified sources through a Web services interface. Such a system would also allow users to add additional operations (methods) that they can respond to based on their organizational roles within a workgroup. Further, a PWS would maintain an active context of the coordinative activities that individuals need to manage, dramatically increasing their abilities to handle the loads created under emergency situations. The PWS would leverage fault-tolerant UDDI directories of individual service engines, enabling peer discovery of local and distant capabilities. Instant messaging and presence could be leveraged by the system to add additional context to each PWS Engine, and allow system-to-system SOAP invocation leveraging real-time (IM) channels that cross existing organizational boundaries.

"A PWS Engine would be capable of being leveraged by other Web services aware initiatives, including software agent-based architectures. In such systems, agents need to perform human interaction, and the proposed system would facilitate a programmatic method of the agents to coordinate with humans. An example of this integration will be demonstrated that works with COUGAAR (Cognitive Agent Architecture) Smart Sensor Web deployed in the infrastructure of facilities and urban communities to create intelligent places.

"In such a distributed system, identity management is critical. The PWS would therefore integrate FIPS (Federal Information Processing Standards) compliant hardware cryptographic tokens to ensure identities of Personal Web Services Engines and provide for secure communications through symmetric and asymmetric cryptography. The PWS would assure that the identity to be managed is more than the guarantee of the personal identity of sender and receiver, but includes a guarantee of which users can fulfill which roles, and access to those roles in a secure and programmatic fashion.

"Building a PWS will demonstrate the increased ability of people to coordinate activities when faced with catastrophic emergency situations. The system could show that computer-augmentation addresses a major need to enable emergency, support, and business personnel to function as the load of activity coordination reaches the limits imposed by human-to-human communications, and centralized systems become compromised or inaccessible."

THE TRUE COST OF INFORMATION

Contrary to the cutesy aphorism of the 1990s, information does *not* want to be free. Information is not sufficiently self-aware to want *anything*. On the other hand, the producers, purveyors, packagers, and controllers of information *do* want something: They want compensation for the intellectual property they produce or control. Producers—including songwriters, authors, and software developers—have to make a living. Purveyors—including ISPs and television networks—have huge infrastructure costs and fixed economic models for revenue production that can ill afford to suffer losses from unauthorized use of their services. Packagers—including the music industry and book and e-book publishers—invest modest-to-large amounts of capital into physical media production and even larger resources into promotion and distribution. Controllers—including Reuters, Web indexers (such as Google), and Lexis-Nexis—make huge investments in maintaining metadata about the otherwise unorganized information amassed on the World Wide Web.

These *infomediaries,* as they are often called, are part of an intricate and delicate financial system. P2P has been instrumental in disrupting the equilibrium of this previously stable system. As we've pointed out previously, P2P:

▼ Significantly affects the amount of bandwidth the average consumer uses. ISPs never foresaw that end users would distribute content to one another, thus requiring symmetric bandwidth.

■ Changes the level of availability and quality of service required from providers. In turn, these changes tend to disrupt a part of the economic model that is based on flat pricing for occasional intermittent access, assumed by connectivity providers from the beginning of the Web era.

■ Removes elements of the existing business models of ISPs by turning them into simple transport providers, thus taking away the "home page advantage," the portal value adds, and additional value adds such as multiple e-mail boxes and on-network storage.

▲ Lowers switching costs for the consumer as well. For example, since the authors have been using Groove as a collaboration space for this book, the extent to which we have a need for on-server services like Yahoo! Calendar, Hotmail, or any sort of portal at all has dropped dramatically. Further, because we own the space and control access to it, we feel insulated from concerns that an ISP might violate our privacy or that we might hit the limit of online storage offered by our respective ISPs. We feel comfortable using Groove as a cheap, distributed, RAID-like system, and worry less about losing information as well. Additionally, we become disinclined to use online vaulting services as well.

As the number and value of ISP attractors decreases owing to individuals and groups producing and consuming larger quantities of their own content and not requiring the assistance of the ISP to publish or consume, the market and profitability picture for the traditional ISP becomes increasingly blurred. ISPs will have to find a new basis for business.

P2P as an Information Utility

Ed Greengrass, of the U.S Department of Defense, is a leading expert in the field of information retrieval, P2P and software agent communities. In much of this book, we have looked at P2P from a somewhat social and personal perspective (i.e., what does P2P enable you to do with other people, how does it allow you to interact with your information resources).

Here, Ed offers an alternative perspective on P2P by contrasting the structure and function of P2P communities with traditional utilities that supply vital but often-unseen services to homes and businesses.

"A P2P community may be considered as a remarkable kind of decentralized 'Information Utility,' an IU for short. The concept is an old one. But viewing P2P in that light can be illuminating.

"How does an IU resemble, and more important, how does it differ from the more familiar utilities we all know and use: electricity, gas, traditional telephone service, etc.?

"First, what do they have in common, that justifies the use of the term 'utility'? They share the following characteristics: (1) they are always 'on,' (2) you can 'plug' into them at any time, and (3) you can plug into them from a great many locations.

"So, how does an IU differ from any of the others? Well, all of the other utilities basically sell one or more commodities. The electric power you draw is basically indistinguishable from the electric power I draw. They differ only in price, amount, time of service, and (perhaps) reliability. Across countries, there may be other minor if annoying differences, e.g., in voltage, current, or frequency. But these differences are readily overcome with some form of standard converter. There is a similar difference between power drawn for running factory equipment versus power for residential use.

"But as soon as we move from power to information, the situation is very different. The information you want or receive may be very different from the information I want or receive. Information can be, and certainly should be, tailored to the individual. It may be tailored based on demographic or personal information collected by vendors. It may be tailored based on profiles that you or I generate. Or (most interesting and tricky of all), it may be tailored based on queries or information needs that we explicitly generate.

"All of these cases, but especially the explicitly generated information need, raise issues that don't arise with the commodities generated or supplied by other utilities. In particular, they raise the question of how you specify your needs, how the IU interprets them, and how they are matched against the vast sea of information 'out there.'

"These issues rarely arise with other utilities. When you connect an electric appliance to a wall socket, the appliance in effect tells the utility what it needs, by withdrawing the amount of power it needs as it needs it. The manufacturer and the utility have agreed-on standards that allow the device to 'talk' to the utility without user intervention, apart from plugging in the device. Trouble arises only in special cases, where you overload the system by attaching too many devices, or attach a device intended for a different kind of line, i.e., one that can handle much higher amperage. In most cases, you don't have to worry about formulating your requirements, except perhaps when your house is being wired, or when you need to add an additional telephone line. Even in such cases, your concern is only with the *amount* of the utility's commodity, e.g., amps, watts, bandwidth, or whatever, that you require. Only with the IU do you need to worry about *what* you want, about how to *express* your information need. Moreover, getting your requirement properly expressed may require *interaction* with the IU. Not only do you need to be able to talk to the IU; the utility needs to be able to talk to you! This makes very natural sense when you realize that the IU is not a faceless corporate entity but a large and dynamic collection of peers, each with her own information resources, interests, and capabilities.

"By the same token, an IU based on P2P technology doesn't necessarily have a 'central office,' or indeed a 'branch office' in the ordinary sense, to which you can report problems or send service requests (as you might if you encounter a standard problem with a traditional utility like a loss of electric power). You need to be able to interact with the IU through your own Information System (IS), a PC, or a wireless device. The IU itself consists of a great many ISs representing the 'peers' with which you will wish to converse. You may have an agent to help you mediate this conversation. Many of the other peers will have them too.

"Moreover, the information you desire may not be available when you request it, either because the IU hasn't yet located or acquired it, or (more important) because the information *doesn't yet exist*. This situation doesn't usually occur with a conventional utility. You may need electric power now or at some time in the future, however (apart from possible overloads due to unusually heavy usage, e.g., during a very hot summer), the power will be available whenever you need it. And you can typically predict when that will be. However, when you request information, it is possible that the information doesn't yet exist, and neither you nor the IU may be able to say when it will come into existence (or even if it ever will). Hence, the IU needs to be able to honor requests that involve monitoring the world, or some relevant part of the world indefinitely, recognizing when the desired information comes into existence, and supplying it (or notifying the user of its creation) at that indefinite time in the future. There is a clear need here for your personal agent, or the agents of the peers with which you are corresponding, to monitor the world of peers and their information sources indefinitely, something agents do very well.

"Another big difference between an IU and the more traditional kind of utility is that with a traditional utility, there is seldom any question about whether the desired service or commodity is being supplied. Either your phone line is active or it isn't. Either electric power is being supplied to the outlets at your house or it isn't. However, with an Information Utility, a different kind of question arises: Given that data are being supplied to you in response to an information need request (perhaps by many peers), does the data contain the information you need? Even if the need has been satisfied, is it buried so far down a list of responses from diverse peers as to be inaccessible for all practical purposes? In general, the IU (that is, the peers who are responding to your request) may not know with any certainty whether 'it' has successfully met your need. Even your personal agent may not know. You, the end user, are the only one who can definitely say whether you have received the information you need, in a usable form. Hence, there is yet another need for you to interact with the IU, perhaps through your personal agent, to indicate success or failure (or something in between), and perhaps to refine the original information request.

"That 'something in between' suggests yet another difference between an IU and the ordinary kind of utility. Perhaps the IU has supplied *part* of the information you need. Or perhaps it has supplied information related to what you need, but not quite on target. Or perhaps it has supplied the same nugget of valuable information 10 times, instead of 10 different nuggets. Or perhaps it has indeed supplied exactly what you asked for, but examining these results makes you realize that you need something additional, or that what you *really* need is not quite what you carelessly *said* you need.

"Finally, the information utility also differs from the traditional utility in the way its output is presented to the user. Information can come in many forms, many data types: freeform text, structured data (textual or numeric), images (bit-mapped or geometric), motion pictures, audio, etc., or combinations of all of these types. Moreover, end users may differ in how they want their information organized and presented.

"Of course, standards (ad hoc, de facto, and formal) already exist for many of these data types. We even have standards for representing complex logical structures, e.g., XML. And we have standards for representing information in certain specialized domains. But these information standards must be extended into (and across) all the other domains that we actual and potential participants in the P2P IU may want to access."

P2P AND WARFIGHTING

Although we have left the topic generally untouched in this book, we cannot ignore the realities of the world in which we now live, and thus should make some mention of P2P's place in warfighting and intelligence.

From the standpoint of the NATO allies, the first wars of the new century are likely to be heavily information-based. That is, our enemies will attempt to break or undermine our civilian and military technology infrastructures including our communications, command control mechanisms. In turn, we will try to break theirs.

There seems little disagreement amongst military and national security planners and analysts that success in the next war will hinge upon information superiority. Further, the next shooting wars are likely to be spread all over the globe, with all the logistics and transport problems that this entails. Finally, armed forces will have to respond quickly to limited conflicts and terrorist organizations. All told, this combination of conditions equates to trading armor for information, weight for mobility, atoms for electrons.

Command and Control Vision

The C2 (Command and Control) vision for future combat systems combines three essential elements:

▼ Achieving superior battlespace understanding and information to negate or defeat potential adversaries

■ Accelerating decision and execution cycles to act before the opponent can react

▲ Optimizing resources to achieve the highest payoff and best exploit the adversary's vulnerabilities

In practice, if these goals are achieved, armed forces should never have to face an adversary whose strength and reaction time are unknown, should be able to airlift or sealift fewer or lighter armaments, and should use weapons capable of more effective destruction. As in any other endeavor of mankind, there are strategic and tactical objectives (akin to "business drivers" in civilian endeavors) in the making of war. General George S. Patton is alleged to have said, "The purpose of war is not to die for your county, rather it's to make the other dumb bastard die for *his*."

The business drivers of military action involve speedy and adaptive threat responses; secure, multi-service (perhaps multinational), cross-organizational activities; superior decision making; and finally, in-band knowledge capture—that is, using each warrior on

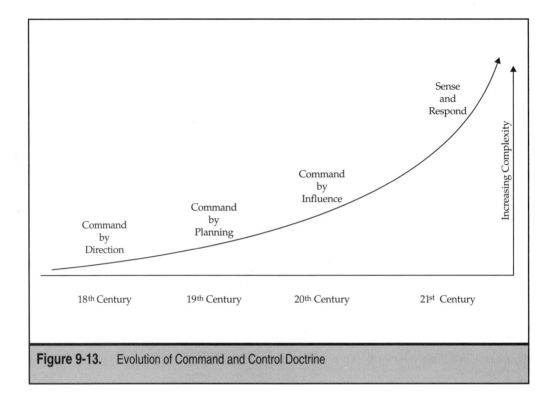

Figure 9-13. Evolution of Command and Control Doctrine

the ground as a human intelligent sensor in a peer-to-peer network. P2P is an excellent paradigm for the evolution of C2 in warfare. Like all organized endeavors of mankind, C2 has experienced a steady evolution in the way it's organized. Figure 9-13 illustrates the evolution of C2 over the last several centuries.

The earliest organization, called *command by direction*, was based on the belief that if a commander could see the entire battlefield, he could control the course of the battle. Unfortunately, any vantage point from which the commander could see the battlefield was sufficiently far from the action that distance prevented him from playing any role other than observer. We might liken this style to the age of the mainframe computer, where computing resources were so tightly controlled and impedance to collaboration was so high that little computer-mediated organizational teamwork was possible or even dreamt of.

The next stage, *command by plan*, originated by Frederick the Great, attempted to mitigate the remoteness from the scene of battle in command by direction. His design for making war was an attempt to plan every move, every contingency, and every logistical need. Frederick's use of a plan to command all of the forces all of the time met with mixed success for the reason that plans seldom are flawlessly executed. Similarly, today's IT departments' attempts to impose firewalls, site filtering, and e-mail control can only be called failed strategies.

Even with the evidence that chaos will always confound the best planning, modern armies continue to use command by plan as the model, and IT departments continue to set up firewalls and DMZs, only to allow exception after exception, making almost all firewalls look like Swiss cheese.

In *command by influence*, beginning in the 20th century, a greater emphasis was placed on authorizing lower levels to issue command decisions and on granting local autonomy based on situational awareness. Essentially, subordinates were allowed wide latitude within the boundaries defined by the CONOP (concept of operations) derived from a commander's intent. One of the small failings of command by influence occurs when local information cannot be correlated, preventing local coordination. There is an obvious analogy to P2P technologies. Because of an increased level of complexity and the growing sophistication and intelligence of the modern warfighter, command by influence is rapidly becoming augmented by "sense and respond" ad hoc organizations and behaviors (see Figure 9-14).

"Sense and respond" organization is much like the flocking that certain animal species demonstrate. For example, migratory birds circulate the leadership of their flying wing; when the leading bird becomes fatigued and drops back to follow the flock, another bird

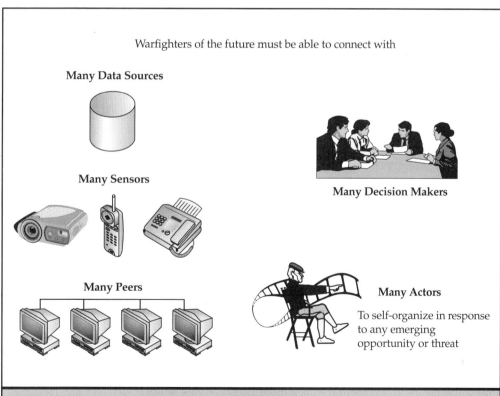

Figure 9-14.   Sense and Respond Organization and Behavior, and Near-Future Warfighting

automatically assumes leadership. An organization can use a similar architecture to recognize targets of opportunity and to gather resources around those opportunities. To the extent that P2P architectures improve local coordination by enabling local collaboration, secure communications, authentication, information access levels, and immediacy, these architectures are an excellent fit for interoperating individual soldiers on the near-future battlefield.

The individual warfighter is a part of a greater whole, of which some elements are automated systems and some are other warfighters.

Likewise, a strong case can be made for "weaponizing" multiple military systems via a P2P collaboration technology. Consider the robustness argument for a technology such as Groove. With a Groove-based weapon space, there is no single point of failure or attack, an ad hoc collaboration in a secure space is trivial to arrange, and all participants use edge devices without having to engineer a specialized (and expensive) C2 system. It should be as easy for an unmanned ground sensor to communicate with a tank commander and an F-16 fighter as it is to create an instant message community. Suppose that UGSs (unmanned ground sensors) the size of a tiny U.S. quarter dollar are made part of a P2P smart sensor Web. The sensors in the Web communicate with each other via a JXTA (www.jxta.org) network, and pick up the acoustic signature of a mobile communication transceiver. The sensors in the Web are equipped with a COUGAAR MicroEdition (www.cougar.org) multi-agent system. Using instant messaging, each sensor checks its view of reality with its closest neighbors. Using their visual and acoustic sensing capabilities, these sensors detect the traffic as well. They reconcile any minor differences in their worldview, and communicate their consensus view to a soldier, who is an authorized member of their JXTA community.

The objective is not in the line of sight for the soldier, so he or she creates a shared Groove space, using a theater-targeting toolset (see Figure 9-15). The targeting toolset template automatically includes an interface to a target identifier bot, which has been automatically invited to the space. (Groove bots are software agents through which people in shared spaces may securely interact with external systems.) The infrared and thermal images and the seismic data from the smart sensor Web are automatically transmitted and collected in a picture tool in the shared space.

The target identifier bot passes images to a target identification system, which uses a Bayesian inference engine to compare the acquired images to thousands of identified target images. The inference engine returns a positive hit on the target. Based on the quality of the information, the bot invites a human analyst agent, this time a targeting analyst aboard J-STARS, an airborne C2 center.

The analyst sees the shared images in the space and decides to get the opinion of an imagery expert. The analyst's choices are to invite another human into the space or to task a Bot close to the scene. The analyst decides on the latter, tasking a bot controlling flight UAVs (unmanned aerial vehicles) in the operational area.

The UAVs return several new aerial photos to the UAV bot, and the new information provided by the additional sensor boosts the confidence in the target identification. The targeting analyst, having confidence in the images, now confirms a target.

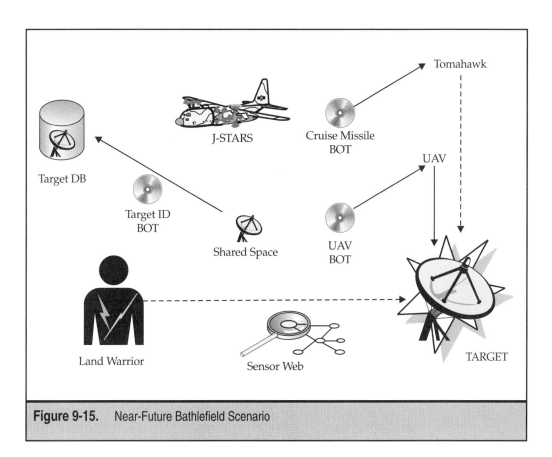

Figure 9-15.   Near-Future Bathlefield Scenario

Finally, the targeting analyst invites a Cruise missile bot, which tracks and communicates with Tomahawk cruise missiles from their launch platforms to their targets. A Tomahawk missile is successfully routed to destroy the enemy target.

This scenario requires no expensive "stovepiped" (specially built) systems. P2P architectures such as JXTA and Groove act as the glue for the actors, human and automated, in this completely ad hoc system. All the participants experience a fully synchronized view of the battlefield. The military target, the context of the situation itself, guides the system's action, not the dictates of a system designed in the past with functional requirements based on assumptions that might not be relevant to the current situation.

Several initiatives at Army Research Laboratories, such as FCS (Future Combat Systems) and SPAWAR (Space and Naval Warfare Command), will spend millions to achieve such capabilities.

Intelligence Analysis

Consider how military intelligence organizations react to the chaotic and unexpected today. During the terrorist action against the U.S.S. *Cole,* traditional ad hoc collaboration strategies included e-mail, instant messaging, fax, and telephone. The most modern part of the analytic and response environment was a Web site used to publish (selected) news and information.

The problems with this approach are myriad. First, there is no process structure in the middle of the situation. Communications are totally out of band (i.e., ad hoc, uncontrolled, not part of a formal collaboration) and generally not (easily) auditable for reuse or analysis.

Further, while the Web is a rich experience in many ways, it is fundamentally difficult to secure and impedes peer publishing. As we have pointed out elsewhere, the Web is not an appropriate bidirectional communication medium. Also, without a tool such as Groove or Magi, there is no real context around which to aggregate documents, images, ideas, discussions, and links. Integration with existing intelligence assets is often difficult and expensive to provide on short notice, and ad hoc systems are inefficient, full of gaps, delays, and missed communications, and makes synchronizing communications, or securely arranging access to new members, much more difficult.

Project GENOA, an ongoing DARPA project, is investigating how it can apply P2P technologies to research it is conducting on developing tools and infrastructure for collaborative crisis analysis and management on behalf of national security. GENOA's objectives are to decrease response and decision cycle time from days to hours, increase by an order of magnitude the number of situations that can be managed simultaneously, and reduce the number of military deployments.

FCS, GENOA, and similar programs reflect an understanding by the U.S. Department of Defense that information superiority on the battlefield hinges on a fully supportive sensor-to-shooter information chain. The next war won't be so much about outfighting the opponent as much as out-knowing, out-communicating, out-maneuvering, and out-reacting him. In short, the objective is to make *him* die for *his* country, just as General Patton advised.

SUMMARY

This chapter offered several predictions about the future of P2P technologies. While we covered issues from peace to war, one theme emerges: Regardless of the area of endeavor, P2P—as implemented in Web services, mobile technologies, and software agents—is a set of essential technologies for these architectures.

John Perry Barlow, former Grateful Dead lyricist, social futurist, and prominent "netizen," says that cyberspace is what happens when you leave the landscape and move onto the map. The implication is that cyberspace is an analog of physical reality, and activities in cyberspace become the electronic analog of those in human space, with all of its chaotic evolution and associated vagaries. Therefore, it is reasonable to expect cyberspace to begin to resemble the development of analogs in human activities (collaboration especially). Indeed, we have already seen at least the first generation of such schemes unfold before us. Since BBN's Ray Tomlinson invented e-mail, the first loosely collaborative space, we have been moving toward the increased sharing of information, entertainment, and experience across time and distance. Many of the current P2P visions are steps along such a path.

One may agree (or disagree) with Barlow's statement. We believe that cyberspace is not a map but a whole new landscape, and that the problem is that the computing industry has not yet created adequate maps for this landscape. However, if cyberspace really is a map, then we contend that we do not yet have adequate meta-maps, or ways of drawing the maps. Prior to the emergence of the many varieties of P2P-based applications, we did not yet have computational or communications structures that

▼   Allowed people to find people, places, and things easily in cyberspace.

◼   Encouraged the structuring of the cyberspace so that is seems less like the old American "Wild West," untamed, unmapped, almost unknowable, and without any sense of "law and order."

▲   Enabled people to project themselves into cyberspace for commerce, entertainment, or myriad other reasons.

Now, perhaps for the first time, these structures are beginning to emerge, and the experiences that these structures yield will be invigorating for some people, technologies, and businesses, challenging for others, and devastating for some. No technological revolution comes without bearing both gifts and trials.

As Tim Berners-Lee said in a piece in the January 2000 *Wired* magazine, "We won't be using the word 'Internet' in 2020, just as today we don't say, 'I saw an interesting article on a piece of paper today.' People will simply talk about the information itself rather than the medium. "We think this starts to address the point of P2P. Berners-Lee has suggested that in a few years, no one will speak about the Internet as though it had any special meaning set aside from the rest of the experience of life. We will take it for granted in the same way that we tend to take electricity for granted. The Internet will simply disappear into the background, woven into the fabric of assumed artifacts. If P2P technologies as the next level of the Internet fulfill their promise, we won't even know the term *P2P* in 2020 either, except as an historical reference. P2P in all its manifestations will simply disappear into the woodwork in such a way that our grandchildren will assume that things were ever such.

Index

▼ D

J

K

L

M

N

INTERNATIONAL CONTACT INFORMATION

AUSTRALIA
McGraw-Hill Book Company Australia Pty. Ltd.
TEL +61-2-9417-9899
FAX +61-2-9417-5687
http://www.mcgraw-hill.com.au
books-it_sydney@mcgraw-hill.com

CANADA
McGraw-Hill Ryerson Ltd.
TEL +905-430-5000
FAX +905-430-5020
http://www.mcgrawhill.ca

GREECE, MIDDLE EAST,
NORTHERN AFRICA
McGraw-Hill Hellas
TEL +30-1-656-0990-3-4
FAX +30-1-654-5525

MEXICO (Also serving Latin America)
McGraw-Hill Interamericana Editores S.A. de C.V.
TEL +525-117-1583
FAX +525-117-1589
http://www.mcgraw-hill.com.mx
fernando_castellanos@mcgraw-hill.com

SINGAPORE (Serving Asia)
McGraw-Hill Book Company
TEL +65-863-1580
FAX +65-862-3354
http://www.mcgraw-hill.com.sg
mghasia@mcgraw-hill.com

SOUTH AFRICA
McGraw-Hill South Africa
TEL +27-11-622-7512
FAX +27-11-622-9045
robyn_swanepoel@mcgraw-hill.com

UNITED KINGDOM & EUROPE
(Excluding Southern Europe)
McGraw-Hill Education Europe
TEL +44-1-628-502500
FAX +44-1-628-770224
http://www.mcgraw-hill.co.uk
computing_neurope@mcgraw-hill.com

ALL OTHER INQUIRIES Contact:
Osborne/McGraw-Hill
TEL +1-510-549-6600
FAX +1-510-883-7600
http://www.osborne.com
omg_international@mcgraw-hill.com